Memoirs of Aaron Burr

Matthew L. Davis

MEMOIRS

OF

AARON BURR.

WITH

MISCELLANEOUS SELECTIONS

FROM

HIS CORRESPONDENCE.

BY MATTHEW L. DAVIS.

"I come to bury Cæsar, not to praise him."

IN TWO VOLUMES.

VOL. II.

NEW-YORK:
PUBLISHED BY HARPER & BROTHERS,
NO. 82 CLIFF-STREET.

1837.

CONTENTS

OF

THE SECOND VOLUME.

CHAPTER I.

CHAPTER II.

CHAPTER III.

CHAPTER IV.

CHAPTER V.

CHAPTER VI.

CHAPTER VII.

CHAPTER VIII.

CHAPTER IX.

CHAPTER X.

CHAPTER XI.

CHAPTER XII.

CHAPTER XIII.

CHAPTER XIV.

CHAPTER XV.

CHAPTER XVI.

CHAPTER XVII.

CHAPTER XVIII.

CHAPTER XIX.

CHAPTER XX.

CHAPTER XXI.

MEMOIRS

OF

AARON BURR.

MEMOIRS

OF

AARON BURR.

CHAPTER I.

Colonel Burr's study of the law* has been already briefly noticed. He brought to that study a classic education as complete as could, at that time, be acquired in our country; and to this was added a knowledge of the world, perhaps nowhere better taught than in the camp, as well as a firmness and hardihood of character which military life usually confers, and which is indispensable to the success of the forensic lawyer. He was connected in the family circle with *two*† eminent jurists, who were at hand to stimulate his young ambition, and to pour, in an almost perpetual stream, legal knowledge into his mind, by conversation and by epistolary correspondence. The time he spent in his studies preparatory to his admission would be considered short at the present day; but (to use the language of another) "it is to be recollected that at that time there were no voluminous treatises upon the mere routine of practice

* For the remarks which I am now about to present to the reader I am principally indebted to two highly intelligent members of the bar. *Either* of whom is fully competent to a development of Colonel Burr's legal character; and *neither* of whom would be disqualified by any prejudices in his *favour*. These gentlemen, it is believed, entertained different views as to the practical value of that species of reading which is necessary to form what is by some termed "a truly learned lawyer."

† Colonel Burr's brother-in-law, Judge *Tappan Reeve*, and his uncle, *Pierpont Edwards*.

to be committed to memory, without adding a single legal principle or useful idea to the mind, and which only teach the law student, as has been said of the art of the rhetorician, 'how to name his tools.' Burr, fortunately for his future professional eminence, was not destined to graze upon this barren moor. He spent his clerkship in reading and abstracting, with pen in hand, Coke and the elementary writers, instead of Sellon and Tidd; and learnt law as a science, and not as a mechanical art."

On the other hand, it has been said "that Colonel Burr was not a deep-read lawyer; that he showed himself abundantly conversant with the general knowledge of the profession, and that he was skilful in suggesting doubts and questions; but that he exhibited no indications of a fondness for the science, nor of researches into its abstruse doctrines; that he seemed, indeed, to hold it and its administration in slight estimation. The best definition of law, he said, was '*whatever is boldly asserted and plausibly maintained.*' This sarcasm was intended full as much for the courts as for the law administered by them."

If Colonel Burr may have been surpassed in legal erudition, he possessed other qualifications for successful practice at the bar which were seldom equalled. He prepared his trials with an industry and forethought that were most surprising. He spared no labour or expense in attaining every piece of evidence that would be useful in his attacks, or guard him against his antagonist. He was absolutely indefatigable in the conduct of his suits. "He pursued (says a legal friend) the opposite party with notices, and motions, and applications, and appeals, and rearguments, never despairing himself, nor allowing to his adversary confidence, nor comfort, nor repose. Always vigilant and always urgent, until a proposition for compromise or a negotiation between the parties ensued. 'Now move slow (he would say); never negotiate in a hurry.' I remember a remark he made on this subject, which appeared to be original and wise. There is a saying, 'Never put off till to-morrow what you can do to-day.' 'This is a maxim,' said he, 'for sluggards. A better reading of the maxim is—*Never do to-day what you can as well do to-morrow*; because something may occur to make you regret your premature action.'"

I was struck, says the same friend, in his legal practice, with that tendency to mystery which was so remarkable in his conduct in other respects. He delighted in surprising his opponents, and in laying, as it were, ambuscades for them. A suit, in which I was not counsel, but which has since passed professionally under my observation, will illustrate this point in his practice. It was an ejectment suit, brought by him to recover a valuable tenement in the lower part of the city, and in which it was supposed, by the able lawyers retained on the part of the defendant, that the only question would be on the construction of the will. On the trial they were surprised to find the whole force of the plaintiff's case brought against the authenticity of an ancient deed, forming a link in their title, and of which, as it had never been questioned nor suspected, they had prepared merely formal proof; and a verdict of the jury, obtained by a sort of *coup-de-main*, pronounced the deed a forgery. Two tribunals have subsequently established the deed as authentic; but the plaintiff lived and died in the possession of the land in consequence of the verdict, while the law doubts, which form the only real questions in the case, are still proceeding, at the customary snail's pace, through our courts to their final solution.

To be employed as an assistant by Mr. Burr was not to receive a sinecure. He commanded and obtained the constant and unremitted exertions of his counsel. It was one of the most remarkable exhibitions of the force of his character, this bending every one who approached him to his use, and compelling their unremitted, though often unwilling, labours in his behalf. His counsel would receive notes from him at midnight, with questions which were sent for immediate replies.

He showed nice discrimination in his selection of his professional assistants. When learning was required, he selected the most erudite. If political influence could be suspected of having effect, he chose his lawyers to meet or *improve* the supposed prejudice or predilection. Eloquence was bought when it was wanted; and the cheaper substitute of brow-beating and vehemence used when they were equivalent or superior. In nothing did he show greater skill than in his measurement and application of his agents; and it was amusing to hear his cool discussion of the obstacles of prejudice, or ignorance, or interest, or political feeling to be encountered in various tribunals, and of the appropriate remedies and antidotes to be employed, and by what persons they should be applied.

Equal discrimination and acuteness was displayed in his political movements. An anecdote which occurred in the contested election of 1800 will exemplify this remark. Funds were required for printing, for committee-rooms, &c. The finance committee took down the names of leading democrats, and attached to each the sum they proposed to solicit from him. Before attempting the collection, the list, at Colonel Burr's request, was presented for his inspection. An individual, an active partisan of wealth, but proverbially parsimonious, was assessed one hundred dollars. Burr directed that his name should be struck from the list; for, said he, you will not get the money, and from the moment the demand is made upon him, his exertions will cease, and you will not see him at the polls during the election. The request was complied with. On proceeding with the examination, the name of another wealthy individual was presented; he was liberal, but indolent; he also was assessed one hundred dollars. Burr requested that this sum should be *doubled*, and that he should be informed that no labour would be expected from him except an occasional attendance at the committee-rooms to assist in folding tickets. He will pay you the two hundred dollars, and thank you for letting him off so easy. The result proved the correctness of these opinions. On that occasion Colonel Burr remarked, *that the knowledge and use of men consisted in placing each in his appropriate position.*

His imperturbable coolness and presence of mind were displayed in his civil as well as in his military life. Against most of the vicissitudes of a trial he guarded by his forethought and minuteness of preparation. I was present myself, says the legal friend already referred to, when he received with great composure a communication which would have startled most men. Mr. P. had long been an inmate of his house; he had been connected with him in many respects and for many years. Colonel Burr and two other lawyers were discussing a proposed motion in a chancery suit in which P. was the plaintiff, the colonel himself having an interest in the result. P. was then out of town. A letter was brought in and handed to the colonel, which, telling us to proceed with our debate, he carefully read, and then placed it, in his customary manner, on the table, with the address downwards. Our discussion proceeded earnestly for ten minutes at least, when the colonel, who had listened with great attention, asked, in his gentlest tone, "What effect would the death of P. have on the suit?" We started, and asked eagerly why he put the question. "P. is dead," he replied, "as this letter informs me; *will the suit abate?*" The colonel was himself ill at the time, and unable to leave his sofa; and even if there was some affectation in his demeanour, there was certainly remarkable collectedness.

Colonel Burr commenced the practice of his profession at the close of the revolution, under the most favourable auspices; and may be said at one bound to have taken rank among the first lawyers of the day, and to have sustained it until he became vice president, at which time, it is believed, he had no superior at the bar, either in this state or in the Union, nor even an equal, except General Hamilton.

The eclat which Burr, yet a beardless boy, had acquired by his adventurous march under Arnold to Canada, through our northeastern wilds, then a trackless desert; his gallant bearing at Quebec and Monmouth; his efficient services in the retreat of our army from Long Island and New-York; and his difficult and delicate command on the lines of Westchester, followed him to private life, gathered around him hosts of admirers and friends among our early patriots, particularly the youthful portion of them, and no doubt essentially aided him in making his successful professional *debut*. The name of the chivalrous aid-de-camp who supported in his youthful arms the dying hero of Quebec was familiar in the mouths of men, and from one end of the continent to the other he was eulogized for his military prowess. Such were the cheering auspices under which he sheathed his sword when his physical energies would permit him no longer to wield it.

"He was indefatigable," says another legal friend, "in business, as he had been in his previous studies, and no lawyer ever appeared before our tribunals with his cause better prepared for trial, his facts and legal points being marshalled for combat with all the regularity and precision of a consummate military tactician. No professional adversary, it is believed, has ever boasted of having broken or thrown into confusion the solid columns into which he had formed them, or having found void spaces in their lengthened line, or to have beaten him by a *ruse de guerre* or a surprise.

"He never heeded expense in completing his preparations for trial; and, while laborious himself to an uncommon degree, he did not stint the labours of others, so far as he could command or procure them. Every pleading or necessary paper connected with his causes was in the first place to be multiplied into numerous copies, and then abstracted or condensed into the smallest possible limits, but no material point or idea was by any means to be omitted. His propensity to concision or condensation was a peculiar trait in his mind. He would reduce an elaborate argument, extending over many sheets of paper, to a single page. Had he written the history of our revolution, which he once commenced, he would probably have compressed the whole of it in a single volume.

In his professional practice, he never solicited from an opponent any favour or indulgence any more than he would have done from an armed foe; but, at the same time, rarely withheld any courtesy that was asked of him, not inconsistent with the interest of his clients. He was a strict practitioner, almost a legal *martinet,* and so fond of legal technicalities, that he never omitted an opportunity of trying his own skill and that of opposite counsel in special pleas, demurrers, and exceptions in chancery, notwithstanding the risk of paying costs sometimes, though rarely incurred, and of protracting a cause.

The labour of drawing his pleadings and briefs, however, at least after his return from Europe in 1812, always devolved upon others; and, with marginal notes of all the authorities which had been consulted, from the year books downward, which were sometimes in law French and law Latin, to the last reports in England and some half a dozen of our states, in which may be properly called *law English,* were submitted to his critical acumen; his thousand doubts, suggestions, hints, and queries, which would start from his mind like a flash, and for a moment seem to throw into inextricable confusion what had been laboriously, and perhaps profoundly studied, at last would most generally be adopted without material alterations or additions.

Colonel Burr's mind cannot be said to have been a comprehensive one. It was acute, analytical, perspicacious, discriminating, unimaginative, quick to conceive things in detail, but not calculated to entertain masses of ideas. He would never have gained celebrity as an author; but as a critic, upon whatever subject, his qualifications have rarely been surpassed, though in literary matters and the fine arts they were only exhibited in conversation. His colloquial powers were impressive and fascinating, though he generally seemed a listener rather than a talker; but never failed to say a proper thing in the proper place."

As a public speaker, his ideas were not diffuse enough; or rather, he appeared to lack fluency to make a long, and what is called an elaborate argument upon any matter, however grave or momentous. In a cause in which he was employed as associate counsel with General Hamilton, an incident occurred, in relation to Chief Justice Yates, not unworthy recording. It speaks a language that cannot be misunderstood, and is demonstrative of the influence which he had over the feelings as well as the minds of his hearers. It was the celebrated case of Le Guen *vs.* Gouverneur and Kemble, one of the most important, in regard to the legal questions and amount of property involved, which at that day had been brought before our tribunals, and in which case he completely triumphed. Only a short period previous to his decease Colonel Burr remarked, that on this occasion he had acquired more money and more reputation as a lawyer than on any other during his long practice at the bar. A letter was addressed to Thurlow Weed, Esq., requesting him to apply to the Hon. John Van Ness Yates, son of the late chief justice, and ascertain whether the incident, as reported, was founded on fact. To that letter Mr. Weed received the following answer.

JOHN VAN NESS YATES TO THURLOW WEED.

Albany, July 8th, 1837.

DEAR SIR,

After some difficulty in finding my father's notes of the argument in the case of Le Guen *vs.* Gouverneur and Kemble, I have ascertained that the account you showed me, given in the letter of M. L. Davis, Esq., is in the main correct. My father's notes of General Hamilton's argument are *very copious.* Those of Colonel Burr's are *limited,* in this way —" Burr for plaintiff, I. The great principles of commercial law which apply to this case are"—then follows a hiatus of some lines. After which, as follows:—

" II. The plaintiff"—another *hiatus.*

" III. !!!!!" and this concludes all I can find.

Hamilton's eloquence was (if I may be allowed the ex pression) *argumentative,* and induced no great elevation or depression of mind, consequently could be easily followed by a note taker. Burr's was more *persuasive* and *imaginative.* He first enslaved the *heart,* and then led captive the *head.* Hamilton addressed himself to the *head* only. I do not, therefore, wonder that Burr engrossed all the faculties of the hearer. Indeed, I have heard him often at the bar myself, and always with the same effect. I do not recollect, in conversation, any particular allusion of my father's to Burr's argument in the case of Le Guen *vs.* Gouverneur and Kemble; but I have frequently heard him say, that of all lawyers at the bar, Burr was the most difficult to follow in the way of taking notes. Yet Burr was very *concise* in his language. He had no pleonasms or expletives. Every word was in its proper place, and seemed to be the only one suited to the place. He made few or no repetitions. If what he said had been immediately committed to the press, it would want no correction.

Yours respectfully,

J. V. N. Yates.

Colonel Burr's style of speaking at the bar was unique, or peculiarly his own; always brief; never loud, vehement, or impassioned, but conciliating, persuasive, and impressive; and when his subject called for gravity or seriousness, his manner was stern and peremptory. He was too dignified ever to be a trifler; and his sarcasm, sometimes indulged in, rarely created a laugh, but powerfully told upon those who had provoked it. His enunciation was slow, distinct, and emphatic; perhaps too emphatic; and this was pronounced, by his early and devoted friend, Judge Paterson,* a fault in his mode of speaking while a youth, and seems never to have been fully corrected, as he did that of rapid utterance, attaining the true medium for public speaking in this respect. He spoke with great apparent ease, but could not be called fluent, although he never appeared at a loss for words, which were always so chaste and appropriate that they seemed to have been as carefully selected before they fell from his lips as if they had been written down in a prepared speech and committed to memory. His manner was dignified and courteous; his self-possession never for an instant forsook him. He never appeared hurried or confused, or betrayed the slighest embarrassment for want of ideas to support his argument, or language in which to clothe it; and possessed a memory so well disciplined as never to forget any thing in the excitement of the legal forum which in the retirement of his study he had intended to use. He has frequently been heard to say that he possessed no oratorical talents; that he never spoke with pleasure, or even self-satisfaction, and seemed unconscious of the effect which he produced upon the minds of his audience.

Colonel Burr accorded the palm of eloquence to General Hamilton, whom he frequently characterized as a man of strong and fertile imagination, of rhetorical and even poetical genius, and a powerful declaimer. Burr's ruling passion was an ardent love for military glory. Next to the career of arms, diplomacy, no doubt, would have been his choice, for which not only his courtly and fascinating manners, but every characteristic of his mind peculiarly adapted him. It is idle now to speculate upon what he might have been had Washington yielded to the importunities of Madison, Monroe, and others, and appointed him minister to the

* See vol. i., p 37.

French republic. Our country, before which he then stood in the original brightness of his character, would have been honoured in the choice, both at home and abroad, and his own destiny, at least, would have been widely different.

Notwithstanding oratory was not his forte, and he never spoke in public with satisfaction to himself, still many anecdotes are told of him which would show that the effect of his speeches were sometimes of unequalled power. It is said, that at the close of his farewell address to the Senate of the United States on his retirement from the vice-presidency, there was scarcely a dry eye to be seen among his grave auditors, many of whom were his bitter political adversaries. His manner of speaking was any thing but declamatory, and more resembled an elevated tone of conversation, by which a man, without any seeming intention, pours his ideas in measured and beautiful language into the minds of some small select circle, dislodging all which they may have previously entertained upon a particular subject, and fixing his own there, by the power of a seeming magical fascination, which he could render, when he chose, almost irresistible. To judge him by his success as a public speaker, few men could be called more eloquent.

As a monument of his legal knowledge and talents, his trial at Richmond may be referred to. The two volumes of Reports which contain it exhibit on almost every page the impress of his great mind, in its singular acuteness and perspicacity, and great powers of analysis and argument. On that trial were engaged some of the ablest lawyers of our country, and he manifestly took the lead of them all. But the abilities which he displayed, hour by hour, and day by day, through that long protracted contest, in which the verdict sought for by those who then wielded the political destinies of our country was an ignominious death, were no less remarkable than his unshaken firmness and high moral elevation of deportment, struggling as he was for honour and for life.

Fiat Justicia ruat cœlum, was the motto of Chief Justice Marshall on the trial of Colonel Burr. He was acquitted, but his acquittal was not owing to the clemency or partiality of his judges. His acuteness as a lawyer, and the adroitness with which he managed his defence, contributed greatly, no doubt, in saving him from becoming a victim, though his innocence of the charge of treason which had been brought against him could hardly have effected that acquittal. Here, then, his talents have done some good to his country, even if it be of a negative character. They saved it from a stain of blood, which would have been as indelible as is that of Admiral Byng upon the escutcheon of England.

After Colonel Burr's return from Europe in 1812, he was engaged in several important causes, in which he was pre-eminently successful. His legal opinion in the great steam-boat cause aided in breaking up that monopoly. He was originally employed in the important land trial of Mrs. Bradstreet, and in the Eden causes, involving a large amount of property in the city of New-York, and turning upon some of the nicest points of the most difficult branch of the law of real property: he triumphed over almost the entire force of the New-York bar, backed by powerful corporations and individuals of great wealth, which they profusely lavished in a long-protracted contest. He commenced the Eden suits in opposition to an opinion which had been given by General Hamilton, Richard Harrison, and other members of the profession of high standing, and on the faith of which opinions the parties in possession of the lands had purchased and held them at the time the suits were commenced.

Had Colonel Burr assiduously pursued the study of law through life, like Marshall, Kent, and others, it is not easy to conjecture to what elevated point he might have risen; but such was not his destiny; the bent of his genius, which had received its inclination at the stirring period of the world when he entered into active life, was military. But to show his persevering industry in his practice as a lawyer, and his power of enduring fatigue, even when almost an octogenarian, the following letter, written by him, is inserted.

Albany, March, 1834.
Germond's, Wednesday Evening.

Arrived this evening between 6 and 7 o'clock, having been *forty-five* hours in the stage without intermission, except to eat a hearty meal. Stages in very bad order—roads excellent for wheels to Peekskill, and thence very good sleighing to this city. The night was uncomfortable; the curtains torn and flying all about, so that we had plenty of fresh air.

The term was closed this day. Nelson will hold the Special Court to-morrow morning—have seen both Wendell and O'Connor this evening—all ready—came neither fatigued nor sleepy. A. B.

CHAPTER II.

Before entering upon the details connected with the election of 1800, a brief history of the rise and progress of political parties in the State of New-York is deemed necessary. By the Constitution adopted during the revolutionary war, the state was divided into four districts, viz., The Southern, the Middle, the Eastern, and the Western. In the Southern District was included the counties of Richmond (*Staten Island*), Kings, Queens, and Suffolk (*Long Island*), New-York (*Manhattan Island*), and Westchester. These six counties, from the autumn of 1776 until the summer of 1783, were in a great measure in the possession of the British forces, and those portions of them which were nominally within the American lines were generally inhabited by tories and refugees. Lord North, or the most unrelenting of his followers, were not as much opposed to American independence as were the tories of the united provinces. The city of New-York became the rendezvous of the most intelligent and influential of this class. From this point they communicated with the British premier, through their correspondents in London. Many of them that were in exile from their late homes in Pennsylvania, New Jersey, and Connecticut, left their families behind them, under the protection of the whigs. By this arrangement facilities were afforded for ascertaining the position, resources, and movements of the rebel armies. These facilities were not neglected, and the information thus obtained was promptly communicated to the British commander-in-chief in New-York, and to the ministry in England. The whigs felt that ingratitude was returned for their hospitality, and, in consequence, they became daily more incensed against the tories.

It is believed that the war would have terminated in 1780 or 1781, if the British minister and his military commanders in America had not been constantly led into errors by the opinions and advice of the refugees, but especially those residing in the city of New-York. Entertaining such views, the suffering whigs, in their most trying hours, consoled themselves with the hope and belief that, when the struggle should terminate and the country become independent, their oppressors and persecutors would no longer be permitted to remain among them. These were the predominant feelings of the men who were perilling their lives and enduring every species of privation and hardship for the freedom of their native land.

During the year 1778, Joseph Galloway, formerly of Philadelphia, sailed for England. His correspondence was extensive, and he became the depository of all the grievances of the American loyalists. He was the medium of communication between them, Lord North, and Lord George Germain. He possessed, in a high degree, the confidence of those who were the conscience keepers of the king. Among the correspondents of Mr. Galloway may be enumerated William Franklin, former governor of New-Jersey, Daniel Cox, and David Ogden, members of his majesty's council in New-Jersey, the Rev. Dr. Inglis, subsequently bishop of Nova Scotia, and Isaac Ogden, counsellor at law of New-York, John Potts, a judge of the Common Pleas in Philadelphia, John Foxcroft, postmaster general of North America, &c., &c. None of Mr. Galloway's correspondents exhibited a more vindictive spirit than the Rev. Bishop Inglis. These letters were private and confidential, excepting so far as the ministry were concerned, for whose use most of them were intended. None of them, it is believed, have ever heretofore found their way into print. They are now matters of history. They are well calculated to develop the secret designs of the tories, and, at the same time, they afford the strongest view that could be given of the patriotism, the sufferings, and the untiring perseverance of the sons of liberty in those days. Some extracts will now be made from the original manuscripts, for the purpose of showing, in a limited degree, the cause, and thus far justifying the hostile feelings of the whigs towards the refugees.

The *Rev. Bishop Inglis*, under date of the 12th December, 1778, says—" Not less than sixty thousand of the rebels have perished by sickness and the sword since the war began, and these chiefly farmers and labourers. I consider it certain that a famine is inevitable if the war continues two years longer; nay, one year war more will bring inexpressible distress on the country with regard to provisions, and this will affect the rebellion not less than the depreciation of their pasteboard dollars. The rebellion, be assured, is on the decline. Its vigour and resources are nearly spent, and nothing but a little perseverance and exertion on the part of Britain is necessary to supress it totally. Butler and Brandt's forces, Indians and loyalists, I am told, amount to five or six thousand men. They have distressed and terrified the rebels more since last spring than the whole royal army.

Isaac Ogden, under date 22d November, 1778, says—

"Thus has ended a campaign (if it deserve the appellation) without anything capital being done or even attempted. How will the historian gain credit who shall relate, that *at least* twenty-four thousand of the best troops in the world were shut up within their own lines by fifteen thousand, *at most*, of poor wretches, who were illy paid, badly fed, and worse clothed, and scarce, at best, deserved the name of soldiers?"

Daniel Cox, under date of 17th December, 1778, says— "Ned Biddle has declined his seat in Congress. The truth is, he means to do more essential service in the assembly, which has ordered the general sense of the people to be taken respecting the present constitution of Pennsylvania. Joe Reed is elected, and accepted the honour of being president and commander-in-chief of the state."

John Potts, under date 1st March, 1779, says—"An opinion prevails here that government (the British) will adopt the mode of devastation. If that should really take place, adieu to all the hopes of the friends of government ever again living in America. Be assured that, should government be restored by such means, her friends would find it impossible to travel this country without a guard to prevent assassination. This is not only my opinion, but the real sentiments of every friend to government. I have conversed with none, except some of the violent tories, indeed, of New England, *who seem to partake of the savage temper of our countrymen.* G—— N——* has said, in a confidential letter to a friend of his, that government wish to get rid of this country, and is only at a loss how to do it without leaving it in a situation to injure her."

Daniel Cox, 28th February, 1779, says—"At any rate, I see absolute ruin attend us poor attainted loyalists should the colonies be given up, or this place (New-York) be evacuated. I once fondly imagined neither would happen. I wish that our old friend, the Black Prince,† could have

* Lord North. † General Vaughan.

the direction here again, and have the glory of conducting the future operations to a happy conclusion. I think he is more calculated for it than somebody* else, who, though he may possess zeal and honesty, wants head."

Isaac Ogden, 8th March, 1779, says—"Admiral Gambier is ordered from this station, to the universal joy of all ranks and conditions. I believe no person was ever more generally detested by navy, army, and citizen, than this penurious old reptile."

Daniel Cox, 10th April, 1779, says—"In an open letter to me, Mrs. Cox speaks of the increasing depreciation of the continental money, under the allegory of an old acquaintance of mine lying in a deep consumption. Should Great Britain be really treating, and give us up, there must be an end to her glory. But such a misfortune I can never believe her subject to, unless from her own folly and internal factions of the accursed opposition."

Thomas Eddy, under date 5th month, 3d, 1779, says—"From accounts received by last packet of the determined resolution of government to pursue the war in America with vigour, I am led to believe that the leaders in the rebellion must give up before fall. Indeed, when I consider the dissatisfaction universally prevalent caused by the badness of their money, I should not be surprised if such an event would take place as soon as General Clinton opens the campaign."

Bishop Inglis, 14th May, 1779, says—"Remonstrate loudly to those in authority against treating with the Congress—treating with them is establishing them, and teaching the Americans to look up to them for deliverance and protection. We have been guilty of a fatal error in this from the beginning; we now see and feel the consequences. This should teach us wisdom and better policy. Though we should conquer the rebels, yet, if an accommodation is settled with the Congress, I shall consider the colonies as eventually lost, and that in a little time, to Great Britain."

John Potts, 15th May, 1779, says—"In my last I mentioned some sanguine hopes which I could not help entertaining, from the prospect of an election to be held in the beginning of April, for a new convention, as they call it, in Pennsylvania. Those hopes are now totally destroyed by the efforts of Joe Reed* and the violent party. Their artful cry of tory against the party in favour of the convention raised a flame too great to be withstood, and procured more than twelve thousand signers to petitions against that measure, in consequence of which the assembly rescinded the resolution for holding the election.

"The person to whom I alluded in my last letter is the woman whom I mentioned to you last fall as so truly enterprising. She has brought three messages through the winter. From her I have this much further to assure you, that great preparations are making at Pittsburgh for the reception of troops.

"The friends of government all agree that they will be content to risk for ever every future hope and prospect of being restored to their estates, provided Great Britain will but secure her own authority fully before any terms are listened to; and, when that is acknowledged and established, then grant terms as liberal as she pleases, consistent with good government and future security."

Bishop Inglis, 3d September, 1779, says—"General Tryon made two or three descents on the coast of Connecticut, and burnt the towns of Fairfield and Norwalk. He was accompanied by a large body of refugees, who were extremely useful, and behaved with a resolution and intrepidity which did them great honour. Had the descents on Connecticut *been longer continued and carried on more extensively, the most salutary consequences might be apprehended.*

"The delusive notion of treating with Congress, I find, still prevails in some degree among you. Yet nothing could

* The Hon. Joseph Reed, whom the British attempted to bribe through the agency of Mrs. Ferguson.

be more destructive to the interest of government. Treating with them would be confirming their usurpation. The loyalists universally dread this above all things. However they may differ in opinion on other points, they are unanimous and united in this; and where so many are perfectly agreed in a matter which is level to all understandings, it must be the evident dictate of truth and reason."

Isaac Ogden, 20th September, 1779, says—"You may well ask what we are doing here. Our army is now (including the garrison from Rhode Island) at least twenty-four thousand men, a number sufficient to march through the whole continent; but what do numbers avail when they are cooped up in this dastardly manner? A want of knowledge of the country, a want of enterprise, or a want of something else, God only knows what, has prevented any and every attempt to interfere with the enemy. It is not a want of sufficient force, neither is it because it was impracticable. These are facts that the warmest of the rebels acknowledge. Their force is really despicable when compared to the army here. How is General Vaughan? I sincerely wish to see him at the head of the army here, as he is the only general that has been here that would listen to the advice of the American loyalists."

Bishop Inglis, 6th of November, 1779, says—"We have now within our lines upward of twenty-six thousand effective men, as I have been informed. Such a force, if led out and exerted with judgment and spirit, could not be resisted by the rebels—it must bear down all opposition. It is reported that Sir Henry Clinton is appointed sole commissioner, with authority to choose five assistants as a counsel, and that he is vested with power to treat with Congress, &c. It may be very proper to have a commissioner here, vested with extensive powers; but as to any hopes of treating with Congress about an accommodation, be assured they are visionary. Congress have done enough to dissipate all such fond expectations, unless their independence is acknowledged; and I should be heartily sorry if a measure so dishonourable to the nation, as treating with the Congress in any respect, were adopted. Insult and obstinacy is all that can be expected from them.

"With respect to the rebellion, I am clearly of opinion that it daily declines. Washington is the man to whom the army look for redress and support. He is *now* in America what Monk was in England in 1659. I wish I could say in every respect. Were he equally disposed, he might effect as sudden and total a revolution here as honest George Monk did then in England."

Isaac Ogden, 16th December, 1779, says—"There is an anecdote of General Grey that I have lately heard and believe to be true, though the fact cannot now be fully ascertained. Just before the battle of Brandywine, an officer was despatched home by General Howe. General Grey undertook to give him his instructions how to demean himself on his arrival in London, &c. A copy of these instructions was found by a countryman, and delivered to Joe Shippen (Secretary *Joe*,) who now has them in Philadelphia. A gentleman here has seen them. As he related them to me, you have them. 'You will first go to Lord George Germain; he will ask you such and such question; you will answer them *so and so*. You will then be sent to Lord North, who will ask you these questions; you will thus answer them. You will then be sent to the king, who will also ask you, &c.; you are also to give him these answers. You will then be examined by the queen. She is a sensible woman. You must answer with caution, but, of all things, be careful that you say nothing that will condemn the conduct of General Howe.' Some pains are taken to procure this paper from Mr. Shippen; if it can be obtained, you will have it."

David Ogden, 3d December, 1779, says—"What gives me great concern is the fear of a dishonourable peace being made with the rebels. My fears arise from what I am told many of the officers in the army give out that America can never be conquered; and the sooner it is given up, and independence admitted by the crown and parliament, the better for Great Britain; and I am also informed that they have wrote to that purpose to their friends in England. What effect this may have on your side of the Atlantic, backed by the anti-ministerial party with you, enemies to monarchy and the great supporters of the rebellion in America, time must show; but I am persuaded that the present ministers will never give the least countenance to the independence of America. The laying the country waste has been called cruelty by the favourers of the rebellion, and said to be below the character of Britons; but in cases of rebellion, it has always, by the most civilized nations, been held justifiable, and no history affords an instance of calling it cruelty. The great mercy shown the rebels since the commencement of the rebellion is esteemed to be the greatest cruelty, as the lives of many thousands would have been preserved by a vigorous exertion of the king's troops to distress the rebels wherever they marched, having a strict regard not to injure the loyalists."

Daniel Cox, 7th December, 1779, says—"Should you see *Joe* Reed's late speech to the assembly of Pennsylvania, you would imagine they felt no shock from the Georgia defeat.* If but common means are actively employed and properly conducted, the rebellion must be crushed totally next campaign. I doubt not every effort in the power of Congress, both abroad and at home, will be made to carry themselves through another year; but, if you are successful at home, they must go to the devil. For God's sake, therefore, do not be frightened nor give us up; all must go right if you are but firm."

Reference has already been made to General Arnold's

* Referring to the discomfiture at Savannah of the combined forces of France and the United States; the former under the command of Count D'Estaing, the latter commanded by General Lincoln.

treason during the summer of 1780.* From the private correspondence of Mr. Galloway, it appears, that as early as the autumn of 1778 Arnold was considered by the refugees as "*lenient*," if not friendly to them, and in this light was represented to the British ministry.

Charles Stewart, under date of the 17th December, 1778, says—"General Arnold is in Philadelphia. It is said that he will be discharged, being thought a *pert tory*. Certain it is that he associates mostly with those people, and is to be married to Miss Shippen, daughter of Edward Shippen, Esq."

David Sproat, 11th January, 1779, says—"You will also hear that General Arnold, commandant in Philadelphia, has behaved with lenity to the tories, and that he is on the eve of marriage to one of Edward Shippen's daughters."

James Humphreys, Jun. (printer), 8th of April, 1779, says —"General Arnold has been accused by the council of sundry misdemeanors. He has insisted upon a trial by a court martial, and was triumphantly acquitted. The Congress, however, have thought proper to remove him from his command in the city of Philadelphia, he being of too lenient a disposition to answer their cruel purposes."

This correspondence also develops the conflicting views which were taken by the tories as to the operations of the British army. So far as it had any influence, it was calculated to embarrass the ministry. Only two very short extracts will be given on this subject. The dividing point between the northern and the southern tories was whether the main army should take possession of Hudson's river, or the isthmus between Newcastle and Chesapeake Bay.

Bishop Inglis, May 14th, 1779, says—"I am still of opinion that taking possession of Hudson's river should be the first object. When that is done, which will effectually divide the rebel forces, circumstances should determine whether our operations should be directed eastward or westward."

John Potts, December 17th, 1778, says—"If government means to pursue this matter, she must spare men enough to take possession of the isthmus between Newcastle and Chesapeake Bay; and, by clearing that country of rebels, procure sufficient provision and forage for the whole British force in America. That country can also supply the fleet with a great quantity of naval stores. The whole trade of Maryland and Pennsylvania will be destroyed, and a great part of Virginia. The interior of that peninsula is better disposed towards the British government than any other country in the middle colonies. If possession of Rhode Island and this place (New-York) is retained, and that post taken, America has no access to sea from any intermediate port but Egg Harbour, which will then be scarcely an object. This is your plan, excepting the possession of Philadelphia and Bordentown, and, as the troops would not be dispersed too much, would, for that reason, be more eligible."

During the winter of 1778–79, the tories had it in contemplation to establish a regular corps for the purpose of plundering the whigs. About this period Colonel Burr took command of the lines in Westchester. His opinion of this system of warfare is expressed in a letter to General McDougall, from which the following is extracted—"Colonel Littlefield, with the party, returned this morning. Notwithstanding the cautions I gave, and notwithstanding Colonel Littlefield's good intentions, I blush to tell you that the party returned loaded with plunder. Sir, till now I never wished for arbitrary power. I could gibbet half a dozen *good* whigs with all the venom of an inveterate tory."* Let the reader compare the above *whig* sentiment with the following *tory* arrangement:—

Christopher Sower, 1st March, 1779, says—"An association is signing here (New-York), according to which the loyalists are to form themselves into companies of fifty men each; choose their own officers; to have the *disposal* of all prisoners by them taken; to make excursions against the rebels, plunder them, sell the spoil, appoint an agent to receive the money, and to divide it among them in equal shares."*

In the autumn of 1779 the refugees in New-York formed a board of delegates from the several provinces. In reference to it, *Daniel Cox*, December 7th, 1779, says—"I have lately brought about a general representation of all the refugees from the respective colonies, which now compose a board, called the board of refugees, and of which I have the honour at present to be president. We vote by colonies, and conduct our debates in quite a parliamentary style."

Christopher Sower, the 5th of December, 1779, says—"The deputies of the refugees from the different provinces meet once a week. Daniel Cox, Esq., was appointed to the chair, to deprive him of the opportunity of speaking, as he has the gift of saying little with many words."

Only one more extract will be given from the correspondence of Mr. Galloway, and that relates to the doings of this board of refugees. Among their labours, the manner of bringing the war to a speedy termination, and the formation of a constitution for the British provinces, engrossed their attention. No comments will be made on the plan; but it will not be found unworthy a careful perusal. Although presented as the individual suggestion of Mr. Ogden, it is evident, from other portions of the correspondence, that it was not unadvised, and, to the American reader, is now an amusing document.

David Ogden, 3d December, 1779, says—"When America submits to the crown of Great Britain, which I take as a matter certain, and will soon happen if proper measures are not neglected—pray, will not a constitution and government, in a manner something similar to the following, be most

* On the back of Mr. Sower's letter Mr. Galloway has made, in his own handwriting, this endorsement—"Mr. Sower is a German refugee at New-York, and a person of the greatest influence among the Germans in Pennsylvania."

for the honour, security, peace, and interest of Great Britain, and also for the happiness and safety of America, and most compatible to the spirit and genius of both?

"That the right of taxation of America by the British parliament be given up. That the several colonies be restored to their former constitutions and forms of government, except in the instances after mentioned. That each colony have a governor and council appointed by the crown, and a house of representatives to be elected by the freeholders, inhabitants of the several counties, not more than forty nor less than thirty for a colony, who shall have power to make all necessary laws for the internal government and benefit of each respective colony that are not repugnant or contradictory to the laws of Great Britain, or the laws of the American parliament, made and enacted to be in force in the colonies for the government, utility, and safety of the whole. That an American parliament be established for all the English colonies on the continent, to consist of a lord lieutenant, barons (to be created for that purpose), not to exceed, at present, more than twelve, nor less than eight from each colony, to be appointed by his majesty out of the freeholders, inhabitants of each colony; a house of commons, not to exceed twelve nor less than eight, from each colony, to be elected by the respective houses of representatives for each colony, which parliament, so constituted, to be three branches of legislature of the northern colonies, and to be styled and called the Lord Lieutenant, the Lords, and Commons of the British Colonies in North America. That they have the power of enacting laws, in all cases whatsoever, for the general good, benefit, and security of the colonies, and for their mutual safety, both defensive and offensive, against the king's enemies, rebels, &c.; proportioning the taxes to be raised in such cases by each colony. The mode for raising the same to be enacted by the general assembly of each colony, which, if refused or neglected, be directed and prescribed by the North American parliament, with power to levy the same. That the laws of the American parliament shall be in force till repealed by his majesty in council; and the laws of the several legislatures of the respective colonies to be in force till the same be repealed by his majesty, or made void by an act and law of the American parliament. That the American parliament have the superintendence and government of the several colleges in North America, most of which have been the grand nurseries of the late rebellion, instilling into the tender minds of youth principles favourable to republican, and against a monarchical government, and other doctrines incompatible to the British constitution.

"A constitution and government something similar to the above, I am convinced, from the knowledge I have of the temper and spirit of the inhabitants of the colonies, will be most acceptable to them in general (it being what they wish for), and will also be conducive to establish a continued and lasting peace and harmony between Great Britain and the colonies. The Congress, no doubt, as it will deprive them of their power, will oppose the same by every artifice, as well as every other plan of accommodation that will lessen their grandeur and consequence. I am therefore persuaded that the Congress had best be altogether disregarded in any overtures of accommodation to be made or proposed, and all treaties with them absolutely refused, either directly with them, or indirectly through the courts of France and Spain, as men void of faith, or even common justice—deceivers of the people, and enemies to the public weal and happiness of mankind. And to facilitate a submission instead of a treaty, proceed with the army against the rebels with vigour and spirit, and issue a proclamation containing a constitution for North America, and a pardon to all who lay down their arms and take the oath of allegiance to his majesty and his government, *excepting*, as necessary examples of justice,

"*First*. The several members of the Continental Congress who have been elected and served as members thereof since the declaration of Independence.

"*Second.* All governors, presidents of the supreme executive councils or of other councils, or of any of the colonies acting under the Congress, or any new and usurped form of government.

"*Third.* All those who have been by his majesty appointed of his council in any of the colonies, and since taken an active part in the civil or military department under the Congress or under any establishment of the rebel government.

"*Fourth.* All judges who have, since the rebellion, passed sentence of death against any of his majesty's liege subjects, for any supposed or real crime, committed or pretended to be committed against any law enacted or made by the Congress, or by any of the usurped or pretended legislatures of the colonies, making the fact or facts criminal for which he, she, or they were condemned to suffer death.

"*Fifth.* All commissaries and others who have seized and sold the estates of any of his majesty's liege subjects, under any pretence whatsoever, unless it was done by the consent and orders of the rightful owner, leaving all such to the mercy of his majesty, to be granted to those only whose conduct merits mercy, and hold up the same in the proclamation, if any should issue.

"Will it not be proper as well as just to have the estates of the rebels who are gone out of the king's lines among the rebels forfeited, confiscated, and sold by commissioners to be appointed for that purpose, and the moneys arising on the sales to be applied to the use of the refugees, to compensate for their sufferings by the rebels in ease of the parliamentary donations? Will not the perfidy of France and Spain justify Great Britain in proposing and entering into an alliance with the courts of Russia, Prussia, and other powers, to unite against France and Spain, the common disturbers of public tranquillity; take and divide among them all their islands in the West Indies?"

CHAPTER III.

THE extracts which have been given from the correspondence of Mr. Galloway present, in a point of view sufficiently clear and distinct, the unquestionable hostility of the tories towards the whigs; the manner in which they wished the British ministry to conduct the contest; the punishment they would have inflicted upon the rebels if they had been successful, and the form in which they would have subsequently governed the country. These views are deemed a sufficient reason for the feelings of the whigs; a justification of those legislative disqualifications of the tories which were adopted by the State of New-York during the war of the revolution, and cause for the patriotic determination that the refugees should not be protected or permitted to remain in the land which they had so zealously struggled to enslave.

At a very early period after the declaration of Independence, parties were formed among the whigs. In the State of New-York, at the first election, in 1777, for governor under the new Constitution, General Schuyler was presented in opposition to George Clinton, but was defeated. With that defeat it is believed commenced political heart-burnings and collisions which, although at times smothered, were never extinguished. Schuyler was a man of great boldness and sagacity. He was personally unpopular, yet he possessed a commanding influence over the mind of those with whom he commingled or was in any manner connected; an ascendency which, in a measure, was to be ascribed to the force of intellect.

On the 12th of September, 1780, General Schuyler was a candidate for Congress. At that time the members were a candidate. The two branches then met together and compared their nominations. If they both designated the same individual, he was declared to be chosen. If not, they proceeded as one body to a ballot, and the person having a majority of all the votes given was duly elected. The house almost unanimously nominated General Schuyler, the vote being for Schuyler thirty-one, for Ezra l'Hommidieu seven. The senate nominated L'Hommidieu. In joint ballot, notwithstanding the vote Schuyler had received in the house, L'Hommidieu was chosen. For some reason not then explained, there was a sudden and extraordinary change of opinion in the legislature in relation to General Schuyler.

About this period certain individuals were for the appointment of a "Supreme dictator, with all the powers conferred by the Roman people." A convention was to be held at Hartford, consisting of delegates from the five New-England states and the state of New-York, for the purpose, among other objects, of devising more efficient measures for the supply of the army. Judge Hobart, Egbert Benson, and General Schuyler were the delegates. "It was for a time contemplated by the legislature to give them instructions to propose that a dictator should be appointed, for which a majority in the more popular branch were believed to be favourable. This 'mad project,' as Colonel Alexander Hamilton designated it, was communicated to him by General Schuyler in a letter of the 16th of September, 1780."*

The scheme was opposed with great ardour and perseverance by Governor George Clinton, Ezra l'Hommidieu, and others; but, through the influence of the former, in a great measure, the "mad project" was defeated. Here again the party lines were drawn between Governor Clinton and General Schuyler. It is highly probable that the plan for appointing a "supreme dictator" was a principal cause for the change of opinion respecting General Schuyler in

* See Life of Hamilton, vol i., p. 316.

the legislature on the 12th of September, and contributed to defeat his election to Congress.

From this period until the adoption of the Federal Constitution, the Clinton and the Schuyler parties continued to exist. In the ranks of the latter there was great concert in action. On an examination of the legislative journals from 1777 to 1788, it will be seen, that with General Schuyler were the Jays, the Livingstons, the Van Rensellaers, and the Bensons, and that they almost uniformly voted together.

And now of the tories. In the year 1779 some of them, who had removed from Albany within the British lines, petitioned the legislature for leave to return, which petition was rejected. At the same session an act was passed requiring all counsellors and attorneys, before they could be permitted to practice in any court, to produce evidence of their attachment to the liberty and independence of the United States. On the 20th of November, 1781, a special act was passed on the same subject, comfirmatory of what had been done in 1779.

The first session of the legislature after the revolutionary war was held in the city of New-York. It was convened by proclamation of the governor on the 6th of January, 1784, and continued its sitting until the 12th of May following. In the first month of the session, numerous petitions were presented by the tories, praying to be relieved from their banishment, and to be permitted a residence within the state. The legislature perceived that, if they did not act promptly, their tables would be covered with these memorials. Therefore, in the language of Governor Clinton at the opening of the session, the assembly said—

"While we recollect the general progress of a war which has been marked with cruelty and rapine; while we survey the ruins of this once flourishing city and its vicinity; while we sympathize in the calamities which have reduced so many of our virtuous fellow-citizens to want and distress, and are anxiously solicitous for means to repair the wastes and misfortunes which we lament," we cannot hearken to these petitions. They were referred to a select committee, which committee in a few days reported against granting their prayer, and the house instantly, without a division, agreed to the report. This was on the 9th of February, 1784.

On the 11th of February, 1784, the assembly passed a resolution directing that the names of those persons that had been attainted should be communicated to the governors of the several states; requesting to be supplied, in like manner, with "a list of the persons proscribed or banished by their respective states, in order that thereby the *principles of federal union* may be adhered to and preserved." In the senate this resolution was permitted to sleep.

Chancellor Robert R. Livingston, in a letter to John Jay dated the 25th of January, 1784, thus speaks of parties at this period. "Our parties are, first, the tories, who still hope for power, under the idea that the remembrance of the past should be lost, though they daily keep it up by their avowed attachment to Great Britain; secondly, the violent whigs, who are for expelling all tories from the state, in hopes, by that means, to preserve the power in their own hands. The third are those who wish to suppress all violence, to soften the rigour of the laws against the loyalists, and not to banish them from that social intercourse which may, by degrees, obliterate the remembrance of past misdeeds."

On the 8th of March, 1784, Peter Yates and three hundred others petitioned the legislature to prevent those persons who had joined or remained with the enemy during the late war from returning, and to prohibit such as have remained from being eligible to any office of profit or trust. On the 31st of the same month strong resolutions were introduced into the house, and adopted by both branches, against the tories, declaring, among other things, "That as, on the one hand, the rules of justice do not require, so, on the other, the public tranquillity will not permit, that such adherents who have been attainted should be restored to the rights of citizenship."

In May, 1784, the legislature passed an act entitled "An act to preserve the freedom and independence of this state, and for other purposes." The object of this law was to prohibit the tories from holding any office. The Council of Revision returned the bill, with objections to its passage, one of which was, "that so large a portion of the citizens remained in parts of the *Southern District* which were possessed by the British armies, that in most places it would be difficult, and in many *absolutely impossible*, to find men to fill the necessary offices, even for *conducting* elections, until a new set of inhabitants could be procured."

This bill of disfranchisement, notwithstanding the objections of the Council of Revision, was passed by more than two thirds of both branches, and thus became a law. Such were the feelings of the "violent whigs;" such the policy of the first legislature after the termination of the war. But, unfortunately, among those who had fought the battles of the revolution, there were some who doubted the capacity of the people for self-government, while there were others who sought power and influence at the hazard of principle. The Schuyler party were in the minority. The Clinton party, designated by Chancellor Livingston as the "violent whigs," were uncompromising on the question of banishing the tories, who were numerous, especially in the Southern District. It seemed probable, therefore, if restored to citizenship, that they would amalgamate with the *third* party, or that class of whigs "who wished to suppress all violence, and to soften the rigour of the laws against the royalists."

In March, 1783, the legislature passed an act entitled "An act for granting more effectual relief in cases of trespass." The object of this act was to enable the whigs at the termination of the war to recover from the tories rent for any landed estate they might have occupied; and in cases of suit for such rent, the act declares "that no defendant or defendants shall be admitted to plead in justification any military order or command whatsoever for such occupancy."

Under this statute an action was commenced by Mrs. Rutgers against Mr. Waddington, in the Mayor's Court of the City of New-York, for the recovery of rent for the occupancy of a brewhouse and malthouse, the property of the said Mrs. Rutgers. The cause was argued on the 29th of June, 1784, James Duane as Mayor, and Richard Varick as Recorder, presiding. On the 27th of August the court gave judgment "that the plea of the defendant was good for so much of the time as he held under the British commander-in-chief; because, in the opinion of the court, a liberal construction of the law of nations would make it so." As this decision involved a great principle, and would materially affect the whigs whose property had been occupied by the tories during the war, it produced great excitement.

A meeting of the whigs was convened on the 13th of September, 1784. A committee was appointed, and an address to the people of the state prepared and published by them. That committee consisted of Melancton Smith, Peter Ricker, Jonathan Lawrence, Anthony Rutgers, Peter T. Curtenius, Thomas Tucker, Daniel Shaw, Adam Gilchrist, Junr., and John Wiley. Of this committee Melancton Smith was the life and soul. He was the author of the address—a clear, able, and unanswerable exposition of the case. It states the determination of Mrs. Rutgers to carry it up to the Supreme Court, and, if defeated there, to the Senate, which, with the judges of the Supreme Court, constituted the Court for the Correction of Errors. Having reference to the contemplated proceedings, the address closes as follows:—

"Preparatory to such an event, we exhort you to be cautious, in your future choice of senators, that none be elected but those on whom, from long and certain experience, you can rely as men attached to the liberty of America, and firm friends to our laws and constitution; men who will spurn at any proposition that has a tendency to curtail the privileges of the people, and who, at the same time that they protect us against *judicial tyranny*, have wisdom to see the propriety of supporting that necessary independence in courts of justice, both of the legislature and people.

"Having confined ourselves to constitutional measures, and now solemnly declaring our disapprobation of all others, we feel a freedom in sounding the alarm to our fellow-citizens. If that independence, which we have obtained at a risk which makes the acquisition little less than miraculous, was worth contending for against a powerful and enraged monarch, and at the expense of the best blood in America, surely its preservation is worth contending for against those *among ourselves who might impiously hope to build their greatness upon the ruins of that fabric which was so dearly established.*

"That the principle of decision in the case of Rutgers *vs.* Waddington is dangerous to the freedom of our government, and that a perseverance in that principle would leave our legislature nothing but a name, and render their sessions nothing more than an expensive form of government, the preceding remarks must evidence.

"Permit us, on this occasion, earnestly to entreat you to join us in watchfulness against every attempt that may be used, either violently and suddenly, or *gently* and *imperceptibly, to effect a revolution* in the *spirit* and *genius* of our government; and *should there be among us characters to whom the simplicity of it is offensive*, let our attention and perseverance be such as to *preclude the hopes of a change.*"

Here again the party lines of 1777 are distinctly marked. Melancton Smith, Jonathan Lawrence, &c., were of the Clinton party, while Mr. Duane and Mr. Varick were attached to the Schuyler interest.

In October, 1784, the case of Rutgers *vs.* Waddington was brought before the legislature, and on the 27th of that month the assembly

"*Resolved*, That this adjudication is subversive of all law and good order; because, if a court instituted for the *benefit and government of a corporation* may take upon themselves to dispense with a law of the state, all other courts may do the like: therefore,

"*Resolved*, That it be recommended to the honourable the Council of Appointment, at their next session, to appoint such persons to be mayor and recorder of the city of New-York as will govern themselves by the known laws of the land."

Subsequently Waddington compromised the claim against him; but the law in similar cases became operative, and remained so until its repeal by the legislature. In the following session, March, 1785, an unsuccessful attempt was made to repeal the act of 1781, disqualifying tory counsellors and attorneys; some modification, however, of other laws of a similar character was effected. In April, 1786, the repealing act passed; and the restriction on the tory lawyers being removed, they were permitted to practise in the several courts of the state. During the same month, "an act for the payment of certain sums of money" was amended by adding a clause, "restoring to the rights of citizenship, on taking the oath of abjuration and allegiance," all such persons as had been disfranchised by the third clause of the act entitled "An act to preserve the freedom and independence of this state," passed the 12th of May, 1784. During this session the Schuyler party had the ascendence, and on all questions having a political aspect the names of Alexander Hamilton, Richard Varick, C. Livingston, Nicholas Bayard, David Brooks, James Livingston, &c., will be found on the same side.

On the 10th of March, 1787, Mr. Hamilton asked leave, which was granted, to bring in a bill to repeal the act entitled "An act for granting relief in case of certain trespasses." This was the act under which the suit had been commenced against Waddington, and which case produced so much excitement in the summer and autumn of 1784. Mr. Hamilton's bill passed; but, lest there should be some forgotten statute that might restrict or limit the political privileges of the tories, it was deemed expedient, on the 13th of April, to introduce and pass an act under the imposing title of "An act to repeal all laws of this state inconsistent with the treaty of peace." As its provisions met every possible case, the tories were now placed on a footing with the whigs. All they wanted was leaders. The rank and file they already possessed.

The Schuyler party sought allies. The tories were numerous, especially in the Southern District. The Clinton party, designated by Chancellor Livingston, in his letter to John Jay, as the "*violent whigs*," were uncompromising on the question of banishing the tories from the state. It seemed probable, therefore, that, sooner or later, if restored to citizenship, they would amalgamate with that class of whigs who wished to suppress "all violence, and to soften the rigour of the laws against the royalists."

The effect of these legislative measures on the tories was anticipated by both friends and foes. Chancellor Livingston, in January, 1784, had said that there were three parties in the state:—

First. The tories.

Second. The violent whigs.

Third. Those who wished "to soften the rigour of the laws against the royalists."

The Council of Revision, composed of Robert R. Livingston, Justice Morris, and Judge Hobart, had solemnly placed on record their opinion, that, in some portions of the Southern District "it would be difficult, and in many *absolutely impossible*, to find whigs to fill the necessary offices even for *conducting* elections." Under such circumstances it was evident that the *first* and *third* parties must amalgamate, and such was the result.

In January, 1788, the legislature met, and directed the

call of a State Convention, to whom was to be submitted the Federal Constitution, as adopted by the General Convention held in Philadelphia in May, 1787. During this session the same party lines continued to be visible, although the respective parties had now assumed, or were designated by new names. The Schuyler was called the Federal party, and the Clinton the anti-Federal party; they were composed, however, of the same individuals, with very few exceptions. The great, and almost the only strength which the federal party possessed in the state was in the Southern District. Here the acquisition of the tories rendered their power and influence irresistible. From this district, composed of the counties of Westchester, New-York, Richmond, King's, Queen's, and Suffolk, the federalists had in the Assembly, during the session of 1788–89, *twenty* votes, and on no *party* question did they command, during the whole session, more than *twenty-three* votes.

In December, 1788, a bill for carrying into operation the federal constitution being under consideration, a proposition was made to choose United States senators; but the federalists having a majority in the Senate, and the anti-federalists a majority in the House of Assembly, no compromise between the parties could be effected, and consequently no senators were chosen.

The following persons may be considered as constituting the strength of the Schuyler, now federal party, in the assembly of 1788–89:—

Brockholst Livingston, of the city of New-York.
William W. Gilbert, " "
Alexander Macomb, " "
Richard Harrison, " "
Nicholas Hoffman, " "
John Watts, Jun., " "
Nicholas Low, " "
Gulian Verplanck, " "
Comfort Sands, " "

Philip Van Cortlandt, Westchester county.
Philip Livingston, " "
Nathaniel Rockwell, " "
Walter Seaman, " "
Jonathan Horton, " "
John Younglove, Albany county.
Henry K. Van Rensellaer, "
Stephen Carman, Queen's county.
Whitehead Cornwell, "
Peter Vandervoort, King's county.
Aquilla Giles, "
Abraham Bancker, Richmond county.
John C. Dongan, "
Samuel A. Barker, Dutchess county.

It will be observed, that all the above Schuyler or federal members, with the exception of *two* from Albany and *one* from Dutchess county, were elected as representatives from the Southern District.

Having stated the origin and progress of the great political parties in the State of New-York, as they appear from the public records, it may be proper to add that Colonel Burr belonged to what was termed by Mr. Livingston "the violent whig party." By that party, while the tories were disfranchised, Mr. Burr was elected in 1784 to represent the city and county of New-York in the legislature. By that party, in 1789, he was appointed attorney-general of the state. By that party, in 1791, he was appointed a senator of the United States. By that party, in 1792, he was appointed a judge of the Supreme Court. By that party, subsequently, he was elected a member of the Assembly and a member of the Convention to revise the Constitution of the State, of which convention he was president; and by that party, in 1800, he was elected vice-president of the United States.

It is not intended to discuss the policy, the humanity, or the justice of the several measures proposed or adopted in relation to the tories by "*the violent whigs*," or by those whigs who wished "*to soften the rigour of the laws against the loyalists*." The historical facts have been given, and the sources from whence they were derived specified. The feelings and opinions of "*the violent whigs*" are expressed by the legislature of the state on the 9th of February, 1784, and by Governor George Clinton at the opening of that session in the city of New-York. They say—"While we recollect the general progress of a war which has been marked with cruelty and rapine; while we survey the ruins of this once flourishing city and its vicinity; while we sympathize in the calamities which have reduced so many of our virtuous fellow-citizens to want and distress, and are anxiously solicitous for means to repair the wastes and misfortunes which we lament, we cannot hearken to these petitions."

On the other hand, the sentiments and views of those whigs who wished "*to soften the rigour of the laws against the loyalists*" are to be found in the following extracts of letters.

JOHN JAY* TO GOVERNOR WILLIAM LIVINGSTON.

"Passay, 9th April, 1783.

"The tories will doubtless cause some difficulty; but that they have always done; and as this will probably be the *last time*, we must make the best of it. A universal, indiscriminate condemnation and expulsion of those people would not redound to our honour, because so harsh a measure would partake more of vengeance than of justice. For my part, I wish that all, except *the faithless and cruel*, may be forgiven. That exception would indeed *extend to very few*; but even if it applied to the case of one only, that one ought, in my opinion, to be saved."

* Jay's Works, vol. i., p. 128.

JOHN JAY TO ROBERT R. LIVINGSTON.

"Passay, 12th September, 1783.

"Europe hears much, and wishes to hear more of divisions, seditions, violences, and confusions among us. The tories are generally and greatly pitied; *more, indeed, than they deserve.* The indiscriminate expulsion and ruin of that whole class and description of men would not do honour to our magnanimity or humanity, especially in the opinion of those nations who consider, with more astonishment than pleasure, the terms of peace which America has obtained."

CHAPTER IV.

It has been seen that the Livingstons were of the Schuyler party during the revolutionary war, and that they continued so until the year 1787, when, in common with their political friends, they were the warm and ardent champions of the Federal Constitution. After its adoption, and the organization of the government under it, they soon became dissatisfied. The cause of that dissatisfaction has been differently explained. On the one hand it was said that they were alarmed at the doctrines of those who had been called to administer the government, and at the assumption of powers not delegated by the people. That they apprehended the government was verging towards a *consolidated national,* instead of a *federal* government of states.

On the other hand it was alleged that the family were disappointed and disgusted at the neglect which they experienced from General Washington. That, as Robert R. Livingston had been, in the state convention which adopted the Constitution, one of its most splendid and efficient supporters, he and his connexions anticipated his appointment to some exalted station; but that, while he was passed by unnoticed, his colleagues in that body, John Jay and Alexander Hamilton, had both received distinguished appointments—the one as Chief Justice of the United States, and the other as Secretary of the Treasury. Whatever may have been the cause of this change, it is certain that they soon abandoned the federal, and united their political destiny with the anti-federal party. Although these gentlemen, as politicians, were acting in concert with Mr. Burr, yet there was no cordiality of feeling between them. In their social intercourse, however, the most perfect comity was observed; and as they were in a minority, struggling to break down a party haughty, proscriptive, and intolerant beyond any thing that the American people had beheld, they zealously united their efforts in effecting the revolution of 1800.

Soon after the adoption of the new constitution, the anti-federal party were recognised by a name more descriptive of their principles and their views. They assumed the title of democrats. They considered themselves anti-consolidationists, but not anti-federalists. They knew that a section of the dominant party were the friends of a splendid national government. That they were the advocates of a system, by means of which all power would have concentrated in the general, and the state governments been reduced to the level of mere corporations. Against this system the democrats reasoned and contended with unabated zeal. They were the early, unflinching, and faithful champions of *state rights*.

From the year 1790 until 1800, the democratic and federal parties were alternately triumphant, both in the city and in the state of New-York. In the former, the result of an election was frequently decided by the operations of some local or exciting topic. No decisive contest took place between the parties previous to 1800, founded on any great or controlling principle of government. But, during the years 1798 and 1799, the whole country was agitated from one extreme to the other. Revolutionary France was convulsed, and, in the midst of her convulsions and sufferings, was daily committing the most cruel and wanton excesses towards her own citizens, while she was offering taunts and insults to foreign nations. The federal party seemed to sigh for a war with France. Pretending that they apprehended a French invasion, a large standing army was raised. At the head of this army, second in command to General Washington, was placed General Alexander Hamilton To support the army and other useless extravagant expenditures, a land tax and an *eight per cent.* loan was found necessary. To silence the murmurs of an oppressed people, a sedition law was enacted. Such were some of the fruits of the elder Mr. Adams's administration.

In the autumn of 1799 and the winter of 1799–1800, the interesting and vital question was presented to the American nation :—Will you sustain this administration and these measures, and thus rivet chains upon yourselves and your posterity? Or will you calmly, but firmly and in union, resort to the constitutional remedy (the ballot-boxes) for relief from wrongs and oppressions which, if permitted to endure, must terminate in the horrors of intestine war? Here was a question of principle; and, it is believed, a question which was to decide the character of the government. Each party felt that it was a mighty struggle, decisive of its future political influence, if not of its existence.

The elections in the state of New-York were held in the month of April. In the year 1799 the federalists had a majority in the city of more than nine hundred. During the summer, it was universally conceded that on the state of New-York the presidential election would depend, and that the result in the city would decide the fate of the state. That this opinion was as universal as it was true, cannot be more distinctly exhibited than by the following extract of a letter from Mr. Jefferson to Mr. Madison, dated 4th March, 1800.

"In New-York all depends on the success of the city election, which is of twelve members, and of course makes a difference of twenty-four, which is sufficient to make the two houses, joined together, republican in their vote. * * * * * * Upon the whole, I consider it as rather more doubtful than the last election (1796), in which I was not deceived in more than a vote or two. * * * * * * In any event, we may say, that if the city election of New-York is in favour of the republican ticket, the issue will be republican; if the federal ticket for the city of New-York prevails, the probabilities will be in favour of a federal issue, because it would then require a republican vote both from New-Jersey and Pennsylvania to preponderate against New-York, on which we could not count with any confidence."

Reference has been made to the conflicting factions of which the democratic party was now composed. The Clinton section, the Livingston section, and the Burr section. The first and last were apparently the same, but not so in reality. Colonel Burr's commanding talents had acquired for him an influence in the ranks of the democratic party in other states, which created some jealousy in the Clinton family, the younger and collateral branches of which were extremely hostile to him. The ambition of Burr, sustained by a daring spirit and unconquerable perseverance, awakened the apprehensions of Governor George Clinton lest he should be supplanted. The governor was a man of great sagacity and shrewdness. But these two sections, or, perhaps, more properly, the heads of them, united in their opposition to the Livingstons.

During the winter of 1800, the efforts of Colonel Burr to bring about a concert in action of these discordant materials were unceasing. With his own personal friends he had no difficulty, for it was ever one of his characteristics to se cure inviolable the attachment of his friends. They were of the most ardent and devoted kind. Confiding in his patriotism and judgment, and feeling that he was incapable of deceiving them, they seemed willing, at all times and under all circumstances, to hazard their lives and fortunes in his support. They were generally young men of gallant bearing and disinterested views. No sordid calculations were made by them. No mercenary considerations influenced their conduct. They beheld in Colonel Burr a patriot hero of the revolution, who had commingled with their fathers in the battle-field, and who had perilled every thing in his country's cause. Such were his friends, and such their zeal in his behalf. It was here that Colonel Burr was all-powerful, for he possessed, in a pre-eminent degree, the art of fascinating the youthful. But with all this tact and talent, he was credulous and easily deceived. He therefore often became the dupe of the most worthless and unprincipled.

Mr. Burr held frequent private meetings with his most intimate and confidential friends. At all these meetings it is believed the success of the democratic party was the only question under consideration. No local or personal interests were permitted to be discussed. The triumph of the party, as a whole, was the great object. By his adherents, it was deemed indispensable that he should be a member of the legislature to be chosen in April, which body was to appoint the presidential electors. While, on the other hand, it was considered not less necessary that he should be free to act at the polls in the city of New-York during the election. How was this to be effected? After much conference and deliberation it was resolved that he should be elected from Orange county, if the arrangement could be made, and the execution of the plan was intrusted principally to Peter Townsend, Esquire, of Chester, who, with the aid of other influential friends, accomplished it.

The next question was, Of whom shall the assembly ticket for the city be composed? On the suggestion of Colonel

Burr, the names of certain distinguished individuals, venerable in years, and respected for their services, for months before the election were put in circulation as candidates; and, among others, Governor George Clinton and General Horatio Gates. At length the nominating committees were chosen; but so general had been the conversations as to suitable candidates, that very little diversity of opinion prevailed in the formation of the ticket.

The following persons were nominated: George Clinton, Horatio Gates, Samuel Osgood, Henry Rutgers, Elias Nexsen, Thomas Storm, George Warner, Philip I. Arcularius, James Hunt, Ezekiel Robins, Brockholst Livingston, and John Swartwout.

In this ticket the three sections of the democratic, but at this election designated the *republican party*, are fully represented. Governor Clinton at the head of one section, Brockholst Livingston representing another, and General Gates, well known to be the personal and political friend of Colonel Burr. This ticket being nominated by the committee, the difficulty was to procure their consent to stand as candidates. A majority of them had no expectation of success. They considered the contest as a forlorn hope, and shrank from being set up as targets to be shot at. Governor Clinton, General Gates, Brockholst Livingston, and others, had repeatedly declared their fixed determination not to permit their names to be used.

A sub-committee was appointed to wait upon the candidates, and obtain permission to present their names for approval to a general meeting of citizens to be convened for that purpose. The sub-committee consisted of Aaron Burr, David Gelston, John Swartwout, John Mills, and Matthew L. Davis. After various communications and much persuasion, *nine* of the candidates consented, some of them conditionally. But Governor Clinton, General Gates, and Brockholst Livingston were for a time immoveable. At length Colonel Burr induced Judge Livingston to agree that he would serve, if Governor Clinton and General Gates consented to serve. The sub-committee next waited upon General Gates, and Colonel Burr appealed to him in the most mild and persuasive language. After much importunity he yielded, provided Governor Clinton was also a candidate.

No terms can give a correct idea of the scenes between Governor Clinton and the sub-committee, for they had an interview with him on three different days. The last was at the house of Colonel Burr, where Mr. Clinton met the committee by appointment. He never did consent to stand, but pledged himself to Colonel Burr and the committee that he would publish nothing in the newspapers, reserving to himself the right (which he subsequently exercised) of stating in conversation that his name was used without his authority or permission. Thus it is evident, that but for the matchless perseverance of Colonel Burr, the ticket, as it stood, never could have been formed, and, when formed, would have been broken up, and the republican party discomfited and beaten.

An imperfect sketch of the scene at the house of Colonel Burr was published in the year 1802, in a pamphlet under the signature of *Aristides*. The following is extracted from it. The note of reference here given is also extracted. Its correctness was never publicly denied by either of the gentlemen named. There exists no longer any reason for concealment on the subject; and it is therefore now admitted that this *note* was written from memorandums made at the time by the author of this volume.

EXTRACT.

"Governor Clinton, however, remained unmoved by the most earnest solicitations; and, with matchless firmness, resisted the arguments of Mr. Burr, who forcibly asserted that it was a right inherent in the community to command the services of an individual when the nature of public exigences seemed to require it. He was inflexible to the last, and then was nominated and elected without a distinct expression of his approbation. Justice, however, induces me to acknowledge, that the reasons he assigned for the reluctance with which he acted were plausible and potent.

"He explicitly declared that he had long entertained an unfavourable opinion of Mr. Jefferson's talents as a statesman and his firmness as a republican. That he conceived him an accommodating trimmer, who would change with times, and bend to circumstances for the purposes of personal promotion. Impressed with these sentiments, he could not, with propriety, he said, acquiesce in the elevation of a man destitute of the qualifications essential to the good administration of the government; and added other expressions too vulgar to be here repeated. 'But,' said he, with energy, 'if you, Mr. Burr, was the candidate for the presidential chair, I would act with pleasure and with vigour.'"*

* "It is so notorious that these were Governor Clinton's sentiments, that it is scarcely necessary to produce authority to prove it. To remove, however, every doubt in the reader's mind, I will refer him to Mr. David Gelston, Mr. John Mills, Mr. John Swartwout, or Mr. Matthew L. Davis, in whose presence these sentiments, and many others more disrespectful, if possible, were uttered. It was at the house of Mr. Burr, who, anticipating the evil consequences that at that critical moment would result from such conduct in Governor Clinton, insisted, before he left the house, that he should promise his friends to desist from using such language previous to or during the election. This was very reluctantly complied with on the part of Mr. Clinton.

"Notwithstanding this, they were continually reiterated by his son, who publicly and loudly animadverted upon the character of Mr. Jefferson with the most vulgar severity. Similar sentiments were certainly entertained by all Governor Clinton's connexions, as their conduct during the election clearly evinced. Mr. Dewitt Clinton, through the whole contest, never appeared at the poll, but observed the most shameful indifference and inactivity."

The nomination of a ticket having been made and approved at a public meeting over which Anthony Lispenard presided, its effect upon both parties was tremendous. The character and standing of the candidates seemed a presage of victory. It elated, and gave life and vigour to the republicans, while it paralyzed and depressed the federalists.

Never before or since has a ticket been presented to the citizens of New-York composed of men combining such talents, patriotism, experience, and public services, as the republican assembly ticket for the year 1800.

Those who possess a knowledge of the character of Colonel Burr know what were his qualifications for execution. The plan of the campaign having been opened, it only remained to be executed. In the performance of this duty, all Mr. Burr's industry, perseverance, and energy were called into operation. Nor were the federal party idle or inactive. They possessed wealth and patronage. Led on to the contest by their talented chieftain, General Hamilton, whose influence in their ranks was unbounded, they made a desperate but ineffectual resistance to the assaults upon their political citadel. If defeated here, their power was gone, and the administration of the government lost. Both General Hamilton and Colonel Burr exerted themselves personally at the polls during the three days of election. They repeatedly addressed the people, and did all that men could do. They frequently met at the same polls, and argued, in the presence of large assemblages, the debatable questions. Their deportment towards each other and towards their opponents was such as comported with the dignity of two of the most accomplished and courtly gentlemen of the age in which they lived.

The polls of the election opened on the morning of the 29th of April, and finally closed at sunset on the 1st of May. Immediately after, the inspectors commenced counting and canvassing the ballots. Sufficient progress was made during the night to render it, in a great measure, certain that the republican ticket had succeeded; and on the 2d of May this result was announced, the average majority being about 490. All doubt as to the presidential vote of the state of New-York was now removed, unless the federal party, in their expiring agonies, could devise some plan by which the will of the people, thus clearly expressed, should be defeated. Such apprehensions were entertained, and, it was soon discovered, not entertained without good reason.

In both branches of the legislature elected in 1799 the federalists had a majority. The time of service of the members would expire on the 1st of July, 1800. After the nomination of the republican assembly ticket, but previous to the election in April, 1800, it was suspected that certain federalists had in contemplation a project to render the city election null and void if the republicans succeeded. When the polls were closed, therefore, discreet and intelligent men were placed at them to guard, if it should be found necessary, the inspectors from committing, inadvertently, any errors, either in canvassing or making their returns. Every movement, subsequently, of leading federal gentlemen was narrowly and cautiously watched. The result of the election was announced on the 2d of May. On the 3d of May, in the evening, a select and confidential federal caucus was held. On the 4th a letter was written to William Duane, editor of the Aurora, stating that such a caucus had been held the preceding night, and that it was determined by the caucus to solicit Governor Jay to convene the existing legislature forthwith, for the purpose of changing the mode of choosing electors for president, and placing it in the hands of the people by districts. The effect of such a measure would have been to neutralize the State of New-York, and, as the result finally proved, would have secured to the federal party their president and vice-president. This letter was published in the Aurora of the 6th of May, and called forth the denunciations of those federal papers whose conductors were not in the secret. The author of the letter was assailed as a *Jacobin* calumniator, and the whole story was pronounced a vile fabrication. One of the New-York city papers reprinted the letter, and thus closes its commentary on it:—"Where is the American who *will not detest the author of this infamous lie?* If there is a man to be found who will sanction this publication, he is worse than

What effect, if any, was produced by this immediate exposure of the caucus proceedings, it is not necessary now to inquire. It is sufficient to say that the development was, in all its parts, literally correct, and the subject is here introduced for the twofold purpose of showing, *first*, the vigilance, promptitude, and arrangement of the republican party of that day; and, *second*, the means to which certain desperate federalists were willing to resort for the purpose of retaining power. That the representations contained in the publication of the Aurora were strictly true, is now matter of recorded history.

In the life of John Jay, vol. i., p. 412, the letter addressed to the governor on this subject is published. It bears date *one day* after the publication in the Aurora, but before the paper reached the city of New-York. The author of the work, after some preliminary remarks, says—" These details will explain the proposal made in the following letter, which was received by the governor *from one of the most distinguished federalists in the United States*."*

TO JOHN JAY.

New-York, May 7, 1800.

Dear Sir,

You have been informed of the loss of our election in this city. It is also known that we have been unfortunate throughout Long Island and in Westchester. According to the returns hitherto, it is too probable that we lose our senator for this district.

The moral certainty, therefore, is, that there will be an anti-federal majority in the ensuing legislature; and the very high probability is, that this will bring Jefferson into the chief magistracy, unless it be prevented by the measure which I shall now submit to your consideration; namely, the immediate calling together of the existing legislature.

* As there were but *few* of " the most distinguished federalists in the United States" residing at that time in the city of New-York, the intelligent reader will form his own conclusions as to the source from whence it emanated.

I am aware that there are weighty objections to the measure; but the reasons for it appear to me to outweigh the objections; and, in times like these in which we live, it will not do to be over scrupulous. It is easy to sacrifice the substantial interests of society by a strict adherence to ordinary rules.

In observing this I shall not be supposed to mean that any thing ought to be done which integrity will forbid; but merely that the scruples of delicacy and propriety, as relative to a common course of things, ought to yield to the extraordinary nature of the crisis. They ought not to hinder the taking of a legal and constitutional step to prevent an atheist in religion and a fanatic in politics from getting possession of the helm of state.

You, sir, know in a great degree the anti-federal party; but I fear you do not know them as well as I do. 'Tis a composition, indeed, of very incongruous materials, but all tending to mischief—some of them to the overthrow of the government, by stripping it of its due energies; others of them to a revolution after the manner of Bonaparte. I speak from indubitable facts, not from conjectures and inferences. In proportion as the true character of the party is understood, is the force of the considerations which urge to every effort to disappoint it; and it seems to me that there is a very solemn obligation to employ the means in our power.

The calling of the legislature will have for object the choosing of electors by the people in districts; this (as Pennsylvania will do nothing) will ensure a majority of votes in the United States for a federal candidate. The measure will not fail to be approved by all the federal party, while it will, no doubt, be condemned by the opposite. As to its intrinsic nature, it is justified by unequivocal reasons of *public safety*.

The reasonable part of the world will, I believe, approve it. They will see it as a proceeding out of the common course, but warranted by the particular nature of the crisis and the great cause of social order.

If done, the motive ought to be frankly avowed. In your communication to the legislature, they ought to be told that temporary circumstances had rendered it probable that, without their interposition, the executive authority of the general government would be transferred to hands hostile to the system heretofore pursued with so much success, and dangerous to the peace, happiness, and order of the country. That under this impression, from facts convincing to your own mind, you had thought it your duty to give the existing legislature an opportunity of deliberating whether it would not be proper to interpose, and endeavour to prevent so great an evil, by referring the choice of electors to the people distributed into districts.

In weighing this suggestion, you will doubtless bear in mind that popular governments must certainly be overturned; and, while they endure, prove engines of mischief, if one party will call to its aid all the resources which vice can give, and if the other (however pressing the emergency) confines itself within all the ordinary forms of delicacy and decorum.

The legislature can be brought together in three weeks, so that there will be full time for the object; but none ought to be lost.

Think well, my dear sir, of this proposition; appreciate the extreme danger of the crisis; and I am unusually mistaken in my view of the matter if you do not see it right and expedient to adopt the measure.

Respectfully and affectionately yours.

Mr. Jay's biographer adds—"On this letter is the following endorsement in the governor's hand, *Proposing a measure for party purposes which I think it would not become me to adopt.*"

CHAPTER V.

During the summer of 1800 General Hamilton prepared for the press his celebrated pamphlet, entitled—"A letter from Alexander Hamilton, concerning the public conduct and character of John Adams, Esq., president of the United States." It was the design of the author of this pamphlet that it should be privately printed, and circulated in South Carolina only a few days before the election, for the purpose of preventing Mr. Adams from getting the vote of South Carolina, but securing it to Mr. Pinckney, who was the federal candidate for the vice-presidency. The consequence would have been to place Mr. Pinckney's electoral vote higher than Mr. Adams's, and thus, if the federal party succeeded, Mr. Pinckney would have been elected president and Mr. Adams vice-president. Colonel Burr ascertained the contents of this pamphlet, and that it was in the press. Its immediate publication, he knew, must distract the federal party, and thus promote the republican cause in those states where the elections had not yet taken place. Arrangements were accordingly made for a copy, as soon as the printing of it was completed; and when obtained, John Swartwout, Robert Swartwout, and Matthew L. Davis, by appointment, met Colonel Burr at his own house. The pamphlet was read, and extracts made for the press. Mr. Davis was charged with forwarding these extracts to William Duane, editor of the Aurora, and to Charles Holt, editor of the Bee, printed in New-London, which was accordingly done, and the extracts immediately published.*

* Mr. Tucker, in his life of Jefferson, ascribes the defeat of the federal party in South Carolina to General Hamilton's pamphlet. Its premature publication, no doubt, contributed largely to produce this result.

The effect of this sudden and unexpected explosion was such as might have been anticipated. It rent the federal party in twain. The publication, from time to time, of extracts, and the excitement which was produced throughout the country by them, at length compelled Mr. Hamilton to authorize the publication of the entire pamphlet; and accordingly, in October, as the electors were to be chosen in November, it was advertised for sale in the Daily Gazette. The editor of the paper explained that it was not the intention of General Hamilton to give publicity to this letter at the time it was made public; but that extracts from it by some unknown means had found their way to the public, and therefore the whole was now given.

Further evidence of the vigilance and efficiency of Colonel Burr in promoting the revolution of 1800 is deemed unnecessary. It is most solemnly believed that the overthrow of the federal party at that time would not have been accomplished but through his zeal, sagacity, and industry. His friends, therefore, have ascribed to him, and not without some foundation, the election of Mr. Jefferson to the presidency.

Governor Jay having refused to comply with the wishes of " one of the most distinguished federalists in the United States," as proposing a measure for party purposes which he (Governor Jay) thought it would not become him to adopt, the legislature did not convene until the fourth day of November, 1800, and on the sixth they proceeded to the choice of electors for president and vice-president. The republican ticket prevailed. It was composed of the following persons :—

Isaac Ledyard, of Queen's County.
Anthony Lispenard, of New-York.
P. Van Courtlandt, of Westchester
James Burt, of Orange.
Gilbert Livingston, of Dutchess.
Thomas Jenkins, of Columbia.

Peter Van Ness, of Columbia.
Robert Ellis, of Saratoga.
John Woodworth, of Rensellaer.
J. Van Rensellaer, of Albany.
Jacob Eacker, of Montgomery, and
William Floyd, of Suffolk.

The vote stood :—

	Republican.	Federal.
In the Senate . .	18	24
In the Assembly . .	64	39

Thus, on joint ballot, the republican majority was nineteen; and consequently, as the city of New-York elected *twelve* members, if the federalists had succeeded in the city, they would have had, in joint ballott, a majority of from six to ten.

As a part of the history of this election, the following letter and extracts from letters are here inserted.

THOMAS JEFFERSON TO AARON BURR.

"Washington, December 15, 1800.

"Dear Sir,

"Although we have not official information of the votes for president and vice-president, and cannot have until the first week in February, yet the state of the votes is given on such evidence as satisfies both parties that the two republican candidates stand highest. From South Carolina we have not even heard of the actual vote, but we have learned who were appointed electors, and with sufficient certainty how they would vote. It is said they would withdraw from yourself one vote. It has also been said that a General Smith, of Tennessee, had declared that he would give his second vote to Mr. Gallatin, not from any indisposition towards you, but extreme reverence to the character of Mr Gallatin. It is also surmised that the vote of Georgia will not be entire. Yet nobody pretends to know these things of a certainty, and we know enough to be certain that what it is surmised will be withheld, will still leave you four or five votes at least above Mr. Adams. However, it was badly managed not to have arranged with certainty what seems to have been left to hazard. It was the more material, because I understand several high-flying federalists have expressed their hope that the two republican tickets may be equal, and their determination in that case to prevent a choice by the House of Representatives (which they are strong enough to do), and let the government devolve on a president of the Senate. Decency required that I should be so entirely passive during the late contest, that I never once asked whether arrangements had been made to prevent so many from dropping votes intentionally as might frustrate half the republican wish; nor did I doubt, till lately, that such had been made.

"While I must congratulate you, my dear sir, on the issue of this contest, because it is more honourable, and, doubtless, more grateful to you than any station within the competence of the chief magistrate, yet, for myself, and for the substantial service of the public, I *feel most sensibly the loss we sustain of your aid in our new administration. It leaves a chasm in my arrangements which cannot be adequately filled up. I had endeavoured to compose an administration whose talents, integrity, names, and dispositions should at once inspire unbounded confidence in the public mind, and ensure a perfect harmony in the conduct of the public business. I lose you from the list,* and am not sure of all the others. Should the gentlemen who possess the public confidence decline taking a part in their affairs, and force us to take persons unknown to the people, the evil genius of this country may realize his avowal that 'he will beat down the administration.' The return of Mr. Van Benthuysen, one of your electors, furnishes me a confidential opportunity of writing this much to you, which I should not have ventured through the postoffice at this prying season. We shall, of course, see you before the fourth of March. Accept my respectful and affectionate salutations."

The letter is, in a great measure, incomprehensible. It indicates nothing but Mr. Jefferson's extreme terror and apprehension lest he should be disappointed in his anticipated elevation to the presidency. It displays the *tact* of the ostrich, and the *sincerity* of a refined Jesuit. What does Mr. Jefferson mean by the declaration that he had formed a cabinet, of which Mr. Burr was to be a member? What when he says—"*I lose you from the list?*" Can any man believe that Mr. Jefferson expected to be elected president, but that Colonel Burr would be defeated; and that, acting upon such a state of facts, he had already selected the members of his administration, and that Mr. Burr was one of them? The supposition is absurd; but, without such a supposition, what becomes of the truth of Mr. Jefferson's declaration when he says—"I feel most sensibly the loss we sustain of your aid in our new administration. *It leaves a chasm in my arrangements* which cannot be adequately filled up?" If this letter is carefully read and analyzed, its object may be comprehended. It was written a few weeks before the balloting was to take place in Congress. Mr. Jefferson expresses doubt as to the vote Mr. Burr will receive, but considers it certain that he will have "four or five votes at least above Mr. Adams." Four days after this letter he writes in a very different tone to a friend.

MR. JEFFERSON TO MR. MADISON.

"Washington, December 19, 1800.

"Dear Sir,

"Mrs. Brown's departure for Virginia enables me to write confidentially what I would not have ventured by the post at this prying season. The election in South Carolina has, in some measure, decided the great contest. Though, as yet, we do not know the actual votes of Tennessee, Kentucky, and Vermont, yet we believe the votes to be, on the whole, Jefferson, 73; Burr, 73; Adams, 65; Pinckney, 64. Rhode Island withdrew one from Pinckney. There is a possibility that Tennessee may withdraw *one* from Burr, and Burr writes that there may be one vote in Vermont for Jefferson. But I hold the latter *impossible*, and the former *not probable*; and that there will be an absolute parity between the two republican candidates. This has produced great dismay and gloom on the republican gentlemen here, and exultation in the federalists, who openly declare they will prevent an election, and will name a president of the Senate *pro tem.* by what, they say, would only be a *stretch* of the constitution. The prospect of preventing this is as follows. Georgia, North Carolina, Tennessee, Kentucky, Vermont, Pennsylvania, and New-York can be counted on for their vote in the House of Representatives, and *it is thought, by some, that* BAER *of Maryland and* LINN *of New-Jersey will come over.*"

The preceding extract shows that Mr. Jefferson entertained no doubt "that there would be an absolute parity between the two republican candidates," notwithstanding his doubting remarks on that subject to Colonel Burr. Hopes were also entertained "that Mr. Baer of Maryland and *Linn of New-Jersey would come over.*" Reference will hereafter be made to these two states. The result of the electoral vote was as Mr. Jefferson anticipated. *Seventy-three* republican and *sixty-five* federal.

Although the ballots for president and vice-president had not been examined officially, yet it was well known that there was a tie between Mr. Jefferson and Colonel Burr.

On the 8th of February, 1801, Mr. Bayard, in the House of Representatives, offered a resolution declaring that, in case of a tie, the house would continue to ballot until a choice of president was made. It was referred to a select committee, and, on the 10th, it, with other rules to govern the house during the balloting, was adopted. The Senate passed a resolution that the ballots should be opened with closed doors. William H. Wells, of Delaware, of the Senate, and John Nicholas, of Virginia, and John Rutledge, of South Carolina, of the House of Representatives, were appointed tellers.

On the 11th of February the ballots were opened. During the performance of this ceremony a most extraordinary incident occurred. As it is known to but few now living, and never been publicly spoken of, it has been deemed proper to record it here, as a part of the history of that exciting contest.

The Aurora of the 16th of February, 1801, remarks, that "the tellers declared that there was some informality in the votes of Georgia; but, believing them to be true votes, reported them as such." No explanation of the nature of this informality was given; nor is it known that any has ever been given since. Had it been announced at the time, there can be no doubt it would have proved fatal to the election of Mr. Jefferson. Whether the interest of our country would or would not have been thereby promoted, is not a question for discussion here.

By the Constitution of the United States at that time it was provided, Art. 2, sect. 1, "The electors shall meet in their respective states, and vote by ballot for two persons, of whom one at least shall not be an inhabitant of the same state with themselves. And they shall make a list of all the persons voted for, and of the number of votes for each, *which list they shall sign, and certify*, and transmit, sealed, to the seat of the government of the United States, directed to the President of the Senate. The President of the Senate shall, in the presence of the Senate and House of Representatives, open *all the certificates*, and the votes shall then be counted. The person having the greatest number of votes shall be the president, if such number be *a majority of the whole number of electors appointed;* and if there be more than one who have such majority, and have an equal number of vôtes, then the House of Representatives shall immediately choose, by ballot, one of them for president; and if no person have a majority, then from the *five highest* on the list the said house shall, in like manner, choose the president. But, in choosing the president, the votes shall be taken by states, and a majority of all the states shall be necessary to a choice."

From the above extract it will be seen that the Constitution is imperative as to the *form* and *manner* in which the electoral returns are to be made. The ceremony of opening was performed in the presence of the two houses. The package of a state having been opened by the vice-president, it was handed by him to the tellers. Mr. Jefferson was the presiding officer. On opening the package endorsed Georgia votes, it was discovered to be totally irregular. The statement now about to be given is derived from an honourable gentleman, a member of Congress from the state of New-York during the administration of Mr. Jefferson, and yet living in this state. He says that Mr. Wells (a teller on the part of the Senate) informed him that the envelope was blank; that the return of the votes was not authenticated *by the signatures of the electors, or any of them, either on the outside or the inside of the envelope, or in any other manner*; that it merely stated in the inside that the votes of Georgia were, for Thomas Jefferson *four*, and for Aaron Burr *four*, without the *signature of any person* whatsoever. Mr. Wells added, that he was very undecided as to the proper course to be pursued by the tellers. It was, however, suggested by one of them that the paper should be handed to the presiding officer, without any statement from the tellers except that the return was informal; that he consented to this arrangement under the firm conviction that Mr. Jefferson would announce the nature of the informality from the chair; but, to his utmost surprise, he (Mr. Jefferson) rapidly declared that the votes of Georgia were *four* for Thomas Jefferson and *four* for Aaron Burr, without noticing their informality, and in a hurried manner put them aside, and then broke the seals and handed to the tellers the package from the next state. Mr. Wells observed, that as soon as Mr. Jefferson looked at the paper purporting to contain a statement of the electoral vote of the state of Georgia, his countenance changed, but that the decision and promptitude with which he acted on that occasion convinced him of that which he (a federalist) and his party had always doubted, that is to say, Mr. Jefferson's decision of character, at least when his own interest was at hazard. Mr. Wells further stated, that if the votes of Georgia had not been thus counted, as it would have brought all the candidates into the house, Mr. Pinckney among the number, Mr. Jefferson could not have been elected president.

The same honourable member of Congress further stated, that some few years after receiving the above information from Mr. Wells, he became intimately acquainted with John Nicholas, who was one of the tellers referred to, and who had removed from Virginia into the western part of the State of New-York. Mr. Nicholas gave to the honourable member the same statement in substance, not knowing that it had been previously derived from Mr. Wells. Mr. Nicholas was a warm personal and political friend of Mr. Jefferson, and declared that he never felt so astounded in his life as when he discovered the irregularity. He claimed some credit for the adroit manner in which he had managed Mr. Rutledge, so far as to obtain his consent to hand the paper to Mr. Jefferson without public explanation from the tellers, and which was effected by a conciliatory appeal to the magnanimity of the member from South Carolina.

The whole number of electoral votes given at the election in 1800 was *one hundred and thirty-eight:* necessary to a choice, *seventy.* Mr. Jefferson and Mr. Burr had each, according to the return made, *seventy-three.* Georgia gave *four* votes. If that number had been deducted from Jefferson and Burr, as illegally returned, of which there is no doubt, they would have had only *sixty-nine* votes each;

consequently they would not have had, in the language of the Constitution, "a majority of the whole number of electors appointed," and the candidates out of which a choice of president must be made would have been Mr. Jefferson, Mr. Burr, Mr. Adams, and Mr. Pinckney. The federal members would then have said to the republicans, We will unite with you in the choice of either of the gentlemen presented to the house except Mr. Jefferson; and if the government is to be brought to a termination by our failure to elect a president, the responsibility will be on you. And is it to be believed, that in such a case the *doubtful* members who were sighing for office, if any such there were, would have rejected the suggestion in toto?

The balloting continued from the 11th until the 17th of February inclusive. *Nine* states were necessary to a choice. On the first ballot Mr. Jefferson had *eight*, Mr. Burr *six*, and *two* states were divided. At every ballot the same result was announced, until the *thirty-sixth* ballot, which was given on the 17th of February, when Mr. Jefferson was declared duly elected, *ten* states having voted for him.

On the first ballot Mr. Jefferson received New-York, New-Jersey, Pennsylvania, Virginia, North Carolina, Kentucky, Georgia, and Tennessee—*eight*.

Mr. Burr received New-Hampshire, Massachusetts, Rhode Island, Connecticut, Delaware, and South Carolina—*six*.

Divided, Vermont and Maryland—*two*.

On the final ballot Mr. Jefferson received New-York, New-Jersey, Pennsylvania, Virginia, North Carolina, Kentucky, Georgia, Tennessee, Maryland (*four* votes and *four* blanks), Vermont (*one* vote and *one* blank)—*ten*.

Mr. Burr received New-Hampshire, Massachusetts, Rhode Island, and Connecticut—*four*.

Delaware *blank*, South Carolina *no vote*.

During the balloting *one hundred and six* members of

the House of Representatives were present. Of this number *fifty-one*, on the first ballot, voted for Mr. Jefferson; and on no subsequent vote was that number increased. The election was effected by the states of Maryland and Vermont giving their vote, instead of remaining *equally divided*, and thus having no vote; and that change was produced in Maryland by Mr. Craick, Mr. Dennis, Mr. Baer, and Mr. Chew Thomas voting *blank*, and Mr. Lewis R. Morris, of Vermont, in like manner voting blank, leaving Mr. Matthew Lyon the sole representative of the state.

Previous to the balloting, Mr. Burr addressed to General S. Smith, of Baltimore, a member of the House of Representatives, the following letter. It will be seen by the date, that as soon as Colonel Burr supposed that there was a probability of a tie, he constituted General Smith his proxy to declare his sentiments.

EXTRACT.

"New-York, 16th December, 1800.

"It is highly improbable that I shall have an equal number of votes with Mr. Jefferson; but, if such should be the result, every man who knows me ought to know that I would utterly disclaim all competition. Be assured that *the federal party can entertain no wish for such an exchange.* As to my friends, they would dishonour my views and insult my feelings by a suspicion that I would submit to be instrumental in counteracting the wishes and the expectations of the United States. And I now constitute you *my proxy to declare these sentiments* if the occasion should require."*

* The effect of this letter upon public opinion may be judged of by the following, among other testimonials which might be inserted.

Baltimore, February 28, 1801.

SIR—Many of the citizens of Baltimore, who have just now heard of your arrival among them, beg leave to congratulate you and themselves upon the success of the late election of President and Vice-president of the United States. They, in a particular manner, appreciate that patriotism which disclaimed competition

CHAPTER VI.

This contest in Congress produced, almost immediately, strong feelings of dissatisfaction between some of the friends of Mr. Jefferson and Colonel Burr. Jealousies and distrust had previously existed. Mr. Jefferson was anxious that Mr. Madison should be his successor in office. The Clinton and Livingston families were prepared to unite in a crusade against Colonel Burr; the chieftains of each section hoping to fill the station from which he was to be expelled. General Hamilton was in favour of the election of Mr. Jefferson, as opposed to Colonel Burr. The result afforded him a triumph, and he was prepared, when opportunity should present, to prostrate his late successful opponent. Such was the state of parties, and such the feelings of leading and distinguished partisans, when Colonel Burr entered upon the vice-presidency, on the fourth of March, 1801. He was hemmed in on every side by political adversaries, ready for the onset so soon as it should be deemed expedient to make it. Every movement, every expression at the convivial board or in the social circle, and every action, was carefully watched and noted for future use, if, by the exercise of ingenuity and misrepresentation, such expression or action could be so tortured as to operate injuriously to him. These several sections, each acting within its own sphere, impelled by conflicting motives, were untiring in their efforts to accomplish the great object—the ruin of the vice-

for the presidential chair with that other eminent character who has finally been called to it—as setting a just value upon the will of the people.

By order of the meeting.

Thomas M'Elderry.

To Aaron Burr, Vice-president elect of the United States of America.

president. They combined wealth, talents, and government patronage.

The following short extracts from letters, written as early as 1794 and 1795, will show what were the wishes of Mr. Jefferson (so far as any reliance can be placed on professions) in relation to Mr. Madison.

THOMAS JEFFERSON TO JAMES MADISON.

"Monticello, December 28, 1794.

"DEAR SIR,

"I do not see in the minds of those with whom I converse a greater affliction than the fear of your retirement;* but this must not be, *unless to a more splendid and more efficacious post.*† There I should rejoice to see you; I hope I may say, I shall rejoice to see you. I have long had much in my mind to say to you on that subject; but double delicacies have kept me silent. I ought, perhaps, to say, *while I would not give up my own retirement for the empire of the universe*, how I can justify wishing one, whose happiness I have so much at heart as yours, to take the front of the battle which is fighting for my security."

THOMAS JEFFERSON TO JAMES MADISON.

"Monticello, April 27, 1795.

"DEAR SIR,

"In mine, to which yours of March the twenty-third was an answer, I expressed my hope of the only change of position I ever wished to see you make, and I expressed it with entire sincerity, because there is not another person in the United States who, being placed at the helm of our affairs, my mind would be so completely at rest for the fortune of our political bark. The wish, too, was pure, and unmixed with any thing respecting myself personally. * * * * * *

"If these general considerations were sufficient to ground

* Mr. Madison was then a member of Congress.

† President of the United States.

a firm resolution never to permit myself to think of the office (president), or be thought of for it, the special ones which have supervened on my retirement still more insuperably bar the door to it. My health is entirely broken down within the last eight months; *my age requires that I should place my affairs* in a clear state; these are sound, if taken care of, but capable of considerable dangers if longer neglected; and, above all things, the delights I feel in the society of my family, and in the agricultural pursuits in which I am so eagerly engaged. *The little spice of ambition which I had in my younger days has long since evaporated, and I set still less store by a posthumous than present name.*"

It is a remarkable fact, that, previous to the balloting in Congress, all parties and sections of parties concurred in the opinion that the election would finally be determined, as it was, by New-York, New-Jersey, and Maryland. These *three* states would render the election of Colonel Burr certain, *two* of them could elect Mr. Jefferson. The vote of New-York was to be decided by *Theodorus Bailey*, of Dutchess county, and *Edward Livingston*, of the city of New-York; the vote of New-Jersey by Mr. *Linn*, and the vote of Maryland by Mr. *Dent* or Mr. *Baer*.

In the Commercial Advertiser of the thirteenth of February, 1801, a paper opposed to the election of Colonel Burr, there is published an extract of a letter from a member of Congress, dated Washington, February 10, which states that, upon the second ballot, it is expected that New-York, New-Jersey, and Maryland will vote for Mr. Burr.

On the sixth of February, 1801, a leading and influential republican member of Congress writes to his correspondent a letter, from which the following is extracted:—

"I have not time to answer your letter as fully as I could wish, as it would have been my desire to communicate to you not only facts, *but some of the reasons which have induced us to adopt the steps we have heretofore taken.* But, at all events, it is important that you should have an immediate knowledge of the present situation of affairs.

"It is reduced to moral certainty, so far as any reliance can be placed on the solemn determinations of men, that either Mr. Jefferson will be chosen, or that there will be no choice made. The republican majorities of eight states (including *Linn** of New-Jersey, and the New-York representation†), the republican half of Maryland, including Mr. *Dent*,‡ and Lyon of Vermont, are *pledged* to persevere in voting for Mr. Jefferson to the end, be the consequence what it will."

Colonel Burr, soon after his election, gave his enemies an opportunity to cavil. It would be impossible to enter into all the details connected with this subject; but the principal charges which were made against the vice-president, and assigned as reasons for opposing his renomination, will be breifly presented. The replies to or explanations of them, by the parties implicated, will also be given.

Late in November, 1801, when Mr. Burr was on his way to Washington to take his seat in Senate as vice-president, he was addressed by certain citizens of Baltimore, on which occasion he remarked, "Time will not allow me to return you a written answer, but I must be permitted to state my disapprobation of the mode of expressing public sentiment by addresses." This gave offence to some, and, by the artful and designing, was misrepresented. Mr. Burr, during the years 1798 and 1799, had beheld, with mortification

* Appointed by Mr. Jefferson supervisor of internal revenue for the state of New-Jersey.

† Edward Livingston and Theodorus Bailey; the former appointed United States district attorney for the district of New-York; the latter subsequently appointed postmaster of the *city* of New-York, and removed from the country, a distance of nearly one hundred miles, to take charge of the office. Cheetham, editor of the *American Citizen*, some time after Mr. Livingston's appointment, in referring to him, says—"Should Mr. Burr's *confidential friend ever become dangerous, we will show what he has been and what he is.*"

‡ Appointed United States marshal for the Potomac district of Maryland.

and disgust, the adulatory, if not sycophantic addresses presented to President Adams. This reproof, therefore, of his friends, evinced his natural independence of character as well as the purest republican notions.

In the month of January, 1802, a bill to repeal what was termed by the republicans the federal midnight judiciary act, was pending before the Senate. On the 27th of January, a motion was made to refer the bill to a committee for the purpose of amendment. On this motion the votes were, *ayes*, 14; *noes*, 14. The vice-president, Colonel Burr, was in the chair. He said—" I am for the affirmative, because I never can resist the reference of a measure where the Senate is so nicely balanced, and when the object is to effect amendment that may accommodate it to the opinions of a large majority, and particularly when I can believe that gentlemen are sincere in wishing a reference for this purpose. Should it, however, at any time appear that delay only is intended, my conduct will be different."

This decision afforded the enemies of Colonel Burr an opportunity to break ground more openly against him. He was now charged with aiding the federal party in their efforts to embarrass the administration, and with the design of defeating the wishes of the American people. As yet, the charge of intriguing and negotiating with the federalists to obtain the presidency in opposition to Mr. Jefferson had not been made. The allies had not yet sufficiently poisoned the public mind against the vice-president, nor had they subsidized the requisite number of presses for carrying on the work of destruction. While the grand assault was meditating, and these *feints* were carrying on against the vice-president, he was constantly receiving approbatory letters from intelligent and well-informed citizens, many of whom cowered beneath the storm when, in the height of its fury, it burst upon the victim. From among a number the following are selected :—

FROM A. J. DALLAS.

Philadelphia, 3d February, 1802.*

DEAR SIR,

On the judiciary question, I wrote my sentiments to Mr. Wilson Nicholas early in the session. I am sorry our friends have taken so peremptory a position, as the very circumstance of having taken it will render it difficult to move them. I cannot concur with them in the policy or expediency of the measure. The business of the court will not allow me to give my reasons in detail, but you shall have my brief.

1. There never was a case in which a party could be more justified in expressing their resentment, on account of the manner of passing the act; the manner of organizing the courts; the nature of the opposition to the repeal, denying its constitutionality, and menacing a civil war.

2. The repeal would be constitutional, from a review of the principles and terms of the constitution itself; of the peculiar situation of the country; its growing population; its extending prospects; its increasing wants, pursuits, and refinements, &c.; of the analogy to the Judiciary Institution of England, where independent of the legislature is not within the policy or provision of the statutes relative to the commissions of the judges; of the analogy to the Judiciary Institutions of the sister states, which have all been subject to legislative interference occasionally. In Pennsylvania particularly, the constitution declares that the judges shall hold their commissions during good behaviour; yet it expressly authorizes the legislature to abolish the Court of Common Pleas, &c.; and of the precedents in the existing act of Congress, which is an exercise of the power *sub modo*.

3. But notwithstanding the indignation I feel, in common with our friends, at the manner of passing the Circuit Court act; and notwithstanding my perfect conviction that Con-

* This letter is dated *seven* days after Mr. Burr's casting vote in the Senate.

gress has the power of repealing the act, I think the repeal would be impolitic and inexpedient. If it would be impolitic acting on party principles, it would be inexpedient of course ; but I mean, also, that it would be inexpedient on account of the use that Pennsylvania (and I presume the same as to other states) has derived from the institution :

1st. *It is impolitic.*

The republicans are not agreed on the constitutionality of the repeal. The people at large have imbibed strong prejudices on the subject of judicial independence. The repeal would be ascribed to party animosity ; and if future amendments should be made, it would be considered as a personal proceeding, merely to remove the present judges : the hazard of loss in public opinion is greater than the hope of gain. There is a mass of the community that will not be fermented by the leaven of party passions. By persons of this description, the motive and effect will be strictly analyzed and purified. The mere resuscitation of the old system will either expose the administration of justice to inconceivable embarrassments, or demonstrate the motive to be abstractedly a party one, by calling for an immediate reform. The clamour of the federalists will at least have a reasonable foundation.

2. *It is inexpedient.*

The mere repeal will reinstate a system which every man of common sense and candour must deprecate. It will entirely destroy institutions susceptible of being modelled into a form economical as well as useful. It will deprive some states of tribunals which have been found highly advantageous to the despatch of business. I allude particularly to Pennsylvania. In this state justice, as far as respects our state courts, is in a state of dissolution, from the excess of business and the parsimony of the legislature.

With this view of the subject you will perceive that I think—*First,* There ought not to be a total repeal. *Second,* There ought to be amendments.

If, however, a repeal should take place, I am clearly of opinion that it would be unjustifiable to make any provision for the ex-judges. On this point and on the introduction of amendments I will, if you desire it, amplify by a future post.

The zealous republicans are exciting some intemperance here, in opposition to a memorial from our bar, which, you will perceive, is confined to the operation of the law in this state as a matter of fact, and not to any controversy of a constitutional or political nature.

I shall be anxious to hear from you as often as you can spare a moment, and particularly while the judiciary bill is pending.

Yours, with great regard,

A. J. DALLAS.

FROM NATHANIEL NILES.

February 17, 1802.

DEAR SIR,

Permit me to thank you most sincerely for the vote you gave in favour of Mr. Dayton's motion to refer the judiciary bill to a select committee; not because I am by any means satisfied it is not best that bill should pass, but because I earnestly desire that republicanism should on every occasion display the spirit of conciliation, as far as can be done without the destruction of principle. I am every day more and more satisfied that the cause is more endangered by the want of such displays than by every thing besides. The fate of parties in and about Congress will ultimately be determined by the great body of the well informed in the middle walks of life. It is happy, in some respects, that these are generally so far from the scene of action as to be tolerably free from the blinding influence of those passions which the scene itself is calculated to excite. They wish for every thing that tends to convince the great public that republicanism, instead of being hostile, is friendly to moderation and harmony. Shall we not do well to mark with great care and precision the sunken rocks and shoals on which self-denominated federalism has dashed itself to pieces? Among these I would enumerate their too eager and violent pursuit of their object. Had they been patient and accommodating, the eyes of the public would have been still hoodwinked, until habit, gradually acquired, would have rendered an expensive monarchy the most agreeable government. But, thank Heaven, they, by overacting, exposed their own feelings and designs. Will not the same pertinacity and precipitation endanger the better—the opposite cause? It is a prevalent idea among us middling people, that a good government must be a moderate one; and we are exceedingly apt to judge of the spirit of the government from the spirit of our rulers. Every thing non-conciliating bears in its very front strong symptoms of a tyrannical spirit.

I am, sir, the more gratified by your moderation because (though I am ashamed to avow it) I have heard you was too impetuous. Pardon my mistake; and suffer me to entreat you to encourage a steady pursuit of republican measures in that way which will convince the bystanders that the actors are uniformly and irresistibly urged to pursue them by cool conviction, resulting from a candid, extensive, and philanthropic survey of the great object. Passion and caprice very illy become so awfully sublime an object as that for which well-informed republicans contend.

With sentiments of respect, your obedient servant,

NATHANIEL NILES.

FROM A. J. DALLAS.

Philadelphia, 3d April, 1802.

DEAR SIR,

The judiciary storm has passed away for the present. I perceive, however, that an effort is making to improve the old system without increasing the number of judges; and we are once more unanimous at the bar of Philadelphia in rejoicing that Paterson, and not Chase, presides in our circuit. I had begun an outline of courts and jurisdictions agreeably to your wish; but I lost the hope of its being adopted when finished, so I abandoned the labour. Perhaps it may be worth while to renew the scheme, with a view to a future session.

There are some rumours of jealousy and dissatisfaction prevailing among the republican leaders, in the executive as well as the legislative departments of the federal as well as of our state government. It will be disgraceful, indeed, if the rumours are true. Very sincerely yours,

A. J. DALLAS.

Such were the sentiments and views of many of the most pure and intelligent of the republican party in relation to a repeal of the judiciary act of 1800. The preceding letters express the opinions entertained by thousands who were opposed to federal men and federal measures, but who wanted time for reflection; and yet, when Colonel Burr voted to recommit the repealing bill for the purpose of ascertaining whether it could not be rendered more satisfactory, the conspirators cried aloud, *Crucify him—crucify him.*

The plot now began to thicken. During the year 1801, a Scotchman by the name of Wood was employed to write "*A History of John Adams's Administration.*" Ward & Barlas, booksellers in New-York, were the proprietors of the copyright, and printed 1250 copies. William Duane, editor of the Aurora, furnished the author a portion of his materials, and became the agent to negotiate with a London bookseller for the publication of an edition in England. In the summer or autumn of 1801 Colonel Burr was informed of the progress of the work, and procured a copy before it was ready for publication. On examining it, he came to the conclusion that it was calculated to do the republican party more injury than good. It abounded with misrepresentations, errors, and libels. Mr. Burr, through a friend, agreed to pay a stipulated sum for the suppression of the work, under the most solemn assurance that no copy or copies would be permitted to go into the hands of any third person, but that the whole edition should be delivered to the agent who was to pay the money. Before the time of payment arrived, it was ascertained that a copy or copies had been parted with, and would not be returned. The contract was, therefore, never carried into effect. Pending this negotiation, Mr. Duane, through Wood or Ward & Barlas, was made acquainted with the arrangements which were in progress. Cheetham, the editor of the American Citizen, was also informed of what was doing. This was considered a most favourable opportunity for assailing the vice-president, and charging him with the design of suppressing the History of John Adams's Administration for the purpose of keeping the people in ignorance of the wrong doings of the federal party. Although the assailants had a full view of the whole ground, yet the attack was commenced by innuendoes, indicating ignorance of the true state of facts. The charge operated most injuriously upon the republican character of Colonel Burr. The injury was irreparable, and the attacks continued with unexampled malignity.

This brief statement, it is hoped, will be found sufficiently explicit to be intelligible. And now for the conduct of Mr. Duane on the occasion. His object, and the object of his employers, was accomplished; but whether a short development of the whole case will or will not add to his fame, the reader must determine.

On or about the 27th of February, 1802, the editor of the Aurora, in his paper, states that a curious fact has lately been brought to light in New-York; that Wood had completed his engagement with Ward & Barlas to furnish a history of John Adams's Administration, and that 1250 copies were printed, but suppressed at the desire of some person. Mr. Duane then animadverts with harshness, and expresses a wish to get a clew to the names of the person or persons who suppressed the work.

On the 31st of May, 1802, the Aurora states that the American Citizen and the Evening Post have commenced a warfare, of which Mr. Burr is the object; that the principal matter of charge is the suppression of Wood's History of John Adams's Administration; and then adds—"We are fully possessed of one side of the subject, and have perused the suppressed book attentively."

On the 12th of July, 1802, the Aurora says—"So far as it relates to Mr. Burr, my opinions have been uniform and reiterated to his particular friends, that if the motives for the suppression of the book were not *satisfactorily explained to the public*, his standing with the republican interest was gone."

During the period between February and July, 1802, the Aurora reprinted the slanders of Cheetham against Mr. Burr in relation to the suppressed book, and continued, from time to time, his own attacks upon the vice-president. While thus *publicly* giving currency to these calumnies, would it be believed (if asserted) that Mr. Duane was *privately* writing Colonel Burr, and approving of his conduct in suppressing the work? One of his letters on this subject is deemed sufficient to a right understanding of the case. It will now be given without comment.

FROM WILLIAM DUANE.

Thursday, April 15, 1802.

DEAR SIR,

I think it fortunate that the pamphlet of Mr. Wood has not yet been published, and that it would be much more so if it were not ever to see the light. It has disappointed my expectations of finding in it at least some useful reflections and reasonings, however little novelty there might be in the facts. But, even in the narration of facts, I find numerous errors, and not a few misrepresentations of things notorious to every man who has attended with understanding to the course of public affairs. There is in it a *something*, too, of a character very different from what was represented to me; the adoption of the story of Hamilton* and Lafayette, if it is not the effect of an indifference to accuracy, or a coldness in pursuit of truth, is something much worse, and at least is suspicious: there is more of the same kind of matter, and less attention to the influence and views of such characters, than the subject required. I consider it, upon the whole, as a hasty, crude, and inconsistent production, calculated rather to produce evil than the least good—as it would be attributed to the republicans, with all its faults and inconsistencies, and a credit assumed from it as a party confession of merit, in a particular character, which is not founded, at least in the way stated in the pamphlet. Were some parts of it omitted, and false statements rectified, it might not do any harm; and perhaps it might be found advisable to adopt some plan of that kind, making a careful *record of the omissions* to insert any future *misrepresentations*, and a like record of such *additions* or *alterations*. This might be very easily done by printing the pages anew which contain the exceptionable parts, and, if necessary, substituting reflections or anecdotes, founded in fact, in their places. This

* The story here referred to is thus related by Wood in his history: "In the year 1780, he (Hamilton) was promoted to the rank of colonel, and at the siege of Yorktown commanded the attack on one of the redoubts, the capture of which decided the fate of Lord Cornwallis and his army. The conduct of Mr. Hamilton on this occasion was truly honourable, and, in the history of his life, ought to weigh against several of those scars that have since stained his character. Previous to the attack, the Marquis de Lafayette proposed to General Washington to put to death all the British troops that should be found in the redoubts, as a retaliation for several acts of barbarity committed by the royal army. The steady and nervous mind of Washington, which was ever known to yield to the virtuous prejudice of compassion, gave his assent to the bloody order. But Mr. Hamilton (the tenderness of whose feelings has led him into error), after the redoubts were subdued, took the conquered under his protection, and proved to his enemies that Americans know how to fight, but not to murder." [General Hamilton, in a letter referring to this same story, says—"Positively and unequivocally, I declare that no such or similar order, or any intimation or hint resembling it, was ever by me received or understood to have been given."

might be done at a small expense. The thing, thus corrected, published; and, if any effort should be made to misrepresent, credit would be derived even by the defence, and the exposure of the motives for suppressing the misstatements.

This I have thought proper to write you, and I hope will, in its object and motives, find with you an excuse for doing so.

I am, with respect, your obedient servant,

William Duane.

CHAPTER VII.

Colonel Burr's silence under these reiterated attacks, with such means of defence as his enemies knew that he possessed, encouraged and imboldened them to make other and more daring assaults. He was now charged, in general terms, with intriguing for the presidency, in opposition to Mr. Jefferson; with endeavouring to obtain federal electoral votes, and thus to defeat Mr. Jefferson and promote his own elevation; with having entered into terms and conditions with federal members of Congress in the winter of 1800; and with having committed himself to that party, in the event of success through their instrumentality. These slanders were countenanced and circulated in whispers by men high in authority, until the political integrity of Colonel Burr was so far ruined as to render any defence, on his part or on the part of his friends, useless and unavailing. The hireling press now boldly entered upon specific charges; naming the parties with whom Colonel Burr or his friends had negotiated, and the agents whom the vice-president had employed to effect his purposes. These details were given in a manner so circumstantial, as, by their audacity, seemingly to command confidence. The slanders were circulated with industry and rapidity, while the contradictions rarely met the public eye, except through the medium of a federal press, which publication, with the already prejudiced republican, was construed as evidence of the truth of the charge. The principal instances of specific cases will now be presented as briefly as practicable.

The presidential electors of the state of New-Jersey were federal. Dr. Samuel S. Smith, president of Princeton College, was an elector. The Hon. Jno. B. Prevost, son of Mrs. Burr by her first husband, was married to the daughter of Dr. Smith. This circumstance rendered plausible a story invented and propagated by the calumniators of Colonel Burr. They boldly charged that "*Dr. Smith, of New-Jersey, was secretly to have voted for Mr. Burr, and thus made him President of the United States.*" To this charge Dr. Smith replied as follows :—

TO THE EDITOR OF THE EVENING POST.

"Princeton, July 29, 1802.

"Sir,

"In your paper of Monday, July 26, under the article entitled *A View of the Political Conduct of Aaron Burr, Esq.*, by the author of the *Narrative*, I observe some very gross misrepresentations, which I conceive it to be a duty that I owe to Mr. Burr, the New-Jersey electors, and myself, to declare to be absolutely false. Mr. Burr never visited me on the subject of the late election for president and vice-president—Mr. Burr never conversed with me a single second on the subject of that election, either before or since the event. No project or plan of the kind mentioned in that paper was proposed or hinted at among the electors of New-Jersey. I am assured that Mr. Burr held no intrigue with them on that occasion, either collectively or individually. They were men above intrigue; and I do not know that he was disposed to use it. At their meeting, they unanimously declared that a fair and manly vote, according to their sentiments, was the only conduct which was worthy of their own characters or of their cause.

"SAMUEL. S. SMITH."

It was next charged that Colonel Burr had sent, at his own expense, special agents to different states, previous to the choice of electors, with the view of influencing their selection, and to promote his own elevation to the exclusion of Mr. Jefferson. The agents named were Mr. Abraham Bishop, of New-Haven, and Mr. Timothy Green, of New-York. It was asserted that Mr. Bishop was Mr. Burr's agent at Lancaster, Pennsylvania, during the session of the legislature that appointed the presidential electors.

In August, 1802, Mr. Bishop published a full and explicit refutation of the charge. He denied that Mr. Burr sent him to Lancaster, or that he went there for any purposes personally or politically regarding that gentleman. The publication of Mr. Bishop is not readily to be found; but he is still living, and subsequently was appointed by Mr. Jefferson collector of the port of New-Haven.

In relation to Mr. Green, it was alleged that he was sent to Columbia, South Carolina, for similar purposes, and that he "*corresponded with the vice-president on the subject of the then approaching election, under cover to John Swartwout.*" The replies of Mr. Green and Mr. Swartwout were as follows:—

"New-York, October 11, 1802.

"MESSRS. DENNISTON AND CHEETHAM,

"In the *American Citizen* of this day you have made a publication, to which you have affixed your names. In this you have stated, 1st, That Timothy Green, of this city, was despatched as an agent to Columbia, the seat of government of the state of South Carolina, by the vice-president. 2dly, That he was the eulogist and intercessor for the vice-president. 3dly, That he sent the vice-president despatches regularly, addressed to Mr. John Swartwout, of this city, under cover.

"Now, as you have been most egregiously imposed upon by some disorganizing person, it is your duty and mine that the public be immediately furnished with both what were and what were not my inducements and motives in making a journey in November, 1800, to Columbia, and of my conduct while there. For this purpose you will please to insert in your paper of to-morrow the following corrections to your statement:—

"1st, I aver that I never went on any message of a political nature to Columbia, in South Carolina, or to any other place for the vice-president or any other person; neither was I ever requested or desired by the vice-president or by any other person to go to Columbia, in South Carolina, or any other place, on any political or electioneering mission, of any name or nature whatsoever. On the contrary, my journey to Columbia, in South Carolina, in the year of our Lord 1800, and my engagements until my return in 1801, was wholly unsolicited by any person (except my debtors in South Carolina), and were solely of a commercial nature, and for which I had been preparing eight months before.

"2dly, That I never wrote a letter to the vice-president of a political nature; neither did I write him any information relative to the presidential election in South Carolina, neither did I ever enclose a letter, directed to the vice-president, in a letter or cover directed to Mr. John Swartwout.

"3dly, That my letters to Mr. Swartwout while in South Carolina were unsolicited, and written solely with the motive to relieve the minds of my friends from the anxiety necessarily attendant on a state of suspense, while an important event is hourly expected to take place.

"4thly, That I never was in the habit of eulogizing public men, neither did I vary from my usual manners while in

South Carolina. I had no occasion to intercede for the election of Colonel Burr: all the fear I had while there was lest a compromise should take place, as the political parties were nearly balanced in the state legislature. This I did, as far as in my power, conscientiously endeavour to prevent; knowing that, if union and good faith were not inviolably preserved among the constitutional republicans, our past, present, and future exertions would be unavailing.

"TIMOTHY GREEN."

FOR THE AMERICAN CITIZEN.

"New-York, October 13, 1802.

"MESSRS. DENNISTON AND CHEETHAM,

"In your seventh letter addressed to Aaron Burr, Esq., Vice-president of the United States, published in the American Citizen of the 11th instant, I notice the following paragraph, viz.:—

"Meantime, sir, you had your eye on South Carolina; you despatched an agent, Mr. Timothy Green, of this city, to Columbia, the seat of government of that state. It was questionable whether South Carolina would give you a single vote. At that period you were scarcely known in the state. Mr. Green was at Columbia at least two months. He was your eulogist; your intercessor; he sent you despatches regularly; they were addressed to Mr. John Swartwout, of this city, under cover, and by him communicated to you.

"You will please to inform the public, through the medium of your paper, that the above paragraph, so far as relates to my receiving letters under cover, or communications from Timothy Green for Aaron Burr, is utterly destitute of truth.

"JOHN SWARTWOUT."

In a pamphlet entitled "A View of Aaron Burr's Political Conduct," it was charged that "Mr. Burr, while in the city of New-York, carried on a negotiation with the heads of the federal party at Washington with a view to his election as President of the United States. A person was authorized by them to confer with him on the subject, who accordingly did so. Mr. Burr assented to the propositions of the negotiator, and referred him to his confidential friend to complete the negotiation. Mr. Burr stated that, after the first vote taken in the House of Representatives, New-York and Tennessee would give in to the federalists."

To this Colonel Burr replied, in a letter to *Governor Bloomfield*, of New-Jersey, under date September 21, 1802:—

"You are at liberty to declare from me that all those charges and insinuations which aver or intimate that I advised or countenanced the opposition made to Mr. Jefferson pending the late election and balloting for president; that I proposed or agreed to any terms with the federal party; that I assented to be held up in opposition to him, or attempted to withdraw from him the vote or support of any man, whether in or out of Congress; THAT ALL SUCH ASSERTIONS AND INTIMATIONS ARE FALSE AND GROUNDLESS."

In the pamphlet already referred to, and various newspaper publications, it was alleged that General Hamilton had personal knowledge of Colonel Burr's negotiations with the federalists. On the 13th of October, 1802, the editor of the New-York Evening Post (William Coleman) states that he is authorized to say that General Hamilton, at a dinner at Edward Livingston's, declared that he had no personal knowledge of any negotiation in reference to the presidency between Colonel Burr and any person whatever.

It will be recollected that Colonel Burr, in his letter to Governor Bloomfield, denied the charge of "having proposed or agreed to any terms with the federal party." The person named as being the agent of the federalists, with authority to confer with Colonel Burr, was David A. Ogden, Esq., of the city of New-York, who was intimately connected with General Hamilton in professional business. Dr. Peter Irving was at that time the proprietor and editor of a highly respectable daily journal (Morning Chronicle) published in the city of New-York. The facts in relation to this charge are developed in the following letters.

P. IRVING TO DANIEL A. OGDEN.

"New-York, November 24, 1802.

"SIR,

"Though I have not the pleasure of a personal acquaintance with you, I flatter myself that the contents of this letter will preclude the necessity of an apology for addressing you.

"It has been asserted in various publications that Mr. Burr, during the late election for president and vice-president, entered into negotiations and agreed to terms with the federal party, or with certain individuals of that party, with a view to advance himself to the office of president to the exclusion of Mr. Jefferson. Mr. Burr, in a letter to Governor Bloomfield, dated the 21st of September last, declared that all such allegations were false and groundless; and the charges have been renewed in more recent publications, which point to you by name as the person through whom such negotiations were carried on and terms concluded. It has now become interesting to a great portion of the community to be informed how far these assertions and charges have been authorized by you, or are warranted by your knowledge of facts.

"Having received frequent anonymous communications for the Morning Chronicle relative to these matters, and being unwilling to occupy the paper with vague and unsubstantial conjectures or remarks on a subject of such importance, I am induced to apply directly to yourself as an authentic source of information. I do this with the more confidence, from a persuasion that you can have no wish to suffer false reports to circulate under the authority of your name for mere party purposes; and that, in the actual posture of things, you cannot be averse to declare publicly and explicitly your agency, if any, in the business. I take the liberty, therefore, of requesting your written declaration to the points above stated, together with any circumstances you may be pleased to communicate tending to establish the truth or falsehood of the charges in question.

"I have the honour to be, very respectfully, your obedient servant, P. IRVING."

DAVID A. OGDEN TO P. IRVING.

"New-York, November 24, 1802.

"SIR,

"Though I did not conceive it to be incumbent upon me, or in itself proper to notice a publication in a newspaper in which my name was used without my permission or knowledge, yet I have no objection to reply to an inquiry which comes in the shape of that contained in your letter, and from a person of your standing in society.

"I declare that my journey to the city of Washington, in the year 1800, was purely on private business, and without any understanding or concert whatever with Colonel Burr, whom I met at the stage-office on his way to Trenton, not having had before the least intimation of such a meeting; and that I was not then or at any time charged by him with any commission or errand of a political nature. In the course of our journey, no political conversation took place but of a general nature and in the presence of the passengers.

"When about to return from the city of Washington, two or three members of Congress, of the federal party, spoke to me about their views as to the election of president, desiring me to converse with Colonel Burr on the subject, and to ascertain whether he would enter into terms. On my return to New-York I called on Colonel Burr, and communicated the above to him. He explicitly declined the explanation, and did neither propose nor agree to any terms. I had no other interview or communication with him on the subject; and so little was I satisfied with this, that in a letter which I soon afterward wrote to a member of Congress, and which was the only one I wrote, I dissuaded from giving support to Colonel Burr, and advised rather to acquiesce in the election of Mr. Jefferson, as the less dangerous man of the two to that cause with which I believed the public interest to be inseparably connected.

"There are no facts within my knowledge tending to establish the truth of the charges specified in your letter.

"With due respect, I am, sir, your obedient servant,

"DAVID A. OGDEN.

"DR. P. IRVING."

It was then boldly asserted that Edward Livingston was "the confidential friend" to whom Mr. Ogden was referred "to complete the negotiation;" whereupon Mr. Burr made a call upon Mr. Livingston, to which the following reply was given:—

"SIR,

"In consequence of certain insinuations lately circulated, I think it proper to declare that you did not, in any verbal or written communication to me, during the late presidential election, express any sentiment inconsistent with those contained in your letter to General Smith,* which was published, or evincing any desire that the vote of the state should be transferred from Mr. Jefferson to yourself.

"I am, very respectfully, your most obedient servant,

(Signed) "EDWARD LIVINGSTON.

"The Vice-president of the United States."

In the hope of giving some support to these calumnies, Mr. William S. Pennington, of New-Jersey, addressed a

* See page 75 of this volume.

letter to the editors of the American Citizen, in which he asserted that General John Swartwout had written to Robert Williams, of Poughkeepsie, pending the election, recommending or countenancing the support of Mr. Burr for president to the exclusion of Mr. Jefferson. To this General Swartwout replied :—

TO THE PUBLIC.

"The false colouring given by the relation of one William S. Pennington, in a letter to Denniston & Cheetham, which appeared in the American Citizen of the 22d inst., and their subsequent malicious remarks, oblige me once more to ask pardon for obtruding myself on the public attention.

"I declare, on my honour, that I did not at any time advise the election of Mr. Burr as president of the United States to the exclusion of Mr. Jefferson; nor did I ever write to any person or persons to that effect; and I hereby authorize Mr. Robert Williams to publish any letter or letters he may have received from me on the subject of the late presidential election. I am induced to contradict the base slanders of those exclusive patriots by a regard to truth only, and not from a conviction that it would have been either dishonourable to me, or disadvantageous to the country or the republican party, to have promoted the election of Mr. Burr to the presidential chair.

"JOHN SWARTWOUT.

"New-York, January 23."

The principal specifications, intended as explanatory of the general charge against Colonel Burr of intriguing for the presidency, have now been given. The replies of the parties implicated accompany them. A whole generation has passed away since these scenes occurred, and yet the time has not arrived when they can be calmly reviewed with impartiality and free from prejudice. They may serve, however, as beacon-lights for those who are now figuring or may hereafter figure on the great political theatre of our country. Through life, Colonel Burr committed an error, if he did not display a weakness, in permitting his reputation to be assailed, without contradiction, in cases where it was perfectly defensible. His enemies took advantage of the sullen silence which he was known to preserve in regard to newspaper attacks. Under these attacks he fell from the proud eminence he once enjoyed to a condition more mortifying and more prostrate than any distinguished man has ever experienced in the United States.

Different individuals, to gratify different feelings, have ascribed this unprecedented fall to different causes. But one who is not altogether ignorant of the springs of human actions; whose partialities and prejudices are mellowed by more than threescore years of experience; who has carefully and laboriously, in this case, examined cause and effect, hesitates not in declaring that, from the moment Aaron Burr was elected vice-president, his doom was unalterably decided, if that decision could be accomplished by a combination of wealth, of talent, of government patronage, of favouritism and proscription, inflamed by the worst passions, and nurtured by the hope of gratifying a sordid ambition. The contest in Congress fixed his fate. Subsequent events were only consequences resulting from antecedent acts.

In the progress of this work no desire has been evinced, none is felt to screen Colonel Burr from censure where it is merited. But the man who can read, unmoved, the evidence which has already been presented of the injustice done him in the charge of having intrigued and negotiated with the federal party for the presidency, must possess more of philosophic than of generous or magnanimous feelings. It would seem that the task of recording the presidential contest in Congress, in the spring of 1801, was now brought to a close. But not so. There yet remains another and imposing view to be presented. Whatever may have been the wishes of Colonel Burr, it is certain that they were so far under his own control as to prevent him from entering into any negotiation, bargain, or intrigue to obtain the presidency. There is not the slightest evidence of any such attempt on his part, while there is strong, if not conclusive proof to the contrary. Can as much be said in favour of his great competitor on that occasion? This is the view that remains to be taken. But, before presenting the testimony in the case, some explanation is necessary as to the manner in which it was first obtained and subsequently made public.

In the year 1804, a suit was instituted by Colonel Burr against James Cheetham, editor of the American Citizen, for a libel, in charging him with intriguing for the presidency. This suit was commenced by Mr. Burr with reluctance, and only to gratify personal friends. It progressed tardily, impediments having been thrown in the way of bringing it to trial by the defendant, and probably the cause not sufficiently pressed by the complainant. In 1805 or 1806, some persons who were really desirous of ascertaining not only the truth or falsity of the charge, but whether there was any foundation for it, determined on having a *wager-suit* placed at issue on the records of the court, and then take out a commission to examine witnesses. Accordingly, the names of *James Gillespie*, plaintiff, and *Abraham Smith*, defendant, were used. The latter at the time being a clerk in the store of Matthew L. Davis, then in the mercantile business, trading under the firm of Strong & Davis.

It was universally believed, that if there were two men in Congress that could unfold the whole negotiation if any had taken place, those two men were James A. Bayard, of Delaware, and Samuel Smith, of Baltimore. The former, a federal gentleman of high standing, the sole representative of a state in the Congress of 1800, and thus possessing, at any moment, the power of deciding the contest in favour of Mr. Jefferson. The latter, a political and personal friend of Mr. Jefferson, and the very individual whom Colonel Burr had previously selected as his proxy to declare his sentiments, in case there was a tie between Mr. Jefferson and himself. A commission was accordingly taken out, and, on the 3d of April, 1806, Mr. Bayard and Mr. Smith were examined. No use, however, was made of these depositions until December, 1830, being a period of nearly twenty-five years.

On the publication of Mr. Jefferson's writings, the sons of the late James A. Bayard felt that the memory of their father had been wrongfully and unjustly assailed in two paragraphs in the fourth volume of this work. The first of these paragraphs, on the 28th of January, 1830, was read in the United States Senate by the Hon. Mr. Clayton, of Delaware, General Samuel Smith and Edward Livingston both being members of the Senate and present. He read the following:

"*February* 12, 1801. Edward Livingston tells me that Bayard applied to-day or last night to General Samuel Smith, and represented to him the expediency of coming over to the states who vote for Burr; that there was nothing in the way of appointment which he might not command, and particularly mentioned the secretaryship of the navy. Smith asked him if he was authorized to make the offer. He said he was authorized. Smith told this to Livingston and W. C. Nicholas, who confirms it to me," &c.

Mr. Clayton then called upon the senator from Maryland (Mr. Smith) and the senator from Louisiana (Mr. Livingston) to disprove the statement here made by Mr. Jefferson.

Mr. Smith, of Maryland, rose and said "that he had read the paragraph before he came here to-day, and was, therefore, aware of its import. He had not the most distant recollection that Mr. Bayard had ever made such a proposition to him. Mr. Bayard, said he, and myself, though politically opposed, were intimate personal friends, and he was an honourable man. Of all men, Mr. Bayard would have been the last to make such a proposition to any man; and I am confident that he had too much respect for me to have made it under any circumstances. I never received from any man any such proposition."

Mr. Livingston, of Louisiana, said, "that as to the precise question which had been put to him by the senator from Delaware, he must say, that having taxed his recollection as far as it could go on so remote a transaction, he had no remembrance of it."

The sons of the late Mr. Bayard, not yet being satisfied as to the other paragraph, resolved on an investigation of the subject, and with this view one of them wrote the following letter.*

FROM RICHARD H. BAYARD.

Wilmington, March 8, 1830.

SIR,

In the fourth volume of Mr. Jefferson's writings, lately published by his grandson, page 521, under the head of a note made April 15, 1806, occurs the following paragraph, after the detail of a conversation held with you about a month previously:—

"I did not commit these things to writing at the time, but I do now, because, in a suit between him and Cheetham, he has had a deposition of Mr. Bayard taken which seems to have no relation to the suit, nor to any other object than to calumniate me. Bayard pretends to have addressed to me, during the pending of the presidential election in February, 1801, through General Samuel Smith, certain conditions on which my election might be obtained; and that General Smith, after conversing with me, gave answers from me. This is absolutely false. No proposition of any kind was ever made to me on that occasion by General Smith,

* It is considered proper to state here that the correspondence which follows is published without the privity or consent of either of the Mr. Bayards. It is found among the papers of Colonel Burr, and is intimately connected with a history of the transaction.

or any answer authorized by me. And this fact General Smith affirms at this moment."

Mr. Jefferson supposes this deposition to have been made in your suit against Cheetham. I have some reason to think he is mistaken as to the precise case in which it was made. However this may be, I am anxious to procure a copy of it, as returned with the commission under which it was taken.

If I may not be considered as trespassing too far on your time and attention, will you permit me to ask whether the deposition referred to by Mr. Jefferson is still in existence? In what case it was taken? And whether a copy of it can be procured?

I have the honour to be, respectfully,

Your obedient servant,

RICHARD H. BAYARD.

TO RICHARD H. BAYARD.

New-York, March 10, 1830.

SIR,

I have this day received your letter of the 8th inst., containing an extract from the fourth volume of the writings of Mr. Jefferson. I have not seen that book, and, on inquiry, do not learn that there is a copy in this city.

The suit referred to is not that of Cheetham, but one instituted, without my agency or knowledge, *on a wager*. The title not now recollected. A commission to take testimony was transmitted to me, then at Washington, and several depositions thereupon taken; copies of all of which may, no doubt, be found among the papers of the late Mr. Bayard.

A gentleman well informed of these matters is now at Albany, where I expect to meet him about the 20th inst., when it may be in my power to give you further satisfaction on the subject of your letter.

I pray in the mean time to be informed whether you are

a son of the late Mr. Bayard. Or how, if at all related to him. And what use it is proposed to make of the communications you may receive. Permit me to add, it will at all times afford me great pleasure to gratify the family of Mr. Bayard on this or on any other occasion.

I have the honour to be, very respectfully,

A. Burr.

TO MATTHEW L. DAVIS.

New-York, March 15, 1830.

Sir,

I enclose you copies of a letter from Mr. Richard H. Bayard, with my answer, and have only to inquire whether I may refer to you to answer this letter of Mr. Bayard; your memory being better than mine, and I not having the depositions in question, or any copies thereof at this moment at my command. If you should write, please to enclose your letter to me. I think it was you who got up that suit. Pray give me the title and date.

I expect to be in Albany early next week. In your answer to this, let me know where to find you. God speed you.

A. Burr.

FROM MATTHEW L. DAVIS.

Albany, March 18, 1830.

Sir,

The irregularity of the mails has prevented my receiving your letter of the 15th inst., with its enclosures, until this day.

I have read Mr. Bayard's letter to you under date of the 8th inst. All the circumstances connected with the subject to which it refers are within my recollection; but, absent as I am from my papers, I am unwilling to speak with great confidence in relation to events which have occurred nearly thirty years since.

The deposition of Mr. Bayard, to which I presume Mr.

Jefferson alludes in his memorandum of the 15th of April, 1806, was taken, as you remark, in the case of *a wager*. The title of the cause I do not now recollect; but Abraham Smith, a clerk in my store, was one of the parties, and I think the period was during the winter of 1805. It may have been a year later.

In that deposition Mr. Bayard states that a negotiation in regard to the pending election between Mr. Jefferson and Colonel Burr, in February, 1801, was entered into with Mr. Jefferson, through Mr. Nicholas, of Virginia, and General Samuel Smith, of Maryland; and that Mr. Jefferson did agree to certain stipulations or conditions therein specified. It is proper for me to add, that to both Robert G. Harper and General Smith the same interrogatories were propounded that were answered by Mr. Bayard, and that the testimony (if my memory is correct) of Mr. Bayard was, in every material point, sustained by both these gentlemen. These examinations were made under a commission issued out of the Supreme Court of our state.

Several copies of these depositions were made from the originals, and I have reason to believe that one copy of them was in the possession of Mr. Bayard or Mr. Harper, and another in the possession of Stephen R. Bradley, Esq., of Vermont. They were read by different gentlemen; among them, I think, was General John P. Van Ness, of Washington city, and Rundolph Bunner, Esq., late a member of Congress from this state, who, I have no doubt, can and would, if asked, detail their contents. I should suppose that General Smith would not only recollect the occurrences in February, 1801, but the contents also of the deposition to which he has sworn.

During the contest I was the advocate of Mr. Jefferson's election, and corresponded with different members of Congress; among the number were Edward Livingston and Albert Gallatin, Esquires. The letters I then received enumerated not only the *doubtful states*, but the *doubtful men* of both parties which were in Congress. These letters have been carefully preserved.

It is due to the character of the late Mr. Bayard to remark, that, so far as the circumstances have come to my knowledge, there was nothing in the transaction calculated in the slightest degree to impeach his fidelity to his party or his honour. The object of the negotiation was not to aggrandize or to elevate himself or his friends, but to secure and perpetuate certain cardinal points of federal policy.

I have not seen the works of Mr. Jefferson, but I will obtain and examine them with care and attention. The history of the times to which these memorandums and documents relate are enveloped in thick darkness. Whether the period has yet arrived when an effort should be made to dispel that darkness is problematical. The means, however, do exist of proving, to the satisfaction of the most skeptical, what are the facts in the case; and, consequently, of doing full justice to all the parties concerned; and that duty, however unpleasant, shall, at a proper crisis, be fairly, impartially, and fearlessly performed.

At my advanced age I do not wish to be drawn into newspaper controversies; nor can I be induced, prematurely, to make any publication on the subject alluded to in this letter. At the same time, you are at liberty to communicate the whole or any part of its contents to Mr. Bayard, in the expectation that it will be used discreetly.

Respectfully, your friend,

M. L. Davis.

GENERAL SAMUEL SMITH TO RICHARD H. BAYARD AND JAMES A. BAYARD.

Washington, April 3, 1830.

Gentlemen,

Ill health, and disinclination to go back to circumstances which happened thirty years past, has prevented an earlier answer to your letter.

In the extract you have sent me from Mr. Jefferson's writings, it is said—"Bayard" (alluding to his deposition) "pretends to have addressed to me, during the pending of the presidential election in February, 1801, through General Smith, certain conditions on which my election might be obtained, and that General Smith, after conversing with me, gave answer for me. This is absolutely false. No proposition of any kind ever was made to me on that occasion by General Smith, or any answer authorized by me; and the fact General Smith affirms at this moment"—to wit, 15th of April, 1806. Yes, gentlemen, it was (I believe) on that day I put into the hands of Mr. Jefferson a press copy of *my deposition in the case of Cheetham*,* in which *I perfectly recollect that I deny having ever received from Mr. Jefferson any proposition of any kind to be made by me to Mr. Bayard or any other person. Not, perhaps, in those words, but in detail to that effect;* or having ever communicated any proposition of the kind as from Mr. Jefferson to Mr. Bayard.

My experience in life has shown that few men take advice unless it comports with their own views. I will, however, recommend that you let well enough alone. Your father was a bitter, most bitter enemy of Mr. Jefferson; his enmity was known to all, and, I presume, to Mr. Jefferson; it was therefore very natural for him to conclude that the suit of Cheetham had been got up for the express purpose of obtaining the oath of your father with the view of injuring him, and that your father had advised such a course. *My recollection of what passed on the occasion is as strong as if it had happened yesterday.* I will give you a detail in as few words as possible.

Two or three days before the election was terminated, a member, who I suppose had been deputed by the federal party, called on me to converse on the subject. I held little

* The suit was James Gillespie *vs.* Abraham Smith. See deposition.

conversation with *him.* Your father then called on me, and said that he was anxious to put an end to the controversy; that, in case of dissolution, Delaware never could expect to obtain her present advantages; that, if satisfied on certain points, he would terminate the contest. He then went on to state those points: they were three or four. I can now remember only *three,* to wit—the funding system, the navy, and the retaining or dismissal of federalists then in office. I answered promptly that I could satisfy him fully on two of the points (which two I do not now recollect), for that I had had frequent conversations with him on them, and I stated what I understood and believed to be his opinions, and what I thought would be his rule of conduct; with which explanation your father expressed his entire satisfaction, and on the third requested that I would inform myself.

I lodged with Mr. Jefferson, and that night had a conversation with him, *without his having the remotest idea of my object.* Mr. Jefferson was a gentleman of *extreme frankness* with his friends; he conversed freely and frankly with them on all subjects, and gave his opinions without reserve. Some of them thought that he did so too freely. Satisfied with his opinion on the third point, I communicated to your father the next day—that, from the conversation that I had had with Mr. Jefferson, I was satisfied in *my own mind* that his conduct on that point would be so and so. But I certainly never did tell your father that I had any authority from Mr. Jefferson to communicate any thing to him or to any other person.

During the session of Congress of 1805–6, your father told me that a little lawyer in Delaware had (he supposed at the instance of Colonel Burr) endeavoured to get from him a deposition touching a conversation with me; that he had refused it; that Burr had, however, trumped up a suit for the sole purpose of coercing his deposition and mine, and said that a commission to take testimony was now in the city, and that he apprized me that I might be prepared.

I asked him what he would state in his deposition. He answered similar to the quotation you have sent. I told him instantly that I had communicated to him my *own opinion*,* derived from conversation with Mr. Jefferson, and not one word from him to your father; and that my testimony would, as to that point, be in direct hostility. He then said, the little fellow will have our testimony by some means or other, and I will give mine. I answered that I would also. A few nights afterward Colonel Burr called on me. I told him that I had written my deposition, and would have a fair copy made of it. He said, trust it to me, and I will get Mr. —— to copy it. I did so, and, on his returning it to me, I found words not mine interpolated in the copy. I struck out those words, had it copied again, and, to prevent all plea of false copying, I had a press copy taken of it. When I appeared before the commission, I found a deposition attached to that of your father, and asked how they came by that. They answered that it had been sent to them. I requested them to take it off; that I had the deposition in my hand to which alone I would swear; they did so, and my deposition was attached. The next day (I think) I called, and told Mr. Jefferson what had passed, read to him the press copy, and asked him if he recollected having given to me the opinions I had detailed. He answered that he did not, but it might be so, for that they were opinions he held and expressed to many of his friends, and as probably to me as any other, and then said that he would wish to have a copy. I told him that I had no use for it; he might, and I gave him the press copy.

You have now a tolerable full view of the case, and will see that no possible censure can attach to Mr. Jefferson; that a diversity of opinion will arise from publication as to your father's credibility or mine, and that both may suffer in the public estimation. I will conclude that, during my

* Will the reader examine the deposition, especially what relates to Mr. M'Lean and Mr. Latimer?

long life, I have scarcely ever known an instance of newspaper publication between A. and B. that some obloquy did not attach to both parties.

I am, gentlemen, with respect,
Your obedient servant,
S. SMITH.

FROM RICHARD H. BAYARD.

Wilmington, Delaware, April 22, 1830.

SIR,

I have just received your letter of the 10th ult., in answer to mine of the 8th, the reason of which delay is to be found in the fact of your having directed it to Wilmington, North Carolina. It was accordingly conveyed to that place, and was returned and received by me this morning.

I reply to your inquiries that I am the eldest son of the late James A. Bayard, and that the object which I have in view is the vindication of his character from the aspersion contained in the passage in Mr. Jefferson's writings, a copy of which I sent you.

It is true that among my father's papers I have found rough copies of the deposition made in your suit against Cheetham, as well as of that made in the wager case. Together with the first-named deposition there is also a copy of the interrogatories; but, in the latter case, simply a rough copy of the deposition, without title, or any memorandum of the names of the parties. You will perceive at once the necessity of accompanying the deposition in the wager case with its *title* and a copy of the interrogatories, in order to show, in the first place, Mr. Jefferson's error in the statement of the *case*, and, secondly, to refute his assertion that the deposition had "nothing to do with the suit, or with any other object than to calumniate him."

The subsequent part of his statement will be met by the deposition itself, by reference to concomitant circumstances, and such corroborating testimony as time has spared.

Being anxious to avoid all room for cavil, by publishing the depositions as returned with the respective commissions, lest, perchance, there should be some slight verbal inaccuracies, I applied to you, believing it was in your power to give the information necessary to enable me to procure certified copies of the record.

You have thus, sir, an entire exposition of my motives for addressing you my letter of the 8th ult.; and, in conformity with the sentiment you are so good as to express in the conclusion of your letter, I doubt not you will furnish me with such information as you possess on the subject.

I wrote some time since to Mr. Edward N. Rogers, of your city, to procure for me copies of my father's and General Samuel Smith's depositions in *both* cases. He informs me, by his letter of the 17th inst., that the depositions in your suit against Cheetham are not to be found in the office; that the case went off by default, and he supposes they were never filed. At all events, the clerk cannot now find them.

You will probably be able to state what became of them, and whether copies can be procured. I will ask of you, therefore, the favour to communicate to him information on this point, as well as the *name* of the *wager case*, that he may be enabled to comply with my request, with the execution of which he has been so kind as to charge himself.

I have the honour to be, respectfully,

Your obedient servant,

RICHARD H. BAYARD.

CHAPTER VIII.

The necessary information having been given to Mr. Bayard to enable him to procure the depositions of his father and General Smith, they were accordingly obtained from Mr. Bradley, of Vermont. Before presenting them, it may not be improper to give the letters of two members of Congress, one of which enters somewhat into a history of the case, and *both* of which negatives, in the most positive manner, any attempt of Colonel Burr, or any person acting in his behalf, to negotiate, bargain, or intrigue with the federal party for the office of president.

WILLIAM COOPER* TO THOMAS MORRIS.

Washington, February 10, 1801.

Dear Sir,

We have this day locked ourselves up by a rule to proceed to choose a president before we adjourn. * * * * * * We shall run Burr perseveringly. You shall hear of the result instantly after the fact is ascertained. *A little good management would have secured our object on the first vote*, but now it is too late for any operations to be gone into, except that of adhering to Burr, and leave the consequences to those who have heretofore been his friends. If we succeed, a faithful support must, on our part, be given to his administration, which, I hope, will be wise and energetic.

Your friend,

W. Cooper.

* Judge Cooper, of Cooperstown, state of New-York.

WILLIAM COOPER TO THOMAS MORRIS.

February 13, 1801.

DEAR SIR,

We have postponed, until to-morrow 11 o'clock, the voting for president. All stand firm. Jefferson eight—Burr six—divided two. *Had Burr done any thing for himself, he would long ere this have been president.* If a majority would answer, he would have it on every vote.

FROM JAMES A. BAYARD TO ALEXANDER HAMILTON.

Washington, January 7, 1801.

DEAR SIR,

I have been but a few days in this city; but, since my arrival, have had the pleasure to receive the letter which you did me the honour to write on the 27th ult. I am fully sensible of the great importance of the subject to which it relates, and am, therefore, extremely obliged by the information you have been so good as to communicate.

* * * * * *

It is considered that at least, in the first instance, Georgia, North Carolina, Virginia, Tennessee, Kentucky, Pennsylvania, New-Jersey, and New-York will vote for Mr. Jefferson. It is probable that Maryland and Vermont will be divided. It is therefore counted, that upon the first ballot it would be possible to give to Mr. Burr six votes. It is calculated, however, and strongly insisted by some gentlemen, that a persevering opposition to Mr. Jefferson would bring over *New-York*, *New-Jersey*, and *Maryland*. What is the probability relative to New-York?—your means enable you to form the most correct opinion. As to New-Jersey and Maryland, it would depend on Mr. Linn of the former and Mr. Dent of the latter state.

I assure you, sir, there appears to be a strong inclination in a majority of the federal party to support Mr. Burr. The current has already acquired considerable force, and is manifestly increasing. The vote which the representation of a state enables me to give would decide the question in favour of Mr. Jefferson. At present I am by no means decided as to the object of preference. If the federal party should take up Mr. Burr, I ought certainly to be impressed with the most undoubting conviction before I separated myself from them. I cannot, however, deny that there are strong considerations which give a preference to Mr. Jefferson. The subject admits of many and very doubtful views; and, before I resolve on the part I shall take, I will await the approach of the crisis, which may probably bring with it circumstances decisive of the event.

The federal party meet on Friday for the purpose of forming a resolution as to their line of conduct. I have not the least doubt of their agreeing to support Colonel Burr. Their determination will not bind me; for though it might cost me a painful struggle to disappoint the views and wishes of many gentlemen with whom I have been accustomed to act, yet the magnitude of the subject forbids the sacrifice of a strong conviction.

I cannot answer for the coherence of my letter, as I have undertaken to write to you from the chamber of representatives, with an attention divided by the debate which occupies the house. I have not considered myself at liberty to show your letter to any one, though I think it would be serviceable, if you could trust my discretion in the communication of it.

With great consideration,
Your obedient servant,
JAMES A. BAYARD.

GEORGE BAER TO RICHARD H. BAYARD.

Frederick, April 19, 1830

SIR,

In compliance with your request, I now communicate to you my recollections of the events of the presidential elec tion by the House of Representatives in 1801. There has been no period of our political history more misunderstood and more grossly misrepresented. The course adopted by the federal party was one of principle, and not of faction; and I think the present a suitable occasion for explaining the views and motives at least of those gentlemen who, having it in their power to decide the election at any moment, were induced to protract it for a time, but ultimately to withdraw their opposition to Mr. Jefferson.

I have no hesitation in saying that the facts stated in the deposition of your father, the late James A. Bayard, so far as they came to my knowledge, are substantially correct; and although nearly thirty years have elapsed since that eventful period, my recollection is vivid as to the principal circumstances, which, from the part I was called upon to act, were deeply graven on my memory. As soon as it was generally known that the two democratic candidates, Jefferson and Burr, had the highest and an equal number of votes, and that the election would consequently devolve on the House of Representatives, Mr. Dent, who had hitherto acted with the federal party, declared his intention to vote for Mr. Jefferson, in consequence of which determination the vote of Maryland was divided.

It was soon ascertained that there were six individuals, the vote of any one of whom could at any moment decide the election. These were, your father, the late James A. Bayard, who held the vote of the state of Delaware; General Morris, of Vermont, who held the divided vote of that state; and Mr. Craik, Mr. Thomas, Mr. Dennis, and myself, who held the divided vote of Maryland. Much anxiety was shown by the friends of Mr. Jefferson, and much ingenuity used to discover the line of conduct which would be pursued by them. Deeply impressed with the responsibility which attached to their peculiar situation, and conscious that the American people looked to them for a president, they could not rashly determine either to surrender their constitutional discretion, or disappoint the expectations of their fellow-citizens.

Your father, Mr. Craik, and myself having compared ideas upon the subject, and finding that we entertained the same views and opinions, resolved to act together, and accordingly entered into a solemn and mutual pledge that we would in the first instance yield to the wishes of the great majority of the party with whom we acted, and vote for Mr. Burr, but that no consideration should induce us to protract the contest beyond a reasonable period for the purpose of ascertaining whether he could be elected. We determined that a president should be chosen, but were willing thus far to defer to the opinions of our political friends, whose preference of Mr. Burr was founded upon a belief that he was less hostile to federal men and federal measures than Mr. Jefferson. General Morris and Mr. Dennis concurred in this arrangement.

The views by which the federal party were governed were these:—They held that the Constitution had vested in the House of Representatives a high discretion in a case like the present, to be exercised for the benefit of the nation; and that, in the execution of this delegated power, an honest and unbiased judgment was the measure of their responsibility. They were less certain of the hostility of Mr. Burr to federal policy than of that of Mr. Jefferson, which was known and decided. Mr. Jefferson had identified himself with, and was at the head of the party in Congress who had opposed every measure deemed necessary by the federalists for putting the country in a posture of defence; such as fortifying the harbours and seaports, establishing manufactories of arms; erecting arsenals, and filling them with arms and ammunition; erecting a navy for the defence of commerce, &c. His speculative opinions were known to be hostile to the independence of the judiciary, to the financial system of the country, and to internal improvements.

All these matters the federalists believed to be intimately blended with the prosperity of the nation, and they deprecated, therefore, the elevation of a man to the head of the government whose hostility to them was open and avowed. It was feared, too, from his prejudices against the party which supported them, that he would dismiss all public officers who differed with him in sentiment, without regard to their qualifications and honesty, but on the ground only of political character. The House of Representatives adopted certain resolutions for their government during the election, one of which was that there should be no adjournment till it was decided.

On the 11th February, 1801, being the day appointed by law for counting the votes of the electoral colleges, the House of Representatives proceeded in a body to the Senate chamber, where the vice-president, in view of both houses of Congress, opened the certificates of the electors of the different states; and, as the votes were read, the tellers on the part of each house counted and took lists of them, which, being compared and delivered to him, he announced to both houses the state of the votes; which was, for Thomas Jefferson 73 votes, for Aaron Burr 73 votes, for John Adams 65 votes, for Charles Pinckney 64 votes, for John Jay one vote; and then declared that the greatest number and majority of votes being equal, the choice had devolved on the House of Representatives. The members of the house then withdrew to their own chamber, and proceeded to ballot for a president. On the first ballot it was found that Thomas Jefferson had the votes of eight states, Aaron Burr of six states, and that two were divided. As there were sixteen states, and a majority was necessary to determine the election, Mr. Jefferson wanted the vote of one state. Thus the result which had been anticipated was realized.

The balloting continued throughout that day and the following night, at short intervals, with the same result, the 26th ballot being taken at 8 o'clock on the morning of the

12th of February. The balloting continued with the same result from day to day till the 17th of February, without any adjournment of the house. On the previous day (February 16), a consultation was held by the gentlemen I have mentioned, when, being satisfied that Mr. Burr could not be elected, as no change had taken place in his favour, and there was no evidence of any effort on the part of himself or his personal friends to procure his election, it was resolved to abandon the contest. This determination was made known to the federal members generally, and excited some discontent among the violent of the party, who thought it better to go without a president than to elect Mr. Jefferson. A general meeting, however, of the federal members was called, and the subject explained, when it was admitted that Mr. Burr could not be elected. A few individuals persisted in their resolution not to vote for Mr. Jefferson, but the great majority wished the election terminated and a president chosen. *Having also received assurances from a source on which we placed reliance that our wishes with regard to certain points of federal policy in which we felt a deep interest would be observed in case Mr. Jefferson was elected*, the opposition of Vermont, Delaware, and Maryland was withdrawn, and on the 36th ballot your father, the late James A. Bayard, put in a blank ballot, myself and my colleagues did the same, and General Morris absented himself. The South Carolina federalists also put in blank ballots. Thus terminated that memorable contest.

Previous to and pending the election, rumours were industriously circulated, and letters written to different parts of the country, charging the federalists with the design to prevent the election of a president, and to usurp the government by an act of legislative power. Great anxiety and apprehensions were created in the minds of all, and of none more than the federalists generally, who were not apprized of the determination of those gentlemen who held the power, and were resolved to terminate the contest when the proper period arrived. But neither these rumours, nor the excitement produced by them, nor the threats made by their opponents to resist by force such a measure, had the least influence on the conduct of those gentlemen. They knew the power which they possessed, and were conscious of the uprightness of their views, and of the safety and constitutional character of the course they had adopted. I was privy to all the arrangements made, and attended all the meetings of the federal party when consulting on the course to be pursued in relation to the election; and I pledge my most solemn asseveration that no such measure was ever for a moment contemplated by that party; that no such proposition was ever made; and that, if it had ever been, it would not only have been discouraged, but instantly put down by those gentlemen who possessed the power, and were pledged to each other to elect a president before the close of the session.

I am respectfully, sir,

Your most obedient servant,

GEORGE BAER.

INTERROGATORIES to be administered to James A. Bayard, Esq., of the state of Delaware, late a member of Congress for the United States from the said state of Delaware, a witness to be produced, sworn, and examined in a cause now depending in the Supreme Court of Judicature of the state of New-York, between Aaron Burr, plaintiff, and James Cheetham, defendant, on the part of the defendant.

1st. Do you know the parties, plaintiff and defendant, or either and which of them, and how long have you known them respectively?

2d. Were you a member of the House of Representatives, in Congress of the United States, from the state of Delaware, in the sessions holden in the months of January and February, in the year 1801?

3d. Was there not an equal number of votes for Thomas

Jefferson and Aaron Burr, as president and vice-president of the said United States, at the election for those officers in the December preceding, and did not the choice of a president consequently devolve on the said House of Representatives?

4th. Did not the said house ballot for the president several times before a choice was made? if so, how many times? Was not the frequency of balloting occasioned by an attempt on the part of several members of Congress to elect the said plaintiff, Aaron Burr, as president? Do you know who such members were? if so, what were their names?

5th. Do you know that any measures were suggested or pursued by any person or persons to secure the election of Aaron Burr to the presidency? if so, who were such person or persons? Did *he*, the said Aaron Burr, know thereof? Were there any letter or letters written communicating such an intention? if so, were such letter or letters forwarded to him through the postoffice by any person, and who? Has he not informed you, or have you not understood (and if so, how?) that he was apprized that an attempt would be made to secure his election?

6th. Did he or any other person (and if so, who?) ever communicate to you, by writing or otherwise, or to any other person or persons to your knowledge, that any measure had been suggested or would be pursued to secure his election? When were these communications made?

7th. Had not some of the federal members of Congress a meeting at Washington, in the month of December, 1800, or of January or of February, 1801, at which it was determined to support Aaron Burr for the presidency? Or if there were any meeting or meetings to your knowledge, in respect to the ensuing election for a president of the United States in the said House of Representatives, what was advised or concluded upon, to the best of your remembrance or belief? Was not David A. Ogden, of the city of New-York, attorney at law, authorized or requested by you, or some other member or members of Congress, or some other person, and who in particular; to call upon the plaintiff and inquire of him—

1st. What conduct he would pursue in respect to certain cardinal points of federal policy?

2d. What co-operation or aid the plaintiff could or would afford towards securing his own election to the presidency? or if you or some other person did not authorize or request the said David A. Ogden to make such communication to the plaintiff in exact terms, what, in substance, was such authority or request? Do you know, or were you informed by the said David A. Ogden or otherwise, that he or any other person had made the said communication to the plaintiff, or the same in substance? Do you know, or have you been informed (and if so, how?) that the plaintiff declared, as to the first question, it would not be expedient to enter into explanations, or words to that effect? That, as to the second question, New-York and Tennessee would vote for him on a second ballot, and New-Jersey might be induced to do the same, or words to that effect? Did you ever communicate with the plaintiff, or he with you, on the subject? Do you know any person who did communicate with him? and if so, what did he say?

Did you not receive a letter or letters from Alexander Hamilton, of New-York, and late Secretary of the Treasury of the United States, now deceased, in the month of January or February, 1801, or at some other time, and when, respecting the election of a president of the United States? Did he not communicate to you that the said David A. Ogden had been requested to see the plaintiff for the purposes aforesaid? And what in particular were the contents of such letters or letter, or communication? Do you know that any, and if so, what measures were suggested or pursued to secure the election of said plaintiff as president; and did the said plaintiff know, or was he informed thereof, or what did he know, or of what was he informed? Had you any reason or reasons to believe that any of the states would relinquish Thomas Jefferson and vote for Aaron Burr as president in the said election in the said House of Representatives, or that the said Aaron Burr calculated on such relinquishment? If so, which state or states, and what was the reason or reasons of such belief?

8th. Do you know any matter, circumstance, or thing which can be material to the defendant in this cause? If yea, set the same forth fully and particularly.

Interrogatory on the part of the plaintiff.—Do you know of any matter or thing that may be beneficial to the plaintiff on the trial of this cause? If so, declare the same fully and at length, in the same manner as if you had been particularly interrogated thereto.

MILLER & VAN WYCK, Attorneys for Defendant.

Approved, March 6, 1805.

B. LIVINGSTON.

The deposition of JAMES A BAYARD, sworn and examined on the twenty —— day of ——, in the year of our Lord 1805, at Wilmington, in the state of Delaware, by virtue of a commission issuing out of the Supreme Court of Judicature of the state of New-York, to John Vaughan, —— or any two of them, directed for the examination of the said James A. Bayard, in a cause there depending between Aaron Burr, plaintiff, and James Cheetham, defendant, on the part and behalf of the defendant.

1st. To the first interrogatory this deponent answers and says, As a member of the House of Representatives, I paid a visit of ceremony to the plaintiff on the fourth of March, in the year 1801, and was introduced to him. I had no acquaintance with him before that period. I had no knowledge of the defendant but what was derived from his general reputation before the last session of Congress, when a personal acquaintance commenced upon my becoming a member of the Senate.

2d. To the second interrogatory, this deponent saith, I was.

3d. To the third interrogatory this deponent saith, There was an equality of electoral votes for Mr. Jefferson and Mr. Burr, and the choice of one of them did, of consequence, devolve on the House of Representatives.

4th. To the fourth interrogatory this deponent saith, The house resolved into states, balloted for a president a number of times, the exact number is not at present in my recollection, before a choice was made. The frequency of balloting was occasioned by the preference given by the federal side of the house to Mr. Burr. With the exception of Mr. Huger, of South Carolina, I recollect no federal member who did not concur in the general course of balloting for Mr. Burr. I cannot name each member. The federal members at that time composed a majority of the house, though not of the states. Their names can be ascertained by the journals of the House of Representatives.

5th. To the fifth interrogatory this deponent saith, I know of no measures but those of argument and persuasion which were used to secure the election of Mr. Burr to the presidency. Several gentlemen of the federal party doubted the practicability of electing Mr. Burr, and the policy of attempting it. Before the election came on there were several meetings of the party to consider the subject. It was frequently debated, and most of the gentlemen who had adopted a decided opinion in favour of his election employed their influence and address to convince those who doubted of the propriety of the measure. I cannot tell whether Mr. Burr was acquainted with what passed at our meetings. But I neither knew nor heard of any letter being written to him on the subject. He never informed me, nor have I reason to believe, further than inference, from the open professions and public course pursued by the federal party, that he was apprized that an attempt would be made to secure his election.

6th. To the sixth interrogatory the deponent saith, Mr.

Burr, or any person on his behalf, never did communicate to me in writing or otherwise, or to any other persons of which I have any knowledge, that any measures had been suggested or would be pursued to secure his election. Preceding the day of the election, in the course of the session, the federal members of Congress had a number of general meetings, the professed and sole purpose of which was to consider the propriety of giving their support to the election of Mr. Burr. The general sentiment of the party was strongly in his favour. Mr. Huger, I think, could not be brought to vote for him. Mr. Craik and Mr. Baer, of Maryland, and myself, were those who acquiesced with the greatest difficulty and hesitation. I did not believe Mr. Burr could be elected, and thought it vain to make the attempt; but I was chiefly influenced by the current of public sentiment, which I thought it neither safe nor politic to counteract. It was, however, determined by the party, without consulting Mr. Burr, to make the experiment whether he could be elected. Mr. Ogden never was authorized or requested by me, nor any member of the house to my knowledge, to call upon Mr. Burr, and to make any propositions to him of any kind or nature. I remember Mr. Ogden's being at Washington while the election was depending. I spent one or two evenings in his company at Stiller's hotel, in small parties, and we recalled an acquaintance of very early life, which had been suspended by a separation of eighteen or twenty years. I spent not a moment with Mr. Ogden in private. It was reported that he was an agent for Mr. Burr, or it was understood that he was in possession of declarations of Mr. Burr that he would serve as president if elected. I never questioned him on the subject. Although I considered Mr. Burr personally better qualified to fill the office of president than Mr. Jefferson, yet, for a reason above suggested, I felt no anxiety for his election, and I presumed if Mr. Ogden came on any errand from Mr. Burr, or was desirous of making any disclosures relative to his election, he would do it without any application from me. But Mr. Ogden or any other person never did make any communication to me from Mr. Burr, nor do I remember having any conversation with him relative to the election. I never had any communication, directly or indirectly, with Mr. Burr in relation to his election to the presidency. I was one of those who thought from the beginning that the election of Mr. Burr was not practicable. The sentiment was frequently and openly expressed. I remember it was generally said by those who wished a perseverance in the opposition to Mr. Jefferson, that several democratic states were more disposed to vote for Mr. Burr than for Mr. Jefferson; that, out of complaisance to the known intention of the party, they would vote a decent length of time for Mr. Jefferson, and, as soon as they could excuse themselves by the imperious situation of affairs, would give their votes for Mr. Burr, the man they really preferred. The states relied upon for this change were New-York, New-Jersey, Vermont, and Tennessee. I never, however, understood that any assurance to this effect came from Mr. Burr. Early in the election it was reported that Mr. Edward Livingston, the representative of the city of New-York, was the confidential agent for Mr. Burr, and that Mr. Burr had committed himself entirely to the discretion of Mr. Livingston, having agreed to adopt all his acts. I took an occasion to sound Mr. Livingston on the subject, and intimated that, having it in my power to terminate the contest, I should do so, unless he could give me some assurance that we might calculate upon a change in the votes of some of the members of his party. Mr. Livingston stated that he felt no great concern as to the event of the election, but he disclaimed any agency from Mr. Burr, or any connexion with him on the subject, and any knowledge of Mr. Burr's designing to co-operate in support of his election

7th. The deponent, answering that part of the seventh interrogatory which relates to letters received from the late Alexander Hamilton, says, I did receive, in the course of the winter of 1801, several letters from General Hamilton on the subject of the election, but the name of David A. Ogden is not mentioned in any of them. The general design and effect of these letters was to persuade me to vote for Mr. Jefferson, and not for Mr. Burr. The letters contain very strong reasons, and a very earnest opinion against the election of Mr. Burr. In answer to the residue of the same interrogatory, the deponent saith, I repeat that I know of no means used to promote the election of Mr. Burr but persuasion. I am wholly ignorant of what the plaintiff was apprized of in relation to the election, as I had no communication with him directly or indirectly; and as to the expectation of a change of votes from Mr. Jefferson to Mr. Burr, I never knew a better ground for it than the opinions and calculations of a number of members.

8th. In answer to the eighth interrogatory the deponent saith, I know of nothing which, in my opinion, can be of service to the defendant in the cause.

To the interrogatory on the part of the plaintiff the deponent answers, Having yielded, with Messrs. Craik and Baer, of Maryland, to the strong desire of the great body of the party with whom we usually acted, and agreed to vote for Mr. Burr, and those gentlemen and myself being governed by the same views and motives, we pledged ourselves to each other to pursue the same line of conduct and act together. We felt that *some concession* was due to the judgment of the great majority of our political friends who differed with us in opinion, but we determined that no consideration should make us lose sight for a moment of the necessity of a president being chosen. We therefore resolved, that as soon as it was fairly ascertained that Mr. Burr could not be elected, to give our votes to Mr. Jefferson. General Morris, of Vermont, shortly after acceded to this arrangement. The result of the ballot of the states had uniformly been eight states for Mr. Jefferson, six for Mr. Burr, and two divided. Mr. Jefferson wanted the vote of one state only; those three gentlemen belonged to the divided states; I held the vote of the state of Delaware; it was therefore in the power of either of us to terminate the election. These gentlemen, knowing the strong interest of my state to have a president, and knowing the sincerity of my determination to make one, left it to me to fix the time when the opposition should cease, and to make terms, if any could be accomplished, with the friends of Mr. Jefferson. I took pains to disclose this state of things in such a manner that it might be known to the friends of Mr. Burr, and to those gentlemen who were believed to be most disposed to change their votes in his favour. I repeatedly stated to many gentlemen with whom I was acting that it was a vain thing to protract the election, as it had become manifest that Mr. Burr would not assist us, and as we could do nothing without his aid. I expected, under these circumstances, if there were any latent engines at work in Mr. Burr's favour, the plan of operations would be disclosed to me; but, although I had the power, and threatened to terminate the election, I had not even an intimation from any friend of Mr. Burr's that it would be desirable to them to protract it. I never did discover that Mr. Burr used the least influence to promote the object we had in view. And being completely persuaded that Mr. Burr would not co-operate with us, I determined to end the contest by voting for Mr. Jefferson. I publicly announced the intention, which I designed to carry into effect the next day. In the morning of the day there was a general meeting of the party, where it was generally admitted Mr. Burr could not be elected; but some thought it was better to persist in our vote, and to go without a president rather than to elect Mr. Jefferson. The greater number, however, wished the election terminated, and a president made; and in the course of the day the manner was settled, which was afterward adopted, to end the business.

Mr. Burr probably might have put an end sooner to the

election by coming forward and declaring that he would not serve if chosen; but I have no reason to believe, and never did think that he interfered, even to the point of personal influence, to obstruct the election of Mr. Jefferson or to promote his own.

INTERROGATORIES to be administered to witnesses to be produced, sworn, and examined in a certain cause now depending and at issue in the Supreme Court of Judicature of the people of the state of New-York, wherein James Gillespie is plaintiff, and Abraham Smith defendant, on the behalf of the defendant.

1st. Do you or do you not know Thomas Jefferson, president of the United States? If yea, declare the same, together with the time when you first became acquainted with him.

2d. Was you a member of the House of Representatives of the United States, at Washington, in the session of 1800 and 1801? If yea, state the time particularly.

3d. Do you or do you not know that in the years 1800 and 1801, Thomas Jefferson and Aaron Burr had each an equal number of votes given by the electors for president and vice-president of the United States, and that consequently the right of electing a president devolved upon the House of Representatives of the United States? State your knowledge herein particularly.

4th. Do you or do you not know, or have you heard so that you believe, of any negotiations, bargains, or agreements, in the year 1800 or 1801, after the said equality became known and before the choice of the president, by or on behalf of any person, and whom, with the parties called federal or republican, or either of them, or with any individual or individuals, and whom, of either of the said parties, relative to the office of president of the United States? If yea, declare the particulars thereof, and the reasons of such your belief.

5th. Do you or do you not know Aaron Burr, late vice-president of the United States? If yea, declare the same, with the time when your acquaintance commenced.

6th. Do you know, or have you heard so that you believe, of any negotiations, bargains, or agreements in the year 1800 or 1801, by or on behalf of the said Aaron Burr, or by or on behalf of any other person, and whom, with the parties called federal or republican, or either of them, or with any individual, and whom, of the said parties, relative to the office of president of the United States? If yea, declare the same, with all the particulars thereof, and the reasons of such your belief.

7th. Did you receive any letters from the said Aaron Burr after the said equality of votes was known and before the final choice of a president? If yea, what was the tenour of such letter? Did the conduct of the said Aaron Burr correspond with the declarations contained in the said letter? Declare your knowledge and belief, together with the grounds and reasons thereof.

Deposition of the Honourable James A. Bayard, a witness produced, sworn, and examined in a cause depending in the Supreme Court of the state of New-York, between James Gillespie, plaintiff, and Abraham Smith, defendant, on the part of the plaintiff, follows.

To the first interrogatory deponent answers and says, I do not know either the plaintiff or defendant.

To the second interrogatory he answers and says, I was personally acquainted with Thomas Jefferson before he became president of the United States, the precise length of time I do not recollect. The acquaintance did not extend beyond the common salutation upon meeting, and accidental conversation upon such meetings.

To the third interrogatory he answers and says, I was a member of the House of Representatives of the United

States, during the fifth, sixth, and seventh Congresses, from the 3d of March, 1797, to the 3d of May, 1803.

To the fourth interrogatory he answers and says, The electoral votes for Thomas Jefferson and Aaron Burr for president of the United States were equal, and that the choice of one of them as president did devolve on the House of Representatives.

To the fifth interrogatory he answers and says, I presume this interrogatory points to an occurrence which took place before the choice of president was made, and after the balloting had continued for several days, of which I have often publicly spoken. My memory enables me to state the transaction in substance correctly, but not to be answerable for the precise words which were used upon the occasion. Messrs. Baer and Craik, members of the House of Representatives from Maryland, and General Morris, a member of the house from Vermont, and myself, having the power to determine the votes of the states from similarity of views and opinions during the pendency of the election, made an agreement to vote together. We foresaw that a crisis was approaching which might probably force us to separate in our votes from the party with whom we usually acted. We were determined to make a president, and the period of Mr. Adams's administration was rapidly approaching.

In determining to recede from the opposition to Mr. Jefferson, it occurred to us that probably, instead of being obliged to surrender at discretion, we might obtain terms of capitulation. The gentlemen whose names I have mentioned authorized me to declare their concurrence with me upon the best terms that could be procured. The vote of either of us was sufficient to decide the choice. With a view to the end mentioned, I applied to Mr. John Nicholas, a member of the house from Virginia, who was a particular friend of Mr. Jefferson. I stated to Mr. Nicholas that if certain points of the future administration could be understood and arranged with Mr. Jefferson, I was authorized to say that three states would withdraw from an opposition to his election. He asked me what those points were: I answered, First, sir, the support of the public credit; secondly, the maintenance of the naval system; and, lastly, that subordinate public officers employed only in the execution of details established by law shall not be removed from office on the ground of their political character, nor without complaint against their conduct. I explained myself that I considered it not only reasonable, but necessary, that offices of high discretion and confidence should be filled by men of Mr. Jefferson's choice. I exemplified by mentioning, on the one hand, the offices of the secretaries of state, treasury, foreign ministers, &c., and, on the other, the collectors of ports, &c. Mr. Nicholas answered me that he considered the points as very reasonable; that he was satisfied that they corresponded with the views and intentions of Mr. Jefferson, and knew him well. That he was acquainted with most of the gentlemen who would probably be about him and enjoying his confidence in case he became president, and that, if I would be satisfied with *his* assurance, he could solemnly declare it as his opinion that Mr. Jefferson, in his administration, would not depart from the points I had proposed. I replied to Mr. Nicholas that I had not the least doubt of the sincerity of his declaration, and that his opinion was perfectly correct; but that I wanted an engagement, and that, if the points could in any form be understood as conceded by Mr. Jefferson, the election should be ended; and proposed to him to consult Mr. Jefferson. This he declined, and said he could do no more than give me the assurance of his own opinion as to the sentiments and designs of Mr. Jefferson and his friends. I told him that was not sufficient—that we should not surrender without better terms. Upon this we separated; and I shortly after met with General Smith, to whom I unfolded myself in the same manner that I had done to Mr. Nicholas. In explaining myself to him in relation to the nature of the offices alluded to

I mentioned the offices of George Latimer,* collector of the port of Philadelphia, and Allen M'Lane, collector of Wilmington. General Smith gave me the same assurances as to the observance by Mr. Jefferson of the points which I had stated which Mr. Nicholas had done. I told him I should not be satisfied or agree to yield till I had the assurance of Mr. Jefferson himself; but that, if he would consult Mr. Jefferson, and bring the assurance from him, the election should be ended. The general made no difficulty in consulting Mr. Jefferson, and proposed giving me his answer the next morning. The next day, upon our meeting, General Smith informed me that he had seen Mr. Jefferson, and stated to him the points mentioned, and was authorized by him to say that they corresponded with his views and intentions, and that we might confide in him accordingly. The opposition of Vermont, Maryland, and Delaware was immediately withdrawn, and Mr. Jefferson was made president by the votes of ten states.

To the sixth interrogatory the deponent answers and says, I was introduced to Mr. Burr the day of Mr. Jefferson's inauguration as president. I had no acquaintance with him before, and very little afterward, till the last winter of his vice-presidency, when I became a member of the Senate of the United States.

To the seventh interrogatory the deponent answers and says, I do not know, nor did I ever believe, from any information I received, that Mr. Burr entered into any negoti-

* During the year 1802 unsuccessful efforts were made by the democracy of Philadelphia to have Mr. Latimer removed from the office of collector. The federal party complained of the number of removals which had already been made. The Aurora of June 29, 1802, referring to this subject, says—"We can tell them (the federalists) that the most lucrative office under the government of the United States in this commonwealth, the emoluments of which amount to triple the salary of the governor of this commonwealth, is now held by *George Latimer*, collector of the customs;" and on the 29th September, he adds, "Let any man of candour say if Latimer ought not long since to have been discharged from his office." Mr. Duane had not then read the depositions of Messrs. Bayard and Smith, and perhaps was ignorant of the *arrangements* by virtue of which this gentleman and Mr. M'Lane, of Delaware, were retained in office.

ation or agreement with any member of either party in relation to the presidential election which depended before the House of Representatives.

To the eighth interrogotary the deponent answers and says, Upon the subject of this interrogatory I can express only a loose opinion, founded upon the conjectures at the time of what could be effected by Mr. Burr by mortgaging the patronage of the executive. I can only say, generally, that I did believe at the time that he had the means of making himself president. But this opinion has no other ground than conjecture, derived from a knowledge of means which existed, and, if applied, their probable operation on individual characters. In answer to the last part of the interrogatory, deponent says, I know of nothing of which Mr. Burr was apprized which related to the election.

(Signed) J. A. BAYARD.

District of Columbia, Washington.

The deposition of the Honourable James A. Bayard, consisting of six pages, was taken and sworn to before us, this 3d day of April, A. D. 1806.

STEPHEN R. BRADLEY.
GEORGE LOGAN.

DEPOSITION of the Honourable Samuel Smith, Senator of the United States for the state of Maryland, a witness produced, sworn, and examined in a cause depending in the Supreme Court of the state of New-York, between James Gillespie, plaintiff, and Abraham Smith, defendant, on the part and behalf of the defendant, as follows:

1st. I knew Thomas Jefferson some years previous to 1800; the precise time when our acquaintance commenced I do not recollect.

2d and 3d. I was a member of the House of Representatives of the United States in 1800 and 1801, and know that Thomas Jefferson and Aaron Burr had an equal number of the votes given by the electors of president and vice-president of the United States.

4th. Presuming that this question may have reference to conversations (for I know of no bargains or agreements) which took place at the time of the balloting, I will relate those which I well recollect to have had with three gentlemen, separately, of the federal party. On the Wednesday preceding the termination of the election, Colonel Josiah Parker asked a conversation with me in private. He said that many gentlemen were desirous of putting an end to the election; that they only wanted to know what would be the conduct of Mr. Jefferson in case he should be elected president, particularly as it related to the public debt, to commerce, and the navy. I had heard Mr. Jefferson converse on all those subjects lately, and informed him what I understood were the opinions of that gentleman. I lived in the house with Mr. Jefferson, and, that I might be certain that what I had said was correct, I sought and had a conversation that evening with him on those points, and, I presume, though I do not precisely recollect, that I communicated to him the conversation which I had with Colonel Parker.

The next day General Dayton (a senator), after some jesting conversation, asked me to converse with him in private. We retired. He said that he, with some other gentlemen, wished to have a termination put to the pending election; but he wished to know what were the opinions or conversations of Mr. Jefferson respecting the navy, commerce, and the public debt. In answer, I said that I had last night had conversation with Mr. Jefferson on all those subjects; that he had told me that any opinion he should give at this time might be attributed to improper motives; that to me he had no hesitation in saying that, as to the public debt, he had been averse to the manner of funding it, but that he did not believe there was any man who respected his own character who would or could think of injuring its credit at this time; that, on commerce, he thought that a correct idea of his opinions on that subject might be derived from his writings, and particularly from his conduct while he was minister at Paris, when he thought he had evinced his attention to the commercial interest of his country; that he had not changed opinion, and still did consider the prosperity of our commerce as essential to the true interest of the nation; that on the navy he had fully expressed his opinions in his Notes on Virginia; that he adhered still to his ideas then given; that he believed our growing commerce would call for protection; that he had been averse to a too rapid increase of our navy; that he believed a navy must naturally grow out of our commerce, but thought prudence would advise its increase to progress with the increase of the nation, and that in this way he was friendly to the establishment. General Dayton appeared pleased with the conversation, and (I think) said, that if this conversation had taken place earlier, much trouble might have been saved, or words to that effect.

At the funeral of Mr. Jones (of Georgia) I walked with Mr. Bayard (of Delaware). The approaching election be came the subject of conversation. I recollect no part of that conversation except his saying that he thought that a half hour's conversation between us might settle the business. That idea was not again repeated. On the day after I had held the conversation with General Dayton, I was asked by Mr. Bayard to go into the committee-room. He then stated that he had it in his power (and was so disposed) to terminate the election, but he wished information as to Mr. Jefferson's opinions on certain subjects, and mentioned, I think, the same three points already alluded to as asked by Colonel Parker and General Dayton, and received from me the same answer in substance (if not in words) that I have given to General Dayton. He added a fourth, to wit: What would be Mr. Jefferson's conduct as to the public officers? He said he did not mean confidential officers, but, by elucidating his question, he added, such as Mr. Latimer, of

Philadelphia, and Mr. M'Lane, of Delaware. I answered, that I never had heard Mr. Jefferson say any thing on that subject. He requested that I would inquire, and inform him the next day. *I did so. And the next day (Saturday) told him that Mr. Jefferson had said that he did not think that such officers ought to be dismissed on political grounds only, except in cases where they had made improper use of their offices to force the officers under them to vote contrary to their judgment. That, as to Mr. M'Lane, he had already been spoken to in his behalf by Major Eccleston, and, from the character given him by that gentleman, he considered him a meritorious officer; of course, that he would not be displaced, or ought not to be displaced. I further added, that Mr. Bayard might rest assured (or words to that effect) that Mr. Jefferson would conduct, as to those points, agreeably to the opinions I had stated as his.* Mr. Bayard then said, We will give the vote on Monday; and then separated. Early in the election my colleague, Mr. Baer, told me that we should have a president; that they would not get up without electing one or the other of the gentlemen. Mr. Baer had voted against Mr. Jefferson until the final vote, when I believe he withdrew, or voted blank, but do not perfectly recollect.

5th. I became acquainted with Colonel Burr some time in the revolutionary war.

6th. I know of no agreement or bargain in the years 1800 and 1801 with any person or persons whatsoever respecting the office of president in behalf of Aaron Burr, nor have I any reason to believe that any such existed.

7th. I received a letter from Colonel Burr, dated, I believe, 16th December, 1800, in reply to one which I had just before written him. The letter of Colonel Burr is as follows:—

"It is highly improbable that I shall have an equal number of votes with Mr. Jefferson; but, if such should be the result, every man who knows me ought to know that I would utterly disclaim all competition. Be assured that the federal party can entertain no wish for such an exchange. As to my friends, they would dishonour my views and insult my feelings by a suspicion that I would submit to be instrumental in counteracting the wishes and expectations of the people of the United States. And I now constitute you my proxy to declare these sentiments if the occasion shall require."

I have not now that letter by me, nor any other letter from him to refer to; the preceding is taken from a printed copy, which corresponds with my recollection, and which I believe to be correct. My correspondence with him continued till the close of the election. In none of his letters to me, or to any other person that I saw, was there any thing that contradicted the sentiments contained in that letter.

(Signed) S. SMITH.

City of Washington, in the District of Columbia.

The deposition of the Honourable Samuel Smith, written upon five pages, was duly taken and sworn to before us, two of the commissioners named in the annexed commission, at the capitol in the said city of Washington, on the fifteenth day of April, in the year of our Lord one thousand eight hundred and six, and of the independence of the United States the thirtieth.

(Signed) GEORGE LOGAN.
DAVID STONE.

CHAPTER IX.

A HISTORY of the presidential contest in Congress in the spring of 1801, with an account of some of the circumstances which preceded and followed it, has now been presented. It afforded the enemies of Colonel Burr an opportunity to lay a foundation deep and broad, from which to assail him with the battering-rams of detraction, falsehood, and calumny. From that day until the period when he was driven into exile from the land of his fathers, he was pursued with an intolerance relentless as the grave. The assailants of his reputation and their more wicked employers felt and knew the wrongs they had done. Self-abased with reflecting on the motives which had impelled them to action, their zeal for his ruin became more fiery, and they faltered at no means, however dishonourable, to effect their object. The power of the press is great. But, painful as the remark is, it is nevertheless true—the power of the press to do evil is much greater than to do good. The power of the press is too often irresistible when conducted by unprincipled and corrupt men, pampered by the smiles and the patronage of those filling high places. A stronger illustration of this remark cannot be found in history than the case of Aaron Burr from 1801 to 1804. At the height of his popularity, influence, and glory in the commencement of 1801, before the close of 1804 he was suspected—contemned—derided, and prostrated; and this mighty revolution in public opinion was effected without any wrong act or deed on the part of the vice-president.

The charge against him was that he had been faithless to the political party which had sustained him through life; that he had negotiated, bargained, or intrigued with the federalists to promote his own election to the exclusion of Mr. Jefferson. The public mind became poisoned; suspicions were engendered; his revilers were cherished; the few stout hearts that confided in his political integrity, and nobly clustered around him, were anathematized and proscribed. The mercenary, the selfish, and the timid united in the cry—down with him.

It has been seen, that whenever and wherever the charge was rendered tangible by specification, it was met and repelled. For a refutation of the general charge, Mr. Bayard's and Mr. Smith's testimony is sufficiently explicit. Concurring testimony could be piled upon pile; but, if there remains an individual in the community who will not be convinced by the evidence which has been produced, then that individual would not be convinced "though one were to rise from the dead" and bear testimony to the falsity of the charge.

The details in relation to the presidential contest of 1801 have occupied much time and space. This could not be avoided. It fixed the destiny of Colonel Burr. Besides, it forms a great epoch in the history of our country and its government, and has been but imperfectly understood.

Mr. Jefferson's malignity towards Colonel Burr never ceased but with his last breath. His writings abound with proof of that malignity, smothered, but rankling in his heart. Let the highminded man read the following extracts. Mr. Jefferson, in a long and laboured letter to Colonel Burr, written uninvited, not in reply to one received, dated Philadelphia, 17th June, 1797, says—"The newspapers give so minutely what is passing in Congress, that nothing of detail can be wanting for your information. Perhaps, however, some general view of our situation and prospects since you left us *may not be unacceptable. At any rate, it will give me an opportunity of recalling myself to your memory, and of* EVIDENCING MY ESTEEM FOR YOU."

In his *Ana*, under date of the 26th of January, 1804, he

says—"I had never seen Colonel Burr till he came as a member of Senate.* *His conduct very soon inspired me with distrust. I habitually cautioned Mr. Madison against trusting him too much.*"

Thus, according to his own showing, while he was endeavouring "*to recall himself to the memory*" of Colonel Burr "*and evidencing his esteem for him,*" he was "*habitually cautioning Mr. Madison against trusting him too much.*"

Again. January 26, 1804, he says—"Colonel Burr, the vice-president, called on me in the evening, having previously asked an opportunity of conversing with me. He began by recapitulating summarily *that he had come to New-York a stranger some years ago; that he found the country in possession of two rich families (the Livingstons and Clintons); that his pursuits were not political, and he meddled not,*" &c.

Now who that knows the history of Colonel Burr's life will believe one sentence or one word of this statement? In the year 1778, Colonel Burr was in command on the lines in Westchester. In July of that year he was appointed by General Washington to receive from the commissioners for conspiracies the suspected persons. He remained at this post during the winter of 1778–79. Ill health compelled him, in March, 1779, to resign. In the autumn of 1780 he commenced the study of law with Judge Paterson, of New-Jersey, where he remained until the spring of 1781, when he removed to Orange county, in the state of New-York, and continued the study of law. In 1782 he was licensed by the Supreme Court of the state of New-York as counsellor and attorney, and immediately commenced practice in Albany. In July of that year he was married, then twenty-six years old. In April, 1783, through an agent, he hired a house in the city of New-York, and removed his family into it as soon as the British evacuated the city. In the spring of 1784, six months after his

* Mr. Burr had left the Senate previous to the date of this memorandum.

removal into the city, he was elected to represent it in the state legislature.* In the face of these facts, to talk of his "*having come to New-York a stranger some years ago, and finding the state in possession of two rich families,*" &c. What absurdity! But, shrinking from these disgusting and revolting exposures, the reader, it is believed, will cheerfully turn to the perusal of those letters which again presents to his view Colonel Burr in the domestic and social scenes of life.

TO THEODOSIA.

Trenton, January 2, 1800.

The question—*When shall we meet?* is already answered; but I must now answer it anew, and for a more distant day; perhaps Wednesday, perhaps Thursday; but you will hear again. Your letters amuse me; your recovery rejoices me; your determination not to torment yourself is neither from philosophy nor spleen—it is mere words, and an attempt to deceive yourself, which may succeed for the moment; *ergo*, no determination; *ergo*, not founded on philosophy; *ergo*, not on resentment; *ergo*, neither. I have no doubt but *chose* is on the way; the journey cannot at this season be performed in thirty days.

My compliments to A. C. M., and am very much obliged to them. It is the most fatiguing thing imaginable for such crude tastes as those of Theodosia and A. B. You had better apologize. You are sick and I am absent. But you have not mentioned the day—neither that of the beauty's ball, for which I owe you much ill will, and therefore my next shall be to *Natalie*, to whom all good wishes.

A. Burr.

* This is not all. It has already been demonstrated, and the fact is notorious, that, from the year 1777 until after the adoption of the Federal Constitution, the Livingstons and Clintons were not acting in concert. The Livingstons were of the Schuyler party. Before the revolutionary war there were two great contending families in the state of New-York; but they were the Van Rensellaers and the Delancies. The former espoused the whig cause, the latter the cause of the tories.

TO THEODOSIA.

Albany, January 29, 1800.

You must be weary of hearing that "I have not yet a line from you, and that John and Alexis are not arrived," but you must submit to hear often of what so often employs my thoughts.

Most of all, I amuse and torment myself by fancying your occupations, your thoughts, your attitudes at different hours in the day and night—generally I find you reading or studying; sometimes musing; now and then counting the time of my probable absence. In comes C. C.—a pleasant interruption, or a note from C. C., and then follows trouble and embarrassments, and sometimes scolding. They are always answered, however.

We have agreed that the cause of Le Guen shall come on next Tuesday. It will last the whole week. The week following I shall hope to leave this place; but I may be deceived, for the court may take a week to consider of the business, and I cannot leave the ground till the thing be determined.

Adieu, chere amiè,

AARON BURR.

TO THEODOSIA.

Albany, February 13, 1800.

Your etter by this day's mail, dated the 13th, and post-marked the 12th, is one of those hasty and unsatisfactory scraps which neither improve you nor amuse me. I pray you never to write to me with the mere motive of getting rid of the task. These performances always lead me to fear that all other tasks are performed in the same manner; but adieu to tasks and reproaches. I will endure your haste or your silence without a murmur. One is not always in the humour to write, and one always writes as much as the humour prompts.

I am here sentinel over the interest of Le Guen, and cannot

leave the post until the final decision be had, of which, at present, I form no conjecture as to the period, but I entertain no doubt of Le Guen's eventual success.

Among the letters forwarded by you is one recommending to me in very high terms a Mr. Irving, or Irwin,* from London; pray inquire who he is, and where to be found, and be able to inform me, on my return, if I *should* happen to return.

Mr. Eacker has offered his services to take a letter. You see that I cannot refrain from improving every occasion of assuring you how very truly I am your faithful friend and affectionate father, A. BURR

TO THEODOSIA.

Albany, February 15, 1800.

This will be handed you by Mr. Brown,† secretary to General Hamilton. By the two preceding mails I had nothing from you; by that of this day I am again disappointed. I do indeed receive a very pleasant little letter, but I expected a volume. Would it be an intolerable labour, if, precisely at half past nine o'clock every evening, you should say, "I will now devote an hour to papa?" Or even half an hour. Your last letter, though not illy written, has evident marks of haste.

I agree entirely with your eulogium on our amiable friend; but one point you overlook. Her heart is as cold as marble, and you mistake the effusions of politeness, mingled with respect, for symptoms of tender emotions.

The argument of the cause of Le Guen is concluded I fear that I must wait for the final decision of the court before I can leave Albany. To-morrow I go with John to Schenectady. I am more impatient to return than I can express. A. BURR.

* George W Irwin, subsequently minister to the court of Spain.

† Major General Jacob Brown, late of the United States army.

TO THEODOSIA.

Albany, March 5, 1800.

I had taken my passage for this day, and anticipated the pleasure of dining with you on Saturday. But—but—these buts—how they mar all the fine theories of life! But our friend Thomas Morris* has entreated in such terms that I would devote this day and night to certain subjects of the utmost moment to him, that I could not, without the appearance of unkindness, refuse. He would, I know, at any time, devote a week or month, on like occasion, to serve me. How, then, could I refuse him one day? I could not.

But, again, more buts. *But* after I had consented to give him a day, I sent to take passage for to-morrow, and lo! the stage is taken by the sheriff to transport criminals to the state prison. I should not be much gratified with this kind of association on the road, and thus I apprehend that my journey will be (must be) postponed until Friday, and my engagement to dine with you until Monday.

A. Burr.

TO JOSEPH ALSTON.

New-York, January 15, 1801.

My dear Sir,

Your two letters have been received, and gave me great pleasure. We are about to begin our journey to Albany. I propose to remain there till the 10th of February; possibly till the 20th. If you should come northward, you will find a letter for you in the postoffice of this city.

The equality of Jefferson and Burr excites great speculation and much anxiety. I believe that all will be well, and that Jefferson will be our president. Your friend,

A. Burr.

* Former United States Marshal of the Southern District of the state of New-York, and son of that distinguished revolutionary financier, the Honourable Robert Morris.

THEODOSIA TO JOSEPH ALSTON.

Poughkeepsie, January 24, 1801.

Thus far have we advanced on this *terrible* journey, from which you predicted so many evils, without meeting even with inconvenience. How strange that Mr. Alston should be wrong. Do not, however, pray for misfortunes to befall us that your character may be retrieved; it were useless, I assure you; although I am very sensible how anxious you must now be to inspire me with all due respect and reverence, I should prefer to feel it in any other way.

We shall go from hence to Albany in a sleigh, and hope to arrive on Sunday evening, that we may be *settled* on Thursday. Adieu. Health and happiness.

THEODOSIA.

TO MRS. THEODOSIA B. ALSTON.

Albany, February 17, 1801.

I have heard that you reached Fishkill on Sunday, and thence conclude that you got home on Monday night.

When in Philadelphia, send a note to Charles Biddle, inquiring, &c., and to inform him that you are going South. He will call and see you, being one of your great admirers. Desire Doctor Edwards to give Mr. Alston a line to Cesar Rodney, of Wilmington, a very respectable young man. He will introduce you to the venerable Dickenson, who, knowing my great respect for him (which you will also take care to let him know), will be pleased to see Mr. Alston and you on that footing. At Baltimore, either call immediately on Mrs. Smith, or let her know of your arrival. You are to wait in Baltimore until I overtake you, which will be on the 28th at the latest. Adieu.

A. BURR.

TO THEODOSIA.

Washington, March 8, 1801.

Your little letter from Alexandria assured me of your safety, and for a moment consoled me for your absence. The only solid consolation is the belief that you will be happy, and the certainty that we shall often meet.

I am to be detained here yet a week. Immediately on my return to New-York I shall prepare for a tour to George-town or to Charleston; probably a water passage.

I. B. Prevost has been hurrying off Senat and Natalie; but for his interposition they would have relied wholly on me, and I had already proposed that they should go with the chancellor some time in the summer or autumn, which would have been then or never, as I had pleased; but he (I. B. P.) has advised otherwise, and strongly urged their immediate departure. I think I shall be able to prevent it.

Would Mr. Alston be willing to go as secretary to Chancellor Livingston? I beg his immediate answer.

Adieu, ma chere amie.

A. Burr.

TO THEODOSIA.

Washington, March 11, 1830.

By the time the enclosed shall reach Mr. Alston, it will have travelled about three thousand miles. It will certainly deserve a kind reception. I leave mine open for your perusal; the other appears to be from *Miss Burr*.

Your Dumfries letter was received yesterday. To pass a day in Dumfries is what you could not at any time very much desire; but to pass one there against your will, and a rainy day too, was indeed enough to try your tempers.

On Sunday, the 15th, I commence my journey to New-York; there I shall not arrive till the 25th. Nothing but *matrimony* will prevent my voyage to Charleston and Georgetown; and even so great an event shall only postpone, but not defeat the project I am sorry, however, to add that I have no expectations or decided views on this subject. I mean Hymen.

It gives me very great pleasure to hear that Colonel W. Hampton is become, in some sort, your neighbour, by having purchased a plantation within fifteen or twenty miles (as is said) of Georgetown. Write me if this be so.

I have written to Frederick* as you commanded; that I might not err in expressing your ideas, I enclosed to him your letter. You have no warmer friend on earth; no one who would so readily hazard his life to serve you. It always seemed to me that you did not know his value.

Certain parts of your letter I cannot answer. Let us think of the expected meeting, and not of the present separation. God bless thee ever.

A. Burr.

TO THEODOSIA.

New-York, March 29, 1801.

On Wednesday, the 18th, I left the great city. At the Susquehannah the wind was rude; the river, swollen by recent rains, was rapid. The ferrymen pronounced it to be impossible to pass with horses, and unsafe to attempt it. By the logic of money and brandy I persuaded them to attempt it. We embarked; the wind was, indeed, too mighty for us, and we drove on the rocks; but the boat did not bilge or fill, as in all reason it ought to have done. I left Alexis and Harry to work out their way; got my precious carcass transported in a skiff, and went on in a stage to pass a day with "thee and thou." I was received by the father with parental affection—but of "thee." How charming, how enviable is this equanimity, if real. There is one invaluable attainment in the education of this sect; one which you and I never thought of: it is "*tacere*." How particularly desirable this in a wife.

* Frederick Prevost, son of Mrs. Burr by her first husband.

At Philadelphia I saw many—many, who inquired after you with great interest—*sans doubte.* Among others I saw B., lovely and interesting; but adieu to that. It cannot, must not, will not be; and the next time I meet B., which will be in a few days, I will frankly say so.

I approached home as I would approach the sepulchre of all my friends. Dreary, solitary, comfortless. It was no longer *home.* Natalie and ma bonne amie have been with me most of the time since my return (about twenty-four hours past). My letters from Washington broke up that cursed plan of J. B. P.; they do not go in the parliamentaire; they do not know when they go; and, in short, they rely wholly on me, so that thing is all right.

The elegant and accomplished Mrs. Edward Livingston died about ten days ago. Mrs. Allen is in town; she is in better health than for years past. As to my dear self, I am preparing with all imaginable zeal for a voyage to Charleston One obstacle interposes; that you can conjecture. That removed, and I shall be off in forty-eight hours. I hope to be at sea by the 20th of April; but, alas! perhaps not. In eight days you shall know more of this.

Your letters have been received as far as Halifax. We conclude that you got home on the 16th. It has been snowing here this whole day most vehemently. You are blessed with "gentler skies." May all other blessings unite.

A. Burr.

TO THEODOSIA.

New-York, April 15, 1801.

Your letters of the 24th and 25th March, received yesterday, give me the first advice of your safe arrival at Clifton. The cordial and affectionate reception which you have met consoles me, as far as any thing can console me, for your absence.

My last will have advised you of the alteration in the plans of Natalie. Of all this she will write you; but I must say a word of my own plans. The ship South Carolina is now in port, and will sail on Monday next. I wish to take passage in her; but a thousand concerns of business and obstacles of various kinds appear to oppose. I shall combat them all with the zeal which my ardent wishes for the voyage inspire; yet I dare hardly hope to succeed. You shall hear again by the mail of Saturday.

Your female friends here complain of your silence; particularly Miss C., and, I am sure, *elle a raison.*

The reasons which you and your husband give against the voyage to France concur with my judgment. You can go a few years hence more respectably, more agreeably. Adieu, chere enfant.

A. BURR.

TO JOSEPH ALSTON.

New-York, April 27, 1801.

Our election commences to-morrow, and will be open for three days. The republican members of assembly for this city will be carried by a greater majority than last year, unless some fraud be practised at the polls. The corporation have had the indecent hardiness to appoint known and warm federalists (and no others) to be inspectors of the election in every ward. Hamilton works day and night with the most intemperate and outrageous zeal, but I think wholly without effect.

If any reliance may be placed on our information from the country, Clinton will be elected by a large majority. The best evidence of dispassionate opinion on this subject is, that bets are two to one in his favour, and that the friends of Van Rensellaer wager with reluctance with such odds.

A. BURR.

TO THEODOSIA.

New-York, April 29, 1801.

This morning will sail the brig Echo, the only vessel in harbour destined for South Carolina. I do not go in her. With unspeakable regret, therefore, the projected visit is abandoned—wholly and absolutely abandoned. The pain of my own disappointment leaves me no room for any sympathy with yours. There is one insurmountable obstacle, which I leave you to conjecture. If that were removed, it would yet, for other reasons, be barely possible for me to go at this time. But enough of disappointment; let us talk of indemnifications.

On the 5th of June I must be at the city of Washington. After the 12th I shall be at leisure, and will meet you anywhere. Write me of your projects, and address me at that place. How can Mr. Alston, consistently with his views of business, leave the state for five or six months, as you have proposed, for your Northern tour?

Of the voyage to France I have written to you both about a fortnight ago. I heartily applaud your judgment, and the motives which have influenced it. You may by-and-by go in a manner much more satisfactory.

How very oddly your letters travel. That of the 30th March arrived on the 15th instant; and yesterday, those of the 6th and 13th by the *same* mail. To solve this phenomenon, I am led to believe that they have moved with a velocity proportioned to the spirit which was infused in them by the writer. Thus, the first crawled with a torpor corresponding with its character. It reminded me of the letter of a French lady, which I have shown you as a model of elegance. "*Mon cher mari, je vous ecris parceque je n'ai rien a faire: je finis parceque je n'ai rien a dire.*" This was, indeed, the substance of yours; but, being spread over a whole page, the laconic beauty was lost, and the inanity only remained. The second, a grave, decent performance, marched with becoming gravity, and performed the journey in two-and-twenty days; but the third, replete with sprightliness and beauty, burst from the thraldom of dulness, and made a transit unparalleled in the history of the country.

You will find in this theory some incentive to the exertion of genius; and I entertain no doubt but that, ere long, your letters will be sped with the rapidity of a ray of light.

We have laughed at your horse negro, and have been very much amused by the other charming little details. Thus letters should be written.

By this vessel I send two dozen pairs of long coloured kid gloves, and half a dozen pretty little short ones, *pour monter a cheval.* They are directed to your husband. I wish you would often give me orders, that I may have the pleasure of doing something for you or your amiable family.

I had like to have forgotten to say a word in reply to your inquiries of matrimony, which would seem to indicate that I have no plan on the subject. Such is the fact. You are or were my projector in this line. If perchance I should have one, it will be executed before you will hear of the design. Yet I ought not to conceal that I have had a most amiable overture from a lady "who is always employed in something useful." She was, you know, a few months past, engaged to another; that other is suspended, if not quite dismissed. If I should meet her, and she should challenge me, I should probably strike at once. She is not of that cast, yet a preference to rank only is not very flattering to vanity; a remark which may remind you of "*Le moi.*"

Adieu, chere enfante.

AARON BURR.

TO THEODOSIA.

New-York, May 26, 1801.

Another parlementaire is preparing in this port, and *ma bonne amie* and Natalie are again preparing to sail; but you may rest assured that they will not go. Their preparations are evidently mere form, and they are ready to yield to gentle persuasion. Yet you must not delay your voyage hither, to aid, if necessary.

But, for a reason much more weighty, you must hasten—*il faut.* I want your counsel and your exertions in an important negotiation, actually commenced, but not advancing, and which will probably be stationary until your arrival; more probably it may, however, in the mean time, retrograde. Quite a new subject.

Who should present himself a few days ago but A. Burr Reeve. He has come, with the consent of his father, to pass some weeks with me—more astonishment. I have put him in the hands of Natalie. She will find it a hard job, but she has entered on the duty with great zeal and confident hopes of complete success.

By the time this can reach you you will be ready to embark for New-York. You will find me in Broadway. Richmond Hill will remain vacant till your arrival. Adieu.

A. Burr.

TO THEODOSIA.

New-York, August 20, 1801.

Mr. Astor, if he should not meet you to deliver this letter, will send it after you. Yet I dare not trust to such hazards the letters which I have received for Mr. Alston and you. I persevere, therefore, in the determination to retain them.

I was so very solicitous that you should see Niagara, that I was constantly filled with apprehension lest something might prevent it. Your letter of the 29th of July relieves me. You had actually seen it. Your determination to visit Brandt gives me great pleasure, particularly as I have lately received a very friendly letter from him, in which he recapitulates your hospitality to him in *ancient days*, and makes very kind inquiries respecting you; all this before he could have entertained the remotest idea of seeing you in his own kingdom.

Natalie and M. Senat have been for some weeks past

at Trenton; they are now on their return, and will be here to-morrow. Vanderlyn, of whom I said something in my last, will immediately set about her picture. They (Natalie and Senat) are to go with the chancellor about the last of September.

Wheeler will be here in a few days. Hampton is actually married to a charming young girl—so General M'Pherson tells me. I forget her name. Mr. Ewing is appointed consul to London, and has sailed. Mrs. Allen is still at Elizabethtown. Adieu.

A. Burr.

TO THOMAS MORRIS.

New-York, September 18, 1801.

Mr. Vanderlyn, the young painter from Esopus, who went about six years ago to Paris, has recently returned, having improved his time and talents in a manner that does very great honour to himself, his friends, and his country; proposing to return to France in the spring, he wishes to take with him some American views, and for this purpose he is now on his way through your country to Niagara. I beg your advice and protection. He is a perfect stranger to the roads, the country, and the customs of the people, and, in short, knows nothing but what immediately concerns painting. From some samples which he has left here, he is pronounced to be the first painter that now is or ever has been in America. Your affectionate friend,

A. Burr.

FROM P. BUTLER

Philadelphia, September 19, 1801.

Dear Sir,

I was yesterday afternoon favoured with your friendly letter of the 16th. On the subject of removal from office, it appears to my finite judgment that it should be done sparingly, and only where it was absolutely necessary. It is

appears to my finite judgment that it should be done sparingly, and only where it was absolutely necessary. It is true, that the appointments during the latter part of Mr. Washington's administration, and the whole of Mr. Adams's, were partial. It will, I think, be prudent not to follow their examples. Every man removed adds twenty enemies to republicanism and the present administration, while it gives us not one new friend; for that man whose patriotism depended on his getting a place for himself or connexion, is neither worth attending to nor keeping right. You must be sensible that a general assault from one end of the line to the other will be made on the present administration. It is, therefore, highly incumbent to be moderate, though firm, to prove to the great body of the landed interest, the true support of good government, that the present administration are the friends of an equal, mild, economic, and just government. We may expect the political vessel to be assailed by waves, but we must steer an even straightforward course—united as friends in the same fate.

Your observation respecting the political state of South Carolina is more flattering to me than I merit. My offering for senator is out of the question; but I am not, neither shall I be inactive on that occasion I shall always feel happy in meeting you anywhere.

You will shortly see a statement of the Carolina election in print, by a gentleman who was present. I was not present, though I believe I know the facts. The thing will not be passed over without notice. Circumstantial facts are collecting. I regret that my two letters from Carolina at that time did not get to your hand. Your friend,

P. BUTLER.

TO JOSEPH ALSTON.

Albany, October 15, 1801.

Our Convention* met on Tuesday the 13th, and will probably continue in session five or six days longer. I shall

* A Convention to revise the Constitution of the State: of which Convention Colonel Burr was president.

forthwith return to New-York, beyond which I have no plan for the month of November, except, negatively, that it will not be in my power to visit South Carolina till spring.

On the road I passed half an hour with Mrs. L., late Mary A. She appeared most sincerely glad to see me. She is still beautiful; something ennuyed with the monotony of a country life; talked of you with the warmest affection. It is really a fraud on society to keep that woman perpetually buried in woods and solitude.

I am extremely solicitous to know how you get on. Pray make easy journeys, and be not too impatient to get forward. Never ride after dark, unless in case of unavoidable necessity, and then on horseback. What a volume of parental advice. God bless you both.

A. BURR.

TO THEODOSIA

New-York, November 3, 1801.

It is very kind indeed to write me so often. Your last is from Petersburgh. "Like gods," forsooth; why, you travel like ——; that, however, was a very pretty allusion. I have repeated it a dozen times and more. Your other letters also contain now and then a spark of Promethean fire: a *spark*, mind ye; don't be vain.

And so ——— has returned *sans femme;* just now arrived. He saw you and spoke to you, which rendered him doubly welcome to A. B.

You made two, perhaps more conquests on your Northern tour—King Brandt and the stage-driver; both of whom have been profuse in their eulogies. Brandt has written me two letters on the subject. It would have been quite in style if he had scalped your husband and made you Queen of the Mohawks.

Bartow, &c., are well. Mrs. Allen better. Mrs. Brockholst Livingston dead. Mrs. Van Ness has this day a son.

Thus, you see, the rotation is preserved, and the balance kept up.

There are no swaar apples this year; some others you shall have, and "a set of cheap chimney ornaments." I have not asked the price, but not exceeding *eight hundred dollars!* Did you take away "The man of Nature?" I proposed to have sent that with some others to L. N., but you have thus marred the project.

Since I began this letter I am summoned to leave town two hours before daylight to-morrow morning, to return next day, when I shall know definitely the result of the sale, which, indeed, is the object of the journey. On my return I passed a day with M. A. Monsieur is cold, formal, monotonous, repulsive. Gods! what a mansion is that bosom for the sensitive heart of poor M. Lovely victim! I wish she would break her pretty little neck. Yet, on second thought, would it not be better that he break his? *He* is often absent days and weeks. *She* has not seen the smoke of a city in five years; but this is dull. I had something more cheerful to say; this, however, came first, and would have place. And here am I, at midnight, talking such stuff to bagatelle, and twenty unanswered letters of *vast importance* before me! Get to bed, you hussy.

A. BURR.

November 5.

This letter was nicely sealed up and laid on my table; late last night I returned from the country, and found the letter just where I left it. Very surprising! This was so like my dear self, that I laughed and opened it, to add that Richmond Hill will probably be sold within ten days for *one hundred and forty thousand dollars*, which, though not half the worth, is enough and more.

A. BURR.

TO THEODOSIA.

New-York, November 9, 1801.

This fine day brings me your two letters from Raleigh and Fayetteville, 28th and 30th of October. It is quite consoling to find that you will have taken the precaution to inquire the state of health before you venture your precious carcass into Charleston. A fever would certainly mistake you for strangers, and snap at two such plump, ruddy animals as you were when you left New-York.

You shall have apples, and nuts, and a cook, and *lucerne* seed. As to *femme de chambre*, I cannot speak with certainty. I have put in motion the whole French republic on the occasion. Mrs. Kemble's friend cannot be found. Most probably Madame S. has tortured into Gamble some name which has not a letter of Kemble or Gamble in it.

Natalie sailed the Thursday after you left town, and she is probably *now* in Havre with her mother. A letter received from Madame d'Lage* since Natalie sailed, advises us that she is there waiting for her, which is indeed most fortunate, and relieves me from a small portion of the anxiety which I suffer for that charming girl. Yet, alas! there is room for too much. I expect to see her here within a year.

Anna wonders you do not write to her. It never occurred to her that she had not written to you: so she is now occupied, and you may soon expect at least twenty pages from her indefatigable pen. I am going to see Board. There is an ancient story of a man who once gave life and spirit to marble (you may read it in the form of a drama in Rousseau). Why may not this be done again? The sale of Richmond Hill goes on, and will, I believe, be completed within eight days. The price and the terms are agreed; some little under works retard the conclusion.

Adieu, my dear Theodosia.

A. BURR.

* The mother of Natalie.

O JOSEPH ALSTON.

New-York, November 15, 1801.

I send the enclosed newspaper merely on account of the proceedings of the Rhode Island legislature. They are on the second page. That, in New-England, men should be found hardy enough to oppose, in public speeches, the recommendation of a thanksgiving sanctioned by the usage of one hundred and fifty years; that this opposition should prevail, and the recommendation be rejected by a large majority of a House of Assembly, are events the most extraordinary which the present generation hath beheld.

It has been announced in your gazettes that I am to visit Charleston this month. Nothing is more true than that my warmest wishes have urged me to verify this expectation; but it is equally certain that I shall do no such thing. When I expressed the hope of seeing your state previously to the session of Congress, I did not know that I was chosen a member of the Convention by the county of Orange, much less could I foresee that I should be president of that Convention; and no individual suspected that fifteen days would have been consumed in accomplishing the business of six hours. These circumstances ought to redeem my character, in this instance, at least, from the charge of versatility or caprice. Vale.

A. Burr.

FROM THOMAS JEFFERSON.

Washington, November 18, 1801.

Dear Sir,

Your favour of the 10th has been received, as have been those also of September 4th and 23d, in due time. These letters, all relating to office, fall within the general rule which even the very first week of my being engaged in the administration obliged me to establish, to wit, that of not answering letters on office specifically, but leaving the answer to be found in what is done or not done on them. You will readily conceive into what scrapes one would get by saying *no*, either with or without reasons; by using a softer language, which might excite false hopes, or by saying *yes* prematurely; and, to take away all offence from this silent answer, it is necessary to adhere to it in every case rigidly, as well with bosom friends as strangers.

Captain Sterret is arrived here from the Mediterranean. Congress will have a question as to all the Barbary powers of some difficulty. We have had under consideration Mr. Pusy's plans of fortification. They are scientifically done and expounded. He seems to prove that no works at either the Narrows or Governor's Island can stop a vessel; but to stop them at the Hook by a fort of *eight thousand* men, and protecting army of *twenty-nine thousand*, is beyond our present ideas of the scale of defence which we can adopt for all our seaport towns. His estimate of *four millions of dollars*, which experience teaches us to double always, in a case where the law allows, but (I believe) *half a million* ties our hands at once. We refer the case back to Governor Clinton, to select half a dozen persons of judgment, of American ideas, and to present such a plan, within our limits, as these shall agree on. In the mean time, the general subject will be laid before Congress. Accept assurances of my high respect and consideration.

THOMAS JEFFERSON.

TO THEODOSIA.

New-York, November 20, 1801.

It is several days since I wrote to you, and many more since I received a letter from you. That from Fayetteville is still the last.

"Gamble's" protegée could not be found. You will probably gain by the exchange. That whom I shall send you is a good, steady-looking animal, *agée vingt trois*. From appearance, she has been used to count her beads and work hard, and never thought of love or finery. The enclosed recommendation of Madame Dupont, the elder, will tell you more. You are in equal luck with a cook. I have had him on trial a fortnight, and he is the best I ever had in the house; for cakes, pastry, and jimcracks, far superior to Anthony. In short, he is too good for you, and I have a great mind not to send him; you will be for ever giving good dinners. He has something of the manner and phisiognomy of Wood, your teacher. *M'lle la femme de chambre and Monsieur le Cuisinier* are both pure French (not creole), and speak well the language. He will take with him a quantity of casseroles and other implements of his etat. They will be shipped off next week.

The sale of Richmond Hill is all off; blown up at the moment of counting the money, partly by whim and partly by accident; something else will be done to produce the effect. I go to Philadelphia in two or three days; but shall return, and not set off for Washington till near Christmas. Mrs. A.'s health is much improved. God bless thee.

A. Burr.

TO THEODOSIA.

Philadelphia, November 26, 1801.

Your letter of the 7th of November, from *Yaahanee*, is received at this place. Though I am in the house with Mr. and Mrs. Lowndes, and several other Carolinians, yet we are wholly ignorant of your position. No one ever heard of Yaahanee. I suspect it to be some Mohawk word, which T. B. A. has been pleased to retain and apply—a very pretty name, I acknowledge. Your reception has, indeed, been charming; it reads more like an extract from some romance than matter of fact happening in the nineteenth century within the United States. I will ride fifty miles out of my way to see that lady.

The great business, as you are pleased to call it, has brought me hither. Not merely to see the statue, nor have I yet seen it; but am in the way. It will be a heavy job, considering that B. is on the spot. To return to the business. It will go on; it must go on; it shall go on. It will be Christmas before I see the city of Washington. My lodgings are near the capitol, and next door to Law, who has removed since we were together at his house. Your cook and maid must be detained at New-York till my return, which will be in about eight days.

Your letter is pretty and lively, and indicates health, content, and cheerfulness, which is much better than if you had told me so, for then I should not have believed a word of it.

You have learned from the newspapers (which you never read) the death of Philip Hamilton.* Shot in a duel with Eacker, the lawyer. Some dispute at a theatre, arising, as is said, out of politics. The story is variously related; will give you a concise summary of the facts, in fifteen sheets of paper, with comments, and moral and sentimental reflections. To this I take the liberty of referring you.

A. Burr.

TO THEODOSIA.

New-York, December 8, 1801.

By the ship Protectress you will receive all your things, together with cook and maid. To sail on the 14th. On the day of sailing I will write to you, enclosing the bills of lading.

Your interesting letter of the 23d is this day received. It brings me to the familiar acquaintance with your amiable circle, and admits me to your fireside more than any thing you have written. Mrs. Allen is here. Anna will, to all appearance, be married before spring to a merchant of the name of Pierpont. Catharine is astonished that she has not yet an answer to her letter. I have told her that she can by no possibility have one before Christmas.

* Son of General Alexander Hamilton.

In your reading, I wish you would learn to read newspapers; not to become a partisan in politics, God forbid; but they contain the occurrences of the day, and furnish the standing topics of conversation. The reading of newspapers is a knack which you will acquire in six weeks, by reading, during that time, every thing. With the aid of a gazetteer and atlas, you must find every place that is spoken of. Pray, madam, do you know of what consist the "Republic of the Seven Islands?" Do you know the present boundaries of the French republic? Neither, in all probability. Then hunt them.

Now, one word of self. I came here on the 6th, and shall remain in New-York till near the 20th. Then to Washington. The business is in a prosperous way. My great love for the fine arts, especially sculpture, may detain me a week in Philadelphia. Adieu, ma belle.

A. BURR.

CHAPTER X.

TO JOSEPH ALSTON.

New-York, December 13, 1801.

HEREWITH is enclosed a duplicate of the bill of lading, specifying the articles shipped for you on board the Protectress. She sailed this afternoon. The president's message, of which a copy was sent you by this ship, will have reached you through other channels long before her arrival.

One idea contained in this message is much applauded by our ladies. They unite in the opinion that the "energies of the men ought to be principally employed in the multiplication of the human race," and in this they promise an ardent and active co-operation. Thus, then, is established the point of universal coincidence in political opinion, and thus is verified the prophetic dictum, "we are all republicans, we are all federalists." I hope the fair of your state will equally testify their applause of this sentiment; and I enjoin it on you to manifest your patriotism and your attachment to the administration by "exerting your energies" in the manner indicated.

"To kill is brutal, to create Divine."

I propose—now observe, this is not to be published—I propose early in the spring to take a ramble with you through your mountains. You had best say nothing of your project of a location in the hills until it shall be executed; for, if competition should arise before you shall be suited, it would increase the expense of an establishment. I am impatient to hear that you are settled and at work. Very affectionately,

A. BURR.

FROM DAVENPORT PHELPS.

New-York, December 15, 1801.

SIR,

The enclosed copy of a letter from Captain Brandt to Isaac Chapin, Esq., superintendent of Indian affairs in the state of New-York, comprising (I conceive) the plan by him committed to me, and to which he alludes in his letter to yourself, for introducing moral instruction among the Indians. This plan, agreeably to his request, was recommended by the superintendent, and, so far as it respects the ordination of a missionary, has been accomplished.

It yet remains, sir, to provide means of support; and when the question respecting the instruction of their youth can be determined, by what means and in what manner this shall be effected.

I will, at present, only use the freedom to suggest whether it might not conduce to the furtherance and facilitating the above design to appropriate for their accommodation a suitable portion of land at or in the vicinity of Sandusky.

Were the scattering tribes concentrated, and with them some of their countrymen and others as patterns of industry and morality, such circumstances must be highly favourable to attempts to bring them into the habits of civilization.

I am, with great respect,

DAVENPORT PHELPS.

FROM JOSEPH BRANDT.

Grand River, May 7, 1800.

SIR,

About three weeks since I received a message from Obeel to attend a council at Buffalo, where I expected the pleasure of seeing you. We attended and waited a few days; but the chiefs there not being ready to meet us, and we having business which required our attendance at this place, were under the necessity of coming away. Had I been so fortunate as to have met you there, it was my intention to have conversed with you upon a subject which I have long considered as most important and interesting to the present and future well being of the Indians, on *both sides* of the lakes and at large; namely, their situation in a moral point of view, and concerning measures proper to be taken in order that regular and stated religious instruction might be introduced among them.

You well know, sir, the general state of the Indians residing on the Grand River, as well as in other parts. A considerable number of some of these nations have long since embraced Christianity, and the conversion of others must depend, under the influence of the Great Spirit, on the faithful labours of a resident minister, who might visit and instruct both here and elsewhere, as ways and doors might, from time to time, be opened for him.

The establishment and enlargement of civilization and Christianity among the natives must be most earnestly desired by all good men; and as religion and morality respect mankind at large, without any reference to the bound aries of civil governments, I flatter myself that you, sir, will approve what many of the chiefs here, with myself, are so greatly desirous of.

I have in view, as I have before suggested, the welfare of the Indians at large, being fully persuaded that nothing can so greatly contribute to their present and future happiness as their being brought into the habits of virtue and morality, which, I trust, may and will be gradually effected by instruction, if properly attended and enforced by example.

I well know the difficulty of finding a gentleman suitably qualified, and willing to devote his life to the work of a missionary among them; and especially one of talents and manners to render him agreeable in a degree highly to favour his usefulness. And, in order to satisfy myself in this respect, I have faithfully inquired and consulted, and am clearly of opinion that Mr. Davenport Phelps, who is recommended as a gentleman of virtue and respectable accomplishments, is the most suitable character for this office of any one within my knowledge. My long acquaintance with his family, and particular knowledge of him, as well as the opinion and wishes of the most respectable characters among the white people in this vicinity, who earnestly wish, for themselves as well as for us, that he may be ordained a missionary, make me earnestly hope that you will officially recommend both the design and him to the right reverend bishops in the United States, or to some one of them, and to such other characters as you may think proper.

From the consideration that religion and politics are distinct subjects, we should not only be well satisfied to receive a missionary from a bishop in the United States, but, for various other reasons, would prefer one from thence.

We shall be able here to do something considerable towards Mr. Phelps's support; and I doubt not but others, who have ability, will be disposed to assist in promoting so good a work. I will add no more than that I have great satisfaction in being confident of your friendly and influential exertions in this important affair, and that I am, with great sincerity, yours, &c.,

JOSEPH BRANDT.

TO THEODOSIA.

New-York, December 15, 1801.

Yesterday Mr. Phelps, mentioned in the enclosed, delivered to me two pairs of moccasins, directed—"From Captain Joseph Brandt to Mr. and Mrs. Alston." Your ship having sailed, I don't know how or when I shall forward them to you; but we will see. I send the original letter of Captain Brandt merely to show how an Indian can write. It is his own handwriting and composition. Upon this notice of his attention you should write him a letter of acknowledgment for his hospitality, &c., which you may enclose to me at Washington.

Dear little Anna is shortly to be married to a Mr. Pierpont, whom I do not personally know; but he is said to be rich and handsome—a young man of industry and credit as a merchant. I think it will do pretty well. E. has a lover—a man of consideration and property—measures six feet eight inches and a half, shoes off; but so very modest that they never will come to an explanation unless she shall begin. So no more at present from your loving father,

A. BURR.

FROM JUDGE WILLIAM P. VAN NESS.

New-York, January 2, 1802.

Since your departure the affair with Wood* has assumed a very singular aspect. When I told the printers that the negotiation was at an end unless they acceded to my proposition, it produced much agitation; and yesterday they

* The author of "A History of John Adams's Administration." This letter relates to the suppression of that book, which, although its publication was suspended for a time, was published according to the advice of General John Swartwout and M. L. Davis.

called to inform me that they had taken the opinion of good counsel on the subject; that their determination was not to publish, but to hold you liable for the expenses. Wood informs them that he acted merely as your agent; that all his proposals were in strict conformity to your directions.

Davis and Swartwout are of the opinion that we ought to get the work published in its present form, if possible:

1. Because our opponents say it unfolds the views of the federal party; that it exposes their principal men, &c., and therefore *we* wish to withhold it:

2. Because, if a new edition appears with the *same facts and character*, they will say it has been subsequently introduced:

3. Because, if *it* is brought out now, the attempt to check *it* will have a favourable tendency.

How far these ideas are correct, and what steps are best to take, you will now be able to determine, and instruct me accordingly. The truth is, that instead of being unwilling and reluctant to suppress, they dare not publish the work without indemnity. I am anxious to know your opinion on the subject, and hope to hear from you on Tuesday next.

W. P. Van Ness.

TO THEODOSIA.

Washington, January 12, 1802.

Just arrived at the city of Washington, this 12th day of January, A. D. 1802. I have only time, before closing of the mail, "to send you these few lines, hoping they may find you in good health, as I am at this present time," &c.

A form of salutation to be found in a public letter of Julius Cesar, and in one of Cicero's familiar epistles.

Your letters which greet me here are of the 2d and 20th of December only; only two. Why, I expected to find a dozen, and some of them down to within three or four days of this date. Having a hundred letters before me *un*read, I must defer writing to you for the present. Adieu.

TO THEODOSIA.

Washington, January 16, 1802.

Your letter of the 20th December (the venison letter) is still the last, though the Carolinians here have so late as the 3d and 4th of January, of which I am a little jealous. It is quite unlucky that you have been out of Charleston when your things arrived. How cook and maid will dispose of themselves for the interim, I know not. Mighty meek and humble we are grown. You really expect to do the honours of your house *equal* to, &c. I know better. It will be one of the most cheerful and amiable houses in the United States. I am gratified that you do not start with splendour; to descend with dignity is rare.

Pray make no definitive arrangements against the mountains. My heart is set on running over them with Mr. Alston in the spring. Why may not Papa Alston be weaned as well as Papa Burr? My movements must depend on the adjournment of Congress. Some say we shall adjourn the middle of April, and some the middle of June. As yet, I know nothing of the matter; for, during the few days I have been here, I have been enveloped in ceremonies. I am pleasantly lodged near the capitol. Eustis opposite to me. Law and Iruko my nearest neighbours.

Good venison is not to be had at this season, and to send indifferent any thing (except a wife) from New-York would be treason. Yet, on this important subject, venison meaning, I have written to New-York. You need not expect it, for I repeat that the best cannot now be had.

You must walk a great deal. It is the only exercise you can take with safety and advantage, and, being in Charleston, I fear you will neglect it. I do entreat you to get a very stout pair of over shoes, or short boots, to draw on over your shoes. But shoes to come up to the ankle bone, with one button to keep them on, will be best; thick enough, however, to turn water. The weather has not yet required this precaution, but very soon it will, and I pray you to write me that you are so provided: without them you will not, cannot walk, and without exercise you will suffer in the month of May. To be at ease on this subject, you must learn to walk without your husband—alone—or, if you must be in form, with ten negroes at your heels. Your husband will often be occupied at the hours you would desire to walk, and you must not *gener* him: oh, never. Adiéu.

A. Burr.

TO BARNABAS BIDWELL.

Washington, February 1, 1802.

Dear Sir,

The newspapers will have shown the position of the bill now before the Senate for the repeal of the act of last session establishing a new judiciary system; and that the bill, when on its third reading, was, by the casting vote of the vice-president, referred to a select committee. This day notice has been given that a motion to discharge that committee will be made to-morrow. It should be noted that the arrival of Mr. Bradley has given a vote to the republican side; hence it may be presumed that the committee will be discharged, and that the bill will pass the Senate to-morrow, and that in the course of three weeks it will become a law. I state this, however, as mere conjecture.

The constitutional right and power of abolishing one judiciary system and establishing another cannot be doubted. The *power* thus to deprive judges of their offices and salaries must also be admitted; but whether it would be *constitutionally moral*, if I may use the expression, and, if so, whether it would be *politic* and expedient, are questions on which I could wish to be further advised. Your opinion on these points would be particularly acceptable.

With entire respect and esteem,

Your obedient servant,

A. Burr.

TO THEODOSIA.

Washington, January 22, 1802.

Still silent. Yet is 20th December the latest date which I have received from you; hence I infer that you have remained at Georgetown much longer than was intended. Five weeks without hearing from you! Intolerable. Now I think to repose myself in sullen silence for five weeks from this date. I know that the apples and nuts will bring you out again. Thus children are moved; but I also thought that a pretty little letter, even without bonbons, would have done the same. I have a very beautiful elegy on a lady whom you love better than any one in the world; even better, I suspect, than L. N., and I was about to send it, but I won't till I hear from you: a nice, handsome letter; none of your little white ink scrawls. They talk of adjourning. No; I won't tell you that either. I have nothing to say of myself, nor any thing to ask of you which has not been often asked. Tell me that Mari is happy, and I shall know that you are so. Adieu, my dear little negligent baggage. Yes; one question. Do you leave your cards T. B. A. or Joseph A.? What are L. N.'s? And one injunction repeated. Do not suffer a tooth to be drawn, or any operation to be performed on your teeth.

A. Burr.

TO JOSEPH ALSTON.

Washington, February 2, 1802.

Your letter of the 10th of January was the first evidence of your existence which I had received for near a month preceding. I hope your wife is allowed the use of pen, ink, and paper. Her letter, three days later, has been also received. The successful "execution of your energies" is highly grateful to me. It *seems probable* that I shall pronounce, in person, on the merit of the workmanship somewhere about May day.

The repeal of the judicial system of 1801 engrosses the

attention of both houses of Congress. The bill is yet before the Senate. You may have observed that some days ago it was referred to a special committee by the casting vote of the vice-president. Bradley having arrived two days ago, and the republicans having thus an additional vote, the committee was this day discharged, and it is highly probable that the bill will pass the Senate to-morrow. On this subject I hesitate, though it is not probable that my vote will be required. Of the constitutionality of repealing the law I have no doubt, but the equity and expediency of depriving the twenty-six judges of office and pay is not quite so obvious. Read the Constitution, and, having informed yourself of the out-door talk, write me how you view the thing.

It has for months past been asserted that Spain has ceded Louisiana and the Floridas to France; and it may, I believe, be assumed as a fact. How do you account for the apathy of the public on this subject? To me the arrangement appears to be pregnant with evil to the United States. I wish you to think of it, and endeavour to excite attention to it through the newspapers. If you publish any thing, send me the papers which may contain it.

Truxton is going out to the Mediterranean with three large and one small frigate. Apprehensions are entertained that our good ally, George III., does secretly instigate and aid the Barbary powers. We do not know that Tunis has declared war, but such an event will not surprise me.

I have not heard a syllable of any changes made or to be made in offices in your state, and, for reasons well known to you, I shall neither make an inquiry nor offer advice. C. Pinckney's nomination was confirmed by *one vote.* All the other nominations have been confirmed, mostly without opposition.

Theodosia writes me that the mountain plan is wholly abandoned for Sullivan's Island. I do not, however, as yet abandon it; and, if I can get hence early in April, I think of going direct to Columbia, there to establish myself till you shall both condescend to visit me.

When you shall be both settled in your own house, I crave a history of *one day*, in the manner of Swift's journal to Stella ; or, as you do not like imitation, in your own manner. Vale.

A. Burr.

TO THEODOSIA.

Washington, February 2, 1802.

I have just received a pretty little letter from C. C., all on nice, pretty figured paper, such as you love, and she talks a great deal about you ; the substance of it is, that you are an ugly, little, lazy, stupid, good-for-nothing knurle, and that she is very sorry she ever wrote you a line. I can't vouch for the very words, but I think this is a fair abridgment of that part of her letter which concerns T. B. A. I wish you would teach half a dozen of your negroes to write ; then you might lay on the sofa, and, if you could submit to the labour of thinking and dictating, the thing would go on.

We make a pleasant society here, so that one may get through the winter without ennui. I live at Mr. Law's, not nominally, but in fact. Mrs. Madison is distant one mile. Anna Payne* is a great belle. Miss Nicholson† ditto, but more retired ; frequently, however, at Mrs. Law's. But pray, miss (madam), as to busts and statues, all the B.'s being out of the question, is there nothing in this line to be found in South Carolina ? I suppose it never came into your head to think or inquire. Pray shake your little noddle, to give the brains, if any there be, a little action ; but who can do two things at once ? That's true. I forgive thee all thy sins, without any further penance than that which you have imposed on yourself. But write C. and poor little Anna, to congratulate her. Tell her what a fine

* Sister of Mrs. Madison.

† Daughter of Commodore James Nicholson, and sister of Mrs. Gallatin.

fellow I learn her husband is. Mrs. Anna Constable Pierpont.

We have a perpetual summer here. I am weary of it, though, in truth, I care nothing about it. With you it must be burning hot.

The cook had only Peggy to aid him; but as Peggy is equal to about forty South Carolina Africans, he is very reasonable if he asks only thirty-five, and ought to be indulged. Your maid will make a miserable housekeeper, and be spoiled as femme de chambre, which last character is, I take it, the more important one. The poem or elegy is not sent, and is not forgotten. I am now going to smoke a segar and pray for you.

A. Burr

FROM CHARLES BIDDLE.

Philadelphia, February 3, 1802.

Dear Sir,

I enclose you a letter for Commodore Truxton. Should he be gone to Norfolk, please to forward it.

Every *gentleman* here, and, what I am sure you think of much more consequence, every *lady*, was much pleased with your vote on the judiciary bill. Those who do not think it unconstitutional to repeal the law are of opinion it would be very injurious to do it. Your friend,

Charles Biddle.

FROM COLONEL MARINUS WILLETT.

New-York, February 4, 1802.

Dear Sir,

What a racket this vile judiciary law makes. It must be repealed; but how the judges, who have their appointment during good behaviour, are to be removed without making a breach in the constitution, is beyond my abilities to develop. It will not, however, be the first assault on that instrument; and, if two wrongs could make one right, this account might be squared. But that horrid law must, indeed it must, be repealed.

I have received your two favours, one dated the 28th of January, and the other without date. The effect of the abolition of the internal taxes on Mr. Osgood* gives me no concern. He has plenty of other business, and money enough without the income from his office.

God bless you; you have my prayers always; and who dare say they are not as good as a bishop's, or any member of a Presbyterian synod? Sometimes I think I'll turn Presbyterian, that I may have the benefit of their prayers not to outlive my useful days; an event I deprecate above all others, and this is a prayer I never heard in our church—I mean my church, which, you know, is the Episcopal. Most sincerely your friend, M. WILLETT.

FROM JOHN M. TAYLOR.

Philadelphia, February 5, 1802.

DEAR SIR,

I had the pleasure of writing you some days ago, since which there are petitions circulating through the city for a repeal of the judiciary system. My own opinion is that there is no necessity for such a measure, as the two houses of Congress have the subject before them, and their decision will be had ere the petitions can be sent forward, and I have no doubt it will be repealed.

I have reasoned with all those who thought you ought to have voted against it being referred to the committee of five, that your intention must have been to afford the opposite party time to discuss the subject fully, so that they might not say of you and your friends (as Governeur Morris has said) that they pertinaciously forced it on the then minority. I think it is better to give them time.

Yours, very respectfully,

JOHN M. TAYLOR.

* Samuel Osgood, Commissioner of Internal Revenue.

FROM MRS. *******.

New-York, February 9, 1802.

At the sight of my writing you will exclaim—"She is unhappy, or she would not write to me." 'Tis not so, my dear friend; I am neither more nor less happy than when you left here. With every passing day I have resolved to inform you of my health, but from day to day it has been deferred, till I suppose my very existence is forgotten. Let me, then, awaken your recollection, by presenting to you the image of my thoughts, and retrace, however faintly, the impression I once flattered myself to have made on your memory.

Tell me how you do, and how you pass your time. Taking lessons of Wisdom from your Minerva? or flying after the Atalanta's of Virginia, more swift than their celebrated racers? or, more probably, poring over musty records; offering your time, your pleasures, your health, at the shrine of Fame; sacrificing your own good for that of the public; pursuing a chimera which ever has and ever will mock the grasp; for, however the end may be crowned with success, the motives will be questioned, and that justice which has been refused to a Regulus, a Brutus, a Publius, who can hope for?

I once admired for device a *skyrocket*, and for motto—"*Let me perish so I be exalted.*" I afterward changed my opinion, and preferred the *glow-worm* twinkling in a hedge. But I now reject them both. They strike for a moment, but neither of them are impressive; and it is thus, in changing, we pursue that something "which prompts the eternal sigh," which never is, which never can be attained. These reflections arise continually on my reading the newspapers, where your actions are so freely canvassed and so illiberally censured. They often excite my wrath; but when I consider that my anger can no more check their calumnies than the splendour of your reputation be clouded by their impotent attempts, my indignation subsides, and I console myself by saying,

"Vain his attempt who strives to please them all."

Z.

TO THEODOSIA.

Washington, February 21, 1802.

Your letter of the 31st, accompanied by a note dated 1st February, came by the mail of yesterday. A few lines from Mr. Alston, received some days before, advised me of your journey to Clifton, and of the distressing occasion. My heart sinks within me when I think of that lovely and disconsolate woman. Your conduct was worthy of you and of my daughter. She must be restored to reason and to life, by being convinced that she has some motive for enduring existence. If no other can be shown, at least she can be persuaded that she is necessary to you. But I learn from your letter, though you say nothing of it, that although she feels with anguish, yet she will not sink into despondency. This testifies a mind of that dignity and firmness which you had taught me to expect.

Nothing could have been more fortunate than the revival of the project. It will divert the attention and summon up the spirits. You must not condemn; it would be better to cherish it. Enter into all the details. Transport yourselves to Europe, and there take a nearer view and more accurate estimate of the dangers and advantages. Let those who oppose it offer something in lieu. What! is she to wear out her youth and beauty, dissipate her talents, and exhaust her spirits without an object in life or a place in society? Without enjoyment, without distinction? These hints will make you think I may hereafter say more.

My life has no variety, and, of course, no incident. To my feelings your letters are the most important occurrence. I am blessed with three of them in three months. It did not use to be so. It would be no excessive encroachment on your precious time to give me an hour twice a week the evening preceding the post days. This I shall expect; *and then*, and after one more communication, to be presently mentioned, I will write definitely as to my spring projects.

It is of sculpture: a hint in your last indicates that you have something in view. Be pleased to give me name and description, in some mystical, sybillistical way, which, in case of robbery of mail, will not disclose too much. One letter may contain the name, and another the comment—"*Car ou l'arreter ?*" is rather too mystical. I can make nothing of it, having studied it a full hour to no purpose.

I entreat that you will always enclose your letter in a blank sheet, on which is to be the seal and superscription. Health and blessings.

A. Burr.

TO THEODOSIA.

Washington, February 23, 1802.

On the 4th day of March next I propose to write you of certain matters and things of high import, heretofore touched, but not elucidated to the entire satisfaction of all the parties concerned, if, in the mean time, you shall be of good behaviour.

This, however, was not what I sat down to say, nor can I by any possible means recollect what it was; but, in truth, I had something to communicate or something to ask. I don't know which. That we have a great snow storm and cold weather (now) will be no news to you, for they will undoubtedly both be at Charleston long before this letter.

I project, as you may have understood, a journey southward at some time, yet nameless, during the current year (or century). Now, if my evil stars or good ones should, against my will and my judgment, take me through Norfolk, I am ruined and done; and there my journey will most infallibly end. That I had better be hanged or drowned, you will readily agree. The antidote or preventative is in your hands, or, if you please, head. The bust, slightly referred to in the letter of the 1st of February, has occupied some of my waking and sleeping moments. Be more particular, and especially the estimated value in dollars and cents; also, in what year or era manufactured, and the character and merit of the work, as it strikes your fancy, but with some minuteness. You know my rage for sculpture has cost me some money and led me into some bad bargains. Thank God, I have got rid of them *all*.

If you will have *Pet* or *Peet*, *Peter*, *Peter Yates*, *Peter Alston*, *Petrus Burr* (or by every other name he may be known) taught to write a good hand, and make me a present of him, I will subscribe myself your very much obliged and humble servant,

A. Burr.

CHAPTER XII

TO THEODOSIA.

Washington, February 22, 1802.

Never were orders obeyed with more promptitude and effect. It is not twelve hours since I desired (directed) you to write, and lo! a letter dated the 9th of February. And even "enclosed in a blank sheet of paper." A zealous manifestation of reciprocity is due to such respectful attention, and thus, in obedience to the high commands of T. B. A., I do most sincerely and devoutly execrate all the postboys and the legislatures of the two most noble states the Carolinas.

You women: it is so with you all. If one wishes to exhibit the best side, one must provoke you. Gratify your wishes and expectations, or, still worse, anticipate them, and it produces a lethargy. How have I laboured for three months, working and writing to please a certain lady: nothing comes but inanity and torpor. I provoke her, and behold the effusions of spirit and genius. Be assured that I shall not speedily relapse into the same error. Indeed, I knew all this before; but I thought it was only one's mistress that was to be thus managed—it is sex.

For certain reasons of state, neither the name nor the epitaph can yet be given; nor can it now be said precisely when. The verses are allowed to be very beautiful. Those on the anniversary of the wedding were received (this day) in the presence of two poets and a poetess, who said handsome things of them. The *ess*, being a maiden of thirty-five, drew a deep sigh.

Indeed, it is impossible to say, for I never before heard of such a thing as that any public body should "ajourn." They do commonly adjourn; and if, perchance, this should be what you mean, and you shall write me so, I will do my best to give you a categorical answer.

Natalie arrived at Orleans on the twenty-sixth day; meaning that she had twenty-six days' passage. She has written both from Orleans and Nantz. Her letters are full of good sense, of acute observation, of levity, of gravity, and affection. No news of her mother. Adieu.

A. Burr.

TO THEODOSIA.

Washington, February 26, 1802.

The arrival of your letter of the 14th justifies me in noticing you by this mail. Your newspapers of the same date, and also of the 15th, contain particulars of the races; but so technically expressed that I comprehend nothing of it. Your story is quite intelligible as far forth as it is legible. I am very glad that Papa Alston has won once. It is, I am told, the first time in his life. Where is Hampton all this while, that you say nothing of him?

Already I have told you that on the 4th of March I shall say something of the adjournment, if, in the mean time, you behave well. I shall *not* go first to New-York. Send back your chairs. General Smith's carriage has just ran away with four ladies, viz.: Mrs. Smith, Miss Speare, Miss Smith, and Mrs. Law. Miss Smith was taken up dead, and brought home dead. After twenty-five minutes she began to show signs of life. In two hours she began to know those about her, and now (three hours) she is perfectly well; and having been stripped and thoroughly examined, it cannot be discovered that she has received the slightest injury, save being frightened to death, as before mentioned. Miss Speare came off unhurt. Mrs. Smith and Mrs. Law are much bruised. You will, I hope, understand that the horses ran off with the carriage, and not that the carriage, of its own mere motion, ran off with the ladies. Adieu.

A. Burr.

TO THEODOSIA.

Washington, February 27, 1802.

Last evening Eustis happened in my room while I was at Smith's (opposite); he saw the cover of your letter, and the few lines which it contains. He wrote what you will find enclosed, and left it on my table. His cure is radical; that which I recommend is temporary.

A dull, raw, misty, vile day. Mrs. Law confined to her bed, as I expected, but not dangerous. The Smiths doing pretty well.

The judiciary bill debating in the House of Representatives, being the last day of the second week devoted *exclusively* to that subject. It may and it may not be finished next week. When this shall be done with, we may be able to make some sort of calculation as to the duration of the session.

Your last letter is pleasant and cheerful. Careless, incorrect, slovenly, illegible. I dare not show a sentence of it [illegible]

TO THEODOSIA.

Washington, March 4, 1802.

You have supposed it to be from malice that I have not written you of the adjournment and of my intentions. The truth is, that I know little more of those matters than you do, and I have chosen rather to postpone it *en badinant* than to write you crude conjectures; yet I can do but little more at present.

I left New-York with a determination not to return till I should have seen you and Charleston, and I arranged my business for an absence of six months. I had hoped that the session of Congress would close by the 15th of March or the 1st of April. On my arrival here every one said so, and I had like to have written it to you; but appearances did not seem to justify the expectation of a short session. The business is hardly commenced, and I see no prospect of an adjournment until some time in May. This is a great embarrassment; and your project of remaining on the coast is another. I could, with pleasure, have passed the summer with you in the mountains; but the heat and dissipation of Sullivan's Island is not so inviting. All this, however, is nothing to the purpose of your inquiry. To come to the point. I still propose to go South the instant I can disengage myself from this place; which may be a very few days before the close of the session. I shall be at least twenty days on the road. I entreat you, however, not to excite any expectation on the subject of my visit; not even to mention my intentions, until we shall see how far it may be in my power to execute them. The judiciary bill being out of the way, I am in hopes we shall engage zealously in the despatch of business. Of this matter I shall write further when I shall receive answers from you to my late letters. They may hasten or retard my movements a little, but not much. Adieu.

A. Burr.

TO THEODOSIA.

Washington, March 8, 1802.

From an accurate attention to the dates of your letters, I discover that you write on Sunday only; that if, by accident or mental indisposition, to which people in warm climates are liable, the business should be put off for that day, it lays over to the next Sunday, and so to a third or fourth, according to exigences, active or passive. Your letter, dated the 22d, but, in fact, written on Sunday the 21st, was received by the mail preceding the last, which brought nothing. This letter is a confirmation of my theory of provocations, which I have lately enlarged and more accurately defined, deducing it from philosophical principles, and adapting it to different *climates*. When this volume shall be ready for publication, I propose to add, in an appendix, by way of illustration, a series of our letters.

What you say of Huger shall receive due attention. Which *Maria* did your husband go for, the biped or the quadruped? It is impossible to determine from any thing in your letter. On the subject of busts you are more whimsical than even your father; just now you had something in view; but, on the 22d of February, "worse than any part of the United States." I have no time to give you now an explanation of your ice phenomenon, but will talk with T. I. and W. E. on the subject. Your last was sealed *on the writing*, a vulgarism which I again condemn. Adieu.

A. BURR.

TO THEODOSIA.

Washington, March 8, 1802.

At the moment of closing your letter, this scrap of a newspaper* caught my eye, and is sent for your amusement. It is aimed at Aaron Burr, by whom, it is well known, the publication of the book† is delayed or suppressed. The

* A paragraph cut from the Aurora.

† Wood's History of John Adams's Administration.

book consists of five hundred pages, principally low scurrility and illy-told private anecdotes ; with about thirty pages of high eulogium on A. B. There may, for aught I know, have been twenty other publications criminating the person by whom the work has been suppressed. They are so utterly lost on me, that I never should have seen even this, but that it came enclosed to me from a friend in New-York, who is solicitous for *my honour*, &c.

You may judge of the purity and decency of the book when I mention that some dozen of persons, by name, are charged with being bribed by British gold, and there is a surmise that General Pinckney is not reputed very *honest.* Of all the federal men, General Hamilton alone is treated with respect, even to flattery. My "solicitous friend" has given me a curious fact, of which I was ignorant till the receipt of his letter. Barlas, a Scotchman, the publisher of the book, is private tutor to the children of General Hamilton. Adieu.

A. BURR.

TO JOSEPH ALSTON.

Washington, March 8, 1802.

I learn, with a good deal of regret, that the mountain plan is abandoned ; at least, that no measures are taken or meditated for its execution. I should cheerfully acquiesce in any reasons founded on motives of economy, convenience, regard to law business, or personal influence ; but the solitary one assigned to me by Theodosia is, that you and she "*may be near papa and mamma.*" Of this, too, I acknowledge the force ; yet it might be considered that the mountain residence was intended for certain months only, and that during the residue (the greater part) of the year, papa and mamma might indulge their fondness. I had seen, or fancied that I saw in this project the assurance of health to yourself and wife, and sound constitutions to your children ; profit in the location ; amusement and economy in the residence, and an increase of your influence and connexions. How far it might comport with professional engagements, if seriously pursued, was not considered. One personal motive, I confess, might have influenced my judgment; the pleasure I had promised to myself in passing the summer with you, and in projecting little schemes of improvement and occupation. It is, indeed, with some hesitation that I shall visit your coast after the middle of May, and there is now no prospect of an adjournment of Congress before that time. Nevertheless, I shall come, though *at your hazard*, which, you know, would be a great consolation to me if I should be caught by a bilious fever in some rice swamp. The situation of Theodosia, so far from being an objection, ought, in my mind, to be an additional and strong motive. With her Northern constitution she will bring you some puny brat that will never last the summer out; but, in your mountains, one might expect to see it climb a precipice at three weeks old. Truly, I mean to be serious, and beg to know whether you have, in fact, resolved, and whether the resolution has, in good faith, been the result of reflection or of inertness. You will pardon the surmise. I allow something for the climate, much for the influence of example; and then, considering the uncommon warmth of the winter! it must be fatiguing even to talk of any thing requiring exertion.

The rapidity, however, with which your house has been furnished and established ought to redeem your wife from any share in this reproach. On the 22d of February I find her fully occupied in those concerns, with hopes of accomplishing the object by the time of my arrival. She was then, however, taking an eight days' repose, that she might renew her labours with more vigour at the expiration of that time. But, again, gravely I inquire where I am to find you about the middle or last of May. I presume, in the place where this will find you. Locomotion is labour.

I entreat your prompt attention to the enclosed memorandum, from my good friend Mr. Law. He says that Chisholm has never informed him of the disposition of the indents mentioned in his letter, of which the enclosed is a copy. Pray inquire and advise me. The thing is of small moment; but I should be gratified in the occasion to show an interest in his concern, for I am daily overwhelmed by the multiplied kindnesses of himself and wife.

The gazettes will tell you better, I suspect, than I can what is doing in the House of Representatives. The sloth with which things move is a daily source of vexation to me, as tending to protract the session. I dine with the president about once a fortnight, and now and then meet the ministers in the street. They are all very busy: quite men of business. The Senate and the vice-president are content with each other, and move on with courtesy.

Your Rutledge will be in Charleston in the course of this month. I hope you are on terms of civility with him, for I receive from him the most marked politeness. He will tell you of many strange things. God bless you ever.

A. Burr.

FROM CHARLES BIDDLE.

Philadelphia, March 13, 1802.

My dear Sir,

Mr. Eckfeldt brought me five medals, four of which I sent by Mr. Ross; the other shall be disposed of as you direct. The die of Truxton's medal broke after fifty-two had been struck. I suppose Truxton will feel more pain for this accident than he would to hear of the death of his friend T. Coxe.

You mentioned that if Murray wrote in favour of Richard Jones, you had no doubt he would be appointed a midshipman. If the Secretary of the Navy sees the enclosed letter, perhaps he will give him a warrant. It could be forwarded by Commodore Truxton, who I do not expect will sail before the 1st of April. Although I frequently trouble you about different persons, believe me, my dear sir, I do not wish you to do any thing whatever that will be disagreeable to you.

Mrs. Wilkinson is much obliged to you for your friendship to the general, which she says she will never forget. When James* sailed he desired I would inform you that he would write you as soon as he had any thing worth writing about. I believe you have no friend feels a warmer attachment to you than James. Sincerely yours,

CHARLES BIDDLE.

FROM JOHN COATS.

Easton (Maryland), March 13, 1802.

MY DEAR SIR,

I have long had it in serious contemplation to address a letter to you, but have frequently been restrained, from a knowledge that your time has been and still is devoted to public service, and that every moment is precious; and often I have been prevented by my own avocations and engagements on this our bustling stage. I have vanity enough to think I possessed a share of your esteem and friendship, which could only originate from your belief that I had a claim to the virtues, truth, candour, and sincerity. I detest the character of a hypocrite, and flatter myself no part of my past conduct can fix it upon me. Then permit me, with solemn truth, to declare, that when I see your name in the prints, I feel involuntarily an animating glow, and it immediately brings to my recollection incidents sometimes producing pleasing, and at others painful sensations, in which we have been mutually engaged and gone hand in hand. Although, to borrow the language of our president, there may exist shades of political difference between us, I have been your defender; and it was well understood and known that I spoke from an intimate acquaintance with you as a soldier and a gentleman.

* The present Commodore James Biddle.

Frequent reflection upon the various scenes we have encountered together has led me to lament the great distance that has so long prevented any social intercourse ; but if the following description of a new route, when you revisit New-York, meets your approbation, I may again have the happiness of a friendly salute of the hand. I have travelled from Philadelphia to Annapolis, *via* Baltimore, and ever thought it a rugged road. I propose that you should come to Annapolis, where exceeding commodious passage-boats constantly ply, and you will in a few hours be landed at Haddaway's, upon our eastern shore, from whence a line of stages run to Philadelphia.

Upon this route you will see a great number of your friends, added to which there will be novelty and ease. I cannot, indeed, promise you any romantic objects, such as *Caratoncka* or Morenci Falls, or gigantic mountains, such as we clambered together in 1775 ; but you will see a country approaching a high state of cultivation, and a number of towns, the most of which bear evident marks of daily improvement. Between these towns are interspersed gentlemen's seats ; some of them beautifully situated, and the inhabitants generally affable, courteous, and hospitable. As to your ease, if you do not travel in your own carriage, you will find the horses and carriages equal to any others ; the public houses comfortable, the country abounding with the good things of this world, whether flesh, fish, or fowl, and the road good, having occasionally what may with propriety be called gentle ascents and descents. My friends, Mr. Robert Wright, of the Senate, and Joseph H. Nicholson, of the House, who live directly on the road I have described, will confirm what I have written. Let me, then, once again enjoy your company, and that at my own hermitage. I shall be gratified by introducing the old lady, my two girls, and my boy to the companion and friend of my youth. They will endeavour to make their *lillapee* of a superior savour to what our cooks in days of yore could do for us. And although, as Partridge says, "non sum qualis eram," I shall certainly use my best exertions, while with us, to render your time agreeable.

Your sincere and old friend,

JOHN COATS.

TO THEODOSIA.

Washington, March 14, 1802.

Your letter of the 1st, postmarked the 3d, was received last evening. I regret that L. N. did not come to town, believing that you only could console her; that she would make you an intelligent companion; and that you could restore the tone of her mind, without diminishing the firmness of your own.

Papa's present was the most gallant and charming thing that could have been imagined. By Mr. Rutledge, who goes to-morrow, I send this papa a little token which has been some weeks waiting for an opportunity. Mr. Rutledge will tell you how I do, and what I do, and, *to an hour*, when Congress will adjourn. He sets off to-morrow, and will be in Chilton about four days after this letter; of course, I do not write by him.

It is probable that the box went with the ship which took your first cargo; but, as no one paid the least attention to the landing of the articles, nor to compare the delivery with the invoice, it may have been left on board. I will, however, write to New-York.

The story of P. is a fable. We are on the best terms, and he calls very often to see me. The elegy may now be seen in the newspaper, which, considering how nearly it touched you, I thought the best mode of communication. Avoid sights. You say nothing of the progress of house-furnishing and housekeeping.

Your last was sealed, as too often before, on the writing. If your *Mari* denies you a sheet of paper to enclose a letter, pray lay out *one* of your four hundred dollars for this purpose. Adieu, ma chere enfante.

A. Burr.

P. S. Somebody (I believe the Spectator) says that a postscript is always the most important part of a lady's letter. This, then, will be feminine.

I have had three letters from Natalie. All full of interest and amusement. Her remarks are equal to those of Lady Mary W. Montague for their truth and spirit, and far superior to any of our diplomatic communications. She is to travel from Nantz to Paris (about four hundred and fifty miles) *with her maid and postillion only:* an enterprise which no woman in France under forty hath executed without shipwreck during the last hundred years. Yet Natalie will do it without injury and without suspicion. I have taught her to rely on *herself*, and *I* rely on her pride.

I have said, and truly, that the story of P. is a fable. It may, however, by remote concatenation, and with the aid of great fancy and a little malice, have grown out of a trifling and ridiculous incident which took place at New-York, and which I am sure you have heard. P. was laughed at, and has behaved better ever since. There are at least twenty (my neighbour, Mrs. Law, says fifty) such anecdotes now circulating in this vicinity, *all equally unfounded.* Without any appeal, therefore, you may contradict all such as are inconsistent not only with truth, but with probability. A lady of rank and consequence, who had a great curiosity to see the vice-president, after several plans and great trouble at length was gratified, and she declared that he was the very ugliest man she had ever seen in her life. His bald head, pale hatchet visage, and harsh countenance, certainly verify the lady's conclusion.

Your very ugly and affectionate father,

A. Burr.

FROM C. A. RODNEY.

Wilmington, March 15, 1802.

HONOURED AND DEAR SIR,

This will be delivered to you by Dr. A. Alexander, of Newcastle, in this state. He has ever been a uniform and firm friend to the principles of our late glorious revolution. He has served many years in the capacity of a senator, and also of a representative in our legislature, and can give you particular information as to the public pulse here. He is a personal friend of mine; one whom I can recommend in the strongest terms.

I had the pleasure of receiving yours of the 10th inst. on yesterday, and was very happy to hear from you. The advice you kindly give me I shall cheerfully take. It has ever been my maxim to be moderate but firm. *Suaviter in modo, fortiter in re*, should be an axiom with all politicians. We continue to progress in the high way of republicanism, and you will find, by our toasts, we have not forgot one of its ablest supporters.* With great personal regard,

Your sincere friend.

C. A. RODNEY.

TO THEODOSIA.

Washington, March 19, 1802.

From your letter of the 6th, received last evening, I infer that you are in some sort settled in your own house; that you pleased yourself on that day is very grateful; that, too, I should have inferred from the spirit of your letter. By the "attack on Sullivan's Island" was intended an attack on the plan of residence.

I am just going on an errand to Baltimore, *de retour* on Tuesday; so that by the next mail you will have nothing from me. Where will you be from the 10th to 15th May? In Charleston, Sullivan's Island, or Clifton? Is L. N. com-

* The vice-president, Colonel Burr. This letter was written more than a year after the presidential contest in Congress.

ing to live with you? I am quite charmed with John and Sally. Preparations for Baltimore occupy me so entirely that I cannot even think of you by this mail. Adieu.

A. B.

March 20.

The preceding was written the morning of yesterday. I folded, and directed, and took it to Senate, thinking there to add a word. At ten last night I found it lying in my pocket. The weather (rain) has prevented my Baltimore jaunt which was planned for this day. The hope of an early adjournment recedes. In short, all is uncertainty. It will depend more on the thermometer than on the progress of business. When the heat shall be intolerable here, shall I set my face towards the sun? I think I will. If you had been in the mountains! but that is not so.

Natalie arrived in Paris the 31st December; her mother not there; but numerous friends, who fatigue her with civilities. Her heart is in the United States.

This will remain in the postoffice till the 23d. If, in the mean time, I receive a letter from you, a supplement will accompany this. Adieu.

A. Burr.

FROM C. A. RODNEY.

Wilmington, March 20, 1802.

Dear Sir,

I have perused with much pleasure the papers enclosed in your highly-acceptable favours. The proposed state will possess the republican tone, and give additional weight to the scale which already so strongly preponderates.

The repeal of all internal taxation will be sensibly felt by the people, and will *popularize* our administration. The expense of collecting those taxes, in consequence of the swarm of pensioners attached to them, points them out as the proper object of retrenchment. The brown-sugar gentry in Congress; your tea-sippers and salts-men (not Attic), who, by-the-by, have laid all those duties, cannot *agitate* the public mind on those topics.

I am happy to discover in the proceedings of the republicans so much moderation, firmness, and unanimity. I trust their opponents will not hereafter think they want *nerve*. This conduct forms a striking contrast with federal gasconade; and the effect of those things, in a free country, is not easily calculated by common rule.

The polite and kind invitation you give me I should certainly accept of if in my power. I had thought seriously of it some weeks back; but you must know I have purchased a little tract of land adjoining Dr. Tilton's, which I once showed you, and have cut out abundant work for the season. This, Dr. Tilton says, is to restore my health perfectly. There are many friends at Washington it would give me great pleasure to see, but none more than yourself.

Most sincerely yours,

C. A. RODNEY.

FROM URIAH TRACEY.*

Washington, March 29, 1802.

The sermon, for which I am indebted to your goodness, is now returned, with many thanks for the loan.

I have perused it with pleasure, and, I hope, profit. It is an excellent treatise, worthy of the attention of every man, and more emphatically so of men in high and responsible stations in government.

Our time is short, my friend, too short to allow an opportunity of retrieving almost any misspense of it; much more so to allow a redemption for any neglect to perform great public services when once happily in our power. God grant that you may be profited by this, and, in turn, be more profitable to this distracted nation.

U. TRACY.

* At that time a member of the United States Senate.

FROM GENERAL HORATIO GATES.

New-York, March 30, 1802.

My dear Sir,

Yesterday I was favoured with your obliging letter of the 23d inst. by Mr. Peter Townsend; also, with a most beautiful silver medal from the die I have presented you. It is in the highest polish and perfection. In respect to the tin medal and its case, I have only heard of them from you, as I never received either, or a single line from Mr. Dallas. But men so much engaged in business seldom have time to attend to such small affairs.

When you see Dr. Murray, present my affectionate respects to him; he is, indeed, an old and highly esteemed friend. As to news, I never expect any from statesmen high in office. So far as the session of the Congress has proceeded, *I*, poor little *I*, am satisfied with what they have done. Taxes and law diminished should be approved of by the many. The stricken deer will weep; but the powerful will, I trust, be generous to those who are not malignant.

The charming Miss Church was, on Thursday, married to Mr. Cruger. But I have a more serious piece of news for your private ear. Young Secretary Sumter, on the passage to Europe, fell desperately in love with Miss Natalie d'Lage. They landed at Nantz, near her mother's chateau. The old lady is a furious royalist, and will not hear of her daughter's being married to a republican; perhaps you know more than I can tell you what is likely to be the result.

Mr. Townsend goes so immediately to Orange county, that he prevents my intended civilities; but I trust he will hereafter put it in my power to cultivate his acquaintance. For any thing I see, your session will be shortly over.

Judge Brockholst Livingston took his seat in the City Hall yesterday. This phenomenon (what shall I call it?) in office or in policy has caused a grumbling in the legislature, where it seems to be laid aside for future contention;

but you will hear more from your correspondents. I am told it is nicknamed the Livingston act. My Mary is well, and has every desire to oblige you.

Affectionately yours,

HORATIO GATES.

FROM DAVID GELSTON.

New-York, April 3, 1802.

DEAR SIR,

I am favoured with yours of the 30th ult., with its enclosure. The subject contained in my letter of the 22d to you has, in several instances, become so important, that I wrote yesterday to Mr. Gallatin on the same business.

You are, in general, so apt to decide promptly and correctly, that if you had at once told me my construction of the law referred to was right, I should have wanted no more. We begin to look better in the city—alarms are less frequent, confidence is gaining, and business increasing.

I have just received permission from the secretary of the treasury to make some additional inspectors. Mr. L. shall be gratified, but my authority is limited to the 15th of November next. If you have a particular wish for any other person, please let me know immediately. Yours, truly,

D. GELSTON.

TO THEODOSIA.

Washington, April 5, 1802.

MA CHERE ENFANTE,

Different accidents and interruptions prevented me from writing by the two last mails; a very unusual omission, and thus happens what, I believe, has never before occurred, that I have two of your letters unanswered, those of the 19th and 22d, both affecting and interesting. The last of them acknowledges the receipt of a letter from me dated March 9th. Now, I did not write any letter under that date, it must be a forgery. On the 8th and 12th I did write to you.

It is, I hope and believe, true that Richmond Hill is competent to all purposes; but nothing is done nor can be speedily done. The thing constantly eludes a conclusion, and matters are, in fact, now as badly circumstanced as one year ago. When I left New-York I arranged my affairs of *all kinds* for six months' absence, which would extend to the middle of June, with the determination to go hence to South Carolina, in which determination I persist; yet you know that *a single letter may take me in a contrary direction*, and mar all my plans of pleasure. This, and this only, produces the instability of my resolutions, and the equivocal tenour of my letters on the subject of the visit.

Nothing certain can be predicated of the adjournment; but I am quite resolved not to remain here beyond the 25th, more probable that I may leave it on the 19th. In either case, it will be vain to address a letter to me at Washington after the receipt of this, as I shall not be here to receive it. My route will be through Richmond and Petersburgh to Fayetteville, and thence to Georgetown and Clifton, where I presume I shall find Papa Alston, Ellen, &c. You may address me a line to Richmond, and another to Fayetteville, merely to say how you are, and who more are dead. Recollecting, when you write, that it will be very uncertain whether they will reach me; still, on my arrival at those places, I shall be quite out of humour if I find no letter from you, and *will stay a week* at each place in hopes of receiving one.

I have ordered Vanderlyn to send you, from New-York, both his and Stuart's picture of A. Burr; and have told him to ship himself for the port of Charleston on the 1st of May.

I have also desired that my beautiful little bust of Bonaparte be sent to Mr. William Alston.

You may send a letter to meet me at Clifton, and two or three to each place if you find my movements so retarded as to admit a probability of their being received. Adieu.

A. Burr.

TO THEODOSIA.

Washington, April 12, 1802.

Your letter of the 29th came by the last mail, exactly, as heretofore, on the eighth day after the date of your last preceding. Whether it be invariably Sunday or not, at least it is always octo-diurnal. Pray get an eight-day clock, and then all family matters will move on in strict uniformity. Thank your husband for his letter about Mr. Law's indents.

The instability of all human concerns has been a theme of remark for the last 4000 years. Lately, very lately, I wrote you of my determination to leave this city on the 26th. I then thought so, as you will readily believe; because, why should I deceive my dear little Theodosia? Now this thing is altered, for reasons too numerous and mighty to be here enumerated; and, besides, you know our doctrine is not to give reasons, but to let the facts speak for themselves. On this occasion, however, even your hard heart would yield to the motives which govern me. The plan, I say, is all altered. Instead of leaving this fair region, as was gravely proposed, on the 26th of this month, the present project is to part from all I here hold dear on the 20th (the *twentieth*) inst., which piece of caprice I hope you will pardon. If no letter intervenes before that day, Papa Alston may expect to see me in some twelve or fifteen days thereafter. I shall hope to find letters at Richmond, Fayetteville, &c. Adieu.

A. BURR.

TO THEODOSIA.

Clifton, May 3, 1802.

At the moment of my arrival on Friday evening I wrote you from Mr. Kinlock's. The day following (May 1) I came here, and, being without horses, sent on Sunday morning to engage the whole stage, which was to go to-morrow, and, as I understand, reaches Charleston in a day. Unfortunately, the stage was full—not even a seat vacant for the vice-president. I am, therefore, doomed to remain here one day longer, and to be two days on the road. My horses not having arrived, Mr. Alston will, on Wednesday morning, set out with me in his curricle. We shall dine and stay the night of Wednesday at Mrs. Mott's, and on the day following, Thursday evening, reach Charleston.

I now send my man George (late Azor Le Guen, now George d'Grasse) to Georgetown. If he can get a place in the stage, he goes on with my baggage; if not, he sends this letter, with all affectionate good wishes. William arrived here this afternoon, and tells us that you are *well*, and your husband *ill*. This is exactly wrong, unless he means to take the whole trouble off your hands, as some good husbands have heretofore done; so, at least, Darwin records. God bless thee, my dear Theodosia.

A. Burr.

FROM MIDSHIPMAN JAMES BIDDLE.

U. S. Ship Constellation,
at Gibraltar, May 8, 1802.

Dear Sir,

As the frigate Philadelphia will sail in a few days for America, I cannot neglect so good an opportunity of writing, and returning you my sincere thanks for the marked civilities I have received at all times from you, particularly at New-York in the summer of 1800. Be assured, sir, I feel the liveliest sense of the obligations I am under for the many favours conferred upon me, and shall ever feel extremely happy to have it in my power to render you any service.

Owing to our being perplexed with almost constant easterly winds, we did not make the land until the 24th ult., when we made Cape Canter, on the coast of Africa. On the 28th we got into the Straits of Gibraltar, but the wind heading us off the rock, we were obliged to bear away for Malaga. There we found the Essex and Philadelphia at anchor. On the 3d inst. we left Malaga, and arrived here in company with the Philadelphia and Essex on the 5th, and I expect to remain until Commodore Truxton arrives on the station.

While the ship lay at Malaga I had an opportunity of seeing every thing that could attract the eye of a stranger. The country round the city is extremely fertile, abounding with all the different kinds of fruit-trees. Indeed, the lower class of the Spaniards subsist almost entirely upon fruit, the produce of the country. The chief articles of exportation are grapes, figs, raisins, oranges, anchovies, wines, &c. Their streets are very narrow, running at random in every direction. Their houses are mostly built of marble, four stories high, different families occupying different stories of the same house. They have two or three forts, built on eminences adjacent to the city for its protection, but they are out of order and decaying.

I anticipate enjoying a very pleasant cruise, as we seem to be favoured with every thing that could render our situation agreeable. Captain Murray is one of the best of men, and treats us with all the kindness and attention we could wish. The climate is mild and healthy. The Tripolitans keep among themselves, and never venture out, so that we shall have nothing to do but to visit the different ports of the Mediterranean. The closest friendship and harmony prevails among the officers of the ship. Every thing, in short, that we could wish, we seem to have, to make our situation comfortable. Pray remember me kindly to Mrs. Alston, and believe me, with esteem and respect, your most obedient servant,

James Biddle.

FROM JOHN TAYLOR, OF CAROLINE.

Virginia, Caroline, May 25, 1802.

Dear Sir,

Your favour, covering the medal struck to commemorate the most brilliant exploit of the American war, from some cause unknown to me, never arrived until this instant. It is particularly acceptable from the circumstance of my having imbibed a personal affection for General Gates by having served under him for a few months.

It would be quite premature in me to consider whether I would go into Congress unless it was probable that I could. The government have no means of providing for the gentleman you mention; and if they had, to do so for the purpose of making room for another might expose them to censures which they will hardly encounter. As to a voluntary resignation of his station, there are some circumstances in his case which do really justify him in refusing to do it, unless for some better prospect of public benefit.

Not until some days after you left this was it discovered that you had forgotten your travelling map. I lamented the inconveniences to which the oversight would expose you, but had no mode of removing them, despairing, from a recollection of your horses, that either of mine would be fleet enough to overtake you. The map could, therefore, only be taken care of for the purpose of being restored to you. Permit me to hope that you will allow me to do this at my own house as you return; and that you will apprize me of your resolution to do so, both that I may be at home and that I may enjoy the hope of your company before the pleasure is realized. Farewell.

JOHN TAYLOR.

CHAPTER XIII.

THEODOSIA TO JOSEPH ALSTON.

New-York, June 24, 1802.

We arrived yesterday morning, exactly the eighth day since I left you. Our passage was pleasant, inasmuch as we had no storms, and the most obliging, attentive captain. I never met with more unremitted politeness. He was constantly endeavouring to tempt my appetite by all the delicacies in his own stores. To the child he proved an excellent nurse when I was fatigued and the rest sick. We are now in my father's town-house. Mrs. Allen had gone up the North River before my arrival; thus I have seen neither her nor her sons. John is to return and be married in a few days.

I have just returned from a ride in the country and a visit to Richmond Hill. Never did I behold this island so beautiful. The variety of vivid greens; the finely-cultivated fields and gaudy gardens; the neat, cool air of the cit's boxes, peeping through straight rows of tall poplars, and the elegance of some gentlemen's seats, commanding a view of the majestic Hudson, and the high, dark shores of New-Jersey, altogether form a scene so lively, so touching, and to me now so new, that I was in constant rapture. How much did I wish for you to join with me in admiring it. With how much regret did I recollect some rides we took together last summer. Ah, my husband, why are we separated? I had rather have been ill on Sullivan's Island with you, than well separated from you. Even my amusements serve to increase my unhappiness; for if any thing affords me pleasure, the thought that, were you here, you also would feel pleasure, and thus redouble mine, at once puts an end to enjoyment. You do not know how constantly my whole mind is employed in thinking of you. Do you, my husband, think as frequently of your Theo., and wish for her? Do you really feel a vacuum in your pleasures? As for your wife, she has bid adieu to pleasure till next October. When, when will that month come? It appears to me a century off. I can scarcely yet realize to myself that we are to be so long separated. Do not imagine, however, that I mean to beg you to join me this summer. No, my husband, I know your reasons, and approve them. Your wife feels a consolation in talking of her sorrows to you; but she would think herself unworthy of you could she not find fortitude enough to bear them! God knows how delighted I shall be when once again in your arms; but how much would my happiness be diminished by recollecting that your advancement and interest suffered. When we meet, let there be nothing to alloy a happiness so pure, so unbounded. Our little boy grows charmingly; he is much admired here. The colour of his eyes is not yet determined. You shall know when it is.

As our papers were mixed, I left my writing-desk open; pray lock the drawers and desk both, and keep the key yourself.

Have you any rice on hand yet? It sells here for five dollars cash. If you have any, had you not better send it? Papa intends writing to you on the subject.

I began a letter to you this morning in time for the mail, but was prevented by innumerable visits, which commenced before I was dressed for breakfast. I am most impatiently waiting for a letter from you. I hope you wrote soon after my departure. I am counting every minute to next Wednesday, when I hope to receive one, though I have many fears it is too early. With how much anxiety do I expect a letter. Maybe, one of these days, I may tell you of a piece of weakness of mine on that subject; maybe, for I do not know whether it is quite right for a wife to display all her foibles in that way to her husband. We have not determined when or where we shall move in the country. It shall certainly not be long ere we leave the city.

Anna Pierpont is well. She and husband go on merrily. They love each other very much, and that is half the battle. She begged me not to omit giving a thousand loves to you My love to the Hugers. Tell them I have seen Nancy. She looks better than they ever saw her. She has got a colour, and is so much more beautiful that I scarcely recognised her. Adieu, mon bien aimi.

THEODOSIA.

THEODOSIA TO JOSEPH ALSTON.

New-York, June 26, 1802.

When, when will the month of October come? It appears to recede instead of approaching; and time, which extinguishes all other sorrows, serves but to increase mine; every moment I feel that I have lost so much of your society which can never be regained. Ah, my husband, what can be pleasure to your Theo., unassisted by the charms of your presence and participation? Nothing. It is an idea which has no place in my mind unconnected with you.

I send you M'Kenzie; there is no London edition in town more elegantly bound. Before my departure you complained grievously of the bad cigars sold in Charleston. In the hope that this city affords better, I send you a box containing a thousand; the seller took some trouble to choose the best for me, and I have added some Vanilla and Tonka beans to them. May the offering please my great Apollo! If you should do so rash a thing as to visit the city during the summer, pray smoke all the time you remain there; it creates an atmosphere round you, and prevents impure air from reaching you.

I wish, also, that you would never be in town before or after the middle of the day. I have somewhere heard that persons were less apt to catch infectious disorders at that time than any other, and I believe it. Have you never remarked how highly scented the air is before sunrise in a flower-garden, so much so as to render the smell of any flower totally imperceptible if you put it to your nose? That is, I suppose, because, when the sun acts with all his force, the air becomes so rarefied, that the quantity of perfume you inhale at a breath can have no effect; while, on the contrary, during the night, the vapours become so condensed that you perceive them in every blast. May not the same be the case with noxious vapours? It is said that the fever in Charleston does not arise from that, but the filth of the streets are quite enough to make one think otherwise. Perhaps I am wrong both in my reason and opinion. If so, you are able to correct; only do as you think best, and be prudent. It is all I ask. I imagine the subject worth a reflection, and you cannot err. Montesquieu says he writes to make people think; and why may not Theodosia?

We have this evening been to visit Mrs. Caines (late Mrs. Verplanck) at her country place. The marriage was thus published—Married, G. C., Esq., counsellor of law, from the West Indies, *and now having a work in the press*, to Mrs., &c. That work has been the cause of some curiosity and not a little amusement.

I dined the other day with Mrs. Montgomery. The chancellor has sent her out a list of statues, which are to be so exactly imitated in plaster as to leave the difference of materials only. The statues are, the Apollo Belvidere, Venus de Medicis, Laocoon and his children, Antinous, and some others. The patriotic citizens of New-York are now subscribing to the importation of a set here for the good of the public. If they are really perfect imitations, they will be a great acquisition to this city. But, *selon moi*, there is the difficulty. Our son looks charmingly. Adieu.

THEODOSIA.

THEODOSIA TO JOSEPH ALSTON.

New-York, June 28, 1802.

And do you, indeed, miss your Theo.? Do you really find happiness indissolubly blended with her presence? Ah! my husband, how much more amiable you are as the man than as the philosopher! How much better your wife can love you! The latter character produces a distance between us; it so resembles coldness, that it annihilates all that free communication of the heart, that certainty of the most perfect sympathy and concord of feeling, which affords so much real happiness. Believe me, it is a very mistaken idea, that to discover sensibility at parting with a friend increases their sorrow. No; it consoles them. That apparent indifference, instead of lessening their pain at separation, only adds to it the mortification of finding themselves alone; wounds their feelings by the idea that, where they expected the most sincere reciprocity, they meet with the most calm tranquillity; and, above all, it is apt to make them involuntarily exclaim—If I am thus regretted, how little shall I be thought of! How soon forgotten! Never, then, my beloved, attempt to play the philosopher. If you see a friend weeping, weep with them. Sympathy is the sovereign cure for all wounds of the heart.

Your letter of the 16th, which I received yesterday, delighted me the more as it was unexpected. I did not *hope* you would have written so soon; still less did I imagine a letter from Charleston would reach this on the eleventh day after date. How anxious I am for to-morrow. Perhaps I may hear from you again.

S. appears more pleased with New-York than any person I ever saw from South Carolina. With the beauty of the country it is impossible not to be delighted, whether that delight is confessed or not; and every woman cannot fail to prefer the style of society, whatever she may say. If she denies it, she is set down in my mind as insincere and weakly prejudiced.

Pray write your journal this summer; you have little else to do. I should be charmed to find it finished on my return. Adieu.

THEODOSIA.

TO JOSEPH ALSTON.

New-York, July 3, 1802.

Your letter of the 19th of June, covering two for Theodosia, was received this morning. She, with Lady Nisbett and your boy, sailed yesterday for Red Hook (120 miles north) on a visit to Mrs. A., who had solicited this attention in terms and under circumstances which admitted of no refusal. The boy has grown surprisingly. The mother has recovered her appetite and spirits. I shall go up to take care of them in ten or fifteen days.

I desired your father to bring or send a barrel of rough rice (rice unpounded). The young Scotchman of whom I spoke to him has already invented a machine which I think will clean ten times as much as your pounding machine with the same power; that is, ten times as fast. Send the rice that we may try.

As to the publications of Cheetham and Wood, it is not worth while to write any thing by way of comment or explanation. It will, in due time, be known what they are, and what is Dewitt Clinton, their colleague and instigator. These things will do no harm to me personally. What effect they may have on the cause is a problem.

I forgot to pay Placide for two or three times bathing. Give him a guinea for me. Yours, affectionately,

A. BURR.

TO NATALIE.

New-York, July 5, 1802.

Your letter of the 22d of February, announcing your intended marriage, is this minute received. Nothing could be more grateful to me than your proposed connexion with Mr.

more grateful to me than your proposed connexion with Mr.

Sumter. I know little of him personally, but his reputation and standing in society fully justify your choice, and I pray you to assure him that I shall most cordially take him to my bosom as a son. With his father I have been long acquainted, and always greatly respected him. We were fellow-soldiers during our revolutionary war, in which he acted a most distinguished part, though we were not then known to each other. We served together some years in Congress, and laboured in the same party. These circumstances never fail to generate attachments, and I am truly happy in being more closely allied to him.

I perceive, and with pleasure, that I shall pass much of my time in South Carolina, and shall divide it between you and Theodosia; but the mountains are my favourite residence. Which is my favourite daughter I have not yet been able to decide. We must not, however, abandon New-York. I will have you both here, if possible, every year, and at Richmond Hill you shall renew the recollection of the happy hours of your childhood.

I have been long impatient, my dear Natalie, to write you on this subject, but I waited for advice from yourself. I was mortified to learn from common report *only* an event so nearly interesting, and which I had supposed you would have communicated to me the first. Your letter, however, has been long in America, and has travelled nearly two thousand miles in pursuit of me, having come in this morning from Charleston.

I arrived here on the 23d with Theodosia, her boy—a most lovely boy, and her sister, Lady Nisbett, who salutes you as a sister, and longs to embrace you. We had a most charming passage of seven days.

This is a great holyday. We are celebrating, with show and much noise, the 4th of July. This may appear to you a little ridiculous when you look at the date of this letter; but, *madame*, please to look at your almanac, and you will see that yesterday was Sunday. I should not have attempted to write to you amid so much bustle ; but the good Mr. Arcambal came in just as I received your letter, and informed me that there was an immediate and safe opportunity to France, and I was impatient to express to you and your husband my participation in your joys, and hearty approbation of your union. God bless you, my dear child.

A. BURR.

P. S. I have not received a line from your mamma in some years. I am not at all surprised at her repugnance to your marriage with a democrat, the son of a rebel. She must hate, above all things, democrats and rebels. But tell her, as doubtless you have told her a thousand times, that she is wrong ; and that we are not like your French democrats. Encore, adieu.

A. BURR.

THEODOSIA TO JOSEPH ALSTON.

New-York, September 3, 1802

What a pity minds could not be made sensible of each other's approach ! Why were we not so formed, that when your thoughts, your soul were with your Theo., hers could be enabled, by the finest sensation of sympathy, to meet it. How superior to writing would that be ! A letter is a month old before it is received ; by that time other thoughts and subjects engage the writer. The sentiments expressed in it seem no longer warm from the heart. I have been all this evening divining your occupation. Sometimes I imagine you writing or reading, and then the hope that you are thinking of me arises. Pray what have you been doing ? If you can possibly recollect, let me know. After all, it is more than probable that you have been smoking with Huger, entirely absorbed in your society and segar.

How does your election advance ? I am anxious to know something of it; not from patriotism, however. It little concerns me which party succeeds. Where you are, there is my country, and in you are centred all my wishes.

Were you a Brutus, I should be a Roman. But were you a Cæsar, I should only wish glory to Rome that glory might be yours. As long as you love me, I am nothing on earth but your wife and your friend: contented and proud to be that.

Mr. M'Pherson is much better. He sits up—I mean out of bed, a great part of the day. Mr. —— spent about three hours with him yesterday. What a Chesterfieldian that is; he has not had the civility to call on me, although you were so attentive to him. He has grown sentimental. He caught a moscheto the other day, and kept it under a tumbler to meditate on, because it reminded him of Carolina, and consequently of Miss ——. What man under heaven ever before discovered an analogy between a moscheto and his mistress? I am very happy you have chosen chess for your amusement. It keeps you constantly in mind how poor kings fare without their queens. Our little one has been very amiable to-day. Adieu.

THEODOSIA.

TO JOSEPH ALSTON.

New-York, July 19, 1802.

On Saturday (17th) Mr. and Mrs. Alston, Lady Nisbett, and Charlotte took passage for Red Hook. The wind has been so favourable that they undoubtedly arrived yesterday before dinner. Charlotte had three or four fits of ague and fever, but had escaped two days before she sailed, and was again in health.

You will herewith receive the second book. The malice and the motives are in this so obvious, that it will tend to discredit the whole. The charges which are of any moment will be shown to be mere fabrications. But there seems at present to be no medium of communication. The printers, called republican in this city (Denniston and Cheetham), are devoted to the Clintons, one of them (Denniston) being nephew of the governor, and, of course, cousin to Dewitt. Wood, after absconding for some time, returned to this city, was put in jail, where he lay some days and until taken out by *Coleman*. You will shortly receive an explanation of this controversy, but not from me. Very affectionately yours,

A. Burr.

TO JOSEPH ALSTON.

New-York, August 2, 1802.

Your letter of the 18th is received. Mr. Williams had before shown me the pamphlet, and had informed me that it had produced all the effect that the writer could have wished, which is the best evidence of the merit of the work. It is evidently a hasty performance, and incorrectly printed, yet it displays ability as a writer, and sentiments honourable to him as a man.

Wood's book has surprised us. We all expected a new series of abuse against A. B. It should be entitled "The Confessions of John Wood, one of the Conspirators lately associated with James Cheetham and Dewitt Clinton against the vice-president." It shows pretty clearly the motives and views of this clan.

The enclosed paper will give you the particulars of the affair of Swartwout and Clinton. You will perceive that the latter indirectly acknowledges that he is an agent in the calumnies against me.

I am about to take possession of Richmond Hill for the reception of Theodosia and her boy, and shall go for them in about ten days. We propose to pass part of September in Orange county.

The letter herewith enclosed came to me under a *blank* cover; through inattention, I broke the seal without looking at the superscription. The first sentence betrayed my error, and I have scolded her a good deal for her blank cover.

Affectionately yours,

A. Burr.

TO THEODOSIA.

New-York, August 8, 1802.

With extreme reluctance, *madame*, I am constrained to resign to Dr. Brown the honour of escorting you hither. The circumstances which have led to this measure are briefly noted in a letter which I have this day written you by the mail.

By Tuesday the 9th inst. I shall be settled at Richmond Hill, ready to receive you and your incumbrances. Tell Mr. and Mrs. Alston, &c., that I hope there to have the pleasure of accommodating them more to their satisfaction than was in my power in the little mansion in Broadway.

The moment you shall receive this, send a line for me to the postoffice, saying how you are, when you will move, &c. Leave with the postmaster a written direction to forward to New-York all letters for Mrs. Joseph Alston. I recommend to you to go round by Stockbridge to see Binney. She is there at the house of Mr. Bidwell. You will also there see your old great-uncle Edwards. But this is left to your discretion. If you go through Pittsfield, you should call and see H. Van Schaack, for whom Dr. Brown has a letter of credence. Make your journey perfectly at your ease; *id est*, with dignified leisure. Write me at every post-town, for I shall have a deal of impatience and anxiety about you and your little nonentity.

All your friends here are well except George's dog and one of his South Carolina birds. We are all in the bustle of moving. Heighho! for Richmond Hill. What a pity you were not here, you do so love a bustle; and then you, and the brat, and the maid, and thirty trunks would add so charmingly to the confusion. Adieu.

A. Burr.

TO JOSEPH ALSTON.

New-York, September 8, 1802.

The debility and loss of appetite which your wife has experienced alarmed me; yet I was totally ignorant of the cause. I was first informed of it by Dr. Bard, who came accidentally to this city about a fortnight ago. He, with Hosack and Brown, all of whom I consulted, joined with me in opinion that she ought immediately to wean her child or provide a wet nurse. This she peremptorily refused, and the bare proposition occasioned so many tears and so much distress that I abandoned it. Within the last three days, however, she has such a loss of appetite and prostration of strength, that she is satisfied of the necessity of the measure for the sake of the child, if not for herself; and I have this day sent off a man to the country to find a suitable nurse. The complaint continued from the period of her *confinement* during the whole time that she remained in Charleston.

It is most unfortunate that she left the Springs. While she was there, either by means of the air or the water, or perhaps both, she had got quite rid of the complaint, and there is no doubt but that, had she remained there a fortnight longer, the cure would have been radical. The ride to Hudson, only thirty miles, brought on a relapse; and, with slight variations, the affliction was increased and her strength diminished. Bard advised the Springs, and was quite angry that she left them.

There is nothing in this disorder which immediately threatens life; nor is it, at present, attended with pain; but if it should become fixed upon her, of which there is danger unless speedily cured, it will unfit her for every duty and every enjoyment in life. The medicines, which under the direction of Bard she used at Lebanon, have hitherto proved ineffectual since her return. I have written fully to Eustis, and expect his answer within two or three days.

The present state of her health and strength will not, I think, admit of an attempt to take her to either of the Springs, or I should not hesitate to go off immediately with her. I have, however, strong and well-grounded hopes that, when she shall have a nurse, and resume the use of proper remedies, a cure will be effected.

I have thought that you ought to be informed of these facts, as well to explain the varied accounts which you may have received of her health, as to anticipate the vague or exaggerated relations which you may receive through other channels.

Most affectionately yours,

A. Burr.

THEODOSIA TO JOSEPH ALSTON.

New-York, September 30, 1802.

Another mail has arrived, but to your Theo. it has brought only unhappiness. It is now a week since I received your last letter. You are ill. You have been imprudent, and all my fears are fulfilled. Without any one near you to feel for you, to attend to you, to watch every change and share every pain. Your wife only could do that. It is her whose soul clings to yours, and vibrates but in harmony with it; whose happiness, whose every emotion, more than entirely dependant on yours, are exchanged for them. It is she only who forgets herself in you, and who, in gratifying your wishes or alleviating your pain, serves the interest nearest her heart. I know you have friends with you; but, when you lose your vivacity, and your society is robbed of its usual charms, they will find your chamber dull, and leave it for some more amusing place. They cannot, like your little Theo., hang over you in your sleep, and, with a beating heart, listen to every groan and tremble at every noise. Your son, too, were we with you, would charm away your cares. His smiles could not fail to sooth any pain. They possess a magic which you cannot conceive till you see him Would we were with you, my beloved. I am miserable about you. Adieu. Heaven bless my husband, and I am happy.

THEODOSIA.

THEODOSIA TO JOSEPH ALSTON.

New-York, October 30, 1802.

I have just received yours of the 21st. You already know the result of my confinement in bed. It certainly relieved me for some time, which proves how easily that cure would have succeeded at first. I have now abandoned all hope of recovery. I do not say it in a moment of depression, but with all my reason about me. I am endeavouring to resign myself with cheerfulness; and you also, my husband, must summon up your fortitude to bear with a sick wife the rest of her life. At present, my general health is very good; indeed, my appearance so perfectly announces it, that physicians smile at the idea of my being an invalid. The great misfortune of this complaint is, that one may vegetate forty years in a sort of middle state between life and death, without the enjoyment of one or the rest of the other.

You will now see your boy in a few days, and you will really be very much pleased with him. He is a sweet little rascal. If Heaven grant him but to live, I shall never repent what he has cost me. Adieu.

THEODOSIA.

TO JOSEPH ALSTON.

New-York, October 15, 1802.

In my letter of yesterday I said nothing of your son. He is well, and growing as you could wish. If I can see without prejudice, there never was a finer boy.

Of yourself I have a good deal to say; more than I can find time to write, and some things which cannot be written. Except the little practical knowledge which you may have gained by mingling with your committee-men, &c., your summer and autumn have, I perceive, been lost—lost, I mean, as to literary acquirements. From your companions, I presume, little is to be gained save the pastime of a social hour. Yet time goes on, and you have much to do.

To the execution of any project, however, health is a sine qua non. Whether you can ever enjoy it in Charleston or on Sullivan's Island has become a problem in my mind. I was quite shocked with your wan appearance when I first met you last spring. How different from that which you took hence the fall preceding. With every advantage attainable in your climate, you have scarcely been free from fever during the season. This cannot fail to debilitate both mind and body. If these hazards are to be annually encountered with similar effects, and worse may be apprehended, it is a price far beyond the value of any benefits which Charleston can offer. The *mountains*, a more *Northern latitude*, or the *grave*, must be your refuge. Pray think of these things. If I should not go to South Carolina this fall, nor you come hither, let us meet in Washington next winter. After the rising of your legislature, you may find time for that journey. But I should prefer to see you here immediately after your election, if there be time for your return before the session of the legislature. Your health must require this change. *Here* you may freeze out all your "miasmata" and surplus bile in ten days, and go to Columbia with nerves well strung and blood well purified.

My solicitude for your frequent appearance in courts is *no way* diminished. The applause which I heard bestowed upon you sunk into my heart. I could distinguish that which you merited from the fulsome eulogy which was uttered through politeness. Your talent for writing is enviable, and, with cultivation, will be unrivalled (nothing without cultivation, remember). No one wishes so ardently as I do, not even you, that these advantages should be improved. But these considerations are unimportant compared with those which regard your health.

If you should leave Charleston, give special orders about

your letters, for I may write what I should wish no one but you to see. Affectionately adieu.

A. Burr.

TO JOSEPH ALSTON.

New-York, November 5, 1802.

The cold weather of the last ten days has had a happy effect on Theodosia. She is so far restored that I can with confidence assure you she will return in health. The boy, too, grows fat and rosy with the frost. They have taken passage in the brig Enterprise, Captain Tombs, the same with whom we came last June. She will have the control of the cabin, and will be perfectly well accommodated. I regret she will sail so soon (the 12th), as well because I cannot attend her as that I could have wished her health and that of the boy to have been still more confirmed. Yet I cannot any longer resist her impatience. You must not delay your journey to Columbia in expectation of her arrival. It is important that you be on the ground the first day, and it is to be desired that you could be there two or three days before the commencement of the session. If you should be gone, she projects to follow you, of which I advise you, that you may leave your directions. When you shall see her and son, you will not regret this five months' separation.

I rejoice that you are to meet Major Pinckney on the floor of your assembly. "*The Citizen*" (Cheetham and Denniston's), in publishing a list of members chosen in Charleston and its vicinity, omitted your name; but took care to add, by way of extract from a pretended letter, that the Alstons were of no consideration or influence in South Carolina. There is no bound to the malice of these people. The conspiracy was formed last winter at Washington. A little reflection will indicate to you the description of men, the motives, and the object of this combination.

Apologize for me to Ch. Marshall that I do not fulfil my engagement to accompany him from Charleston to Washington. I hope you will bring him with you.

Would Charles Lee accept the place of secretary of the Senate? It is worth twenty-three hundred dollars per annum, and not laborious. The secretary, you know, is chosen by the Senate. Otis, the present incumbent, will probably decline. If you should think that Lee would desire it, and the thing should appear to you proper, it should be suggested to your senators. Of the legislative subjects mentioned in one of your letters, I hope to find time to say a word on Sunday (7th inst.). God bless you.

A. Burr.

TO THEODOSIA.

New-York, December 4, 1802.

So you arrived on the 24th, after a passage of ten days; you and the Charleston packet on the same day. All this I learned last night; not from you. Vanderlyn and I drank a bottle of Champagne on the occasion.

Though this relieves me from the great anxiety under which I laboured, still there are many details of your passage, your arrival, &c., on which nothing but your letter can satisfy me. For some unknown reason, the mail is now eighteen days on the road.

Vanderlyn has finished your picture in the most beautiful style imaginable. When it was done, he exclaimed with enthusiasm, "There is the best work I have ever done in America."

Your letter must be addressed to Washington. The dear little boy, I hope, made a good sailor. Adieu.

A. Burr.

TO THEODOSIA.

New-York, December 16, 1802.

Your letter of the 26th November came yesterday, that of the 25th the day preceding. You see, therefore, that twenty-one days had elapsed from the time of your arrival to the receipt of your first letter. This is not by way of reproach, for it is an unpleasant truth that, for the last six or eight weeks, the Charleston mail has been twenty days on the way. Had it not been for the intelligence by water of your safe arrival, we should have concluded that you and Kate* were now dancing with Amphitrite. How jealous her majesty would have been at the presence of two such rivals.

The day after you left us, though the weather was mild, not even a frost, the leaves of the trees about the house began to fall, and in three days they were as bare as in midwinter, though you may recollect that you left them in perfect verdure. This, I am sure, was sympathy and regret. I shall respect these trees for their sensibility. It was in harmony with my feelings; for, truly, all was dreary.

Yes, I enter into all your little vexations; but while I write, and long before, they probably have passed away, and are succeeded by new ones. Kate will help you to laugh them off. Kiss her for me. Not a word, not a line from your husband since the 30th of October. We ought, nay, we must, every day add something to our experience, and usually at some cost.

I expect to leave this in about a week. Henceforth, therefore, address me at Washington. On my arrival there we will begin to talk of our spring and summer plans. You did well, very well to give up the Columbia project. I really wish you had given the pair of horses in your own name. In all such cases, that which is most grateful to you will be so to me. Butter shall be sent. The card plate must be altered.

Maybe I may write you from Philadelphia; not again from this city, unless I should receive from you something very pretty. Vanderlyn projects to visit Charleston, but I am sure he will not. He is run down with applications for portraits, all of which, without discrimination, he refuses. He is greatly occupied in finishing his Niagara views, which,

* Her cousin, Catharine Brown, daughter of Dr. Joseph Brown.

indeed, will do him honour. They will be four in number, and he thinks of having them engraved in France. You hear the roaring of the cataract when you look at them Kiss the dear little boy. Adieu, ma belle.

A. Burr.

TO THEODOSIA.

Washington, January 26, 1803.

Your last letter, and the only one received within a month, is dated the 14th inst., and written, I suppose, at your plantation. It gives me the satisfaction of knowing that you and your boy are well, and nothing more. How long you are to remain there, where next to go, and every thing leading to a knowledge of your occupations and intentions, is omitted. One half of the letter is a complaint of my silence, and the other half (nearly) an apology for yours, You know (or am I now to tell you) that you and your concerns are the highest, the dearest interest I have in this world; one in comparison with which all others are insignificant.

Recollect, my dear Theodosia, that in five weeks Congress will adjourn (3d March); that I shall then go in some direction, but in what is yet unsettled; that my movements will depend essentially on yours. Tell me, therefore, where you are to pass the summer, when you are to leave Charleston, and all the details. If these matters should not yet be settled, let it be forthwith done. If you are not to go northward, it is not probable that I shall see you in some time, for I have thoughts of going on a tour through the western country, which, if executed, will consume the whole summer. I offer you and your family Richmond Hill for the season, and will meet you there in May or June, or when you please. Perhaps would come to make the voyage with you, by land or water. Sullivan's Island will not, I hope, be thought of. How is it that I have not a line from *Mari*, in answer to several letters which I wrote him from New-York?

I entreat you to answer this letter distinctly, and in all its parts; for there will not be time for another letter and reply before I shall be off. My love to Kate. You do not say whether she grows handsome or ugly, nor is it any matter which while on the plantation.

I can't conceive how you all stow yourselves in that little wreck of a mansion. Please to write over, in some way, the erased part of your letter. You must be very destitute of wit and contrivance. No essence in Washington. I still prefer musk, but not to be had. One would think you had suffered some injury from perfumes. Your message and commission to Mrs. Madison will be delivered. My mode of life, establishment, &c., are the same as last year, except that I bought a chariot, having some hope of seeing you and your husband here. As I shall not write again until I hear where you are, I may as well say now all that occurs to me.

On my way through Philadelphia I rode out to Lansdown, to see our beautiful little K. and Mrs. L. They appear to love you with all their hearts. K. especially talked of you with an interest which could not be affected. The ladies find fault with her dress, her person, her manners; in short, with every thing appertaining to her. Mrs. L. has also her full share of the eulogium. K. is *toujours belle.* At Wilmington I did not see friend S. She had gone to church. God bless thee.

A. BURR

TO DR. JOHN COATS.

Washington, February 23, 1803.

It is from me, my dear sir, that apologies are due; but you have kindly anticipated all I could make. I thank you for this instance of your goodness; for your friendly recollection; above all, for the justice you do to my heart and feelings. Your last letter has been received. It is without date, and came by the mail of yesterday. You see that I

feelings. Your last letter has been received. It is without date, and came by the mail of yesterday. You see that I
K 2

am resolved not to furnish a new occasion for apologies by further negligence.

Whether, after the adjournment, I shall go North or South, is yet undetermined. If northward, I propose to take the route which you had the goodness to describe, and to pass at least some hours with you. I shall insist on a dish of lillipee, in order to give a more dramatic effect to the review which we will take of past scenes.

Dearborn, now minister of war, was our fellow-traveller through the wilderness. If you will designate more particularly the papers you wish to recover, I will with pleasure make search for them. Accept, I pray you, the assurance of my undiminished regard and esteem.

A. Burr.

FROM THEODOSIA.

Clifton, March 17, 1802.

Ever since the date of my last letter, for it was not forwarded till some days after, I have been quite ill; till within these two or three days totally unable to write. The whole family, as well as myself, had begun to think pretty seriously of my last journey; but, fortunately, I have had the pleasure of keeping them up a few nights, and drawing forth all their sensibility, without giving them the trouble of burying, mourning, &c.

I was one night so ill as to have lost my senses in a great measure; about daylight, as a last resource, they began plying me with old wine, and blisters to my feet. But, on recovering a little, I kicked off the blisters, and declared I would be dressed; be carried in the open air, and have free use of cold water. I was indulged. I was carried below, where I drank plentifully of cold water, and I had my face, neck, and arms bathed with it, and it assisted most astonishingly in recovering me. The day before yesterday I was put on a bed in a boat and brought here. The change of air and scene have assisted me wonderfully. I am again getting well. Indeed, the rapidity with which I gain strength surprises the whole family. The secret is, that my constitution is good. I exert myself to the utmost, feeling none of that pride, so common to my sex, of being weak and ill. Delicacy and debility are sometimes fascinating when affected by a coquette, adorned with the freshness of health; but a pale, thin face; sunken, instead of languishing eyes; and a form, evidently tottering, not gracefully bending, never, I suspect, made, far less could they retain a conquest, or even please a friend. I therefore encourage spirits, try to appear well, and am rewarded. In a few days I shall be on the high road to health. Mari is well, and the boy charming. Adieu.

THEODOSIA.

TO THEODOSIA.

Philadelphia, June 3, 1803.

I have only to announce my safe arrival yesterday noon. Went forthwith to see the B.'s. They were all out of town. Will be back to-day.

Send me the number of volumes of the American Encyclopedia. I wish to complete the set, and must, therefore, know the deficiencies. I have seen none of your acquaintance save the Biddles. To-morrow (if I should in the mean time receive a letter from you) I shall add something.

You are the two most spiritless young persons I ever knew. Pray muster up energy enough to do something more than lounge on sofas. Go on Sunday to Ludlow's. Ask some of your friends often to dine with you.

There is a little boy right opposite my window who has something of the way of "mammy's treasure." Don't be jealous; not half so handsome. I have had him over to my room, and have already taught him to *bang*. Adieu.

A. BURR.

FROM THEODOSIA.

New-York, June 4, 1803.

Encore stupid. For Heaven's sake, what do you imagine I can find to say once a day that is worth saying, shut up thus, either tinkling on the harp or holding a tête-à-tête conversation? You must, indeed, have a high opinion of my genius and the fertility of my imagination.

Pray how do you advance? Heavy business, is it not? I beg you will perform your promise, and write me the history of it. I'll bind it in red morocco, and keep it for the advantage and instruction of the boy. Adieu. Do not forget my commission, and return soon.

A. Burr.

TO THEODOSIA.

Philadelphia, June 5, 1803.

I received yesterday your first letter. Pray no more apologies about your stupidity, &c., because on that subject I am perfectly informed. Be pleased to recollect that your letters cannot be answered the day they are received. We are now even. I wrote you on Friday.

I went this morning to see L. and Keene. The former, as usual, polite, friendly, and cheerful. The latter something improved by a very slight acquisition of embonpoint; so very slight, however, as not to be obvious to common optics. They will pass their summer at their present residence, and I have almost promised that you shall make them a visit.

But I should have narrated in the order of events according to their dates or in the order of the importance. Neither hath been observed, which argues ill of my temper of mind for the principal pursuit. Cette —— spoils me. From that intercourse I return faintly to the line of duty.

On Friday I saw the inamorata, and it happened as we had feared; for really I did not know whom I had the honour to address; nor could I, with certainty, discover during the interview, for I saw but one. The appearance was pleasing. There was something pensive and interesting. It exceeded my expectations. It was a visit of ceremony, and passed off as such. This day I met the whole four at dinner. My attentions were pointed, and met a cheerful return. There was more sprightliness than before. Le pere leaves town to-morrow for eight days, and I am now meditating whether to take the fatal step to-morrow. I falter and hesitate, which you know is not the way. I tremble at the success I desire. You will not know my determination till Wednesday. In the mean time I crave your prayers.

I entreat you to ride about. Your monotonous life can never restore your health; nay, it is hostile to recovery. The business part of my journey assumes some importance, but the result is uncertain. Adieu.

A. Burr.

TO THEODOSIA.

Philadelphia, June 6, 1803.

The plot thickens, and I do not find it possible to communicate faithfully the details, without hazarding too much in case of loss of the letter. Something, however, may be said.

I called at the house this morning; before I had asked for any one in particular, the servant bid me in, and in a few minutes Inamorat sole appeared. This looked like secret understanding or sympathy; perhaps, however, it was only as head and representative of the family. She looked well; but, unfortunately, a trifling carelessness in dress had nearly concluded the farce. Recollecting, however, that they were packing up for a temporary removal, to take place this very day, an apology was obvious. Having made to myself the apology, I went further, and found that there was politeness, *at least,* in receiving me, and in so prompt an attendance under such circumstances. After ten minutes le pere came in; conversation became general, and I took leave.

at least, in receiving me, and in so prompt an attendance under such circumstances. After ten minutes le pere came in; conversation became general, and I took leave.

Returning home, and pondering on the subject most profoundly for full five minutes, I boldly took up my pen, and wrote le pere that I wished a few minutes' conversation with him at his own house in the course of the day. Within an hour he was at *my room* to receive the communication. Now paint to yourself a desperate miscreant on the point of committing self-murder, trembling with anxiety, choking for want of utterance, &c. Having formed the portrait to your own taste, I must tell you that there was no such figure. The salutations, on meeting, passed as usual. An expression or two of sensibility to the courtesy which anticipated so promptly the intended visit, and then some unembarrassed direct questions and monosyllabic answers. "Is ——— under any engagement?" *None.* "Would it be agreeable to you that ——— should make overtures?" &c. *Certainly.* A very complimentary thing, however, was said by le pere. It was agreed that the suiter should make known his pretensions, he (le pere) declining to intermeddle. *End of the first act.*

I have the honour to acknowledge the receipt of your two letters, both dated June 4. Evidently they cost you great labour.

June 7.

I left this open that I might acknowledge the receipt of one by this morning's mail. I am gratified to have it in my power. The accident to the harp has been very fortunate, inasmuch as it enabled you to make out a long letter on the subject. However it may be broken, nothing is so easy to be repaired. Kiss dear little *bang*.

A. Burr.

TO THEODOSIA.

Philadelphia, June 7, 1803.

As you were informed yesterday, my *Celeste* has gone with the family (le pere excepted) to pass a fortnight six miles from town. I go to-morrow morning to recommend myself; and that no time may be wasted, and these six mile rides may not be too often repeated to no purpose, I shall not go much round about the subject, but come pretty directly to the point; of all which you will be duly informed.

Truly, if my head be as confused as my narrative, it will be of little use to me in the negotiation. I should have begun by relating what happened this morning. There are, however, two ways of telling a story. One by beginning with the oldest event, and so travelling down to the close of the tale, and this is the mode commonly used by philosophers and historians. The other is by commencing with the most recent fact or earliest incident, which is the mode universally practised by lovers, and, generally, by poets. I could even quote Homer and Virgil as authorities in support of this latter method. Further I may add, that this retro-progressive arrangement seems more congenial with the temper and feelings of the fair sex. Thus, you see, most ladies turn first to the last chapter of a novel or romance. In defence of this practice I could dilate to the utmost extent of many sheets; but, intending soon to publish an essay on the subject, I leave for the present the residue to your reflections, and return to the interview of this morning.

I was admitted without hesitation, and was presently joined by Celeste, though I had not particularized any one as the object of my visit. For some minutes she led the conversation, and did it with grace and *sprightliness*, and with admirable good sense. I made several attempts to divert it to other subjects—subjects which might have nearer affinity, again, to others; unsuccessfully, however; yet, whether I was foiled through art or accident, I could not discover. Be assured she is much superior to l'ainée.

"I would be wooed, and, not unsought, be won."

So I conjectured she thought, and she was right.

A. BURR.

TO THEODOSIA.

Philadelphia, June 8, 1803.

I told you the negotiation should not be long. It is finished —concluded—for ever abandoned—*liber sum*. Celeste never means to marry; "firmly resolved." I am very sorry to hear it, madam; had promised myself great happiness, but cannot blame your determination. "No, certainly, sir, you cannot; for I recollect to have heard you express surprise that any woman would marry, &c., and you gave such reasons, and with so much eloquence, as made an indelible impression on my mind." Have you any commands to town, madam? I wish you a good-morning. *End of the second and last act.*

The interview was about an hour. Celeste was greatly agitated; behaved, however, with great propriety. The parting was full of courtesy, and there is reason to hope that there will be no hanging or drowning.

I dined to-day chez Rush. The two elder daughters are in Canada. The little Julia, now about ten, is growing up very lovely and *tres gentile*. Afterward called to see your friend, Mrs. Stewart, and her beautiful daughter. She is really beautiful. To-morrow I dine chez la Raz.

The law business goes on slowly; may be finished about Tuesday next, after which I shall hasten to those who love me, when I shall endeavour to rouse them from their lethargy, and give them a little zest for life. Just now I recollect that I have no letter from you this morning, at which I was confoundedly vexed. I stop, therefore, and shall withhold even this for a day, by way of punishment. You will say that you were not well, that you were engaged in company, that the servant neglected to take the letter, or some such trite thing. All nonsense. Bon soir.

Thursday morning.

Your letter of Tuesday, containing the history of the dinner, is received this morning. Truly, I think that Mr. and

Mrs. Moore and Clem might, with any tolerable aid, have made the dinner gay. Mr. and Mrs. Moore have both a great deal of wit, and are both well bred. Clem is by no means deficient. It must, therefore, have been the fault of yourself and husband. If the harp is not essentially injured, I would not purchase a new one. Kiss little *bang*.

A. Burr.

FROM THEODOSIA.

New-York, June 9, 1803.

I received yesterday your three letters of the 5th and 6th. They made me laugh, yet I pity you, and have really a fellow feeling for you. Poor little Rippy, so you are mortgaged! But you bear it charmingly; do you think this courage will last, or is it only a spasm? Spasmodic love. It is really quite new. The trifling incident in relation to dress you must pardon. I am a *connoisseur* in these things, and can assure you they are very pardonable.

I am all anxiety and impatience for to-day's mail. But it surprises me that *primo mobile* is forgotten. Pray, have you lived altogether on pepper? We shall ride to Montalto this afternoon, and you shall know our reception. I am too anxious for my letters to add a word more. Poor Starling!

Theodosia.

TO THEODOSIA.

Philadelphia, June 10, 1803.

Yesterday I dined chez la Raz; a very pleasant party. The farce of eight days past had been forgotten, or recollected only as a dream.

Just as I sit down to write to you I receive a note from Celeste, advising me that she is in town for a few hours, and will be happy to see me. What in the name of love and matrimony can this mean? The conclusion was definitive, and a mutual promise that neither would ever renew the subject. I am all impatience, and I go to hear. You shall know to-morrow.

A. Burr.

FROM THEODOSIA.

New-York, June 10, 1803.

My apology for not writing this morning is enclosed. We have been dining with Mrs. Laight to-day, and have been much amused. We are to take them, with Miss Laight and Miss Brown, in curricle and coachee to Montalto to-morrow afternoon. We are absolutely two demonstrations of two laws in mechanics. When we repose it requires a great exertion to move us, and when put in motion we go on.

My interruption last evening prevented me from wishing you joy at the declaration of independence. What are your plans now. Cher petit pere, the boy kisses you; but I do not, because you remain so long in Philadelphia.

Theodosia.

CHAPTER XIV.

TO THEODOSIA.

Philadelphia, June 11, 1803.

Continuation of the Story of the Loves of Reubon and Celeste.

Your recollection must be recalled to the fatal and decisive interview of Wednesday. The result only was stated in a former letter. It would have required too much time to compress into the compass of one or two sheets a conversation of two hours. The details are therefore omitted; but a circumstance which will increase your surprise at the incident related yesterday morning is, that, on Wednesday night, Reubon received by the hands of a servant of Celeste, sent for the sole purpose seven miles, a letter from her, couched in civil terms, but expressing " an unalterable determination never to listen again to his suit, and requesting that the subject might never be renewed." Reubon returned home late last evening, and was told that a boy had been three times in the course of the afternoon and evening to deliver him a message, but refused to say from whom he came. The last time the servant of Reubon traced the boy to the house of Celeste in town. It was not known that Celeste had been that day in town, and no conjecture could be formed as to the owner of the boy or the object of his message. The note received by Reubon this morning explains the mystery. The letter which I wrote you by the mail left Reubon puzzling his brain to discover the meaning of that note, and just going out to obey the challenge which it conveyed. He went, as you were apprized, and has just now returned and communicated what you shall now hear.

Some years ago, a worthy country judge, having heard a cause very ingeniously debated by lawyers on each side, when he came to charge the jury, did it in the words following: " Gentlemen of the jury, you must get along with this cause as well as you can; for my part, I am swamp'd." Now Reubon is exactly in the case of this judge, and I am at a loss what to advise him. You could unravel this thing in five minutes. Would to God you were here ; but to the story.

He found Celeste with a visiter; some female neighbour, who sat a full half hour. Celeste betrayed considerable agitation when Reubon came in, and the most palpable impatience at the long stay of the lady visiter. At length she went, and the parties were alone. As she had desired the interview, it was her place to speak first. After a pause and several efforts, she, with some trepidation, said that she feared the letter which she had writen had not been expressed in terms sufficiently polite and respectful; she had wished an opportunity to apologize; and here she stuck. Reubon ought in mercy and in politeness to have taken up the conversation; but he, expecting no such thing, was taken by surprise, and remained dumb, with a kind of half grin. The duette, at this moment, would have made a charming subject for the pencil of Vanderlyn. Celeste was profoundly occupied in tearing up some roses which she held in her hand, and Reubon was equally industrious in twirling his hat, and pinching some new corners and angles in the brim. At length he recovered himself so far as to gain utterance. He denied, plumply, that there was want of politeness or respect in the letter; and, after many awkward detours and half-finished sentences, he said he would return the letter, and would consider it as cancelling the determination which it contained, and proposed to call on her in the country to-morrow morning to renew his suit. This was *faintly* opposed. He changed the course of conversation, without insisting on a formal permission or refusal, and then went into the subject of celibacy and matrimony, and passed an hour tête-à-tête. It may be worth noting that, towards the close of the conversation, some one knocked, and that she went out and ordered the servant to deny her, from which it may be inferred that she was not disagreeably engaged, and that she did not wish to be interrupted.

Now, ma Minerve, is not this a very ridiculous posture for so grave an affair? And is not Reubon in a way to be coquetted, with his eyes open? I rather think he erred in giving to the apology of Celeste any other meaning than she literally expressed. Thus he might have compelled her to be more explicit. On the other hand, if she did in fact repent, and so suddenly, it would seem too harsh and fastidious to shut the door against all treaty and negotiation. Upon the whole, however, I conclude that if she wished, for any kind reason, to retreat, she should have gone further, and held out something like encouragement; in short, have met him half way. It may, I know, be replied, that her habits of life and singular education forbid every thing like advance; and that a lady may always presume that her lover, if sincere, will seize the slightest ground for hope; and that, in the logic of love, an equivocal refusal is assent. Certainly, this last interview has been illy managed on the part of Reubon, but I have not yet resolved what to advise. This is left open till morning, when perhaps a word may be added.

Saturday morning.

From the state of things it is obvious that there can, at this hour, be no new fact to communicate; but I have no longer any doubts as to the meaning of the late scene, nor as to the line of conduct to be pursued by Reubon. The note of Celeste is one of those trifling incidents which are too small for calculation, which may have arisen from the trifling motive assigned. Perhaps from a little spirit of coquetry, perhaps a mere piece of sport. He shall, therefore, take no further notice of it; not even to go out this morning to see her, as he had solicited and engaged; and, when he shall next meet her, make some slight apology. Thus the thing is settled.

A. BURR.

TO THEODOSIA.

Philadelphia, June 12, 1803.

I am weary, and so must you be, of this story of Reubon and Celeste. It is, however, closed, and you will, after this letter, hear no more of it.

Reubon agreed to comport himself in the manner advised in my last. Immediately after this determination, Celeste sent a servant to inform him that she was in town! He called to see her; returned the offensive letter, and told her that, as he understood that it was the manner and not the substance of the letter which had induced her to recall it, it would be quite unnecessary for her to take the trouble of writing another. They talked of indifferent matters. Reubon, quite at ease, played the man of the world, and, in my opinion, the man of sense. Before they parted, her face was flushed like a full-blown rose. She begged his permission to destroy the letter, which was certainly a very useless request, considering that the letter was wholly in her power. During the interview, Celeste, having no roses to occupy her hands, twisted off two corners of a pocket-handkerchief.

This reference (the law business), of which I informed you something, has become extremely troublesome and disagreeable. I am apprehensive that it will detain me here nearly the whole of this week.

Binny looks remarkably well, and talks much about you. Dennis and wife, from Savannah, are here. *Madame est toujours belle.* I can't express to you my impatience to be with you, your husband, and little one. Truly I think with horror of passing five days more here. Pray form no plans of distant rides until my return.

A. Burr.

FROM THEODOSIA.

New-York, June 14, 1803.

As to Celeste, *voila mon* opinion. She meant, from the beginning, to say that awful word—*yes* ; but not choosing to say it immediately, she told you that *you* had furnished her with arguments against matrimony, which in French means, Please, sir, to persuade me out of them again. But you took it as a plump refusal, and walked off. She called you back. What more could she do ? I would have seen you to Japan before I should have done so much. I still, however, like your plan. My opinion is not, perhaps, well founded, and it is best to be on the safe side. If she is determined to be kind, she will find out a way of expressing it, or she is not worth having. I am quite pleased with her, and am waiting the arrival of the mail with the utmost impatience.

"Treasure" is well, notwithstanding all predictions on my folly in his dress. You must be home for my birthday (the 20th inst.), or I'll never forgive you; or, rather, I shall not spend it pleasantly.

THEODOSIA

TO THEODOSIA.

Philadelphia, June 16, 1803.

No letter by this mail; being the fourth omission and violation of promise since the 1st inst.

The birthday must be kept. It shall be "honoured by my presence." You will therefore make your preparations, and, among other articles for your feast or party, I recommend two fiddlers, not barbacued or roasted, but *en plein vie.*

If this should be received on Friday morning, in season to be answered by that day's mail, I beg to have a line from you, if only a *bon jour;* after which, no more letters can be received. You shall not have any distant parties or jaunts until I can partake. I am even jealous of the Fort Washington tour. Indeed, you can't go there without me, for no one can so well show you the ground.

If Mr. Kane and his wife (late Miss Clarke) should be in town, pray call on them immediately, and make them and the sister of the party. Recollect they have many claims to your civilities. His sister, Mrs. Thomas Morris, was very kind to you at Genesee. Mr. Kane himself overwhelmed us with good offices on a certain occasion at Albany, and the frequent hospitalities of John Innes Clarke can never be forgotten. Be prompt, therefore, and courteous.

A. BURR.

FROM THEODOSIA.

Ballston, July 20, 1803

Behold us, *cher pere,* at this fountain of health; and now my only wish is to leave it as soon as possible. On arriving

30

Behold us, cher pere, at this fountain of health; and now my only wish is to leave it as soon as possible. On arriving
30

here we found that your letter to H. Walton had not been received; but we have been very fortunate in getting a house entirely to ourselves, and one quite as pleasantly sit uated as that you mentioned. Mr. Walton has been extremely polite to us. We dined there on Monday, and in the evening went to a ball, which surpassed my expectations in brilliancy. I danced twice, but I am unable to tell you whether I looked well or danced well; for you are the only person in the world who says any thing to me about my appearance. Mari generally looks pleased, but rarely makes remarks. On my return, therefore, I wished for you to learn some account of myself; for vanity and diffidence had a combat in which each so well maintained its ground that the affair is still left undecided.

General Smith and family are here. Never was ennui more strongly depicted than in the countenance of madame and sister. They appear absolutely bereft of every thing like exertion. Mr. ——, on the contrary, while he owns that this is not one of the most pleasant places he has ever seen, is still lively and agreeable. Such are the baneful effects of our education. Put out of our usual sphere of acquaintance, or the old routine of amusement and occupation, we rarely have knowledge of the world enough to discover any pleasant qualification that may exist in a stranger, and to put it to any use if it obtrude itself on our notice; and still less are we taught to create amusements for ourselves.

The boy is pretty well, but I confess I have many doubts as to the healthiness of this place for children. Every morning since our arrival there has been a thick mist, which the sun does not disperse till nine or ten o'clock. I kiss you with all my heart.

THEODOSIA.

FROM CHARLES BIDDLE.

Philadelphia, February 3, 1803.

DEAR SIR,

The business of New-Orleans is much talked of here. In my opinion, and it is the opinion of many others, we should immediately take possession, and then treat about it. We have no business to make excuses for the conduct of the Spanish government, by saying that they gave no orders to treat us in this manner. For my own part I do not fear a war with France and Spain. We could do more injury to them than they could do us. If we were at war with them, and Great Britain did not join us, we should have our ports filled with their seamen, and the coasts of France and Spain would soon swarm with our cruisers.

I remember, just before the commencement of the revolutionary war, my mother was disputing with an English officer. He said the Americans, of right, should not go to war; they could do nothing; they could get no person to head them. She replied, that the Americans would have no difficulty in finding some person to command their army; that she had seven sons, and, if necessary, would lead them herself to oppose their army. *Two* of her sons fell during the war in the service of their country. I have seven sons, whom I would much sooner lead to the field than suffer our country to be insulted. Your friend,

CHARLES BIDDLE.

FROM JOHN TAYLOR, OF CAROLINA.

Virginia, near Port Royal, March 25, 1803.

DEAR SIR,

By your note from the Bowling Green I find you are under two mistakes. One, that I am a candidate for Congress; the other, that I am making a book. As to the first, I have withstood all solicitation; and, although a few gentlemen have been pleased, without my knowledge, to make a

I have withstood all solicitation; and, although a few gentlemen have been pleased, without my knowledge, to make a stir, as it is called, nothing will come of it, and the old colonel will once more be felicitated.

As to the second, writing is one of my amusements, but in a wild, careless, and desultory way. Judge, then, how unlikely such scraps are to come out a book. Not that I would hesitate to publish any thing which might do these people good, however it might effect my own name, about which the fifty years which have passed over my head have rendered me quite indifferent. My time goes along tolerably enough, one way or another. Fancy furnishes me with passions and amusements, and about one hundred dollars a year more than meets every want I have which money can gratify.

This election affair has, however, exposed me to five or six essays in the newspapers, composed of lies, malice, and nonsense. One writer (an old tory) charges yourself and Colonel Smith with having met in caucus here, to plot the expulsion of Anthony New from Congress. I would have given five guineas had you called again, for it is probable you would have met Smith at my gate, and another pretty piece would have appeared most prodigiously entertaining.

Well, if you will call in June, I will give you a hearty welcome to the best I have. May you be happy.

Your friend,

JOHN TAYLOR.

FROM PIERCE BUTLER.

Near Darien, Georgia, March 30, 1803.

DEAR SIR,

The letter you did me the honour of writing, with the accompaniments you so kindly forwarded, have my warm and grateful acknowledgments. The selection of *ten miles square* for the seat of government appeared to me at the time, and has continued, an excrescence on the Constitution like a wart on a fair skin. Neither the foreign ministers nor the resident citizens in the federal city have any thing to alarm them under state laws. There is no finger of blood in the laws of Maryland or Virginia. I am of Mr. Bacon's opinion—return the sovereignty to the states. I hope we shall preserve peace with Spain. I observe, with much gratification, that the debates in Congress are much more decorous than they were last session.

The object or end of Mr. Monroe's mission I am ignorant of, as I do not correspond with any public character but yourself. I suppose an explanation with France respecting New-Orleans. I leave my farm in a few days for Philadelphia, where it would afford me pleasure to see you.

Your friend,

P. BUTLER.

TO THEODOSIA.

New-York, July 30, 1803.

It was kind to announce to me, by the earliest opportunity, your safe arrival at Lebanon. Tell me more precisely the movements and intentions of the family, as they will in some measure control mine. I am negotiating for the possession of Richmond Hill, by exchanging with Colonel F. for my house in town. It will be interesting indeed to have you and your boy at the house where you have been once so happy. We will trace back our childish sports and our more grave amusements. In the sale of this estate I reserve the house and a due portion of the ground about it; yet a good price will tempt me to part with it.

Some obscure hints in one of your letters have saddened my heart. From *son pere* I have merited neither suspicion nor reserve. Is it, then, criminal that a person of mature age should converse on a subject most highly interesting with the friend most likely informed? Yet did I not even give advice; invariably and inflexibly I declared that I would never interfere in the matter unless son pere concurred. Have you forgotten the mad project of going to England? the anxiety and misery it cost us for some days? I should have thanked the man who had thus treated my child. Indeed, my dear Theodosia, such things sink into my soul. They seem to invade the very sanctuary of happiness. Had I any thing so much at heart as to render him happy? That I love him, you best know. God bless my dear Theodosia.

A. BURR.

TO THEODOSIA.

Providence, R. I., August 1, 1803.

I left New-York two days after you, that is, on Saturday, and had a pretty little passage of forty-eight hours. We were, on board, a British custom-house officer, a sensible, pleasant man, who played chess with me; two ladies, rather pretty, who did not molest us, *point exigentes*, bien amiable; five little children, who neither cried nor quarrelled the whole way! yet cheerful and playful.

Six days have I passed here very pleasantly. To-morrow I go, whither is not determined. You may, however, address me at New-York, which will most probably be my destination.

All those you saw when you were last here inquire about you with great civility and interest, and say pretty things of you. Don't be vain, madam, for I take this to be a kind of flattery to me, or to be so intended. Miss C. talks much of you, and L. N., and Miss A. Can you imagine what are Miss C.'s occupations and arrangements? Never; so I'll tell you. Why, she instructs two nieces and a nephew (things of twelve or thirteen) in astronomy, natural philosophy, and principles of botany! Her boudoir has globes, several mathematical instruments, &c. All this I discovered by accident; for she denies it all most strenuously, and with some pretty, unaffected embarrassment. Be assured this is an amiable, sensible girl. I don't believe you know her value: so I pray you to study her. She left town yesterday with her mother for Lebanon. Mr. C. went on Friday to New-York. What care you for all that?

Are you a good girl? Do you drink the waters, and bathe, and ride, and walk? I hear Mrs. W. is handsomer than during her widowhood, of which I am very glad. Mr. Russel left this on Thursday, intending to pass through Albany and Ballston on his way to Niagara. If he should come into your vicinage, desire Mr. Alston to recollect him. His wife is with him. I never saw her.

Tell me who you see, and what you do, and what are your plans. You had best return by Boston and Providence if you should have time. Can you make little *chose* drink the water? I dare say not. If I were there I would force some down his little throat. God bless you all.

A. Burr.

TO THEODOSIA.

New-York, August 6, 1803.

Your letter of the 20th of July was received from the post-office on my arrival last evening. There must be some anachronism in the date, for you left New-York on the 21st. I learn, however, that you arrived, were well, and had danced. Lord, how I should have liked to see you dance. It is so long; how long is it? It is certain that you dance better than anybody and looked better. Not a word of the Spring waters, their effects, &c.

I made the journey from Providence by land in four days. Near town, yesterday, P. M., I met Mr. and Mrs. Harper, of Baltimore. They are to breakfast with me this morning; so I must make haste, for it is now eight o'clock. How bad I write to-day. With Mr. and Mrs. Harper was a pretty-looking, black-eyed lass, whose name I did not hear. I hope she is coming out to breakfast, for I like her. There was also that Liverpool merchant, who used to hang on Butler so in Charleston. I hope he won't come.

I wrote you from Providence, on Monday last, all I had

ler so in Charleston. I hope he won't come.
I wrote you from Providence, on Monday last, all I had

to say of it and its inhabitants. I found the whole country, from Providence to this place, greatly alarmed about the yellow fever, said to be in New-York, and dreadful stories in circulation, as usual. There have been some suspicious cases, and some decided instances of yellow fever. Our practising physicians, however, our mayor and police-officers deny its existence. There is no alarm in town. The coffee-house is attended as usual. This length of intolerable heat has, I fear, prepared an atmosphere for the kind reception, if not for the generation of the fever. Now I hear the carriage. *Bon jour.* Be a good girl. Love to H. 'Twas nothing but a cart.

L. and her little *bang* are here (*chez nous*); how happy are you mothers. She will descant on its beauties by the hour; will point them out to you distinctly, lest they might escape notice. The hair, the nose, the mouth, and, in short, every feature, limb, and muscle, is admirable and is admired. To all which I agreed.

Jerome Bonaparte is not here; nor is it certain that he is on the continent. The French consul, whom I met in the road, told me, with *un maniere mysterieuse*, that he had something to communicate on that subject. Maybe he is come, maybe he isn't. I conjecture that he is come or coming.

Here they come, in earnest. I see only one lady in the carriage; so miss has not come; well, she may stay.

A. Burr.

TO THEODOSIA.

New-York, August 8, 1803.

Your amiable letter of the 1st inst. has not *yet* come to hand, and therefore cannot *yet* be acknowledged; perhaps it has not *yet* been written.

Indeed, we are about to be scourged with the plague called yellow fever. John Bard dead; but, to keep the account good, Billy B. has twins (boys). Catharine Church

Cruger (Mrs. Peter C.) has a son. But of the deaths. We die reasonably fast. Six or eight new cases reported yesterday. Of those who take the fever three fourths die. The coffee-house was, nevertheless, pretty well attended. No appearances of alarm until to-day. Several families have removed from the neighbourhood of the Tontine Coffee-house, and five times the number will remove to-morrow. Laight claimed Mr. Alston's promise of Montalto, and I have admitted his pretensions. He will take possession to-morrow or next day. Our pretty (beautiful) Mrs. Talbot, late Miss Truxton, more lately Mrs. Cox, is in my neighbourhood.

I write in town, and in the most outrageous hurry, having nothing to do, but having, according to custom, omitted writing till the moment of closing the mail. Mr. and Mrs. Harper did come, and with them that black-eyed young lady, which proved to be Miss Chase, of Baltimore. Mr. —— came also.

Do you know Miss Joanna Livingston? Pray recollect all her good and amiable qualities. Reflect profoundly. Adieu, ma chere amie.

A. BURR.

FROM THEODOSIA.

Washington, October 16, 1803.

We arrived here yesterday somewhat fatigued. I was, however, very happy to find myself at Washington, for we had, in the morning, been near taking quite a different route. Some part of our harness having broken on the top of a pretty long descent, fortunately the leaders were frightened by the wheel horses crowding on them; and running aside, one got his leg over the pole and was stopped, or you would not have had the pleasure of receiving this interesting scribleriad, and the *poor world* would have been deprived of the heir-apparent to all its admiration and glory.

Our friend L. I have not seen. She was not to be seen.

She has gone to Lancaster, and intends returning by the way of Harper's Ferry. Her journey is taken with a view to recruit herself after a severe attack of the bilious fever; with which, also, her little daughter has been at the point of death—literally, I am told. Lest I might lose the pleasure of seeing her by some mistake, I would not trust to the information of Tunnecliffe as to her absence, but made him send directly to her house. There; is not that little incident related in the true heroic style? Mrs. Madison and myself have made an interchange of visits to-day. She is still pretty; but oh, that unfortunate propensity to snuff-taking. We drank tea with Mr. and Mrs. Gallatin by invitation. Nobody asked us to eat. The markets are bad, I hear. We live very well, however, and, if you have not engaged lodgings, I advise to apply here also.

To-morrow takes us to Dumfries, and the next day beyond Fredericksburgh. *Le pere* is at Bowling Green. I bear travelling remarkably well. Headaches have disappeared, and my appetite increases; but poor little *gampy* does not like the confinement of the carriage.

On inquiry, we find that the one-eyed Nicholas who was in Congress is named John, and has only three brothers, Wilson, Robert, and Normond; so your man is an impostor, consequently you have been imposed on and cheated out of fifty dollars. Wade Hampton arrived here this evening.

THEODOSIA.

FROM THEODOSIA.

Petersburgh, October 21, 1803.

We reached this last night without any accident or even incident, but with great fatigue. Mr. Alston appears so distressed and worn out with the child's fretting, that it returns on me with redoubled force.

Le pere et frere are here. *Toujours honnête et bon.* They breakfasted with us, for we are obliged to take separate lodgings, and my husband has now gone to the races with them; a party of pleasure I was very willing to resign for you and repose. The longer I live, the more frequently the truth of your advice evinces itself, and never was there any thing more true than that occupation is necessary to give one command over themselves. I confess I feel myself growing quite cross on the journey, and it is really to be feared that, unless we soon finish it, the serene tranquillity of my placid temper may be injured. Novel reading has, I find, not only the ill effect of rendering people romantic, which, thanks to my father on earth, I am long past, but they really furnish no occupation to the mind. A series of events follow so rapidly, and are interwoven with remarks so commonplace and so spun out, that there is nothing left to reflect upon. A collection of images, which amuse only from their variety and rapid succession, like the pictures of a magic lantern; not like a piece of Vanderlyn, where the painter makes fine touches, and leaves to your vanity at least the merit of discovering them. Oh! would I had my friend Sterne. Half he says has no meaning, and, therefore, every time I read him I find a different one.

The boy has perfectly recovered. He remembers you astonishingly. He is constantly repeating that you are gone, and calling after you. When I told him to call Mr. Alston grandfather—"Grandfather gone," says he. I kiss you from my heart.

THEODOSIA.

FROM THEODOSIA.

Lumberton, S. C., October 29, 1803.

Thank Heaven, my dear father, I am at Lumberton, and within a few days of rest. I am sick, fatigued, out of patience, and on the very brink of being out of temper. Judge, therefore, if I am not in great need of repose. What conduces to render the journey unpleasant is, that it frets the boy, who has acquired two jaw teeth since he left you, and still talks of *gampy*. We travel in company with the two

boy, who has acquired two jaw teeth since he left you, and still talks of *gampy*. We travel in company with the two
L 2

Alstons. Pray teach me how to write two *A's* without producing something like an *Ass.*

We expect to reach Georgetown on the 1st of November. There we shall remain three or four days, and then proceed to Charleston. Adieu. *Mille baises.*

THEODOSIA.

FROM THEODOSIA.

Clifton, November 8, 1803.

You are surprised at my date, but my last must have prepared you for it in some degree. I received such warm and repeated solicitations to come here, that I accepted. We came on the 3d, and shall remain here till the day after to-morrow, when—oh!—oh! I go to Hagley, where we shall remain till Natalie's arrival, which will carry me to Charleston. It might appear ill-natured and ungrateful for the kindness John and Sally show me to regret residing at Hagley. But you, who always put the best construction on my words and deeds, will allow, that a place in which we have suffered much and run a risk of suffering more must be unpleasant.

We have visited the Oaks house since our arrival. The lazy workmen have been wasting their time, and have not yet finished what two Northern workmen would have done in a month. They are in the act of plastering, and that will not be dry enough to admit us in some time. Thus I shall remain with John till Mr. Alston returns from Columbia. Do you not think we may safely enter the house then? The plastering will be finished in less than a week hence; and the legislature, you know, adjourns at Christmas. I am particular on this subject, because I have known persons to suffer much from inhabiting a house too newly finished, and I wish to have your opinion.

I am extremely anxious to hear from you. When we parted you were engaged in talking over a bargain with Mr. Astor. Pray tell me the event of your deliberations. I had almost forgotten to tell you that we have every prospect of a capital crop.

THEODOSIA.

TO THEODOSIA.

New-York, November 7, 1803.

Your letter from Chester was received in due time; that from Washington came only yesterday, having lain there fourteen days before it was put into the office. By this time you must have received all those which I have written to you since your departure—not a single one. This is the first time that I have put pen to paper at you; but I have been too busy, selling. All is sold, and well sold; not all, however. The house, outhouses, and some three or four acres remain. Enough to keep up the appearance, and all the pleasant recollections of your infantine days, and some of your matronly days also, are reserved with interest. This weighty business, however, is completed, and a huge weight it has taken from the head and shoulders, and every other part, animal and intellectual, of A. B.

Mr. M'Kinnon wrote me, last June, a letter, which I received a few days ago, and with it came two shawls or cloaks (a kind of worked muslin, all the rage in Paris and London at that date), some visiting cards, and ornamented message paper. Half his letter is to you and of you. He begs you to accept one of the shawls, and to give Frances the other. I executed his instructions by giving F. one. Surely it is not worth while to send the other to the Oaks for the admiration of your Africans. It is, in my opinion, beautiful; though, at first sight, I thought so little of it that I was going to give it to Peggy or Nancy. Of the cards I enclose a sample.

If little *gamp* could read, I should write to him volumes. I find my thoughts straying to him every hour in the day, and think more of him twenty fold than of you two together.

Mrs. Laight and child are well. They move to town in six or eight days. Anna is well. Cath. C. la la.

A. Burr.

TO THEODOSIA.

New-York, November 22, 1803.

My last went by water, in care of young Gibbs, the baker's son, with the curricle box, and some other articles which I have forgotten. The letter contained some samples of M'Kinnon's present. The shawl is still retained as being too precious to be sent by sea or land. Is this right?

Mr. Astor left with me some days ago for Mr. Alston a very beautiful map of Lower Canada, price *ten* dollars, and two views of Montreal and its vicinity, *two guineas*. I am particularly charged by Mr. Astor to inform Mr. Alston that his landlord at Montreal paid to him (Mr. Astor), for the account of Joseph Alston, Esq., the sum of *one half guinea;* the said landlord having discovered, after the departure of the said Joseph Alston *et ux.*, that they had not taken with them two bottles of Madeira wine which the said landlord had charged in the bill of the said Joseph Alston, and for which he had received payment. Thus I have discharged myself of a commission which has been enjoined upon me at least ten times.

Roger Morris's place, the large handsome house on the height beyond Mrs. Watkins, is for sale. I can get it for Richmond Hill with *four* acres. Shall I exchange? R. M.'s has one hundred and thirty acres. If I leave Richmond Hill, however, had I not better buy in town, that you may have a resting-place there? Dear little *gampy;* tell me a great deal about him, or I shall not value your letters. Indeed, I will return them unopened. Is not that good Irish?

Mr. Law has arrived. Miss Wheeler* is also at Washington, and A. B. at New-York—*tant mieux*. Would you

* Subsequently Mrs. Commodore Decatur.

think it? I have been coquetted by a rich widow, and really I had some thoughts of yielding.

Jerome Bonaparte is here, and he will keep me three days to dine him. We have exchanged visits, but have not yet met. I think I have mixed up here every thing I have to say to T. B. A. or J. A. No one word of politics; but, on further reflection, Mari will be at Columbia when this arrives.

A. BURR.

TO THEODOSIA.

Washington, December 4, 1803.

I arrived this afternoon, and found here your three letters from Petersburgh, Lumberton, and Georgetown. The last is dated the 2d of November. How very long ago. These letters are very satisfactory, except on the article of your health; of that you must speak a little more plainly. How long are you to stay in Charleston? Without knowing this, I am at a loss where to address you. I shall conclude that you will remain there till the return of Mr. Alston from the legislature.

The manner of your letters pleases me "prodigiously." There is ease, good sense, and sprightliness. That from Petersburgh merits still higher encomium. Tell dear little *gampy* that I have read over his letter a great many times, and with great admiration. Mrs. Law, to whom I showed it, thinks it a production of genius.

That good and ill fortune never come in single strokes, but in sequences, you have heard since you were four years old. Since we parted I have been almost daily surprised by some pleasant occurrence or discovery of a personal nature. I pray it may continue a little longer; even till a bust is found and obtained.

Mrs. Law was vexed and mortified beyond measure at missing you. She has bid me say more things than this sheet would hold. The Misses Butler are all here. I shall

missing you. She has bid me say more things than this
sheet would hold. The Misses Butler are all here. I shall

see them to-morrow. Mary Allen, that was, now Mrs. Livingston; that beautiful little Miss Gray, whom we saw in Boston; she became Mrs. Dobel, then a widow, and now Mrs. Payne.

At Philadelphia Mrs. Lenox and K. almost quarrelled with me for your passing their gate without calling. They had made some preparation, and, in good faith, desired your visit. Miss Boadley, too, talked of you with great interest. At Wilmington I saw no one of your acquaintance; nor at Baltimore, except Susan Smith, who is there on a visit from Princeton.

To go back to New-York. All things are much as you left them, except that what regards gamp is a good deal better. Mrs. Laight, and child, and sisters all in good condition and in high spirits. Have already been dancing—I believe twice. At Mrs. General G.'s I met by accident Mrs. Rogers. She is a pleasant, cheerful, comely woman, to appearance not past thirty-eight or forty. You know we had heard otherwise. Eustis has sprained his ankle, which puts him, for the present, out of the gay world. I have not been abroad except to dine with Mrs. L. I am rejoiced at what you tell me of La Grec.

Pray take immediately in hand some book which requires attention and study. You will, I fear, lose the habit of study, which would be a greater misfortune than to lose your head. M'Kinnon has sent me out a beautiful picture of the celebrated Madame Ricammier. It is a good deal like your pretty widow, Mrs. Wright. *Bon soir.*

A. Burr.

FROM THEODOSIA.

Charleston, November 19, 1803.

All your trouble, good precepts, and better example have been thrown away on me. I am still a child. Your letter of the 7th inst. reached me yesterday. Of course it made me very happy; but those pretty little playthings from D.

M'Kinnon delighted me. I looked at them over and over, with as much pleasure as a miser over his hoard. But you must send me the shawl. I shall be down at the races, and want to have the gratification of displaying it.

From my date and my last letter you imagine that Natalie is in town, but you are mistaken. I came down in the hope of meeting her, and to buy some furniture for the Oaks. Mari on business. I return to Waccamaw to-morrow morning early. My husband left me to-day for Columbia. He received your letter too late to answer it hence, but will do so from Columbia. As for me, I am in the height of bustle and confusion. Before seven this morning I had packed up two or three trunks, and unpacked them all again. Is not that industry? I write as if I were in a hurry. You may perceive the state of my head and house from the style of my letter. More from Hagley. Good-by.

THEODOSIA.

TO THEODOSIA.

Washington, December 6, 1803.

Since closing a letter to you last evening, I have received two more, 8th and 19th of November. You are a good girl to write so often. Oh, yes! I knew how much of a child you were when I sent the pretty things. Just such another child is *son pere*.

I write from my breakfast-table, having not yet been abroad, and having denied myself to everybody. I have, therefore, nothing now to say, and should not so soon have *troubled* you again, but for that part of your letter which speaks of the condition of your house. I hasten to say that, in my opinion, your house will not be a fit or healthy residence for your boy before the middle of April or 1st of May. The walls may, to the touch, appear dry in three or four weeks; but shut up any room for twelve or twenty-four hours, and enter before it be aired, you will meet an offensive, and, as I believe, a pernicious effluvia; an air totally unfit for respiration, unelastic, and which, when inhaled, leaves the lungs unsatisfied. This is the air you will breathe if you inhabit the house. I could, perhaps, show chymically how the atmosphere of the closed rooms becomes thus azotic, but I prefer to submit to the test of your senses.

The shawl shall be ordered on, since you will risk it. Yes, go to the races, and appear to be amused. Be more social.

A. Burr.

TO THEODOSIA.

Washington, December 9, 1803.

When any thing amuses me, my first thought is whether it would not also amuse you; and the pleasure is but half enjoyed until it is communicated. The enclosed has suggested this prologue.

Perhaps I did not tell you that Kate made breakfast for Bonaparte one morning at my house: a breakfast *à la François*, at twelve o'clock. Of four ladies, she was the only one who spoke French, and she really seemed inspired. No Parisian could have been more fluent, graceful, or sprightly.

I have nothing to add of A. B., nor of any of the rest of the alphabet; and my breakfast being on table, farewell.

A. Burr.

FROM THEODOSIA.

Clifton, December 1, 1803.

I have been here about a week, *cher pere*. Since your letter by Gibbs, have not received a line from you. I do not know whether to be most sorry or mad: a little of both troubles me at present; but, to punish you for your silence, I will not tell you which preponderates. Pray write to me immediately.

On the morning after writing to you in Charleston, I set off for the country, as determined on; and, since my arrival, have learned that Natalie was at my house in less than three hours after my departure. Sumter's business will not allow him time to come here, so that I shall go there. William drives me down in his curricle, and we shall set off to-day—this morning—now. The flat is in the canal; the curricle on board; my clothes not yet packed up; so good-by. Before I finish I must tell you that I have again heard from La Greque; she is astonishingly improved in appearance, so say others, and is very happy. She has sent me a Parisian bonnet, two beautiful handkerchiefs, and a pair of walking shoes. To the boy a French and English library; and to Mari a beautiful little golden candlestick, and wax tapers to light his segar.

My health is infinitely improved, and I attribute it to nothing but the continual bustle I have been kept in for three weeks past. What a charming thing a bustle is. Oh, dear, delightful confusion. It gives a circulation to the blood, an activity to the mind, and a spring to the spirits.

THEODOSIA.

TO THEODOSIA.

Washington, December 27, 1803.

Indeed, indeed, my dear little Theodosia, I will write to you very soon. Don't scold and pout so, and I will tell you *how* I visited Annapolis, and *how* I returned about an hour ago. All that, however, may be told in half a line. I went and returned in my own little coachee. But what I did and who I saw are other matters. Something, too, about Celeste, and something about Madame G., whom you are pleased to term the rich widow. This, I think, will keep you quiet a week.

Your letter, written on your return from seeing Natalie, is received. You are a dear good little girl to write me so; and of dear little *gampy*, too, so much, yet never enough. God bless thee.

A. BURR.

FROM THEODOSIA.

Clifton, December 10, 1803.

Behold me again at Clifton; and, in good truth, I begin to be cloyed with the delights of bustle. William and myself left this the day after the date of my last. Some difficulty in crossing the horses delayed us till then. We reached Charleston on the second day, and I found Natalie delighted to see me, and still pretty. She has grown thinner, much thinner; but her complexion is still good, though more languid. The loss of her hair is, however, an alteration much for the worse. Her crop is pretty, but not half so much so as her fine brown hair. I write you all these foolish little particulars because you enter into them all, or, rather, are sensible of all their importance to us. Natalie has a lovely little daughter called after her.

Mr. Sumter is very affectionate and attentive to her, and polite to me. I like him infinitely better than I did. He is an amiable, good-hearted man, with talents to render him respectable. The people of Charleston have paid Natalie every possible attention; indeed, much more than I ever received.

Your letter of the 22d of November greeted me on my arrival here. The exchange has employed my thoughts ever since. Richmond Hill will, for a few years to come, be more valuable than Morris's; and to you, who are so fond of town, a place so far from it would be useless. So much for my reasoning on one side; now for the other. Richmond Hill has lost many of its beauties, and is daily losing more. If you mean it for a residence, what avail its intrinsic value? If you sell part, you deprive it of every beauty save the mere view. Morris's is the most commanding view on the island. It is reputed to be indescribably beautiful. The grounds are pretty. How many delightful walks can be made on one hundred and thirty acres! How much of your taste displayed! In ten or twenty years hence, one hundred and thirty acres on New-York island will be a principality; and there is to me something stylish, elegant, respectable, and suitable to you in having a handsome country-seat. So that, upon the whole, I vote for Morris's.

You, perhaps, have not yet heard of the death of J. M'Pherson. He expired on the road from town to his brother's. Poor Sally was with him, and John here. He has gone for her, and thus Hagley will be deserted for a long time.

Men are indubitably born monkeys. *Gampy* imitates me in every thing I do, and to-day I had a lesson not to be forgotten. He was playing in my room while I was dressing; quite at the commencement of my toilet, *toute a fais en desabille*, I ran out in the entry to call my maid; while engaged in that operation, I turned round and saw my brother's door opening within a few yards of me; girl-like, or rather babylike, I ran to my room, threw the door open violently, and uttering a scream, was at the other end of it in one jump. The boy, who was busily engaged in eating mint-drops, no sooner heard me scream and appear frightened than he yelled most loudly, and, running to me, caught my clothes, clinched his fists, and appeared really alarmed for two minutes. It was not affectation. Do you think this trait ominous of a coward? You know my abhorrence and contempt of those animals. Really I have been uneasy ever since it happened. You see I follow your injunction to the letter. How do you like this essay? Have you enough of *gampy* now?

THEODOSIA.

TO CHARLES BIDDLE.

New-York, July 20, 1800.

MY DEAR SIR,

The President has hauled out into the stream. Your boys left my house yesterday and went on board. They have gained very much of my esteem and attachment by their amiable manners, their modesty, and good sense; the friendship which I formerly bore them on your account is now

gained very much of my
amiable manners, their modesty, and good sense; the friendship which I formerly bore them on your account is now

The more I reflect on the destination of these young men, the more I am pleased with it ; and if I had but one son, I think I should place him in the navy.

If the object be ambition, our navy presents the best prospect of honour and advancement. A young man of merit may be sure of rapid promotion and opportunities of distinction. If the pursuit be wealth, still the navy offers the fairest and most honourable means of acquiring it.

But another reason, perhaps not often attended to nor generally believed, would weigh very much with me. The young men of our day, those, I mean, who are deemed to be in the higher ranks of life, are addicted to gross and vicious habits, which are often ruinous to their health and constitutions, and always corrupt the morals and enfeeble the mind. In naval life they are certainly much less exposed to these vices. The profession calls for the active exertions both of body and mind; and I have always remarked that sailors, I mean those among them who are men of education, and are stimulated by motives of honour or ambition, have a generosity of temper, a frankness and manliness of character, which is much more seldom seen in other orders of life.

I am, therefore, firmly persuaded that, situated as our country now is, a young man of activity and talents has the best chance for health, fortune, and honour by entering the navy. Your sons are under peculiar advantages, for you may be assured that they will find not only a friend, but truly a parent in Captain Truxton. We have talked much about them, and I am happy to find that his dispositions towards them are such as you could wish.

I am, dear sir,

Your very affectionate friend and servant,

A. Burr.

Recollect, if you please, the Trenton bridge, and find me a copy of the law—any information with regard to the difficulties—the expense, and probable income—also the doings of the commissioners, if indeed they have done any thing.

FROM JAMES BIDDLE.

Tripoli Prison, November 29, 1803.

MY DEAR SIR,

I sit down to fulfil the promise made at parting, of writing you upon our arrival in the Mediterranean. I had flattered myself with the pleasure of hearing from you frequently during the long and happy cruise which I had contemplated; for, although the greater part of our time was to be spent far up the Mediterranean, where opportunities to America rarely occur, yet I should have written you from every port we visited, sealed, and forwarded my letters as a conveyance offered. But fate, it seems, had cruelly ordained that we should not realize those prospects of pleasure and gratification which we had, with so much certainty, calculated upon; and that this cruise, which had promised to be so agreeable, should be suddenly terminated, in its very commencement, by events the most distressing to ourselves and our friends, and which may involve our country in difficulties and perplexities with this regency.

For the unfortunate events of the thirty-first ultimo, the lamentable day which terminated in the loss of our ship* by being wrecked on rocks within a few miles of this town, and in ourselves becoming prisoners of war to the Bashaw of Tripoli (I should have said slaves, for we certainly are in the most abject slavery, our very lives being within the power and at the very nod of a most capricious tyrant), let me refer you to statements which I presume you will already have seen before the receipt of this. Suffice it to say, that the shoal we run upon was never laid down on any chart yet published, nor ever before discovered by any of our vessels cruising off this coast; consequently, the charts and soundings justifying as near an approach to the land as we made, not the smallest degree of censure can be attached to Captain Bainbridge for the loss of the ship. That, after

* The Philadelphia

having grounded, every effort was made, and every expedient tried, without effect, that could have the remotest probability of getting her afloat; and that, after having sustained the fire of the enemy's gunboats for upward of four hours, and a re-enforcement approaching from the town, while our guns were rendered almost useless from the careening of the ship, there seemed no alternative left but the cruel, mortifying one of hauling down our colours. Let me also tell you that the treatment we received from these savages was such as raised our utmost indignation. Our swords were snatched from us; the money, and every thing in our pockets was stolen; some had their boots pulled off to examine if something was not concealed there; and some had their very coats stripped off their backs, which the barbarians exultingly put upon themselves; and, as if the trophies of some signal victory, seemed to triumph in obtaining what fortune alone had put them in possession of. To murmur at their treatment was only to expose ourselves to repeated and more provoking insults; to resist was only hazarding our lives. We were therefore obliged, however degrading in our own opinion, to submit to these lawless, unfeeling robbers.

We were all conducted, amid the shouts and acclamations of the rabble multitude, to the palace, and there ushered into the presence of the mighty bashaw, who, seated in state, with his council about him, and surrounded by guards, awaited our coming. He asked a variety of questions, principally concerning our ship and our squadron; and, after having us all paraded before him, and taken a full survey of each of us, at which a gracious smile appeared upon his countenance, expressive of his inward satisfaction at so unexpected a piece of good fortune, we were carried by our guards to the house allotted for us during our imprisonment in this country. It was the American consular house formerly occupied by Mr. Catchcart.

Here we were left undisturbed to our own reflections till

the fifteenth instant. A few days previous to this the prime minister had written to inform Captain Bainbridge that a letter had been received from the Tripolitan captain of the ship captured by the U. S. Frigate John Adams, in which he complained of being ill treated by Captain Rogers; that, in consequence of this, he should be under the necessity of retaliating such ill treatment upon us, unless Captain B. would immediately write to Commodore Preble, and *order* him to deliver up all the prisoners he had, in which latter case we should continue to be treated as heretofore. No exchange was proposed, but we were to deliver up seventy-eight prisoners merely to ensure our not being cruelly treated. Captain B. told him that he would write to Commodore Preble, and acquaint him with their demands; but as to ordering or requesting him to deliver up the prisoners in question, he would not do it. We were, therefore, conducted to the castle, under the idea of being put to work. The change, indeed, was an unpleasant one, from a large, commodious house, to what they called a castle, which was, in fact, a most loathsome prison. We were crammed into the same room with all our ship's company—how well calculated to contain such a number, you may be enabled to judge, when I tell you that the place was about eighty feet by twenty-five. How comfortable, when I tell you that the only place to admit the air was through a small aperture in the top of the house, grated over, with no floor, nor a single article of furniture, so that, when we were tired standing up, we were obliged to lay down on the ground. While there, Lisle, the admiral, *accidentally* passed, and was very much *surprised* at our removal. He came to inquire the cause, observing that he had understood a letter was received, mentioning that the Tripolitan prisoners had been illy treated by Captain Rogers. Captain Bainbridge told him, that if such a letter had been written, the writer had asserted a most malicious falsehood; that the laws of the United States absolutely forbid any prisoners being illy treated; and that

most malicious falsehood; that the laws of the United States
absolutely forbid any prisoners being illy treated; and that

he knew Captain Rogers had given no just cause of complaint; that, even supposing he had, that could not justify their retaliating upon us; it would not tend to produce a reconciliation, but would have a quite opposite effect; that, however, we were in their power, and they might sacrifice the whole of us; but the United States had men and ships enough to send in our places.

In the evening we were reconducted to our former house, probably in consequence of the interposition of the Danish and French consuls in our behalf. The reason of our removal to the castle, as given out to us, was in order to retaliate upon us ill treatment which they say their prisoners received from us. A more probable reason was this:—

When our ship was plundered, all our chests and trunks, with every article of clothing, was carried off. The prime minister, with the view of making money, bought in at reduced prices as many of our clothes as he could collect, and offered them to us for twelve hundred dollars. Captain Bainbridge would not purchase them. Disappointed in his expectations of pecuniary profit, and, instead of gain, sustaining loss, he probably sought consolation in his disappointment by increasing the weight of our misfortunes. The prime minister and admiral are both renegadoes, the former a Prussian, the latter a Frenchman.

How long we are to remain in this savage country God only knows. No doubt it must depend in a great measure upon the exertions that are made in our favour. We rely with implicit confidence that the government of our country will make the most speedy, as well as effectual measures for our release. While we are here, our lives must be in constant jeopardy and uncertainty. Adieu. Remember me affectionately to Mrs. Alston; and believe me,

With much esteem and respect,

Your most obedient servant,

JAMES BIDDLE.*

* Now Commodore Biddle, and son of the late Charles Biddle.

CHAPTER XV.

An amendment to the Constitution of the United States having been proposed by Congress, and doubts existing as to the manner in which it should be authenticated and transmitted to the several states, Mr. Burr, as president of the Senate, addressed a note on the subject to the secretary of state, Mr. Madison, and to the secretary of the Senate, Mr. Otis, to which the following replies were made.

FROM MR. MADISON.

Department of State, December 11, 1803.

J. Madison presents his respects to the vice-president, who will find in the enclosed the information afforded by the office of state on the subject of former amendments to the Constitution. Mr. Beckley recollects, that in one of the instances, copies equal to the number of the states were made out in the clerk's office of the House of Representatives. In the other, I understood from him that the copies were not furnished to the executive; but it does not appear, from any thing in the office of state, whether this was or was not the case.

J. WAGNER TO MR. MADISON.

Department of State, December 10, 1803.

Dear Sir,

I find that all the amendments to the Constitution, though none of them are signed by the president, have been enrolled in this office. I do not find that the first set was forwarded by this department to the states, though the president was requested to communicate them, as appears by the journals. The last amendment was forwarded by the secretary of

requested to communicate them, as appears by the journals. The last amendment was forwarded by the secretary of state, by direction of the president, to the governors of the states.

The vice-president called this morning and stated two questions, which I was then unable to answer, *viz.*, Whether the enrolment took place here, and whether the amendments were forwarded to the states from hence ?

It is to enable you to give him satisfaction on these points that I have written this. With great respect, your obedient servant,

J. WAGNER.

FROM SAMUEL A. OTIS.

Senate Chamber, December 15, 1803.

SIR,

In answer to the note you did me the honour to send this morning, my first impression was that the amendments for each state should be enrolled in the office of the secretary of the Senate, as the resolution commenced in Senate. This impression arose from the proceeding in the *first* instance, when the enrolments were made in the House of Representatives, where the amendments commenced. This was at a time when the secretary of Senate and clerk of the House of Representatives were empowered to publish the laws. But, since the establishment of the department of state, the amendments to the Constitution have been enrolled in the office of that house where they originated. This enrolment, as a bill, hath been sent to the President of the United States, with a joint resolution that he would forward authenticated copies. This was the case in March, 1794, as you will see by the journals of Senate. To confirm this idea, a resolution is on the table of the House of Representatives for the above purpose. If precedent is of avail, it certainly devolves, in the distribution, on the office of state.

Hearing there was some uncertainty, I have, through a friend, transmitted my opinion to the secretary of state.

Very respectfully,

SAMUEL A. OTIS.

FROM GEORGE DAVIS.

Leghorn, December 3, 1803.

A letter to my brother* of this date will give you a detail of my pursuits since leaving Malaga until my arrival in Leghorn.

I have only to say of Tuscany that two months have passed away in endeavouring to repair the ravages of Italian physicians. My pursuits, though not profitable, have still been flattering to myself. I am at the house of F. C. Degen, who married Miss Russell, of Boston. She is acquainted with you, and often retraces the hours you spent with Mrs. Russell. I may add, that I have been not only a welcome, but most happy guest of this worthy family for six weeks. My hours of relaxation have not been employed in playing the *cavallero cervante*, but in acquiring the Italian; and, with the assistance of a tolerable tutor, I am making great progress. Pisa and Lucca I have been at twice, and about the 20th of this month I shall visit Florence. From thence I proceed to Rome, Naples, Palermo, and Malta, where I am directed to join the commodore, he having given me furlough for the purposed route.

I refrain speaking of those places *all the world* have seen. Should my expectations be realized when at Rome, I shall certainly offer you my first *essay*. Nothing has yet been done in the way of making me rich. The hospital establishment lays over till spring. Commodore Morris offers to leave me as chargé des affaires for Tripoli in the event of peace. If nothing better can be done, I will remain. Eaton has resigned the consulship of Tunis. Who will be appointed? Rufus King is expected daily in Tuscany. He sails early in the spring for the United States.

I ought not to omit mentioning Mrs. Derby, who arrived here a few days since from Florence. I have spent some pleasant hours with her. She is unaffected and untinctured with the licentious manners of Paris and London. We shall meet at Rome. I yesterday dined with Mr. Pinckney, our

* Matthew L. Davis.

minister for the court of Spain. He wants, I think, *ministerial dignity*, whatever may be his talents.

I have written you several times, and although this gives me no claim to expect a letter, yet, when you learn that I have not received a line from the United States since leaving it, you may judge how great is my desire, and what would be my gratification in hearing from you. The beautiful Mrs. D. is in the parlour, and I have been sent for three times. With perfect respect,

George Davis.

FROM CHARLES BIDDLE.

Philadelphia, December 12, 1803.

If you can, without inconvenience, let me know how James stands as a midshipman, I wish you would do it. Having lost a brother, a son, and two nephews in the service, I have some right to expect James will not be neglected. I have not the honour of knowing the secretary of the navy, but I am told he is a very worthy and respectable gentleman.

Yours,

Charles Biddle.

FROM ROBERT SMITH, SECRETARY OF NAVY.

Washington, December 31, 1803.

Sir,

It was my intention to have had the pleasure of calling upon you for the purpose of having some conversation with you about Mr. Biddle, midshipman. Not knowing what is the precise object of his father's inquiries, my communication may not afford the expected explanations. I can only state to you, at present, that the official reports which have been made of him by his commanding officers are highly favourable, and that, of course, I have a strong disposition to afford to him every opportunity of improvement, and to give him every advancement in the navy that can be done consistently with the just pretensions of his fellow-officers.

We regret sincerely that the weather has deprived us of the pleasure of presenting, in person, our reciprocal compliments and solicitations of the season.

Respectfully yours,

R. SMITH.

FROM ROBERT G. HARPER.

Baltimore, December 20, 1803.

Mr. Carroll, my dear sir, requests me to assure you that it will give him very particular pleasure to see you at his house on Christmas day, and as many days before and after as you may find it agreeable to favour him with your company. He regrets that there will not, at that time, be a room which he can offer you; but, in every thing except the article of lodging, he hopes that you will be his guest while you find it agreeable to remain at Annapolis.

Yours truly,

ROBERT G. HARPER.

FROM J. GUILLEMARD.

February 22, 1803.

SIR,

You will not, I hope, think me over intrusive when I take the liberty of introducing to your attentions and kindness the Earl of Selkirk, a young nobleman who has a project of making a settlement for some of his countrymen on the western side of the Atlantic. I need say nothing more of him. His merits will speak for themselves; and give me leave to add, that I am happy in this opportunity of expressing my grateful sense of your kindness and attention to me during my residence in the United States. With great respect, your obedient servant,

J. GUILLEMARD.

FROM JOHN VAUGHAN.

Wilmington (Delaware), January 3, 1804.

Dear Sir,

I cannot resist, until morning, the pleasure of acknowledging how much I am indebted to you for an acquaintance with Doctor Peter Irving and Mr. Bishop. I found them all you intimated, and much more; and sincerely hope the reciprocation you anticipated may have taken place. We spent the evening with Mr. Dickinson, and, I believe, with mutual pleasure; and they have just left my house, Dr. Irving the last. We have many fine tales of the satisfaction inspired by a common sense of *public rights*, but I query whether a just sense of *political wrongs* do not bind men more closely together.

A very curious game, indeed, has been played here since you passed through our borough. A special caucus has been held, to counteract the political machinations which are to arise out of my pleasurable interview with you; but the clamour is unexpectedly checked. Some wicked man in New-York had the assurance to send to Mr. Dickinson and myself each a copy of a pamphlet, entitled, "*An Examination, &c., by Aristides*," and, after perusing it with equal pleasure and avidity, I had the imprudence to hand it to a disinterested republican, who read it with the highest satisfaction. In one week it has passed through several hands, and has excited no inconsiderable interest. Dr. Irving has promised me a supply as soon as practicable.

I am authorized to say that Mr. Dickinson was never prejudiced, and is now highly gratified. He indeed regretted that I had not assured you, when here, that his opinion was untarnished by the malignant clamour of demagogues.

It is a more than lamentable fact, that factions have arisen up in several states which are determined to prostrate every man who might be capable of opposing them, or dared to lisp one expression of dissent to the machinations of favouritism. But, though I have borne too much, I am unalterably resolved to adhere inflexibly to the ground I have taken, and stand or fall in the honest path of political rectitude.

There is a crisis in the affairs of men which sooner or later unveils the hidden features of selfishness ; and there is no position in which my opinion is more fixed than in the utility of a firm union of honest men. If the cabals of the day be not speedily arrested, where shall our political bark be anchored ? The Sylla of oligarchy, or Charybdis of disorganization must be the portion of our government. Of all tyrannies, oligarchies are the most delusive and dreadful, and anarchy is equally to be deplored.

Wishing you, my dear sir, complete retribution for the past, and happy in the reflection of having preserved myself uncontrolled by artifice,

I am sincerely your friend,
John Vaughan.

FROM JOHN DICKINSON.

Wilmington, Delaware, 4th 1st mo, 1804.

My dear Friend,

Thy letter of the 30th of last month was delivered to me yesterday by Abraham Bishop, and I desire thee to accept my thanks for introducing one to the other.

He was so kind as to spend some hours with me, and I was exceedingly pleased with the traits of character displayed in the course of our conversation. He appears to me to be a man who possesses great and well-directed energies of mind. I rejoice in the prospect he opened to me of the advancement of republican principles and measures to the eastward.

I am thy sincere friend,
John Dickinson.

TO CHARLES BIDDLE.

Washington, January 2, 1804.

Last evening I received the answer of Robert Smith, of which a copy is enclosed. It may be satisfactory to you to know, *officially*, that James is favourably spoken of, and is in estimation with the government. A more precise answer could not, perhaps, be expected from a minister. The application may secure him from being forgotten, and the answer from being prejudiced in any future arrangements. He shall be informed of your precise object by

A. BURR.

TO THEODOSIA.

Washington, January 3, 1804.

This is only to assure you that I am in perfect health. That General Jackson is my good friend; that I have had no duel nor quarrel with anybody, and have not been wounded or hurt.

Jerome Bonaparte, wife, maids of honour (Miss Spear *et al.*), &c., &c., will be here to-morrow. There are various opinions about the expediency, policy, decency, propriety, and future prospects of this match. I adhere to Mrs. Caton. To be sure the French laws say something on this subject. As you are a learned lady, I will not say what; but, if you avow ignorance, you shall have all I know: not in my next, for Annapolis is yet on hand. Indeed, matters thicken so fast, that I may possibly leave this within twenty days to go northward, without saying a word about it. I hope the shawl (or cloak) has arrived safe, and that it may be so displayed as to add beauty to grace and grace to beauty.

A. BURR.

TO THEODOSIA.

Washington, January 4th or 5th, 1804.

How could I forget to tell you the very important event of the marriage of Jerome Bonaparte with Miss Patterson.

It took place on Saturday, the 24th ult. Mrs. Caton approves of this match, and therefore A. B. does, for he respects greatly the opinions of Mrs. Caton.

I like much your reasoning about Morris's place and Richmond Hill. Yet would not a permanent residence in town for some, for many, for all reasons, be better? La G. is much better than I had heard—*d'un certaine* age, and well-looking, considering that circumstance. Cheerful, good-tempered, the best of housewives, and, as it is thought, *willing*.

Celeste—(for this I begin a new line) Celeste will be seen on the way home, but that La R. spoils every thing in that place. La Planche; that you will never find out. I bet you thirty guineas against M‘K.'s shawl. By-the-by, the shawl is ordered on; at this moment, perhaps, on the perilous ocean, and unensured. La Planche, I say, was seen on our way hither. All right and pretty; improved since the last inspection. Great friend of La R.; *tant pis*. Lex et ux. ill suited; mischief brewing. *Gamp*, the mutual friend and confidant.

Now for the trip to Annapolis. No, not now either. It is past two o'clock in the morning (no matter of what day, for I don't intend to date this, seeing it will equally suit all dates), and I am (not) sleepy. Yet I will go to bed, and not be kept up by any such baggage. So good-morning. Poor little Natalie, I have not written her a line. What's the matter I don't write to Natalie any more? I say I will go to bed. The fire is out, and I have no wood.

A. Burr.

TO PEGGY GAITIN (A SLAVE).

Washington, January 4, 1804.

You may assure the family that I never was in better health; that I have not been wounded or hurt, and have had no quarrel with anybody. I received your letter of the 29th this evening. Let nothing hinder you from going to school punctually. Make the master teach you arithmetic, so that you may be able to keep the accounts of the family. I am very much obliged to you for teaching Nancy. She will learn more from you than by going to school.

I shall be at home about the last of this month, when I will make you all New Year's presents. Tell Harry that I shall expect to find a good road up to the house. Tell me what Harry is about, and what is doing at Montalto. Sam and George are well.

You must write to Mrs. Alston about Leonora's child. Enclose your letter to me. I hope little Peter is doing well.

A. Burr.

TO THEODOSIA.

Washington, January 17, 1804.

Your kind wishes on the new year are received this evening in your letter dated 3d January, 1803. No matter what date, such things are always welcome. I don't believe it came into my head to say Happy New Year! my heart is so full of good wishes for you every day in the calendar. Yet I like to see attention paid to all *les jours de fête*. I am very sorry for poor Charlotte, and do most sincerely sympathize with Sally. She must know my great attachment for her brother.

Of my plans for the spring nothing can be said, for nothing is resolved. It is not probable that I shall be able to visit you; but I shall expect you very early. If you are to come by land, I will meet you on the road; perhaps in this place, perhaps in Richmond. I do not now see that it will be possible for me to visit South Carolina. Now, what are your plans? The shawl was ordered on the very day I received your commands; whether it has actually been sent I know not, but most probably it has.

Of the boy you never say enough. Nothing about his French in your last. I hope you talk to him much in French, and Eleonore always. A letter from Peggy says that Eleonore's boy was well on the 13th. Your icehouse and vaults are finished. Of Annapolis I find the newspapers have anticipated me. They will tell you where I dined, and supped, and whom I saw.

Madame Bonaparte passed a week here. She is a charming little woman; just the size and nearly the figure of Theodosia Burr Alston; by some thought a little like her; perhaps not so well in the shoulders; dresses with taste and simplicity (by some thought too free); has sense, and spirit, and sprightliness. A little of the style and manner of Susan Smith.

Mrs. Merry* is tall, fair, fat—*pas trop*, however. No more than a desirable embonpoint. Much of grace and dignity, ease and sprightliness; full of intelligence. An Englishwoman who has lived much in Paris, and has all that could be wished of the manners of both countries. An amiable and interesting companion, with whose acquaintance you will, next summer, be much gratified. She proposes to pass some time in New-York.

I want a French translation of the Constitution of the United States, and, for the purpose, send you a copy in English. It will, I fear, be a great labour to you; but I cannot get it done here, and it may not be useless to you to burnish up your French a little. Do you ever hear from Natalie? I have not yet written to her. How scandalous.

You do not say whether the boy knows his letters. I am sure he may now be taught them, and then put a pen into his hand, and set him to imitate them. He may read and write before he is three years old. This, with speaking French, would make him a tolerably accomplished lad of that age, and worthy of his blood.

A most bitter cold day. *Bon jour*.

A. BURR.

* The lady of the then British Minister Plenipotentiary to the United States.

TO JOSEPH ALSTON.

Washington, January 18, 1804.

I have been greatly flattered by the applauses bestowed on your speech at Columbia. Send me half a dozen copies. Why have you not alrėady done it?

The papers herewith enclosed will show you our possession of Louisiana, and the manner of it. The Spanish government will endeavour to limit our west bounds to the Mississippi, with the addition of the Island of Orleans only; on this consideration that government would still hold on the west bank of the Mississippi, from the river Iberville to the 31st degree of latitude, an extent of one hundred miles.

In attempting to legislate for our newly-acquired territory, it is doubted whether the Louisianians can be received into the Union without an amendment to the Constitution. Consider of this. Again; are they citizens of the United States, or can Congress make them such? A bill establishing a form of government is now before the Senate; when it shall have passed that house I will send you a copy. It is at present in too crude a state to merit your notice.

The newspapers will have informed you that a committee has been appointed in the House of Representatives to inquire into the official conduct of Judge Chace. Peters is associated with him, but he is not the object, and the insertion of his name was accidental. This inquiry, as is obvious, is with a view to an impeachment. If it result in an impeachment, and an immediate trial be had, Congress will sit till May or June. Yours very affectionately,

A. Burr.

TO CHARLES BIDDLE.

Washington, January 20, 1804.

Dear Sir,

I thank you for the letter and the newspaper; for a short letter too, written on your return from Lancaster, which has not yet been answered.

It is seriously my intention to visit you next week, if I can get away, which will depend a little on the state of business in Senate. The association of Peters with Chace was, I believe, accidental. It was moved (I think by one of your members), and, as they sat together on the bench, it was not, at the time, seen how they could be separated. I presume it affords him a new subject for wit. On receipt of this, write me one line, saying when Mr. R. will leave Philadelphia. God bless you.

A. Burr.

TO CHARLES BIDDLE.

Washington, January 23, 1804.

My dear Sir,

When I last wrote you (about Thursday, I think), I felt the approaches of a headache, which I concluded would be, as usual, the torment of twenty-four hours only. On the contrary, it has pursued me without intermission. I have undergone cathartic, emetic, and phlebotomy, operations not experienced by me in twenty years, and all to no purpose. The pain continues, but to-day has allowed me to leave my bed for an hour or so at a time. At one of these intervals I now write to you to say that this incident has rendered my journey doubtful, though on the day I last wrote you I informed the Senate that I should have occasion to be absent for two or three weeks.

It is extraordinary that all these medical experiments, and a total abstinence from food for three days, has produced no diminution of strength or spirits. At this instant I feel able to start for Philadelphia (the snow eight inches deep) notwithstanding. It will, however, be impossible to move before Thursday, if at all.

January 24.

After writing, last evening, the nonsense on the other page, I recollected that the mail had closed. This postscript is added to say that I am much better to-day; but little pain, yet my head too weak to bear the least motion, and fear it will not allow me to travel for several days.

I. Brown is again in the chair as president of the Senate. It was a hard election. Ten or twelve ballotings. The Virginia interest supported Mr. Franklin. Yours,

A. BURR.

TO NATALIE DELAGE SUMTER.

Washington, January 25, 1804.

Your safe arrival, my dear Natalie, gave me the greatest joy. Theodosia has given me a detailed account of yourself and your lovely little girl. All as I could wish. I could never realize that you were not lost to me till I heard that you were actually on American ground. Your letter relieved my anxieties and fulfilled my hopes, by assuring me of your unabated affection. But when or where, I pray, are we to meet? Engage Mr. Sumter to come and pass the summer with me at New-York; by the summer I mean from the 1st of May till the middle of November. Theodosia has told you that I am wholly at Richmond Hill, and that her house is only five miles off. You will review with pleasure the scenes of your sportive childhood, and you will gratify the fondest wishes of your affectionate friend and father,

A. BURR.

P. S. I enclose some papers for the amusement of your husband. Pray present them to him with the assurance of my respectful and affectionate regard. You, too, my dear Natalie, will read with instruction and amusement the account of Louisiana. A. B.

TO THEODOSIA.

Washington, January 25, 1804.

A letter from Mari, without a line from Theodosia, is novel. If the compliment should be returned, I should bring an old house about my ears. But no apologies or explanations.

I hate them, and the matter will be forgotten before they can reach me.

I have been a week confined to my room by a headache, but there are no mortal or alarming symptoms. On Saturday I take a ride to Baltimore, where I am to dine with Madame Bonaparte. Then on to Philadelphia ; thence, perhaps, to New-York, and here again by the time your answer can arrive. Have not yet written to Natalie. How shameful !

Fine sleighing here. Eight inches snow ; clear and cold. Having nothing more at present of great importance to add I remain yours, &c.,

A. Burr.

P. S. Since the conclusion of this performance I have set down in a rage, and written a *pretty* little letter to Natalie Lord, how much easier and lighter I feel.

A. B.

TO NATALIE DELAGE SUMTER.

Washington, January 27, 1804.

The *brochure*, containing proclamations and manifestoes regarding Louisiana, was intended to accompany those which I lately transmitted to you for Mr. Sumter.

You will be proud, as a New-Yorker, to see that the first attempt to create a taste for painting and sculpture has been made in our city. We have about forty busts and groups. Lailson's theatre (west side Greenwich-street) has been fitted up for their reception. It forms a circular room of about sixty or seventy feet diameter, lighted by a dome, and to us, who have seen nothing better, the thing, of course, looks well. Come and see our infant efforts.

I am just leaving this place for a few days on a visit to Philadelphia ; a visit, however, of business only. On my return you will hear again from me. In the mean time, pray write me when I may expect you at New-York.

A. Burr.

TO THEODOSIA.

Washington, January 29, 1804.

There is no end to the trouble such a baggage gives me. Another thing occurs, which, forsooth, must be sent to her too. It would not, perhaps, merit so high an honour as that of being perused by your —— eyes and touched by your fair hands, but that it is the production of a youth* of about nineteen, the youngest brother of Dr. Peter Irving, of New-York. *Salut.*

A. BURR.

TO A. R. ELLERY.

Washington, January 29, 1804.

DEAR SIR,

Your letter of the 6th of January is received at the moment that I am leaving this city on a tour to Philadelphia for two or three weeks. I can, therefore, only acknowledge it. The map was a most acceptable present. I value it greatly as the work of Madame Ellery; a circumstance which my vanity has not allowed me to conceal.

You may rely on my zeal and my good will. You can estimate their importance. On my return you will hear again from me.

The bill, or project of law, herewith enclosed, is now under debate in the Senate. You will, therefore, consider it as a project merely, not yet a law. In the course of this discussion it may receive important alterations, and may be finally rejected. Do not, therefore, suffer any copy to be taken of it, still less to get into newspapers, if any you have. You may show it to whom you please. If you have any acquaintance with Mr. Daniel Clarke, pray let him see it. I wish his and your opinions, though they may, probably, be received too late to influence the result. Mr. Clarke is not known to me personally, but very much through our

* Washington Irving.

common friend General Dayton. With respectful compliments and thanks to Mrs. Ellery, I am your friend,

A. Burr.

TO THEODOSIA.

Havre de Grace (Susquehannah), January 30, 1804.

In a former letter I told you we had eight inches snow at Washington. On Saturday last, 28th, fell six or eight inches more, so that we had a foot depth of snow, cold weather, and, of course, good sleighing. The vice-president having, with great judgment and science, calculated the gradations of cold in different latitudes, discovered that for every degree he should go north he might count on *four and a half inches* of snow. Thus he was sure of *sixteen and a half* inches at Philadelphia; *twenty-one inches* at New-York, and so for all the intermediate space. Hence he wisely concluded to take off the wheels from his coachee and to set it on runners. This was no sooner resolved than done. With his sleigh and four horses he arrived at Baltimore at early dinner. Passed the evening with Madame Bonaparte; all very charming. Came off this morning; fine sleighing. A hundred times he applauded the wisdom of his plan. Within *six* miles of the Susquehannah the snow appeared thin; within *four*, the ground was bare. It had not thawed, but none had fallen. He dragged on to this place, and here he is in the midst of the most forlorn dilemma. This is palpable fraud in *monsieur le tems*, to hold out such lures merely to draw one into jeopardy. Having neither wife nor daughter near me on whom to vent my spleen, renders the case more deplorable. It is downright desperation.

After pacing the floor with a very quick step for about five minutes, I determined to call for a good dinner and a bottle of wine, and, after the discussion whereof, I hope to be more able to meet the exigence. You shall presently know.

New-York, February 8, 1804.

Just arrived—all well. The dinner and wine mentioned t'other side operated so happily, that, before the repast was concluded, I ordered my horses to the door, drove over the Susquehannah on the ice, and came that night to the head of Elk. Next day to Chester, having seen friend Dickenson *en passant* (the daughters not visible, on account of the loss of their mother, who died *last summer*), and breakfasted in Philadelphia on the morning of the 1st of February. The ebullition of the 30th January was intended to have been finished at Havre de Grace and sent to the postoffice. I came off in too much haste, and, seeing it now in my writing-case, I thought it a pity that so precious a morceau should be lost to the world.

Tout le monde is marrying at Philadelphia. You will not have a *single single* (decipher that) acquaintance there on your return. Yes, La R., La Planche, and La Bin. may remain. I went to a wedding supper at Mrs. Moore's, whose daughter has married Willing—could any one suppose she was *unwilling?* Execrable! Mr. Boadley died a few days ago. Madame of course was invisible. Ann Stuart will, most likely, marry P. C.—very well. She is very pretty. Mary Rush just married Mannors, a captain in the British army. She looked quite melancholy, being on the point of setting off for Niagara, where her husband is stationed. Binney and Keene look better than I ever saw them. Keene is learning the harp. They are at lodgings in town, and, happening to be near my quarters, I saw them two or three times a day.

I left Philadelphia yesterday, and arrived, as you see, after a very pleasant journey. Fine, mild winter weather. Roads hard and smooth. Note. I left my runners and got wheels at Philadelphia. How could I omit Celeste and her sisters, whom I saw several times? What of that? Pray can it be true that she was engaged to a young man whom we knew and valued, and who lately died in your country? To-morrow I am to see La G. Pray for me.

To-morrow, February 9th.

A most ugly northeast storm of rain, and hail, and mist. Shall not see La G. to-day. God bless thee.

A. Burr.

TO THEODOSIA.

New-York, February 16, 1804.

In one hour I shall be on the west side of the Hudson river, and in the mail stage. Goldsmith is the very book I should have recommended. A critical knowledge of historical events may assist a statesman or form a pedant. For you, something less will do, and something more is necessary. La G. will not do. I have written twice to Natalie.

Say to Mari, the Clintons, Livingstons, &c., had not, at the last advice from Albany, decided on their candidate for governor. Hamilton is intriguing for any candidate who can have a chance of success against A. B. He would, doubtless, become the advocate even of Dewitt Clinton if he should be the opponent. A. Burr.

TO THEODOSIA.

Baltimore, February 21, 1804.

I left New-York on the 16th. The roads were so very bad that I sent back Sam, George, and the horses from Trenton, and came on in the mail stage *sans valet*. One great discovery has been made by the experiment, namely, that George is not only useless on the road, but requires abundance of my care, so that, in fact, I have less trouble without him.

On the way I saw Celeste, and renewed, with some levity, a certain subject. It excited an agitation perfectly astonishing. The emotion was so great as to produce universal tremour, which attracted the notice of the company (there was a room full); I was exceedingly alarmed and perplexed, having imagined the denouement of last summer to have been conclusive, in good faith. Undoubtedly there is some secret agent, some underwork, perhaps restraint, of which I am ignorant. I strongly suspect that she has done violence to her feelings. Shall I or shall I not investigate this point? Humph! heighho!

I have just been visiting Monsieur Dubourg, president of the French College. The visit, indeed, was to the institution rather than to the man. Both please me greatly. It (the college) seems to me to possess some advantages over any other in the United States; more decorous subordination. The living languages, French and Spanish, may there be learned by association and habit. The French, the Spanish, the English (I mean the learners of those languages) are each in separate apartments. Not a word is spoken but in the language intended to be taught. It is even the medium of instruction for every other branch. The Senats speak Spanish fluently. *Bon soir.* A. BURR.

TO THOMAS SUMTER, JUN.

Washington, February 27, 1804.

DEAR SIR,

On my return from New-York a few days past, I had the pleasure to meet here your father, and to receive your letter of the 21st of January. It is not probable that it will be in my power to visit South Carolina this spring. If, fortunately, I should find leisure for a journey which I have so much at heart, my first object would be Statesburgh; but as Mr. and Mrs. Alston will be in New-York early in the season, I entertain hopes that this, with other motives, may induce you to pass the summer and autumn with me. Yet great as is my solicitude to see your wife and child, to renew my acquaintance with you, to tender you my friendship and affection, and to claim a return, I would by no means urge a measure inconsistent with your interest. Of this you only can judge. I should not, perhaps, have repeated the invitation expressed in my last letter to Natalie, but that I learn from your father that her health has suffered materially. Hence I am filled with apprehension of the effects of your long summer on a northern constitution already debilitated.

Presuming that you hear from your father as much as you desire to know of the doings of Congress, I abstain from those subjects. Be assured of the great consideration and esteem with which I am your friend,

A. Burr.

TO CHARLES BIDDLE.

Washington, March 3, 1804.

Your letter of the 28th February, covering a newspaper, was received last evening. It cannot yet be settled whether there will be commissioners to run the boundary line with Spain; but I will mention the thing to the Smiths, who still profess friendship for General Wilkinson. My direct interference otherwise would not probably be useful to him.

Please to put the enclosed, for Truxton, in the postoffice. One of his friends here (not a man in power, for he has, I believe, no such friend) thinks he will certainly be called into service; and he states to me pretty plausible grounds for the opinion. Yet I doubt, which is perhaps the result only of my ignorance.

I shall be with you the last of next week, or, at farthest, within ten days, on my way home.

Very affectionately yours,

A. Burr.

TO FREDERIC A. VANDERKEMP.

Washington, March 6, 1804.

Sir,

Immediately on the receipt of your letter of the 15th of February, I wrote to Mr. Madison for the information you desired. It affords me great pleasure to learn that you are engaged in a literary pursuit so congenial with your taste and your talents. If I can in any way promote your views in this or in any other instance, I entreat that you will command me, *without apology*. I have now the satisfaction to enclose you Mr. Madison's answer, which I this day received.

You speak of a letter written to me some time ago on the subject of Captain Ingraham's voyage. It is impossible, sir, that I can have been guilty of so gross an inattention as to have permitted a letter from you to have remained unnoticed. I have no recollection of that which you mention, and am persuaded that it never came to hand.

Allow me to repeat the assurance of the very great consideration and respect with which I am

Your obedient servant,

A. Burr.

TO WILLIAM P. VAN NESS.

Washington, March 7, 1804.

Friday last was the day assigned for the appearance of Judge Pickering on his impeachment. He did not appear; but an *amicus curiæ* suggested that the judge was insane, and tendered the proof of that fact.

This has given rise to some troublesome questions, rendered more embarrassing by the total want of rule or precedent, and still increased by some dissatisfaction on the part of the managers, which seems to have also infected the House of Representatives. In this dilemma it would be improper that I should leave the Senate. Considerations, however, of a nature which you will more readily approve, have had an influence in detaining me. A decision is hoped this day on the points now under discussion. I take my leave as soon as this business is disposed of, and will be with you in the course of mail-stage.

A. Burr.

TO THEODOSIA.

New-York, March 28, 1804

Your letter, dated early in this month—I don't recollect the very day, having left the letter in town; but you write so seldom that a reference to the month is sufficiently descriptive; your letter, then, of March, announcing your removal to the Oaks, the pretty description of your house and establishment, *and all that*, were very amusing. I had really begun to doubt whether you were not all dead or something worse.

I shall get the speech, no thanks to you; there is a copy in Philadelphia, for which I have written, and it will come endorsed by the fair hand of Celeste: truly her hand and arm are handsome. I did not see her on my way through —*tant mieux;* for I took great affront; thence ensued explanations, &c. Nothing like a quarrel to advance love. La Planche I did see twice in one day; the last a long, very long visit. Lovely in weeds. La G., of whom you inquire, is of the grave age of forty-six; about the age of the vice-president.

They are very busy here about an election between Morgan Lewis and A. Burr. The former supported by the Livingstons and Clintons, the latter *per se.* I would send you some new and amusing libels against the vice-president, but, as you did not send the speech, nor did even acknowledge the receipt of one of the many public documents which I *took the trouble* of forwarding, it may be presumed that this sort of intercourse is not desired.

Ph. Church and Miss Stewart, of Philadelphia, it is said, are to be married; Duer (which Duer I don't know) and Miss M. Denning reported as engaged; Bunner and Miss Church said to be mutually in love; on his part avowed, on hers not denied.

The Earl of Selkirk is here: a frank, unassuming, sensible man of about thirty. Whether he thinks of La R. is unknown to the writer. He dines with me on Monday.

If you had one particle of invention or genius, you would have taught A. B. A. his *a*, *b*, *c* before this. God mend you. His fibbing is an inheritance, which pride, an inheritance, will cure. His mother went through that process. Adieu. A. Burr.

TO THEODOSIA.

New-York, April 3, 1804.

I hasten to acknowledge your long, interesting, and beautiful letter of the 14th. It is received this morning, and finds me in the midst of occupations connected with the approaching election: of course, every moment interruptions.

The History of Frederic II. will amuse you. You will read Montesquieu with interest and instruction. Yet he has a character—I mean that his "*Esprit des Loix*" has a character above its merit. His historical facts are, nevertheless, collected and arranged with judgment, and his reasoning is ingenuous. The political dogmas are not, however, to be received as axioms. They are neither founded on experience nor on a knowledge of human nature.

You improve greatly in your style and manner of writing. A little more pains and a little more reading, and you will exceed Lady Mary W. Montague. Practice, however, is indispensable. The art of writing is an acquirement, as much as music or dancing.

April 7.

Since the 3d I have vainly endeavoured to get a minute to write to you. It will not, I fear, be possible before the 30th inst., when, or soon after, I hope to be in Philadelphia, whence you will hear from me. As you have a great taste for mischief, I send you a new paper* established in this city, by whom edited unknown. Some of the numbers are allowed to have wit. Whether these have any I know not. God bless thee. A. Burr.

* The Corrector, by *Toby Tickler*.

TO MRS. ———.

New-York, April 18, 1804.

Your vanity, if in any degree concerned, will be fully satisfied by the assurance that my heart, my wishes, and my thoughts will be with you. The mortal part of me is indispensably otherwise engaged. As you cannot fail to have admirers, you cannot fail to be amused. Knowing that you are happy, I shall be so by sympathy, though in a less degree, as reflected light is less potent than direct.

A. BURR.

TO THEODOSIA.

New-York, April 25, 1804.

What nice, pretty paper. I verily believe that it would not have entered into my head to write to you; but *Peet* or *Peter* just brought in a ream of paper so handsome looking, that it tempted me to write, and *chose* being generally uppermost in my mind, of course it will be addressed to *chose*, though, for aught that yet appears, it will suit as well *quelque autre chose*.

I, too, write in a storm; an election storm, of the like you have once been a witness. The thing began yesterday, and will terminate to-morrow. My headquarters are in John-street, and I have, since beginning this letter, been already three times interrupted.

A very modest and amiable proposition! that I should ride sixteen hundred miles to see a couple of *varmins*. As to your system of economy, I should rejoice at it if I believed it; but I well know that you will spend double at the Mills that you would here. Now for my plan, which is to be submitted to the judgment and the *feelings* of Mr. Alston.

You take Richmond Hill; bring no horse nor carriage. I have got a nice, new, beautiful little chariot, made purposely to please you. I have also a new coachee, very light, on an entire new construction, invented by the vice-president. Now these two machines are severally adapted to two

entire new construction, invented by the vice-president.
Now these two machines are severally adapted to two

horses, and you may take your choice of them. Of horses I have five; three always and wholly at your devotion, and the whole five occasionally. Harry and Sam are both good coachmen, either at your orders. Of servants there are enough for family purposes. Eleonore, however, must attend you, for the sake of the heir apparent. You will want no others, as there are at my house Peggy, Nancy, and a small girl of about eleven. Mr. Alston may bring a footman. Any thing further will be useless; he may, however, bring six or eight of them, if he like. The cellars and garrets are well stocked with wine, having had a great supply last fall. I shall take rooms (a house, &c.) in town, but will live with you as much or as little as you may please and as we can agree; but my establishment at Richmond Hill must remain, whether you come or not. Great part of the summer I shall be off eight or ten days at a time, but no long journeys. You will have to ride every day or two to Montalto to direct the laying out of the grounds, &c.

In this way you cannot, without wanton extravagance, expend more than four hundred dollars If you insist on bringing your horses, there is now room for them, and plenty of provender. You ought to come by water, but not to be swindled again by taking a cabin. Bring your Ada, if you please, to finish her education.

Tell Mr. Alston that I ordered my booksellers to open a correspondence with him, and to send out, by way of sample, and under the advice of M'Kinnon, not to exceed the value of fifty guineas. M'Kinnon writes me that the articles will be here by the first or before the middle of June, shipped for New-York.

I forgot to speak of the election.* Both parties claim majorities, and there never was, in my opinion, an election, of the result of which so little judgment could be formed. A. B. will have a small majority in this city *if to-morrow should be a fair day*, and not else.

* The election for governor, Morgan Lewis and Aaron Burr being the candi-

You may wonder how I live and mean to live in town. Peter and Alexis are all my attendants. My breakfast is made *a la garçon:* dinners, &c., from a neighbouring eating-house. Adieu.

A. Burr.

TO THEODOSIA.

New-York, May 1, 1804.

Your letter of the 16th of April had better luck than that other of the 1st.; on the road, I mean, for the reception of both was equally kind. The last arrived yesterday. I do not remember exactly what it is about, and it is on my table in the library up stairs, and I am writing in the dining-room beside a good fire on this evening of the first of May. Now *madame pour quelque chose tres interessante.*

How limited is human foresight! How truly are we the sport of accident. To-morrow I had proposed to visit Celeste, and now, alas! *cetera desunt.*

La G. may be forty-one. Something of the style and manners of *la tante de La* R. Is about as silly; talks as much, and as much nonsense; is certainly good-tempered and cheerful; rather comely, abating a flat chest; about two inches taller than Theodosia. Things are not gone to extremities; but there is danger—poor gampy.

The election is lost by a great majority: *tant mieux.* It does not appear possible that I should make you a visit; even if La G. should not prevent it, which ought to be hoped, some other thing of like kind will.

Tell Natalie that I have just now received her letter, which she acknowledges to be in answer to *four of mine.*

Of the boy you have been remarkably reserved in your two last letters. I conclude, however, that he cannot be dead, as you would, probably, have thought that a circumstance worthy of being mentioned, at least in a postscript. Now Natalie has written me a whole page about her girl, for which I am very grateful.

What would you bet that La G. is not in a kind of quandary just now? Gods! what a pathetic love-scene it will make if it shall go on. Adieu.

A. Burr.

TO MISS ——.

New-York, May 20, 1804.

I send you a sample of that species of philosophy which I have thought particularly suited to your cast of mind and the delicacy of your taste. You are to read from the 66th page to the 125th. What precedes and follows will fatigue, without interesting or amusing you. Indeed, some of it will not be very intelligible, and you must not be disgusted in the outset.

The author has not noticed those advantages which personal beauty derives from intellectual improvement, or expansion of the mind tempered by commerce with the world, nor how grace and expression may be thus heightened and improved. I wish some one would write a volume on this subject. Indeed, I have had thoughts of doing it myself, and holding you up as the example to verify my theory. To this some thoughtless ones may object, that, where nature had done so much, nothing was left for the work of art. There cannot be a greater error. The essential difference between the silly and the wise consists in their different capacity for improvement. Bestow what pains, offer what advantages you may to a dull subject, and she will remain stationary. One of taste and talents, on the contrary, extracts improvement from every thing, and approaches perfection in proportion as the means of advancement are afforded.

What grave nonsense, you will say, or at least think, if this should find you, as is probable, surrounded by admirers uniting to persuade you that you are already perfect; and in such company how stupid a compliment will it seem to tell you that you may still improve; that there are no limits to the improvement and approaches which you may make towards perfection. Such, however ungallant, will be the language of your admirer and friend,

A. BURR.

TO THEODOSIA.

New-York, May 8, 1804.

I think I have answered, or at least have noticed, your letter of the 17th, being the last which has been received, and, as usual, postmarked nine days after its date.

The affair of La G. is becoming serious. After due reflection, this does appear to me to be the most discreet thing —prudence, cheerfulness, and good-temper are ingredients of importance. I will offer homage. Are you content? Answer quickly.

Madame Bonaparte and husband are here. I have just seen them and no more. For reasons unknown to me (doubtless some state policy), we are suddenly become strangers.

Of all earthly things I most want to see your boy. Does he yet know his letters? If not, you surely must want skill, for, most certain, he can't want genius. You must tell me of all his acquirements.

It ought to have been mentioned that I have not seen my inamorata since the time of which I wrote you, which you may think passing strange.

May 26, 1804.

I think I will never again be so long without writing to you. It has been a daily and nightly reproach to me since the 8th of May, the date of the preceding part of this letter. The matter there spoken of seemed to be in so precarious a state, that I did not like to send you that page alone, and, in fact, knew not what to add to it. It is just so now; but from that day to this I have not seen La G., owing partly to accident and partly to apathy.

Your long and interesting letter of the 5th and 6th inst

has been received. It shall be answered anon. In the mean time I repeat the injunction that you read, and in sequence. Study philosophy, if nothing should more allure you. Darwin and Harris you have; others I will send. Read over Shakspeare critically, marking the passages which are beautiful, absurd, or obscure. I will do the same, and one of these days we will compare. To improve your style and language is, however, the most interesting point. In this you will be aided by regaining your Latin. Gods! how much you might accomplish this year.

Miss Cruger, youngest daughter of the late widow Cruger, now Mrs. Rogers, married two or three days ago to one of your Haywards, I think William. A runaway job. *La mere et beau pere bien fachés.* How far are you from Natalie?

A. BURR.

TO THEODOSIA.

New-York, June 11, 1804.

Your letter of the 14th of May is the last, and, I believe, unanswered, which is rather scandalous on both sides; but the letter of A. B. A., at the foot of yours, was far the most interesting. I have studied every pothook and trammel of his first literary performance, to see what rays of genius could be discovered. You remember our friend Schweitzer, nephew and pupil of Lavater. He used to insist that as much was to be inferred from the handwriting as from the face. I showed him a letter from a man of great fame, and he saw genius in every stroke. I then produced a letter from an arrant blockhead and great knave, but so like the other as not to be distinguished, at least by my unphysiognomical discernment. He acknowledged that there was resemblance to an ignorant eye; but, said he, triumphantly, this (latter) could never have made that scratch, which sybilistic scratch was the mere prolongation of the last letter of the last word in a sentence. Now it occurs to me that one of A. B. A.'s scratches is exactly in the line of genius according to Schweitzer; and surely more may be presumed from the instinctive effort of untutored infancy than from the laboured essay of scientific cultivation. To aid your observations in this line, I pray you to read Martinus Scriblerius. Mr. and Mrs. Hayward are happily living with the mother.

I am stationary (*not paper, wax, and quills*), but, adjectively speaking, unlocomotive. The affair of La G. has also been perfectly stationary since my last, the parties not having met; but hearing that La G. has expressed a sort of surprise, approaching to vexation, at this apathy, the other party has *kindly* promised an interview to-morrow. If it should take place, you will, in due time, know the result. Your permission or dissent is impatiently expected by

A. BURR.

TO THEODOSIA.

New-York, June 13, 1804.

The joint and several letter of Natalie and Theodosia was received yesterday, and will be answered to-morrow or next day. It seems that you write once a fortnight. Two such idle sluts might find half an hour daily to give a sort of journal to papa.

Another interview yesterday with La G. One more would be fatal and final. I shall seek it to-day; *after which* I will read Moore's fables, you impudence. My time, till near closing the mail, has been occupied in writing to your husband. At present I can only thank you both.

A. BURR.

TO THEODOSIA.

New-York, June 24, 1804.

"To-morrow, did I say? 'Tis nowhere to be found but in the fool's calendar;" and yet I said "to-morrow." The morrow brought me an ague in the face, which I have been nursing from that day to this, in great ill-humour. Till yesterday I could not dispense with my mufflings, and yesterday we kept Theo.'s birthday. The Laights and half a dozen others laughed an hour, and danced an hour, and drank her health at Richmond Hill. We had your picture in the dining-room; but, as it is a profile, and would not look at us, we hung it up, and placed Natalie's at table, which laughs and talks with us.

I do not like the boy looking pale so early in the season. It argues ill; but I like much his heroism and his gallantry. You can't think how much these little details amuse and interest me. If you were quite mistress of natural philosophy, he would now be hourly acquiring a knowledge of various branches, particularly natural history, botany, and chymistry. Pursue these studies, and also that of language. For fifty dollars you may get, in Philadelphia, a chymical apparatus, put up in a small box, with which more than one hundred experiments may be made.

Your idea of dressing up pieces of ancient mythology in the form of amusing tales for children is very good. You *yourself* must write them. Send your performances to me, and, within three weeks after they are received, you shall have them again in print. This will be not only an amusing occupation, but a very useful one to yourself. It will improve your style and your language, give you habits of accuracy, and add a little to your stock of knowledge. Natalie, too, must work at it, and I'll bet that she makes the best tale. I will be your editor and your critic.

You laugh at me so much and so impudently, that I will not say a word more of certain things till something be concluded. Your permission seems to be that I may hang or drown, or make any other apotheosis I may please. Dear indulgent creature, how I thank thee.

Pray, madam, give your orders to Peggy yourself. She writes a better hand than I do, and would be so proud to receive a letter from *Missy*. I have shown her that part of your letter which concerns her, and she is now engaged in executing your commands. A. BURR.

TO THEODOSIA.

New-York, July 1, 1801.

Having been shivering with cold all day, though in perfect health, I have now, just at sunset, had a fire in my library, and am sitting near it and enjoying it, if that word be applicable to any thing done in solitude. Some very wise man, however, has exclaimed,

"Oh! fools, who think it solitude to be alone."

This is but poetry. Let us, therefore, drop the subject, lest it lead to another on which I have imposed silence on myself.

You may recollect, and, if you do not, your husband will, that he has several times requested me to open a correspondence between him and my bookseller in London. To introduce the thing, I desired Mr. White to send with my next parcel of books a parcel for Mr. Alston, not exceeding the value of fifty guineas, and referred him to Mr. M'Kinnon for instructions. The books came out accordingly, and, with respect to my box, all was smooth and fair; but it was alleged by the owners of the ship and by the captain, that the box for Mr. Alston, having been irregularly shipped, occasioned the seizure and detention of the ship, and the owners refused to deliver the box unless I would pay thirty guineas damages. This I declined, and the box was taken to the custom-house, where it has lain these six weeks unopened. After the expiration of nine months it will be opened, and the contents sold at auction by order of the officers of the customs. I shall write to the bookseller, Mr. White, to employ his own agent here to look to the box as his property. This trifling tale would not have been told but to show Mr. Alston that I really have made an attempt to establish a correspondence for him.

You ought to be collecting a few books for your own use. One way of forming a small library, and which I recommend to you, is to note down the title of every book which, either from its reputation or from perusal, you may wish to possess. Make you a small memorandum book for this purpose. If they be written on loose scraps, by the time you get a dozen eleven of them will be lost. I recommend to you a new publication called the Edinburgh Review. One number is issued every three months. The plan of the editors differs from that of similar works in that they give more copious extracts, and notice only books of merit or *reputation.*

I wait impatiently for some of your tales. No hasty scrawls, madam, for I will correct nothing. We have now here three shiploads of South Carolinians, who all find the weather intolerably hot, though I have slept under a blanket every night except one in all June.

Jerome Bonaparte has taken Belvidere for the season. The two French frigates remain here blockaded. C. C. says you are a good-for-nothing, lazy ****** (I really cannot write her words; they are too dreadful, and must be left to your imagination to supply), because you never write to her, nor even answer her letters. I assented to all this.

All strangers go to see Montalto as one of the curiosities or beauties of the island. Your last letter is dated the 31st of May, whence I conclude that you submit to the labour of writing to me once a fortnight only.

A. BURR.

CHAPTER XVI.

In February, 1804, Colonel Burr was nominated, at a public meeting held in the city of New-York, as a candidate for the office of governor. At this meeting Colonel Marinus Willett presided as chairman, and Ezekiel Robbins acted as secretary. Both these gentlemen were well known as efficient members of the democratic party. Judge Morgan Lewis was the opposing and successful candidate. This contest was of an acrimonious character. While the great mass of the democratic party supported Judge Lewis, a section of that party, alike distinguished for their talents and patriotism, sustained Colonel Burr. Nor were these divisions confined to the ranks of the democracy. Among the federalists similar dissensions sprang up. General Hamilton, and all that portion of politicians over whom he had a controlling influence, opposed the election of Colonel Burr with an ardour bordering on fanaticism. The press teemed with libels of the most atrocious character. An event connected with this election has rendered it memorable in the history of our state and country. A letter, written by Dr. Charles D. Cooper, and published pending the election, ultimately led to the hostile and fatal meeting between General Hamilton and Colonel Burr. Immediately after the death of the former gentleman, Judge William P. Van Ness, the second of Colonel Burr, published the correspondence between the parties, with a statement of the conversations he held with General Hamilton and Judge Pendleton, the second of the general. As their accuracy has never been called in question, they are now presented in the form in which they then appeared.

STATEMENT.

On the afternoon of the 17th of June last (1804), says Judge Van Ness, I received a note from Colonel Burr* requesting me to call on him the following morning. Upon my arrival he alleged that it had, of late, been frequently stated to him that General Hamilton had, at different times and upon various occasions, used language and expressed opinions highly injurious to his reputation; that he had for some time felt the necessity of calling on General Hamilton for an explanation of his conduct, but that the statements which had been made to him did not appear sufficiently authentic to justify the measure; that a newspaper had, however, been recently put into his hands, in which he perceived a letter signed Charles D. Cooper, containing something which he thought demanded immediate investigation. Urged by these circumstances, and justified by the evident opinion of his friends, he had determined to write General Hamilton a note upon the subject, which he requested me to deliver. I assented to this request, and, on my return to the city, which was at eleven o'clock the same morning, I delivered to General Hamilton the note which I received from Colonel Burr for that purpose, and of which the following is a copy.

No. I.

New-York, June 18, 1804.

SIR,

I send for your perusal a letter signed Charles D. Cooper, which, though apparently published some time ago, has but very recently come to my knowledge. Mr. Van Ness, who does me the favour to deliver this, will point out to you that clause of the letter to which I particularly request your attention.

* Colonel Burr then resided at Richmond Hill.

You must perceive, sir, the necessity of a prompt and unqualified acknowledgment or denial of the use of any expressions which would warrant the assertions of Mr. Cooper.

I have the honour to be

Your obedient servant,

A. Burr.

General Hamilton.

General Hamilton read the note of Mr. Burr, and the printed letter of Mr. Cooper to which it refers, and remarked that they required some consideration, and that in the course of the day he would send an answer to my office. At half past ten o'clock General Hamilton called at my house, and said that a variety of engagements would demand his attention during the whole of that day and the next; but that on Wednesday, the 20th inst., he would furnish me with such an answer to Colonel Burr's letter as he should deem most suitable and compatible with his feelings. In the evening of Wednesday, the 20th, while I was from home, the following letter, addressed to Colonel Burr, was left at my house, under cover to me.

No. II.

New-York, June 20, 1804.

Sir,

I have maturely reflected on the subject of your letter of the 18th inst., and the more I have reflected the more I have become convinced that I could not, without manifest impropriety, make the avowal or disavowal which you seem to think necessary. The clause pointed out by Mr. Van Ness is in these terms: "I could detail to you *a still more despicable* opinion which General Hamilton *has expressed* of Mr. Burr." To endeavour to discover the meaning of this declaration, I was obliged to seek in the antecedent part of this letter for the opinion to which it referred as having been already disclosed. I found it in these words: "General Hamilton and Judge Kent have declared, in *substance*, that they looked upon Mr. Burr to be a *dangerous man*, and one *who ought not to be trusted with the reins of government.*"

The language of Doctor Cooper plainly implies that *he* considered this opinion of you, which he attributes to me, as a *despicable* one; but he affirms that I have expressed some other *more despicable*, without, however, mentioning to whom, when, or where. 'Tis evident that the phrase "still more despicable" admits of infinite shades, from very light to very dark. How am I to judge of the degree intended? Or how shall I annex any precise idea to language so indefinite?

Between gentlemen, *despicable* and *more despicable* are not worth the pains of distinction; when, therefore, you do not interrogate me as to the opinion which is specifically ascribed to me, I must conclude that you view it as within the limits to which the animadversions of political opponents upon each other may justifiably extend, and, consequently, as not warranting the idea which Doctor Cooper appears to entertain. If so, what precise inference could you draw as a guide for your conduct, were I to acknowledge that I had expressed an opinion of you *still more despicable* than the one which is particularized? How could you be sure that even this opinion had exceeded the bounds which you would yourself deem admissible between political opponents?

But I forbear further comment on the embarrassment to which the requisition you have made naturally leads. The occasion forbids a more ample illustration, though nothing could be more easy than to pursue it.

Repeating that I cannot reconcile it with propriety to make the acknowledgment or denial you desire, I will add, that I deem it inadmissible, on principle, to consent to be interrogated as to the justice of the *inferences* which may be drawn by others from whatever I have said of a political opponent in the course of fifteen years competition. If there were no other objection to it, this is sufficient, that it would tend to expose my sincerity and delicacy to injurious imputations from every person who may at any time have conceived the *import* of my expressions differently from what I may then have intended or may afterward recollect. I stand ready to avow or disavow promptly and explicitly any precise or definite opinion which I may be charged with having declared of any gentleman. More than this cannot fitly be expected from me; and, especially, it cannot be reasonably expected that I shall enter into any explanation upon a basis so vague as that you have adopted. I trust, on more reflection, you will see the matter in the same light with me. If not, I can only regret the circumstance, and must abide the consequences.

The publication of Doctor Cooper was never seen by me till after the receipt of your letter. I have the honour to be, &c., A. HAMILTON.

Colonel BURR.

On the morning of Thursday, the 21st, I delivered to Colonel Burr the above letter, and, in the evening, was furnished with the following letter for General Hamilton, which I delivered to him at 12 o'clock on Friday, the 22d inst.

No. III.

New-York, June 21, 1804.

SIR,

Your letter of the 20th inst. has been this day received. Having considered it attentively, I regret to find in it nothing of that sincerity and delicacy which you profess to value.

Political opposition can never absolve gentlemen from the necessity of a rigid adherence to the laws of honour and the rules of decorum. I neither claim such privilege nor indulge it in others.

The common sense of mankind affixes to the epithet

dulge it in others.
The common sense of mankind affixes to the epithet
38 N 3

adopted by Doctor Cooper the idea of dishonour. It has been publicly applied to me under the sanction of your name. The question is not whether he has understood the meaning of the word, or has used it according to syntax and with grammatical accuracy, but whether you have authorized this application, either directly or by uttering expressions or opinions derogatory to my honour. The time "when" is in your own knowledge, but no way material to me, as the calumny has now first been disclosed so as to become the subject of my notice, and as the effect is present and palpable.

Your letter has furnished me with new reasons for requiring a definite reply.

I have the honour to be,
Sir, your obedient
A. Burr.

General Hamilton.

General Hamilton perused it, and said it was such a letter as he had hoped not to have received; that it contained several offensive expressions, and seemed to close the door to all further reply; that he had hoped the answer he had returned to Colonel Burr's first letter would have given a different direction to the controversy; that he thought Mr. Burr would have perceived that there was a difficulty in his making a more specific reply, and would have desired him to state what had fallen from him that might have given rise to the inference of Doctor Cooper. He would have done this frankly; and he believed it would not have been found to exceed the limits justifiable among political opponents. If Mr. Burr should be disposed to give a different complexion to the discussion, he was willing to consider the last letter not delivered; but if that communication was not withdrawn, he could make no reply, and Mr. Burr must pursue such course as he should deem most proper.

At the request of General Hamilton, I replied that I would

detail these ideas to Colonel Burr; but added, that if in his first letter he had introduced the idea (if it was a correct one) that he could recollect of no terms that would justify the construction made by Dr. Cooper, it would, in my opinion, have opened a door for accommodation. General Hamilton then repeated the same objections to this measure which were stated in substance in his first letter to Colonel Burr.

When I was about leaving him he observed, that if I preferred it, he would commit his refusal to writing. I replied, that if he had resolved not to answer Colonel Burr's letter, that I could report that to him verbally, without giving him the trouble of writing it. He again repeated his determination not to answer; and that Colonel Burr must pursue such course as he should deem most proper.

In the afternoon of this day I reported to Colonel Burr, at his house out of town, the answer and the determination of General Hamilton, and promised to call on him again in the evening to learn his further wishes. I was detained in town, however, this evening, by some private business, and did not call on Colonel Burr until the following morning, Saturday, the 23d June. I then received from him a letter for General Hamilton, which is numbered IV.; but, as will presently be explained, never was delivered. The substance of it will be found in number XII.

When I returned with this letter to the city, which was about two o'clock in the afternoon of the same day, I sent a note to General Hamilton's office, and also to his house, desiring to know when it would be convenient to him to receive a communication. The servant, as he informed me, received for answer at both places that General Hamilton had gone to his country seat. I then wrote the note of which No. V. is a copy, and sent it out to him in the country.

No. V.

June 23, 1804.

SIR,

In the afternoon of yesterday I reported to Colonel Burr the result of my last interview with you, and appointed the evening to receive his further instructions. Some private engagements, however, prevented me from calling on him till this morning. On my return to the city, I found, upon inquiry, both at your office and house, that you had returned to your residence in the country. Lest an interview there might be less agreeable to you than elsewhere, I have taken the liberty of addressing you this note, to inquire when and where it will be most convenient to you to receive a communication.

Your most obedient and very humble servant,

W. P. VAN NESS.

General HAMILTON.

To this I received for answer No. VI., which follows.

No. VI.

Grange, June 23, 1804.

SIR,

I was in town to-day till half past one. I thank you for the delicacy which dictated your note to me. If it is indispensable the communication should be made before Monday morning, I must receive it here; but I should think this cannot be important. On Monday, by nine o'clock, I shall be in town at my house in Cedar-street, No. 52, where I should be glad to see you. An additional reason for preferring this is, that I am unwilling to occasion you trouble.

With esteem I am your obedient servant,

A. HAMILTON.

At nine o'clock on Monday, the 25th of June, I called on General Hamilton, at his house in Cedar-street, to present the letter No. IV. already alluded to, and with instructions for a verbal communication, of which the following notes, No. VII., handed me by Mr. Burr, were to be the basis. The substance of which, though in terms as much softened as my injunctions would permit, was accordingly communicated to General Hamilton.

No. VII.

A. Burr, far from conceiving that rivalship authorizes a latitude not otherwise justifiable, always feels greater delicacy in such cases, and would think it meanness to speak of a rival but in terms of respect; to do justice to his merits; to be silent of his foibles. Such has invariably been his conduct towards Jay, Adams, and Hamilton; the only three who can be supposed to have stood in that relation to him.

That he has too much reason to believe that, in regard to Mr. Hamilton, there has been no reciprocity. For several years his name has been lent to the support of base slanders. He has never had the generosity, the magnanimity, or the candour to contradict or disavow. Burr forbears to particularize, as it could only tend to produce new irritations; but, having made great sacrifices for the sake of harmony; having exercised forbearance until it approached to humiliation, he has seen no effect produced by such conduct but a repetition of injury. He is obliged to conclude that there is, on the part of Mr. Hamilton, a settled and implacable malevolence; that he will never cease, in his conduct towards Mr. Burr, to violate those courtesies of life; and that, hence, he has no alternative but to announce these things to the world; which, consistently with Mr. Burr's ideas of propriety, can be done in no way but that which he has adopted. He is incapable of revenge, still less is he capable of imitating the conduct of Mr. Hamilton, by committing secret depredations on his fame and character. But these things must have an end.

Before I delivered the written communication with which

I was charged, General Hamilton said that he had prepared a written reply to Colonel Burr's letter of the 21st, which he had left with Mr. Pendleton, and wished me to receive. I answered, that the communication I had to make to him was predicated upon the idea that he would make no reply to Mr. Burr's letter of the 21st of June, and that I had so understood him in our conversation of the 22d. General Hamilton said that he believed, before I left him, he had proffered a written reply. I observed that, when he answered verbally, he had offered to put that *refusal* in writing; but that, if he had now prepared a written reply, I would receive it with pleasure. I accordingly called on Mr. Pendleton on the same day (Monday, June 25th), between *one* and *two* o'clock P. M., and stated to him the result of my recent interview with General Hamilton, and the reference he had made to him.

I then received from Mr. Pendleton No. VIII., which follows:—

No. VIII.

New-York, June 22, 1804.

Sir,

Your first letter, in a style too peremptory, made a demand, in my opinion, unprecedented and unwarrantable. My answer, pointing out the embarrassment, gave you an opportunity to take a less exceptionable course. You have not chosen to do it; but, by your last letter, received this day, containing expressions *indecorous* and improper, you have increased the difficulties to explanation intrinsically incident to the nature of your application.

If by a "definite reply" you mean the direct avowal or disavowal required in your first letter, I have no other answer to give than that which has already been given. If you mean any thing different, admitting of greater latitude, it is requisite you should explain.

I have the honour to be, sir, your obedient servant,

Alex. Hamilton.

A. Burr, Esq.

This letter was unsealed, but I did not read it in his presence. After some conversation relative to what General Hamilton would say on the subject of the present controversy, during which Mr. Pendleton read from a paper his ideas on the subject, he left me for the purpose of seeing and consulting Mr. Hamilton, taking the paper with him. In about an hour he called at my house. I informed him that I had shown to Colonel Burr the letter he had given me from General Hamilton; that, in his opinion, it amounted to nothing more than the verbal reply I had already reported; that it left the business precisely where it then was; that Mr. Burr had very explicitly stated the injuries he had received and the reparation he demanded, and that he did not think it proper to be asked now for further explanation. Towards the conclusion of the conversation I informed him that Colonel Burr required a general disavowal of any intention, on the part of General Hamilton, in his various conversations, to convey expressions derogatory to the honour of Mr. Burr. Mr. Pendleton replied that he believed General Hamilton would have no objections to make such declaration, and left me for the purpose of consulting him, requesting me to call in the course of the afternoon for an answer. I called on him, accordingly, about six o'clock. He then observed that General Hamilton declined making such a disavowal as I had stated in our last conversation; that he, Mr. Pendleton, did not then perceive the whole force and extent of it; and presented me with the following paper, No. IX., which I transmitted in the evening to Mr. Burr.

No. IX.

In answer to a letter properly adapted to obtain from General Hamilton a declaration whether he had charged Colonel Burr with any particular instance of dishonourable conduct, or had impeached his private character either in the conversation alluded to by Doctor Cooper, or in any other particular instance to be specified, he would be able to answer consistently with his honour and the truth, in substance, that the conversation to which Doctor Cooper alluded turned wholly on political topics, and did not attribute to Colonel Burr any instance of dishonourable conduct, nor relate to his private character; and in relation to any other language or conversation of General Hamilton which Colonel Burr will specify, a prompt and frank avowal or denial will be given.

The following day (Tuesday, 26th June), as early as was convenient, I had an interview with Colonel Burr, who informed me that he considered General Hamilton's proposition a mere evasion, that evinced a desire to leave the injurious impressions which had arisen from the conversations of General Hamilton in full force; that when he had undertaken to investigate an injury his honour had sustained, it would be unworthy of him not to make that investigation complete. He gave me further instructions, which are substantially contained in the following letter to Mr. Pendleton, No. X.

No. X.

June 26, 1804.

SIR,

The letter which you yesterday delivered to me, and your subsequent communication, in Colonel Burr's opinion, evince no disposition, on the part of General Hamilton, to come to a satisfactory accommodation. The injury complained of and the reparation expected are so definitely expressed in Colonel Burr's letter of the 21st instant, that there is not perceived a necessity for further explanation on his part. The difficulty that would result from confining the inquiry to any particular times and occasions must be manifest. The denial of a specified conversation only would leave strong implication that on other occasions improper language had been used. When and where injurious opinions and expressions had been uttered by General Hamilton must be best known to him, and of him only will Colonel Burr inquire. No denial or declaration will be satisfactory unless it be general, so as wholly to exclude the idea that rumours derogatory to Colonel Burr's honour has originated with General Hamilton, or have been fairly inferred from any thing he has said. A definite reply to a requisition of this nature was demanded by Colonel Burr's letter of the 21st instant. This being refused, invites the alternative alluded to in General Hamilton's letter of the 20th.

It was required by the position in which the controversy was placed by General Hamilton on Friday (June 22d) last, and I was immediately furnished with a communication demanding a personal interview. The necessity of this measure has not, in the opinion of Colonel Burr, been diminished by the general's last letter, or any communication which has since been received. I am, consequently, again instructed to deliver you a message as soon as it may be convenient for you to receive it. I beg, therefore, you will be so good as to inform me at what hour I can have the pleasure of seeing you.

Your most obedient and humble servant,

W. P. Van Ness.

Nathaniel Pendleton, Esq.

In the evening of the same day I received from him the following answer:—

No. XI.

June 26, 1804.

Sir,

I have communicated the letter which you did me the honour to write to me of this date, to General Hamilton. The expectations now disclosed on the part of Colonel Burr appear to him to have greatly extended the original ground of inquiry, and, instead of presenting a particular and definite case for explanation, seem to aim at nothing less than an inquisition into his most confidential conversations, as

nite case for explanation, seem to aim at nothing less than an inquisition into his most confidential conversations, as
39

well as others, through the whole period of his acquaintance with Colonel Burr.

While he was prepared to meet the particular case fairly and fully, he thinks it inadmissible that he should be expected to answer at large as to every thing that he may possibly have said in relation to the character of Colonel Burr at any time or upon any occasion. Though he is not conscious that any charges which are in circulation to the prejudice of Colonel Burr have originated with him, except one which may have been so considered, and which has long since been fully explained between Colonel Burr and himself, yet he cannot consent to be questioned generally as to any rumours which may be afloat derogatory to the character of Colonel Burr, without specification of the several rumours, many of them, probably, unknown to him. He does not, however, mean to authorize any conclusion as to the real nature of his conduct in relation to Colonel Burr by his declining so loose and vague a basis of explanation, and he disavows an unwillingness to come to a satisfactory, provided it be an honourable, accommodation. His objection is the very indefinite ground which Colonel Burr has assumed, in which he is sorry to be able to discern nothing short of predetermined hostility. Presuming, therefore, that it will be adhered to, he has instructed me to receive the message which you have it in charge to deliver. For this purpose I shall be at home and at your command to-morrow morning from eight to ten o'clock.

I have the honour to be, respectfully,

Your obedient servant,

NATHANIEL PENDLETON.

WM. P. VAN NESS, Esq.

I transmitted this to Colonel Burr; and, after a conference with him, in which I received his further instructions, and that no misunderstanding might arise from verbal communication, I committed to writing the remarks contained in No. XII., which follows:

No. XII.

Wednesday morning, June 27, 1804.

SIR,

The letter which I had the honour to receive from you, under date of yesterday, states, among other things, that, in General Hamilton's opinion, Colonel Burr has taken a very indefinite ground, in which he evinces nothing short of predetermined hostility, and General Hamilton thinks it inadmissible that the inquiry should extend to his confidential as well as other conversations. To this Colonel Burr can only reply, that secret whispers traducing his fame and impeaching his honour are at least equally injurious with slanders publicly uttered; that General Hamilton had, at no time and in no place, a right to use any such injurious expression; and that the partial negative he is disposed to give, with the reservations he wishes to make, are proofs that he has done the injury specified.

Colonel Burr's request was, in the first instance, proposed in a form the most simple, in order that General Hamilton might give to the affair that course to which he might be induced by his temper and his knowledge of facts. Colonel Burr trusted with confidence, that, from the frankness of a soldier and the candour of a gentleman, he might expect an ingenuous declaration. That if, as he had reason to believe, General Hamilton had used expressions derogatory to his honour, he would have had the magnanimity to retract them; and that if, from his language, injurious inferences had been improperly drawn, he would have perceived the propriety of correcting errors which might thus have been widely diffused. With these impressions Colonel Burr was greatly surprised at receiving a letter which he considered as evasive, and which, in manner, he deemed not altogether decorous. In one expectation, however, he was not wholly

as evasive, and which, in manner, he deemed not altogether decorous. In one expectation, however, he was not wholly deceived; for the close of General Hamilton's letter contained an intimation that, if Colonel Burr should dislike his refusal to acknowledge or deny, he was ready to meet the consequences. This Colonel Burr deemed a sort of defiance, and would have felt justified in making it the basis of an immediate message; but, as the communication contained something concerning the indefiniteness of the request; as he believed it rather the offspring of false pride than of reflection; and as he felt the utmost reluctance to proceed to extremities while any other hope remained, his request was repeated in terms more explicit. The replies and propositions on the part of General Hamilton have, in Colonel Burr's opinion, been constantly, in substance, the same.

Colonel Burr disavows all motives of predetermined hostility, a charge by which he thinks insult added to injury. He feels as a gentleman should when his honour is impeached or assailed; and, without sensations of hostility or wishes of revenge, he is determined to vindicate that honour at such hazard as the nature of the case demands.

The length to which this correspondence has extended only tending to prove that the satisfactory redress, earnestly desired, cannot be attained, he deems it useless to offer any proposition except the single message which I shall now have the honour to deliver.

With great respect, your obedient servant,

W. P. Van Ness.

Nathaniel Pendleton, Esq.

I handed this to Mr. Pendleton at twelve o'clock on Wednesday the 27th. After he had perused it, agreeable to my instructions, I delivered the message which it is unnecessary to repeat. The request it contained was acceded to. After which Mr. Pendleton remarked that a court was then sitting in which General Hamilton had much business to transact, and that he had also some private arrangements to make, which would render some delay unavoidable. I acceded to his wish, and Mr. Pendleton said he would call on me again in the course of the day or the following morning, to confer further relative to time and place.

Thursday, June 28th, ten o'clock P. M., Mr. Pendleton called on me with a paper which he said contained some views of General Hamilton, and which he had received from him. I replied, that if the paper contained a definite and specific proposition for an accommodation, I would with pleasure receive it, and submit it to the consideration of my principal; if not, that I must decline taking it, as Mr. Burr conceived the correspondence completely terminated by the acceptance of the invitation contained in the message I had yesterday delivered. Mr. Pendleton replied that the paper did not contain any proposition of the kind I alluded to, but remarks on my last letter. I, of course, declined receiving it. Mr. Pendleton then took leave, and said that he would call again in a day or two to arrange time and place.

Tuesday, July 3d, I again saw Mr. Pendleton; and, after a few subsequent interviews, the time when the parties were to meet was ultimately fixed for the morning of the 11th of July instant. The occurrences of that interview will appear from the following statement, No. XIII., which has been drawn up and mutually agreed to by the seconds of the parties.

No. XIII.

Colonel Burr arrived first on the ground, as had been previously agreed. When General Hamilton arrived, the parties exchanged salutations, and the seconds proceeded to make their arrangements. They measured the distance, ten full paces, and cast lots for the choice of position, as also to determine by whom the word should be given, both of which fell to the second of General Hamilton. They then proceeded to load the pistols in each other's presence, after which the parties took their stations. The gentleman who was to give the word then explained to the parties the rules which were to govern them in firing, which were as follows: "The parties being placed at their stations, the second who gives the word shall ask them whether they are ready; being answered in the affirmative, he shall say—*present!* After this the parties shall present and fire *when they please.* If one fires before the other, the opposite second shall say *one, two, three, fire,* and he shall then fire or lose his fire. He then asked if they were prepared; being answered in the affirmative, he gave the word *present,* as had been agreed on, and both parties presented and fired in succession. The intervening time is not expressed, as the seconds do not precisely agree on that point. The fire of Colonel Burr took effect, and General Hamilton almost instantly fell. Colonel Burr advanced towards General Hamilton with a manner and gesture that appeared to General Hamilton's friend to be expressive of regret; but, without speaking, turned about and withdrew, being urged from the field by his friend, as has been subsequently stated, with a view to prevent his being recognised by the surgeon and bargemen who were then approaching. No further communication took place between the principals, and the barge that carried Colonel Burr immediately returned to the city. We conceive it proper to add, that the conduct of the parties in this interview was perfectly proper, as suited the occasion."

In the interviews between Mr. Pendleton and Mr. Van Ness, they were not able to agree in two important facts that passed on the ground. "Mr. Pendleton expressed a confident opinion that General Hamilton did not fire first, and that he did not fire at all at Colonel Burr. Mr. Van Ness seemed equally confident in opinion that General Hamilton did fire first; and, of course, that it must have been *at* his antagonist."

Such was the statement made by the friend of Colonel Burr. It is now proposed to insert such explanations of, or remarks on, the communications between the parties as emanated from the friend of General Hamilton. None were given previous to document No. III. Immediately after that letter, dated 21st June, are the following remarks:—

"On Saturday, the 22d of June, General Hamilton for the first time called on Mr. Pendleton, and communicated to him the preceding correspondence. He informed him that, in a conversation with Mr. Van Ness at the time of receiving the last letter (No. III.), he told Mr. Van Ness that he considered that letter as rude and offensive, and that it was not possible for him to give any other answer than that Mr. Burr must take such steps as he might think proper. He said, further, that Mr. Van Ness requested him to take time to deliberate, and then return an answer, when he might possibly entertain a different opinion, and that he would call on him to receive it. That his reply to Mr. Van Ness was, that he did not perceive it possible for him to give any other answer than that he had mentioned, unless Mr. Burr would take back his last letter, and write one which would admit of a different reply. He then gave Mr. Pendleton the letter hereafter mentioned of the 22d of June, to be delivered to Mr. Van Ness when he should call on Mr. Pendleton for an answer, and went to his country house."

[After No. V., dated June 23d, is the following:—]

"Mr. Pendleton understood from General Hamilton that he immediately answered that, if the communication was pressing, he would receive it at his country house that day; if not, he would be at his house in town the next morning at nine o'clock. But he did not give Mr. Pendleton any copy of this note."

[After No. VIII., dated June 22d, is the following:—]

"This letter, although dated on the 22d of June, remained in Mr. Pendleton's possession until the 25th, within which period he had several conversations with Mr. Van Ness. In these conversations Mr. Pendleton endeavoured to illustrate and enforce the propriety of the ground General Hamilton had taken. Mr. Pendleton mentioned to Mr. Van Ness

trate and enforce the propriety of the ground General Hamilton had taken. Mr. Pendleton mentioned to Mr. Van Ness as the result, that if Colonel Burr would write a letter, requesting to know, in substance, whether, in the conversation to which Dr. Cooper alluded, any particular instance of dishonourable conduct was imputed to Colonel Burr, or whether there was any impeachment of his private character, General Hamilton would declare, to the best of his recollection, what passed in that conversation; and Mr. Pendleton read to Mr. Van Ness a paper containing the substance of what General Hamilton would say on that subject, which is as follows:—

"General Hamilton says he cannot imagine to what Doctor Cooper may have alluded, unless it were to a conversation at Mr. Taylor's, in Albany, last winter (at which he and General Hamilton were present). General Hamilton cannot recollect distinctly the particulars of that conversation, so as to undertake to repeat them without running the risk of varying, or omitting what might be deemed important circumstances. The expressions are entirely forgotten, and the specific ideas imperfectly remembered; but, to the best of his recollection, it consisted of comments on the political principles and views of Colonel Burr, and the results that might be expected from them in the event of his election as governor, without reference to any particular instance of past conduct or to private character."

"After the delivery of the letter of the 22d, as above mentioned, in another interview with Mr. Van Ness, he desired Mr. Pendleton to give him, *in writing*, the substance of what he had proposed on the part of General Hamilton, which Mr. Pendleton did, in the following words." [See No. IX.]

[After No. XII., dated June 27th, is the following:—]

"With this letter a message was received, such as was to be expected, containing an invitation which was accepted, and Mr. Pendleton informed Mr. Van Ness he should hear from him the next day as to further particulars.

"This letter was delivered to General Hamilton on the same evening, and a very short conversation ensued between him and Mr. Pendleton, who was to call on him early the next morning for a further conference. When he did so, General Hamilton said he had not understood whether the message and answer was definitively concluded, or whether another meeting was to take place for that purpose between Mr. Pendleton and Mr. Van Ness. Under the latter impression, and as the last letter contained matter that naturally led to animadversion, he gave Mr. Pendleton a paper of remarks in his own handwriting, to be communicated to Mr. Van Ness, if the state of the affair rendered it proper.

"In an interview with Mr. Van Ness on the same day, after explaining the causes which had induced General Hamilton to suppose that the state of the affair did not render it improper, Mr. Pendleton offered this paper to Mr. Van Ness, but he declined receiving it, alleging that he considered the correspondence as closed by the acceptance of the message that he had delivered.

"Mr. Pendleton then informed Mr. Van Ness of the inducements mentioned by General Hamilton in the paper for at least postponing the meeting until the close of the circuit; and, as this was uncertain, Mr. Pendleton was to let him know when it would be convenient."

Remarks on the letter of June 27, 1804, which Mr. Van Ness declined to receive.

"Whether the observations on this letter are designed merely to justify the result which is indicated in the close of the letter, or may be intended to give an opening for rendering any thing explicit which may have been deemed vague heretofore, can only be judged of by the sequel. At any rate, it appears to me necessary not to be misunderstood. Mr. Pendleton is therefore authorized to say, that in the course of the present discussion, written or verbal, there has been no intention to evade, defy, or insult, but a sincere disposition to avoid extremities, if it could be done with propriety. With this view General Hamilton has been ready to enter into a frank and free explanation on any and every object of a specific nature; but not to answer a general and abstract inquiry, embracing a period too long for any accurate recollection, and exposing him to unpleasant criticisms from, or unpleasant discussions with, any and every person who may have understood him in an unfavourable sense. This (admitting that he could answer in a manner the most satisfactory to Colonel Burr) he should deem inadmissible in principle and precedent, and humiliating in practice. To this, therefore, he can never submit. Frequent allusion has been made to slanders said to be in circulation. Whether they are openly or in whispers, they have a form and shape, and might be specified."

"If the alternative alluded to in the close of the letter is definitively tendered, it must be accepted; the time, place, and manner to be afterward regulated. I should not think it right, in the midst of a circuit court, to withdraw my services from those who may have confided important interests to me, and expose them to the embarrassment of seeking other counsel, who may not have time to be sufficiently instructed in their causes. I shall also want a little time to make some arrangements respecting my own affairs."

"On Friday, the 6th of July, the circuit being closed, Mr. Pendleton informed Mr. Van Ness that General Hamilton would be ready at any time after the Sunday following. On Monday the particulars were arranged. On Wednesday the parties met at Weehawk, on the Jersey shore, at seven o'clock A. M. The particulars of what then took place appear in the statement, as agreed upon and corrected by the seconds of the parties." [See No. XIII.]

DOCTOR DAVID HOSACK TO WILLIAM COLEMAN.

August 17, 1804.

Dear Sir,

To comply with your request is a painful task; but I will repress my feelings while I endeavour to furnish you with an enumeration of such particulars relative to the melancholy end of our beloved friend Hamilton as dwell most forcibly on my recollection.

When called to him upon his receiving the fatal wound, I found him half sitting on the ground, supported in the arms of Mr. Pendleton. His countenance of death I shall never forget. He had at that instant just strength to say, "This is a mortal wound, doctor;" when he sunk away, and became to all appearance lifeless. I immediately stripped up his clothes, and soon, alas! ascertained that the direction of the ball must have been through some vital part.* His pulses were not to be felt, his respiration was entirely suspended, and, upon laying my hand on his heart and perceiving no motion there, I considered him as irrecoverably gone. I, however, observed to Mr. Pendleton, that the only chance for his reviving was immediately to get him upon the water. We therefore lifted him up, and carried him out of the wood to the margin of the bank, where the bargemen aided us in conveying him into the boat, which immediately put off. During all this time I could not discover the least symptom of returning life. I now rubbed his face, lips, and temples with spirits of hartshorn, applied it to his neck and breast, and to the wrists and palms of his hands, and endeavoured to pour some into his mouth. When we had got, as I should judge, about fifty yards from the shore, some imperfect efforts to breathe were for the first time manifest; in a few minutes he sighed, and became sensible to the impression of the hartshorn or the fresh air of the water. He breathed; his eyes, hardly opened, wandered, without fixing upon any object; to our great joy, he at length spoke.

* For the satisfaction of some of General Hamilton's friends, I examined his body after death, in presence of Dr. Post and two other gentlemen. I discovered that the ball struck the second or third false rib, and fractured it about in the middle; it then passed through the liver and diaphragm, and, as far as we could ascertain without a minute examination, lodged in the first or second lumbar vertebra. The vertebra in which it was lodged was considerably splintered, so that the spiculæ were distinctly perceptible to the finger. About a pint of clotted blood was found in the cavity of the belly, which had probably been effused from the divided vessels of the liver.

"My vision is indistinct," were his first words. His pulse became more perceptible, his respiration more regular, his sight returned. I then examined the wound to know if there was any dangerous discharge of blood; upon slightly pressing his side it gave him pain, on which I desisted. Soon after recovering his sight, he happened to cast his eye upon the case of pistols, and observing the one that he had had in his hand lying on the outside, he said, "Take care of that pistol; it is undischarged, and still cocked; it may go off and do harm. Pendleton knows" (attempting to turn his head towards him) "that I did not intend to fire at him." "Yes," said Mr. Pendleton, understanding his wish, "I have already made Dr. Hosack acquainted with your determination as to that." He then closed his eyes and remained calm, without any disposition to speak; nor did he say much afterward, except in reply to my questions. He asked me once or twice how I found his pulse; and he informed me that his lower extremities had lost all feeling, manifesting to me that he entertained no hopes that he should long survive. I changed the posture of his limbs, but to no purpose; they had entirely lost their sensibility. Perceiving that we approached the shore, he said, "Let Mrs. Hamilton be immediately sent for; let the event be gradually broken to her, but give her hopes." Looking up we saw his friend, Mr. Bayard, standing on the wharf in great agitation. He had been told by his servant that General Hamilton, Mr. Pendleton, and myself had crossed the river in a boat together, and too well he conjectured the fatal errand, and foreboded the dreadful result. Perceiving, as we came nearer, that Mr. Pendleton and myself only sat up in the stern sheets, he clasped his hands together in the most violent apprehension; but when I called to him to have a cot prepared, and he at the same moment saw his poor friend lying in the bottom of the boat, he threw up his eyes and burst into a flood of tears and lamentation. Hamilton alone appeared tranquil and composed. We then conveyed him as tenderly as possible up to the house. The distresses of this amiable family were such that, till the first shock was abated, they were scarcely able to summon fortitude enough to yield sufficient assistance to their dying friend.

Upon our reaching the house he became more languid, occasioned probably by the agitation of his removal from the boat. I gave him a little weak wine and water. When he recovered his feelings, he complained of pain in his back; we immediately undressed him, laid him in bed, and darkened the room. I then gave him a large anodyne, which I frequently repeated. During the first day he took upward of an ounce of laudanum; and tepid anodyne fomentations were also applied to those parts nearest the seat of his pain. Yet were his sufferings during the whole of the day almost intolerable.* I had not the shadow of a hope of his recovery; and Dr. Post, whom I requested might be sent for immediately on our reaching Mr. Bayard's house, united with me in this opinion. General Rey, the French consul, also had the goodness to invite the surgeons of the French frigates in our harbour, as they had had much experience in gunshot wounds, to render their assistance. They immediately came; but, to prevent his being disturbed, I stated to them his situation, described the nature of his wound, and the direction of the ball, with all the symptoms that could enable them to form an opinion as to the event. One of the gentlemen then accompanied me to the bedside. The result was a confirmation of the opinion that had already been expressed by Dr. Post and myself.

During the night he had some imperfect sleep, but the succeeding morning his symptoms were aggravated, attended, however, with a diminution of pain. His mind retained all its usual strength and composure. The great source of his anxiety seemed to be in his sympathy with his half-distracted

* As his habit was delicate, and had been lately rendered more feeble by ill health, particularly by a disorder of the stomach and bowels, I carefully avoided all those remedies which are usually indicated on such occasions.

wife and children. He spoke to me frequently of them—"My beloved wife and children" were always his expressions. But his fortitude triumphed over his situation, dreadful as it was; once, indeed, at the sight of his children, brought to the bedside together, seven in number, his utterance forsook him; he opened his eyes, gave them one look, and closed them again till they were taken away. As a proof of his extraordinary composure of mind, let me add, that he alone could calm the frantic grief of their mother. "*Remember, my Eliza, you are a Christian,*" were the expressions with which he frequently, with a firm voice, but in a pathetic and impressive manner, addressed her. His words, and the tone in which they were uttered, will never be effaced from my memory. About two o'clock, as the public well know, he expired—

> "Incorrupta fides—nudaque veritas
> Quando ullum invenient parem?
> Multis ille quidem flebilis occidit."

Your friend and humble servant,

DAVID HOSACK.

"After his death, a note, which had been written the evening before the interview, was found addressed to the gentleman who accompanied him to the field; thanking him with tenderness for his friendship to him, and informing him where would be found the keys of certain drawers in his desk, in which he had deposited such papers as he had thought proper to leave behind him, together with his last will." Among these papers was the following.

On my expected interview with Colonel Burr, I think it proper to make some remarks explanatory of my conduct, motives, and views.

I was certainly desirous of avoiding this interview for the most cogent reasons.

1. My religious and moral principles are strongly opposed to the practice of duelling, and it would ever give me pain

to be obliged to shed the blood of a fellow-creature in a private combat forbidden by the laws.

2. My wife and children are extremely dear to me, and my life is of the utmost importance to them in various views.

3. I feel a sense of obligation towards my creditors; who, in case of accident to me, by the forced sale of my property, may be in some degree sufferers. I did not think myself at liberty, as a man of probity, lightly to expose them to this hazard.

4. I am conscious of no *ill will* to Colonel Burr distinct from political opposition, which, as I trust, has proceeded from pure and upright motives.

Lastly, I shall hazard much, and can possibly gain nothing by the issue of the interview.

But it was, as I conceive, impossible for me to avoid it. There were *intrinsic* difficulties in the thing, and *artificial* embarrassments from the manner of proceeding on the part of Colonel Burr.

Intrinsic, because it is not to be denied that my animadversions on the political principles, character, and views of Colonel Burr have been extremely severe; and, on different occasions, I, in common with many others, have made very unfavourable criticisms on particular instances of the private conduct of this gentleman.

In proportion as these impressions were entertained with sincerity, and uttered with motives and for purposes which might appear to me commendable, would be the difficulty (until they could be removed by evidence of their being erroneous) of explanation or apology. *The disavowal required of me by Colonel Burr, in a general and definite form, was out of my power*, if it had really been proper for me to submit to be so questioned; but I was sincerely of the opinion that this could not be; and in this opinion I was confirmed by that of a very moderate and judicious friend whom I consulted. Besides that, Colonel Burr appeared to me to assume, in the first instance, a tone unnecessarily peremptory and menacing, and, in the second, positively offensive. Yet I wished, as far as might be practicable, to leave a door open for accommodation. This, I think, will be inferred from the written communications made by me and by my direction, and would be confirmed by the conversations between Mr. Van Ness and myself which arose out of the subject.

I am not sure whether, under all the circumstances, I did not go further in the attempt to accommodate than a punctil ious delicacy will justify. If so, I hope the motives I have stated will excuse me.

It is not my design, by what I have said, to affix any odium on the character of Colonel Burr in this case. *He doubtless has heard of animadversions of mine which bore very hard upon him;* and it is probable that, as usual, they were accompanied with some falsehoods. He may have supposed himself under a necessity of acting as he has done. I hope the grounds of his proceeding have been such as ought to satisfy his own conscience.

I trust, at the same time, that the world will do me the iustice to believe *that I have not censured him on light grounds* nor from unworthy inducements. *I certainly have had strong reasons for what I have said, though it is possible that in some particulars I have been influenced by misconstruction or misinformation.* It is also my ardent *wish that I may have been more mistaken than I think I* have been, and that he, by his future conduct, may show himself worthy of all confidence and esteem, and prove an ornament and blessing to the country.

As well, because it is possible that I may have injured Colonel Burr, however convinced myself that my opinions and declarations have been well founded, as from my general principles and temper in relation to similar affairs, I have resolved, if our interview is conducted in the usual manner, and it pleases God to give me the opportunity, to reserve and throw away my first fire, and I have thoughts even of reserving my second fire, and thus giving a double opportunity to Colonel Burr to pause and to reflect.

It is not, however, my intention to enter into any explanations on the ground—apology from principle, I hope, rather than pride, is out of the question.

To those who, with me, abhorring the practice of duelling, may think that I ought on no account to add to the number of bad examples, I answer, that my *relative* situation, as well in public as private, enforcing all the considerations which men of the world denominate honour, imposed on me (as I thought) a peculiar necessity not to decline the call. The ability to be in future useful, whether in resisting mischief or effecting good, in those crises of our public affairs which seem likely to happen, would probably be inseparable from a conformity with prejudice in this particular.

A. H.

The impression which the death of General Hamilton made on every class of people in the city of New-York is best described by simply remarking, that all party distinction was lost in the general sentiment of respect expressed for the illustrious dead. On Wednesday morning, the 11th of July, 1804, the parties met; on Thursday, the 12th, General Hamilton died; and on Saturday, the 14th, he was interred, with military honours, " the Society of the Cincinnati being charged with the direction of the funeral ceremonies of its president-general." About noon, the different bodies forming the procession took their respective places. The body was conducted from the house of his brother-in-law, John B. Church, Esq., to Trinity Church, where an appropriate oration was delivered by the Hon. Gouverneur Morris.

TO THEODOSIA.

New-York, July 10, 1804.

Having lately written my will, and given my private letters and papers in charge to you, I have no other direction to give you on the subject but to request you to burn all such as, if by accident made public, would injure any person. This is more particularly applicable to the letters of my female correspondents. All my letters, and copies of letters, of which I have retained copies, are in the six blue boxes. If your husband or any one else (no one, however, could do it so well as he) should think it worth while to write a sketch of my life, some materials will be found among these letters.

Tell my dear Natalie that I have not left her any thing, for the very good reason that I had nothing to leave to any one. My estate will just about pay my debts and no more —I mean, if I should die this year. If I live a few years, it is probable things may be better. Give Natalie one of the pictures of me. There are three in this house; that of Stewart, and two by Vanderlyn. Give her any other little tokens she may desire. One of those pictures, also, I pray you to give to Doctor Eustis. To Bartow something—what you please.

I pray you and your husband to convey to Peggy the small lot, not numbered, which is the fourth article mentioned in my list of property. It is worth about two hundred and fifty dollars. Give her also fifty dollars in cash as a reward for her fidelity. Dispose of Nancy as you please. She is honest, robust, and good-tempered. Peter is the most intelligent and best-disposed black I have ever known. (I mean the black boy I bought last fall from Mr. Turnbull.) I advise you, by all means, to keep him as the valet of your son. Persuade Peggy to live with you if you can.

I have desired that my wearing apparel be given to Frederic. Give him also a sword or pair of pistols.

Burn immediately a small bundle, tied with a red string,

which you will find in the little flat writing-case—that which we used with the curricle. The bundle is marked "*Put.*"

The letters of *Clara* (the greater part of them) are tied up in a white handkerchief, which you will find in the blue box No. 5. You may hand them to Mari, if you please. My letters to Clara are in the same bundle. You, and by-and-by Aaron Burr Alston, may laugh at *gamp* when you look over this nonsense.

Many of the letters of *Clara* will be found among my ordinary letters, filed and marked, sometimes "*Clara,*" sometimes "L."

I am indebted to you, my dearest Theodosia, for a very great portion of the happiness which I have enjoyed in this life. You have completely satisfied all that my heart and affections had hoped or even wished. With a little more perseverance, determination, and industry, you will obtain all that my ambition or vanity had fondly imagined. Let your son have occasion to be proud that he had a mother. Adieu. Adieu.

A. BURR.

I have directed that the flat writing-case and the blue box No. 5, both in the library, be opened only by you. There are six of these blue boxes, which contain my letters and copies of letters, except those two clumsy quarto volumes, in which letter-press copies are pasted. They are somewhere in the library. The keys of the other five boxes are in No. 5.

It just now occurs to me to give poor dear Frederic my watch. I have already directed my executors here to give him my wearing apparel. When you come hither you must send for Frederic, and open your whole heart to him. He loves *me* almost as much as Theodosia does; and he does love *you* to adoration.

I have just now found four packets of letters between *Clara and Mentor* besides those in the handkerchief. I have thrown them loose into box No. 5. What a medley you will find in that box!

The seal of the late General Washington, which you will find in the blue box No. 5, was given to me by Mr. and Mrs. Law. You may keep it for your son, or give it to whom you please.

Assure Mrs. Law of my latest recollection. Adieu. Adieu.

A. Burr.

TO JOSEPH ALSTON.

New-York, July 10, 1804.

My dear Sir,

You will find enclosed a statement of my affairs. Swartwout and Van Ness are joint executors with you and Theodosia. It was indispensable that there should be an executor on the spot. I have directed them to sell immediately my horses, and to sell nothing else until your pleasure shall be known. I pray that Theodosia may be consulted and gratified in this particular.

Explanations of every concern of my property is given in two sheets of paper which accompany my will. The enclosed is an abstract.

It would have been a great satisfaction to me to have had your assurance that you would assume my debts, and take and dispose of the property at discretion. It may be done in a way which you would find a convenience. My creditors would take your assumption at such time as you might judge convenient. The property will, undoubtedly, produce more than the amount of my debts. What you may not incline to keep may be forthwith turned into cash.

The library, maps, pictures, and wine are articles which you will need, and which you cannot procure without great trouble and more money. I think, too, you would do well to retain Richmond Hill, as a more convenient residence than Montalto, particularly as no expense will be necessary for buildings or improvements.

My private letters I have directed to be put in the hands of Theodosia, that she may select from them her own, those of her mother, and some others. Among them and my copies you will find much of trifling, something of amusement, and a little of interest.

Get from Mr. Taylor (the younger), of Columbia or Camden, my letters to his brother-in-law, the late J. E. Hunt, who was one of your chancellors.

Messrs. R. Bunner, William Duer, John Duer, and J. W. Smith, of this city, and John Van Ness Yates, of Albany, all lawyers and young men of talents, have manifested great and disinterested zeal in my favour on some recent occasions.* I pray you to take some notice of them, and give to each of them, and to William T. Broome, now in Paris, some small token of remembrance of me. William T. Broome, with great defects of temper, unites very considerable literary talents and acquirements. A little attention would attach them all to you.

My very worthy friend, Charles Biddle, of Philadelphia, has six or seven sons—three of them grown up. With different characters and various degrees of intelligence, they will all be men of eminence and of influence. Call to see the father when you pass through Philadelphia, and receive the sons kindly.

I have taught my friends in every quarter to look to you as my representative. There are many of them, your discernment will distinguish which, on whose loyalty and firmness you may rely through all changes.

I have called out General Hamilton, and we meet to-morrow morning. Van Ness will give you the particulars. The preceding has been written in contemplation of this event. If it should be my lot to fall, * * * * * * * * yet

* They supported Colonel Burr for the office of governor in opposition to Morgan Lewis.

I shall live in you and your son. I commit to you all that is most dear to me—my reputation and my daughter. Your talents and your attachment will be the guardian of the one—your kindness and your generosity of the other.

Let me entreat you to stimulate and aid Theodosia in the cultivation of her mind. It is indispensable to her happiness and essential to yours. It is also of the utmost importance to your son. She would presently acquire a critical knowledge of Latin, English, and all branches of natural philosophy. All this would be poured into your son. If you should differ with me as to the importance of this measure, suffer me to ask it of you as a last favour. She will richly compensate your trouble.

Most affectionately adieu,

A. Burr.

The elder Prevost,* Augustine James Frederic Prevost, is a most amiable and honourable man. Under the garb of coarse rusticity you will find, if you know him, refinement, wit, a delicate sense of propriety, the most inflexible intrepidity, incorruptible integrity, and disinterestedness. I wish you could know him; but it would be difficult, by reason of his diffidence and great reluctance to mingle with the world. It has been a source of extreme regret and mortification to me that he should be lost to society and to his friends. The case seems almost remediless, for, alas! *he is married!* A. Burr.

If you can pardon and indulge a folly, I would suggest that Madame Sansay, too well known under the name of Leonora, has claims on my recollection. She is now with her husband at St. Jago of Cuba.

A. Burr.

* Mrs. Burr's son by her first husband, Colonel Prevost, of the British army.

CHAPTER XVII.

TO JOSEPH ALSTON.

New-York, July 13, 1804.

General Hamilton died yesterday. The malignant federalists or tories, and the imbittered Clintonians, unite in endeavouring to excite public sympathy in his favour and indignation against his antagonist. Thousands of absurd falsehoods are circulated with industry. The most illiberal means are practised in order to produce excitement, and, for the moment, with effect.

I propose leaving town for a few days, and meditate also a journey for some weeks, but whither is not resolved. Perhaps to Statesburgh. You will hear from me again in about eight days.

A. Burr.

TO JOSEPH ALSTON.

July 18, 1804.

The event of which you have been advised has driven me into a sort of exile, and may terminate in an actual and permanent ostracism. Our most unprincipled Jacobins are the loudest in their lamentations for the death of General Hamilton, whom, for many years, they have uniformly represented as the most detestable and unprincipled of men—the motives are obvious. Every sort of persecution is to be exercised against me. A coroner's jury will sit this evening, being the *fourth* time. The object of this unexampled measure is to obtain an inquest of murder. Upon this a warrant will issue to apprehend me, and, if I should be taken, no bail would probably be allowed. You know enough of the temper and principles of the generality of the officers of our state government to form a judgment of my position.

The statement* in the Morning Chronicle was not submitted to my perusal, I being absent at the time of the publication. Several circumstances not very favourable to the deceased are suppressed; I presume, from holy reverence for the dead. I am waiting the report of this jury; when that is known, you shall be advised of my movements. At present I have decided on nothing. Write under cover to Charles Biddle, Philadelphia.

A. BURR.

TO THEODOSIA.

July 20, 1804.

La G. has, on a recent occasion, manifested a degree of sensibility and attachment which have their influence on *gamp*. Her conduct is also highly honourable to the independence of her mind, for all her associations and connexions would lead to a different result. An interview is expected this evening, which, if it take place, will terminate in something definitive.

It was, indeed, a pretty ludicrous description which you received. On the other side you may add, real good-temper and cheerfulness; a good education, according to the estimation of the world. I shall journey somewhere within a few days, but whither is not yet decided. My heart will travel southward, and repose on the hills of Santee.

Adieu, my dear child.

A. BURR.

TO JOSEPH ALSTON.

Philadelphia, July 29, 1804.

The coroner's jury continued to the 26th (my last New-York date) to sit and adjourn. Upon suspicion that my friends had some knowledge of the subject, derived either

* The statement made by William P. Van Ness, Colonel Burr's second.

from Van Ness or me, *warrants* have issued to bring them in to testify. Matthew L. Davis was apprehended, and, refusing to answer, was committed to prison, where he now lies; probably Colonel Willett is now also in jail on the same account. Swartwout, Van Ness, and others are secreted. How long this sort of persecution may endure cannot be conjectured.

The ferment, which was with so much industry excited, has subsided, and public opinion begins to take its proper course.

A. Burr.

FROM JOHN SWARTWOUT.

New-York, August 2, 1804.

I was interrupted in my letter yesterday. The jury agreed to their verdict this morning at *two* o'clock, *viz.*, wilful murder by the hand of A. B. William P. Van Ness and Nathaniel Pendleton accessories before the fact. The only evidence, Bishop Moore. Edward Ferris, James Ferris, and a Mr. Milne dissented, and contemplate a protest against the illegal conduct of the coroner. Their counsel is James Woods. At four o'clock this morning I despatched an express to Van Ness. The printers, you perceive, continue their malevolence through the vilest motives; notwithstanding all this, there is a considerable reaction. The public palate has become satiated. The Nicholsons, the Gelstons, the Mills's, and may other demo's are rapidly travelling back to 1800. Mr. P. called and begged that the Chronicle might still be kept silent. He observed, that he mixed with these people, and found it to be the true policy. Although this is not my opinion, yet we must be governed by the advice of the majority.

The oration (by Gouverneur Morris) has displeased many republicans of the first water. Governor Morgan Lewis speaks of the proceedings openly as disgraceful, illiberal, and ungentlemanly. In short, a little more noise on their side, and a little further magnanimity on ours, is all that is necessary. In all this bustle, judicious men see nothing but the workings of the meanest passions. The Salem Gazette and the Boston Chronicle seem to take the most correct ground.

TO JOSEPH ALSTON.

Philadelphia, August 3, 1804.

The preceding is a summary of the intelligence by this day's mail. The purport of the inquest is confirmed by a letter from J. B. P. I am further advised that an application has been made to Governor Lewis, of New-York, requiring him to demand me of the governor of this state, with which Lewis will most probably be obliged to comply. I shall, nevertheless, remain here some days (from 8 to 20), that I may the better know the measures of the enemy. *Have no anxiety about the issue of this business.*

A. BURR.

TO THEODOSIA.

Philadelphia, August 2, 1804.

Your letters of the 8th and 18th of July are received; the latter yesterday. You must not complain or find fault if I omit to answer, or even to write. Don't let me have the idea that you are dissatisfied with me a moment. I can't just now endure it. At another time you may play the Juno if you please. Your letters amuse and console me. Continue to write with this reliance, and without the expectation of pay in kind. I owe you no thanks for a letter if you demand prompt payment to the full amount.

All you write of the boy represents him such as I would have him. His refusal of the peaches reminded me of his mother. Just so she has done fifty times, and just so I kissed her; but then I did not give her peaches.

Nothing can be done with Celeste. There is a strange indecision and timidity which I cannot fathom. The thing, however, is abandoned; and, for a few months, I believe, all such things.

I shall be here for some days. How many cannot now be resolved. I am very well, and not without occupation or amusement. Nothing would give me so much pleasure as to hear that your time, or any part of it, is usefully employed.

A. BURR.

TO THEODOSIA.

Philadelphia, August 3, 1804.

You will have learned, through Mr. Alston, of certain measures pursuing against me in New-York. I absent myself from home merely to give a little time for passions to subside, not from any apprehension of the final effects of proceedings in courts of law. They can, by no possibility, eventually affect my person. You will find the papers filled with all manner of nonsense and lies. Among other things, accounts of attempts to assassinate me. These, I assure you, are mere fables. Those who wish me dead prefer to keep at a very respectful distance. No such attempt has been made nor will be made. I walk and ride about here as usual. A. BURR.

TO THEODOSIA.

Philadelphia, August 11, 1804.

Your letter of the 25th July finds me in a moment of great occupation, being on the point of embarking for St. Simons. Write to me on receipt of this, and enclose to the postmaster at Darien, Georgia. The letter to me to be addressed to A. B., at Hampton, St. Simons; and pray write over again all you have written since the 25th, for the letters now on the way will not be received for some time. I shall lay a plan for meeting you somewhere, but whether I may have it in my power to visit the high hills of Santee is doubtful; I fear improbable. They say there is no going through the flat country at this season without hazard of life. Consult your husband about this, and write me as above directed. You shall hear from me the moment of my arrival anywhere; that is, I shall write, and you may read as soon as you can get the letter.

If any male friend of yours should be dying of ennui, recommend to him to engage in a duel and a courtship at the same time—prob. est.

Celeste seems more pliant. I do believe that eight days would have produced some grave event; but, alas! those eight days, and perhaps eight days more, are to be passed on the ocean.

My love to Natalie; to her girl and your boy. I have received a very charming letter from her, which shall be noticed when I get the other side of you. Adieu.

A. Burr.

TO JOSEPH ALSTON.

Philadelphia, August 11, 1804.

Your letters of the 21st and 25th July are just now received, and I have barely time to read them and transmit your orders to New-York about Montalto.

My plan is to visit the Floridas for five or six weeks. I have desired Theodosia to consult you whether there be any healthy point within a hundred miles or so of St. Simons at which we might meet. Might I safely travel through your low country at this season?

Theodosia fat and the boy pale are bad omens. For God's sake, or rather for theirs, your own, and mine, hurry them off to the mountains. I could, perhaps, as easily find you there as elsewhere.

Warrants have been issued in New-York against all those charged with an agency in the death of General Hamilton, but no requisition or demand has been made by the governor of that state on this or any other, nor does it seem very probable that such demand will be immediately made.

I am negotiating to get an assurance from authority that I shall be bailed, on receipt of which I shall surrender.

The eastern republicans take part against the calumniators in New-York. Swartwout is now here. He thinks the tide has already turned in New-York. You had better open a correspondence with him.

A. BURR.

TO THEODOSIA.

Hampton, St. Simon's, August 28, 1804.

We arrived on Saturday evening, all well. The mail, which arrives but once a week, had just gone. An accidental opportunity enables me to forward this to Savannah.

I am at the house of Major Butler, comfortably settled. A very agreeable family within half a mile. My project is to go next week to Florida, which may take up a fortnight or ten days, and soon after my return to go northward, by Augusta and Columbia, if I can find ways and means to get on; but I have no horse, nor does this country furnish one. In my letter to your husband, written at the moment of leaving Philadelphia, I desired him to name some place (healthy place) at which he could meet me. Enclose to "Mr. R. King, Hampton, St. Simon's."

A. BURR.

TO THEODOSIA.

St. Simon's, August 31, 1804.

I am now quite settled. My establishment consists of a housekeeper, cook, and chambermaid, seamstress, and two footmen. There are, besides, two fishermen and four bargemen always at command. The department of laundress is done abroad. The plantation affords plenty of milk, cream, and butter; turkeys, fowls, kids, pigs, geese, and mutton; fish, of course, in abundance. Of figs, peaches, and melons there are yet a few. Oranges and pomegranates just begin to be eatable. The house affords Madeira wine, brandy, and porter. Yesterday my neighbour, Mr. Couper, sent me an assortment of French wines, consisting of Claret, Sauterne, and Champagne, all excellent; and at least a twelve months' supply of orange shrub, which makes a most delicious punch. Madame Couper added sweetmeats and pickles. The plantations of Butler and Couper are divided by a small creek, and the houses within one quarter of a mile of each other; accessible, however, only by water. We have not a fly, moscheto, or bug. I can sit a whole evening, with open windows and lighted candles, without the least annoyance from insects; a circumstance which I have never beheld in any other place. I have not even seen a cockroach.

At Mr. Couper's, besides his family, there are three young ladies, visiters. One of them arrived about three months ago from France, to join a brother who had been shipwrecked on this coast, liked the country so much that he resolved to settle here, and sent for this sister and a younger brother. About the time of their arrival, the elder brother was accidentally drowned; the younger went with views to make an establishment some miles inland, where he now lies dangerously ill. Both circumstances are concealed from the knowledge of Mademoiselle Nicholson. In any event, she will find refuge and protection in the benevolent house of Mr. Couper.

The cotton in this neighbourhood, on the coast southward to the extremity of Florida, and northward as far as we have heard, has been totally destroyed. The crop of Mr. C. was supposed to be worth one hundred thousand dollars, and not an extravagant estimate, for he has eight hundred slaves. He will not get enough to pay half the expenses of the plantation. Yet he laughs about it with good humour and without affectation. Butler suffers about half this loss Part of his force had been turned to rice. My travelling companion, secretary, and aid-de-camp is Samuel Swartwout, the youngest brother of John, a very amiable young man of twenty or twenty-one.

Now, verily, were it not for the intervention of one hundred miles of low, swampy, pestiferous country, I would insist on your coming to see me, all, all! Little *gamp*, and Mademoiselle Sum*tare*, and their appendages; for they are the principals.

I still propose to visit Florida. To set off in three or four days, and to return hither about the 16th of September; beyond this I have at present no plan. It is my wish, God knows how ardently I wish, to return by land, and pass a week with you; but, being without horses, and there being no possibility of hiring or buying, the thing seems scarcely practicable. Two modes only offer themselves—either to embark in the kind of mail stage which goes from Darien through Savannah, Augusta, and Columbia, to Camden, or to take a water passage either to Charleston or Georgetown. Either of these being accomplished, new difficulties will occur in getting from Statesburgh northward. I must be at New-York the first week in November. Consult your husband, and write me of these matters. Enclose to Mr. Roswell King, which I repeat, lest my former letters should not have been received. Our mail has just arrived, but has brought me no letter.

I erred a little in my history of the family of Mademoiselle N. There are still two brothers here. One a man d'une certaine age. Though not wealthy, they are not destitute of property.

Mr. C. has just now gone with his boat for the dashers who live about thirty miles southwest on the main. He has requested me to escort Madame C. on Sunday to his plantation on the south end of this island, where we are to meet him and his party on Monday, and bring them home in our coach. Madame C. is still young, tall, comely, and well bred.

I have been studying all the maps and gazetteers to discover the best access to Statesburgh. Georgetown seems to be the nearest port; but whether there be thence a direct road, I cannot discover. Does our friend Doctor Blythe still reside at Georgetown? If so, I should repose on him for the means of transportation. Desire Mari to write to him to aid me in case I should take that route. If I should go to Charleston, meaning to Sullivan's Island, for Charleston I shall at this season most certainly avoid, I should put myself on General M'Pherson, who, I hear, is now living there with his family; thence up the Cooper river, about four miles above the town, is a ferryhouse and tavern on the north side, and thence by Strawberry, where is the best tavern in the state, is a very direct and beautiful road, and thence, according to the maps, a very straight road to the high hills of Santee. But how to get from that ferryhouse is a question I cannot resolve. All these circumstances are mentioned that I may have your advice, meaning that of your husband. And, after all, it is possible that I may not be able to find a passage either to Charleston or Georgetown, and so be obliged to sail for New-York. Will close this letter, for to-morrow it must go to the postoffice at Darien, which is only about twenty-two miles distant.

September 1.

In one of Mr. Alston's letters he spoke of taking you and A. B. A. to the mountains; and, in a letter which I wrote him from Philadelphia, I proposed to meet you in the mountains. Now, for aught which I as yet know, it will be as easy for me to get to the mountains, or to the Alps, or the Andes, as to Statesburgh, and therefore, as before, I crave counsel.

Do you recollect the second daughter of Mr. Barclay, of Philadelphia, the sister of Nelly? She has grown up the very image of her sister. I saw her very often while I was last in Philadelphia. She talked perpetually of you, and made me promise that I would tell you so.

Adieu, my dear Theodosia. Remember that I have not received a letter from you since that of the 22d or 25th of July. I forget which was the date. I have no faith in the climate of your high hills, surrounded as they are by noxious swamps. God bless and preserve thee.

A. Burr.

TO THEODOSIA.

St. Simon's, September 3, 1804.

You see me returned from Gaston's Bluff, now called *Hamilton's Bluff*, a London merchant, partner of Mr. Couper. We were four in the carriage; the three ladies and myself.

Mr. Morse informs you that this island is forty-five miles long, and that it lies north of the mouth Altamaha, commonly spelled Alatamaha. It is, in fact, twelve and a half miles in length, and lies southeast of that river. Its width is about two and a half miles. There are now residing on the island about twenty-five white families. Frederica, now known only by the name of *Old Town*, is on the west side of the island, and about midway between its northern and southern extremities. It was first settled by Governor Oglethorpe, and was, about fifty years ago, a very gay place, consisting of perhaps twenty-five or thirty houses. The walls of several of them still remain. Three or four families only now reside here. In the vicinity of the town several ruins were pointed out to me, as having been, formerly, country seats of the governor, and officers of the garrison, and gentlemen of the town. At present, nothing can be more gloomy than what was once called Frederica. The few families now remaining, or rather residing there, for they are all new-comers, have a sickly, melancholy appearance, well assorted with the ruins which surround them. The southern part of this island abounds with fetid swamps, which must render it very unhealthy. On the northern half I have seen no stagnant water.

Mr. Couper, with his escort of ladies, was to have met us this afternoon, but he has sent us word that he is taken ill on the way; that, owing to illness in the family of the ladies who were to have accompanied him, they have been obliged to renounce the visit. We therefore returned as we went. At Frederica and Gaston's Bluff we were convinced that insects can subsist on this island. Moschetoes, flies, and cockroaches abounded.

Thursday, September 6, 1804

Just returned from Darien. And what took you to Darien? To see the plantation of Mr. Butler on an island opposite that town, and to meet a day sooner the letters which I expected from you. In the last object I have been again disappointed, which I ascribe wholly to the irregularity of the mails. It is most mortifying and vexatious to be seven weeks without hearing of you or from you, and now a whole week must elapse before I can expect it.

You are probably ignorant that Darien is a settlement (called a town) on the north bank of the Alatamaha, about eight miles from its mouth. Major Butler's Island in this river is one mile below the town. It must become a fine rice country, for the water is fresh four miles below Major Butler's, and the tide rises from four to five feet, and the flats or swamps are from five to seven miles in width for a considerable distance up the river. The country, of course, presents no scenes for a painter. I visited Little St. Simon's and several other islands; frightened the crocodiles, shot some rice-birds, and caught some trout. Honey of fine flavour is found in great abundance in the woods about the mouth of the river, and, for aught I know, in every part of the country. You perceive that I am constantly discovering new luxuries for my table. Not having been able to kill a crocodile (alligator), I have offered a reward for one, which I mean to eat, dressed in soup, fricassees, and steaks. Oh! how you long to partake of this repast.

Wednesday, September 12, 1804.

On Friday last, hearing that Mr. Couper had returned and was very seriously ill, I took a small canoe with two boys, and went to see him. He lay in a high fever. When about to return in the evening, the wind had risen so that, after an ineffectual attempt, I was obliged to give it up, and remain at Mr. C.'s. In the morning the wind was still higher. It continued to rise, and by noon blew a gale from the north, which, together with the swelling of the water, became alarming. From twelve to three, several of the out-houses had been destroyed; most of the trees about the house were blown down. The house in which we were shook and rocked so much that Mr. C. began to express his apprehensions for our safety. Before three, part of the piazza was carried away; two or three of the windows bursted in. The house was inundated with water, and presently one of the chimneys fell. Mr. C. then commanded a retreat to a storehouse about fifty yards off, and we decamped, men, women, and children. You may imagine, in this scene of confusion and dismay, a good many incidents to amuse one if one had dared to be amused in a moment of much anxiety. The house, however, did not blow down. The storm continued till four, and then very suddenly abated, and in ten minutes it was almost a calm. I seized the moment to return home. Before I had got quite over, the gale rose from the southeast and threatened new destruction. It lasted great part of the night, but did not attain the violence of that from the north; yet it contributed to raise still higher the water, which was the principal instrument of devastation. The flood was about seven feet above the height of an ordinary high tide. This has been sufficient to inundate great part of the coast; to destroy all the rice; to carry off most of the buildings which were on low lands, and to destroy the lives of many blacks. The roads are rendered impassable, and scarcely a boat has been preserved. Thus all intercourse is suspended. The mail-boat, which ought to have passed northward last Saturday, and by which it was intended to forward this letter, has not been heard of. This will go by a man who will attempt to get from Darien to Savannah on foot, being sent express by the manager of

Major Butler; but how, or whether it will go on from Savannah, is not imagined.

Major Butler has lost nineteen negroes (drowned), and I fear his whole crop of rice, being about two hundred and sixty acres. Mr. Brailsford, of Charleston, who cultivates in rice an island at the mouth of the Alatamaha, has lost, reports say, seventy-four blacks. The banks and the buildings on the low lands are greatly injured. We have heard nothing from the southward, nor farther than from Darien northward. I greatly fear that this hurricane, so it is here called, has extended to the Waccama.

The illness of Mr. C., which still continues, and the effects of the storm, have defeated all my plans. To get to Florida seems now impracticable; nor do any present means occur of getting from this island in any direction. Young Swartwout, who went ten days ago to Savannah, has not returned, nor is it possible that he should very speedily return. I have not received a letter since my arrival from any person north of Savannah (yes, one from C. Biddle, of 19th August), nor do I expect one for many days to come.

I had taken up another sheet to say something more, I know not what; but the appearance of a fine sheep's-head smoking on the table has attractions not to be resisted. *Laissez moi diner*, "and then," &c.

Madame j'ais bien diner, and *j'ai fait mettre mon* writing-desk *sur le table a diner*. What a scandalous thing to sit here all alone drinking Champagne—and yet—(*madame je bois a votre santé et a celle de monsieur* votre fils)—and yet, I say, if Champagne be that exhilarating cordial which (*je bois a la santé de Madame Sumtare*) songs and rumour ascribe to it (*a la santé de Mademoiselle Sumtare*), can there be ever an occasion in which its application could be more appropriate, or its virtues more (*mais buvons a la santé de mon hôte et bon ami*, Major Butler). By-the-by, you have no idea—how should you have, seeing that you never heard a word about it?—you have no idea, I was going to say, of the zeal and animation, of the intrepidity and frankness with which he avowed and maintained—but I forget that this letter goes to Savannah by a negro, who has to swim half a dozen creeks, in one of which, *at least*, it is probable he may drown, and that, if he escape drowning, various other accidents may bring it to you through the newspapers, and then how many enemies might my indiscretion create for a man who had the sensibility and the honour to feel and to judge, and the firmness to avow (*a la santé de Celeste un* bumper toast). *La pauvre Celeste.* Adieu.

A. BURR.

TO THEODOSIA.

Frederica, St. Simon's, September 15, 1804.

Having very unexpectedly procured a boat, I left my house yesterday afternoon, came hither by land, and proceed in a few minutes for St. Mary's. It is possible that I may extend my tour to St. John's, and even to St. Augustine's; but, if so, it will be very rapid; a mere flight, for I propose to be at home (Hampton, St. Simon's) again in eight days.

On the 12th I sent by a special messenger, who was to go from Darien to Savannah on foot, my journal for the ten or fifteen days preceding, with some account of the hurricane; but a man this day from Darien says that our express can by no possibility reach Savannah; for that every bridge and causeway is destroyed, and the road so filled with fallen trees as to be utterly impassable. I apprehend that the roads on the whole coast as far north, at least, as Cape Hatteras, are in the same condition. If on my return I should receive intelligence confirming those apprehensions, it will compel me to abandon the hope of seeing you until the last of February. On this, as on all other occasions, let me find that you exhibit the firmness which I have been proud to ascribe to you. Let me hear that you are seriously engaged in some useful pursuit. Let me see the progressive improvement of your mind, and it will console me for all the evils of life.

My young friend Swartwout is still absent, and I suppose at Savannah. It is not probable that I shall see him again before my return to New-York.

A Mr. Bartram, of Philadelphia, travelled through Georgia and the Floridas in 1772. His travels are published in one large octavo volume. Procure and read it, and you will better understand what I may write you. I promise myself much gratification in this little trip. If an opportunity should offer for Charleston by water, I shall venture a letter to you. This will be forwarded before my return; if not, it will lay here. I am writing to you before sunrise, and am now summoned to the boat (canoe).

A. Burr.

TO THEODOSIA.

Hampton, St. Simon's, September 26, 1804.

I returned yesterday from my Florida excursion, about which I wrote you on the 15th inst. The weather prevented me from going farther than the river St. John's, about thirty miles from St. Augustine. I have been making out for you a journal of my tour, but I still entertain a slight hope of seeing you somewhere within a fortnight; if at all, it will be by the 10th of October. Pray keep yourselves in readiness to meet me at Columbia, or still more southward if I should require it.

Not a line from you or your husband since those of the 25th of July. Your letters have either been lost in the hurricane or are now in the mail-boat, which, by some mistake, has brought down the Darien mail and carried it on more southward, so that it will not reach Darien till I am off; yet I entertain a hope of finding letters at Savannah.

A boat has at length been found to take me to Savannah, and thither I go to-morrow, or rather set out, for I shall not reach it till the 30th instant. What course I shall take thence will be determined by what I may hear at that city. You will have a line from me as soon as I arrive there; meaning always that the line will be written, and sent on by the first mail, to get to you as soon as it can.

It is a fact that the Spanish ladies smoke segars. They say that a young lady will take a few puffs and hand it to her favoured lover as a mark of great kindness. This rumour, however, I cannot verify from personal observation, much less have I to boast of any such favour. But we will talk of these things if we should meet; if not, we will write about them.

I was treated with great kindness and respect at St. Mary's, and have everywhere experienced the utmost hospitality. My health has been perfect and uninterrupted. God bless thee.

A. BURR.

TO THEODOSIA.

Savannah, October 1, 1804.

Ten o'clock A. M., arrived in a storm (northeast). They had last evening a minor hurricane here, for the special use of this city. It overset some canoes, drowned a few negroes, unroofed some houses, and forced in a few windows. It was the affair of a few minutes, confined to a small space, and did no other mischief that I learn.

My last letter to you was from St. Simon's, about the 27th ult., the day previous to my departure. My voyage hither was full of variety, and not of the most pleasant kind, but no accident to affect health. My first reflection on landing was that I was one hundred miles nearer to you; but my inquiries since my arrival afford no prospect of getting on by land, except by the purchase of horses, to which there is one insuperable objection. The condition of the roads has not yet admitted of travelling northward or westward in a carriage. The mail goes on horseback.

Not a line from any creature north of this place since I

left Philadelphia. I hear, however, that the Darien mail, which I passed at Frederica, as mentioned with vexation in my last, had letters for me, doubtless from you.

I was kindly interrupted in these idle regrets by visiters, who continued in succession till dinner was announced. At the lodging-house, where rooms were provided for me, were the governor, a Scotch merchant, and a sea captain. In the evening a band of music came under the window, which I supposed to be a compliment to the governor, till one of the gentlemen who accompanied it came in and said that a number of citizens at the door wished to see the vice-president. Interrupted again.

Tuesday, October 2.

Firstly, your pardon is craved for this torn sheet; it was entire when I commenced, but one half went last night to answer a note, there being no paper in the house, and Peter abroad with my key. You have not, I think, been introduced to Peter, my *now* valet. It is a black boy purchased last fall. An intelligent, good-tempered, willing fellow, about fifteen; a dirty, careless dog, who, with the best intentions, is always in trouble by sins of omission or commission. The latter through inadvertence, and often through excess of zeal. About three times a day, sometimes oftener, I get angry enough to choke him, but his honesty and good-nature prevail. In my will, made about the 10th of July, I recommend him to you as valet to A. B. A.

I have been this morning scouring the town and the docks in quest of ways and means to get on. There is a packet which will sail for Charleston on Saturday; a great way off to one so impatient as the writer of this. No stage nor a horse to be hired. Finding that the mail does not close till seven this evening, this letter shall be kept open till the last moment, and shall not be closed till I have settled some plan of getting forward, either to Statesburgh or New-York. It will, I think, be Statesburgh. Six hours hence you shall know. Have patience, my dear child, for six hours.

Lest I should forget it, let me now tell you that I am received with the warmest hospitality. Notwithstanding the desolation occasioned by the hurricane (and it is truly distressing), I have invitations which it would require weeks to satisfy. These attentions are almost exclusively from republicans.

Four o'clock P. M.

Io triumphe! A letter; two, three letters. Two from you and one from your husband. Since writing I have had other good luck; *viz.*, two gentlemen have offered me each an excellent horse to go as far as Statesburgh by any route I may please. Another horse, and I am made. Note, my young friend Swartwout is with me, and I cannot well part with him. If another horse shall be found, I shall take the route through Orangeburgh, as being the most direct to Statesburgh. If the land route shall for any reason be found impracticable, I shall take possession of a Charleston packet, and perhaps take it on to Georgetown. By one way or the other you shall see me within ten or twelve days. Tell Mari that his letter being received this afternoon, and the postmaster having just now sent me word that the mail is about to close, I can only answer him thus.

You are now to keep your ground and expect me at the hills. Pray let A. B. A. know that *gamp* is a black man, otherwise he may be shocked at the appearance of A. B., who is now about the colour of Peter Yates. Not brown, but a true quadroon yellow; whether from the effects of climate, or travelling four hundred miles in a canoe, is no matter. A. Burr.

TO THEODOSIA.

Fayetteville, October 23, 1804.

I get on as usual; arrived here this forenoon, but detained all day by some trifling repairs to the carriage. I promised you a journal in the manner of modern travels, to show you how such books could be made without facts or ideas. My first four days, to wit, from Statesburgh to this place, would, I find, from notes which I have actually taken, make about one hundred pages, and two hundred in the manner of Rochefoucault d'Liancourt; but the labour of so much writing has alarmed and almost discouraged me.

No more pauses, not even for weather, till Richmond, distant two hundred miles, and proposed to be travelled in five days. I know no person in this place but Mr. Grove, late member of Congress, who has not called on me. Tell your husband that I have heard nothing worthy of being communicated. Since I began to write it has begun to rain, as if to test my determination not to be stopped by weather. Adieu, chere T.

A. Burr.

Warrenton, October 27, 1804.

We parted at Fayetteville. The morning following I started one hour before day, the moon showing us the way, and, at about seven or eight in the evening, was at Raleigh, being full fifty miles. It was a hard day's journey, and greater than will be made again on this trip. The fatigues of the day were in some measure compensated by the very hospitable reception which I met from the *negroes* of the capital of North Carolina. I reposed till nine the next morning, and came the next day only to Louisburgh (twenty-nine miles), where I slept in the little up-stairs room which you once occupied; but there is a new landlord. The Jew is broke up. The wind had been two days strong at northeast, threatening a storm, and raining a little from time to time. Last night it came on in earnest, raining and blowing vehemently. So I lay abed again till nine, and, after breakfasting for two hours, set off at eleven in all the storm. At twelve it began to snow, and continued to snow most plentifully till night. The ground looked like the depth of winter in Albany. Poor Andrew was almost perished, and *gamp's* hands were nearly frozen; still we kept on, and got here about five, being twenty-five miles. It will take me full three days more to reach Richmond, and perhaps longer, for the roads are so gullied as to be barely passable. This afternoon, stopping at a tavern and calling for the hostler, the man told me that, *foreseeing* the storm, he had sent him for a load of wood.

A gentleman who passed here yesterday says he left Major Butler on the way, going to Georgia by land. When I sat down to write my head was full of totally different matters; but, having gone on so far with road incidents, the other concerns must be omitted.

My landlord has just been telling me that Swartwout passed here eight days ago. They were three in the stage, all very apprehensive of being overset, as they were to start at two in the morning. In the excess of caution, they desired the landlord to give no rum to the driver. The landlord promised, and gave orders to the barkeeper. When the driver arrived, he called for a dram; was refused, and told the reason. Resenting this indignity, he swore he would get drunk; went to a store, bought rum, and got drunk. Set out at two, and overset the stage the first hour. The passengers were bruised, but not very seriously injured.

TO JOSEPH ALSTON.

Petersburgh, October 31, 1804.

I came here on the morning of the 29th, intending to stay two hours. The hospitalities of the place have detained me three days. A party was prepared for me on the evening of my arrival. There were present between fifty and sixty, all pure republican. An invitation from the republican citizens, communicated through the mayor, to a public dinner, was made in terms and in a manner which could not be declined. We had the dinner yesterday at the hotel. In the evening I was attended by some fifteen or twenty to the theatre, where I was greatly amused, particularly by Mrs.

West, whom I think the best female actress in America, not excepting Mrs. Merry.

I send you a collection of Curran's speeches, compiled, however, only from newspapers. There is reason to hope for one more perfect, made under the inspection of the author. Burk's history has agreeably disappointed me. I speak from the reading of thirty or forty pages. If it should gain your approbation, you may render him a service by procuring him subscriptions at the meeting of your legislature. My horses are at the door to take me to Richmond.

A. BURR.

TO THEODOSIA.

Richmond, October 31 (Evening), 1804.

How faithfully I return you the paper which you *lent* me at Statesburgh. This is the last sheet, and I think you will have received back all but one of them.

My journey hither from Drummond, at which place you left me on Saturday evening, the 27th, just going to bed, beside a comfortable fire in a furnished room (what an unconscionable parenthesis), has been very pleasant; but why and wherefore cannot now be told, because you know it must be reserved for "The Travels of A. Gamp, Esq., A.M., LL.D., V. P. U. S.," &c., &c., &c., which will appear in due time.

Virginia is the last state, and Petersburgh the last town in the state of Virginia, in which I should have expected any open marks of hospitality and respect. You will have seen from my note of this morning to Mr. Alston how illy I have judged.

To think of meeting with such an actress as Mrs. West in such a place. Her voice is as sweet as Mrs. Merry's (the actress, not the other Mrs. Merry), her manners superior. In comedy she is unequalled. They say she excites equally in tragedy. I have no doubt but she is good at every thing. I could make you laugh at a ridiculous embarrassment, but I won't; nay, I dare not, for who knows but you may first see this in the newspaper. Madam, this is Colonel B., V. P. U. S., all out loud. Sir, this is Mrs. ——. Miss, this is, &c., &c. The players stand, and the pit stand, and the gallery stand. No, there is no gallery. Indeed, I don't know when I have been better entertained with a play.

I arrived here about sunset. Am to dine to-morrow with Dr. B., and, from appearances, might be amused here a week. At the utmost I shall stay but two days, desiring to be at Washington on Monday. I am most comfortably lodged.

Young Dr. Rush travels with Major Butler, which I forgot to mention to your husband. Pray exert yourself to please and amuse Major Butler.

A. Burr.

TO JOSEPH ALSTON.

Washington, November 5, 1804.

I arrived last evening. You will have received my two letters of the 30th ult. and 1st instant, communicating, among other things, some information which I received on the road respecting the feelings in Bergen county, New-Jersey. Since that a grand jury has been *empannelled*, who have found an indictment of murder. The witness, Parson Mason. The presiding judge, Boudinot, one of the most vehement of vehement federalists. The particulars shall be communicated as soon as I can find time to write them; they will furnish you with new materials for reflection. They talk of making a demand here.

My house and furniture have been sold for about twenty-five thousand dollars. Seven or eight thousand dollars of debts remain unpaid. My agents have not collected any of my debts, nor sold any of the detached lots. The library and the wine remain. They will, I think, become your property.

A. Burr.

TO THEODOSIA.

Washington, November 17, 1804.

Shall I write to her to-night, or omit it till to-morrow? Oh! to-night, dear pappy. Well, then, to-night it shall be —"*Je vous ecris parceque je n'ai rien a faire*," &c. That's not true; fifty unanswered letters on my table pronounce it false.

But when I deliberated about writing, it was with a view to write you sense—grave sense. What a dull thing is sense. How it mars half the pleasure of life, and yet how contemptible is all that has it not. Too much sense, by which I mean only a great deal, is very troublesome to the possessor and to the world. It is like one carrying a huge pack through a crowd. He is constantly hitting and annoying somebody, and is, in turn, annoyed and jostled by every one, and he must be a very powerful man indeed if he can keep upright and force his way. Now there appears to me to be but two modes of carrying this pack with any tolerable comfort to the owner.

Interrupted. A very extraordinary visit; you shall hear as soon as they go.

The visiters were a middle-aged gentleman; a man of fortune, of family; has travelled, and been received in the first circles on both continents; intelligent and well-informed; prompt, rapid, and decisive. A high federalist, yet a warm and open friend of *gamp* on all occasions. Reputed to be insane, of which this attachment may be deemed an evidence. Such is Mr. Y. The other, Mr. S., a very handsome, genteel young man, who never carried a pack. They sat two hours, and Mr. Y. was not only rational, but amusing. The only evidence of insanity which I have heard is that he quarrels with his dear *rib*; and if this be deemed evidence, I fear our madhouses will soon be filled with married men. I ought to have excepted one incident, which has been related to me as follows:—

Mr. R., a young lawyer of reputable connexions, but who

had committed some follies, called to visit Mr. Y. After sitting some time, " Mr. R.," says Y., " it has been reported that you are a little deranged in mind (there had, in fact, been such a report), and I have heard that whipping has been found a sovereign remedy; indeed, in the case of the King of England, its benefit was manifest. Now as I have a very great regard for you, and doubt whether your friends will take the trouble of administering this discipline, I will take it on myself to do it."

Two stout negroes were called in. The astonished R. was seized, stripped, and tied, and most unmercifully whipped. All, however, with the utmost composure on the part of Y., and mingled with expressions of kindness. When R. was taken down, bloody, lacerated, and exhausted—" Pray, sir, walk in and take a dish of tea." " No; d—n you." " But, as you must be somewhat fatigued with the exercise, perhaps you would prefer some brandy and water." R. walked sullenly off, and, as soon as he had recovered, left the neighbourhood, and has not since been heard of.

But by this digression we have lost sight of the pack. The further discussion of that subject must be reserved for the " Book of Travels." The " grave sense" is still further off, and must wait a more fit occasion. As you are skilled in ancient mythology, I pray you to inform me whether there was ever a goddess of nonsense. A god won't serve my purpose. Momus, for instance, is a loud, boisterous, rude, coarse fellow.

Leave off the *vice-president*, &c., in the direction of your letters. Let it be simply A. B. or Colonel B. Tell Mari so.

A. Burr.

TO THEODOSIA.

Washington, December 4, 1804.

You have doubtless heard that there has subsisted for some time a contention of a very singular nature between the states of New-York and New-Jersey. To what lengths it may go, or how it may terminate, cannot be predicted; but, as you will take some interest in the question, I will state it for your satisfaction and consideration.

The subject in dispute is which shall have the honour of hanging the vice-president. I have not now the leisure to state the various pretensions of the parties, with the arguments on either side; nor is it yet known that the vice-president has made his election, though a paper received this morning asserts, but without authority, that he had determined in favour of the New-York tribunals. You shall have due notice of the time and place. Whenever it may be, you may rely on a great concourse of company, much gayety, and many rare sights; such as the lion, the elephant, &c.

On the subject of books, since I shall write to you only by this mail, tell Mr. Alston to order out from his bookseller the British Critic and the Edinburgh Review from their commencement, and to be continued as they shall come out. To form a library is the work of time, and by having these books you may select and give orders without danger of imposition; for though I disclaim much reliance on the judgments of the editors, yet from their extracts and remarks a pretty correct opinion may be formed. I recommend also that you prohibit the sending out of any folio or quarto, unless particularly ordered. Octavo is at about half the price, and much more convenient.

I hope you read Quintilian in the original, and not in translation; and let me entreat you not to pass a word or sentence without understanding it. If I hear a very good account of you, Stuart shall make a picture to please you. God bless thee. A. BURR.

TO JOSEPH ALSTON.

Washington, December 15, 1804.

The trial of Judge Chace will not come on before the middle of January. He is summoned to appear the 2d January. I regret extremely that you cannot be present.

Biddle and Dallas have written a joint letter to Governor Bloomfield, of New-Jersey, urging a nol. pros. in the case of the vice-president. Dallas has, throughout this business, behaved with an independence, and open, active zeal which I could not have expected, and to which I had no personal claim.

The leading republican members of the United States Senate have addressed a similar joint letter to the governor. Many individuals of the same *sect* co-operate in the measure, and have expressed their opinions by letter and in conversation. Nothing final and favourable will promptly be done. On the other hand, nothing hostile will be attempted. I enclose you the articles of impeachment against Judge Chace, as agreed upon.

A. Burr.

TO THEODOSIA.

Washington, December 31, 1804,

Being the last time I shall write 1804. Now, how much wiser or better are we than this time last year? Have our enjoyments for that period been worth the trouble of living? These are inquiries not wholly congenial with the compliments of the new year, so we will drop them. You would laugh to know the occupation of my New Year's eve. It cannot be written, but it shall at some time be told.

I propose to move my quarters to-morrow, and the confusion has already commenced, and even pervades this letter. Mrs. Merry arrived a few days ago, and looks extremely well. Madame Turreau is supposed to be lost or captured. Mr. Chace's trial will not come on till after the middle of January. Peter Van Ness, the father of General John P., died on the 23d instant. He has left his sons about forty thousand dollars apiece.

Madame, when I enclose you a book or paper, be pleased, at least, to let me know that you or your husband have read it. Pretty business, indeed, for me to be spending hours in cutting and folding pamphlets and papers for people who, perhaps, never open them. Heaven mend you.

A. Burr.

CHAPTER XIX.

TO THEODOSIA.

Washington, January 15, 1805.

At five in the morning I shall start for Philadelphia. The object of this journey has been intimated in a former letter. One motive, however, lays down at the bottom of my heart, and has scarcely, as yet, been avowed to myself. You will conjecture, and rightly, that I mean Celeste. That matter shall receive its final decision. Now, to confess the truth, which, however, I have but just discovered, but for this matter the journey would not have been taken. How little is this truth suspected by the hundreds who are at this moment *ascribing to the movement motives of profound political importance.*

I enclose you a pamphlet written with views the most friendly to A. B. So greatly do I differ from the author, that I have desired a friend to buy them up and burn them. I shall return to this city on the 29th. Adieu.

A. Burr.

TO THEODOSIA.

Washington, January 28, 1805.

Your letter of the 1st of January found me at Philadelphia, and at the moment of leaving it. Your kind wishes came so warm from the heart, that, in a journey of eight hundred miles, at this inclement season, they had not yet cooled.

You treat with too much gravity the New-Jersey affair. It should be considered as a farce, and you will yet see it terminated so as to leave only ridicule and contempt to its abettors. The affair of Celeste is for ever closed, so there is one trouble off hand.

After you get through the book you are now reading, which I think is Anacharsis, or is it Gibbon? you better suspend history till you have gone through B. You do wrong to read so slow the first reading of B. I had rather you went through it like a novel, to get fixed in your mind a kind of map of the whole; after which, when you come to read *scientifically*, you would better see the relations and bearings of one part to another. In all journeys, whether on foot or on horseback, it is a relief to know not only where you start from, but where you are going to, and all the intermediate stages. I beg that in every letter you will give me one line about B., and ask me questions if you please.

A. Burr.

TO THEODOSIA.

Washington, February 23, 1805.

I regret the unprofitable employment of your time, and sincerely hope such long visitations will not be repeated; but you are something to blame to have taken no books with you, and again for not finding one at Clifton, where I know there are many. Still I believe in your good intentions and in their execution. It will add greatly to my happiness to know that the cultivation of your mind is not neglected; because I know that without it you will become unfit for the duties, as well as the enjoyments of life. Perhaps, also, my vanity may be something concerned.

Your last letters are written with more correctness, and apparently with more attention than is your habit. They have amused and pleased me much. By pleased, I mean gratified my pride. Your critical remarks are quite interesting. I advise you, as soon as you have finished a play, novel, pamphlet, or book, immediately to write an account and criticism of it. You can form no idea how much such a work will amuse you on perusal a few years hence. When A. B. A. has got so far as to read stories of the most simple kind, the least pleasing part of his intellectual education is finished. I might, perhaps, have added with truth, the most laborious part.

A. Burr.

The last public duty of any importance performed by Colonel Burr was to preside in the case of Judge Samuel Chace, who was impeached before the Senate of the United States for high crimes and misdemeanours. Colonel Burr evinced his accustomed promptitude, energy, and dignity. His impartiality and fairness won for him the applause of opponents as well as friends; and it may be confidently asserted, that never did president judge, in this or any other country, more justly merit applause than did the vice-president on this occasion.

The Senate Chamber, under his immediate direction, was fitted up in handsome style as a court, and laid out into apartments for the senators, the House of Representatives, the managers, the accused and counsel, the members of the executive departments, besides a semicircular gallery constructed within the area of the chamber, which formed from its front an amphitheatre contiguous with the fixed gallery of the Senate Chamber.

On the right and left of the president of the Senate, and in a right line with his chair, there were two rows of benches, with desks in front, and the whole front and seats covered with crimson cloth, so that the senators fronted the auditory.

The secretary of the Senate retained his usual station in front of the president's chair; on the left of the secretary was placed the sergeant-at-arms of the Senate, and on his right the sergeant-at-arms of the House of Representatives.

A temporary semicircular gallery, which consisted of

three ranges of benches, was elevated on pillars, and the whole front and seats thereof covered with green cloth. At the angles or points of this gallery there were two boxes, which projected into the area about three feet from the line of the front, which saved the abruptness of a square termination, and added considerably to the effect of the coup d'œil. In this gallery ladies were accommodated, and they assembled in numbers.

On the floor beneath this temporary gallery three benches were provided, rising from front to rear, and also covered with green cloth; these benches were occupied by the members of the House of Representatives; on the right there was a spacious box, appropriated for the members of the executive departments, foreign ministers, &c.

A passage was opened in front from the president's chair to the door; on the right and left hand of the president, and in front of the members of the House of Representatives, were two boxes of two rows of seats; that facing the president's right was occupied by the managers, that on the other side of the bar for the accused and his counsel. These boxes were covered with blue cloth. The marshal of the District of Columbia and a number of his officers were stationed in the avenues of the court and in the galleries.

On the 3d of January, 1805, the senators were sworn as judges, and Monday, the 4th of February ensuing, was fixed as "the day for receiving the answer and proceeding on the trial of the impeachment of Samuel Chace." Accordingly, on the day appointed, the senate convened, and

After proclamation was made that Samuel Chace should appear conformable to the summons, or that his default should be recorded, Mr. Chace appeared. The president of the senate (Mr. Burr) then stated to him, that, having been summoned to answer the articles of impeachment exhibited against him by the House of Representatives, the Senate were ready to hear any answer which he had to make; whereupon Mr. Chace addressed the court.

The trial continued until Friday, the first day of March, 1805, when, at half past twelve o'clock, the court took their seats; and the president, having directed the secretary to read the first article of impeachment, observed, that the question would be put to each member, on each article separately, as his name occurred in alphabetical order. The first article was then read. When the question was hereupon put by the president of the court, and repeated after each article as read, viz.:—

Is Samuel Chase, Esquire, guilty of a high crime or misdemeanour in the article of impeachment just read? The decision was as follows:—

Article				
Article 1st.	Guilty	16;	not guilty	18
2d.	"	10;	"	24
3d.	"	18;	"	16
4th.	"	18;	"	16
5th.	Not guilty, *unanimous.*			
6th.	"	4;	"	30
7th.	"	10;	"	24
8th.	"	19;	"	15

The president then said—"*There not being a constitutional majority on any one article, it becomes my duty to pronounce that Samuel Chace, Esquire, is acquitted on the articles of impeachment exhibited against him by the House of Representatives.*"

TO THEODOSIA.

Washington, March 10, 1804.

Still lingering here, being detained by some trifling, important concerns of business, for trifles are important in matters of finance; nothing vexatious, however. That, I hope and believe, is past.

Your anxieties about me evince a sort of sickly sensibility, which indicates that you are not well. I fear that you are suffering a debility, arising from climate or other cause, which affects both mind and body. When you are in health you have no sort of solicitude or apprehension about me; you confide that, under any circumstances, I am able to fulfil your expectations and your wishes. Resume, I pray you, this confidence, so flattering to me, so consoling to yourself, may I add, so justly founded?

On the 13th I shall leave this for Philadelphia. There is no reason to think that I shall this season visit either New-York or New-Jersey. The plan of summer operations is to go from Philadelphia to Fort Pitt (Pittsburg), thence through the states on each side of the Ohio. To visit St. Louis and the mouth of the Missouri; thence through Tennessee (where pass a month) to Orleans; and thence, either by water or land, to the Atlantic coast, not far from Yarnaco or the mouth of the Waccama. Thus you see that you are the end of all plans, and, wherever they may begin, the termination is the same. This tour has other objects than mere curiosity. An operation of business, which promises to render the tour both useful and agreeable. I may be at Philadelphia long enough to receive your answer to this, after which you must *surcease* from writing till further advice. You will hear of me occasionally on my route. Write now, therefore, all you have to say.

Just at the moment of writing the last word I receive a message from the president informing me that Dr. Browne may have the office of secretary of the government of Louisiana (which means the upper district, whereof St. Louis is the capital). General Wilkinson is appointed governor of that territory. St. Louis is on the banks of the Mississippi, about twenty miles below the mouth of the Missouri. It contains about two hundred houses, and some very wealthy people. The inhabitants are French; retain the French manners of the last century; are said to be hospitable; gay to dissipation; the society polished and fashionable. All accounts represent the country as remarkably healthy, fertile, and beautiful. The salary of secretary is, I think, but eight hundred dollars per annum. Certain contingences, however, will make it worth about double that sum. Wilkinson and Browne will suit most admirably as eaters and laughers, and, I believe, in all other particulars.

Charles Williamson has not returned from Europe, but is hourly expected. My right of franking letters will cease on the 23d of this month, so that you are not to expect pamphlets, &c., by the mail. God bless thee.

A. Burr.

TO THEODOSIA.

Washington, March 13, 1805.

The enclosed newspaper is just now put into my hands. It is true, as is there said, that I made a talk, as was decent and proper, to the Senate on leaving them formally. There was nothing written or prepared, except that it had been some days on my mind to say something. It was the solemnity, the anxiety, the expectation, and the interest which I saw strongly painted in the countenances of the auditors, that inspired whatever was said. I neither shed tears nor assumed tenderness; but tears did flow abundantly. The story in this newspaper is rather awkwardly and pompously told. It has been gathered up, I presume, from different relations of the facts. This newspaper (*The Washington Federalist*) has been for months past, and, for aught I know (for I read none of them), still is, one of the most abusive against A. Burr. I am told that several papers lately make some qualified compliments; thus, for instance, referring to Judge Chace's trial—" He conducted with the dignity and impartiality of an angel, but with the rigour of a devil." May God have you in his holy keeping

A. Burr.

From the Washington Federalist, 13th March, 1805.

Having heard much said in commendation of Mr. Burr's valedictory address to the Senate, we have solicited and procured the following, which we present to our readers without comment.

On Saturday, the 2d of March, 1805, Mr. Burr took leave of the Senate. This was done at a time when the doors were closed; the Senate being engaged in executive business, and, of course, there was no spectators. It is, however, said to be the most dignified, sublime, and impressive that ever was uttered; and the effect which it produced justifies these epithets. I will give you the best account I have been able to obtain, from the relation of several senators, as well federal as republican.

"Mr. Burr began by saying that he had intended to pass the day with them, but the increase of a slight indisposition (sore throat) had determined him then to take leave of them. He touched lightly on some of the rules and orders of the house, and recommended, in one or two points, alterations, of which he briefly explained the reasons and principles.

"He said he was sensible he must at times have wounded the feelings of individual members. He had ever avoided entering into explanations at the time, because a moment of irritation was not a moment for explanation; because his position (being in the chair) rendered it impossible to enter into explanations without obvious danger of consequences which might hazard the dignity of the Senate, or prove disagreeable and injurious in more than one point of view; that he had, therefore, preferred to leave to their reflections his justification; that, on his part, he had no injuries to complain of; if any had been done or attempted, he was ignorant of the authors; and if he had ever heard, he had forgotten, for, he thanked God, he had no memory for injuries.

"He doubted not but that they had found occasion to observe, that to be prompt was not therefore to be precipitate; and that to act without delay was not always to act without reflection; that error was often to be preferred to indecision; that his errors, whatever they might have been, were those of rule and principle, and not of caprice; that it could not be deemed arrogance in him to say that, in his official conduct, he had known no party—no cause—no friend; that if, in the opinion of any, the discipline which had been established approached to rigour, they would at least admit that it was uniform and indiscriminate.

"He further remarked, that the ignorant and unthinking affected to treat as unnecessary and fastidious a rigid attention to rules and decorum; but he thought nothing trivial which touched, however remotely, the dignity of that body; and he appealed to their experience for the justice of this sentiment, and urged them in language the most impressive, and in a manner the most commanding, to avoid the smallest relaxation of the habits which he had endeavoured to inculcate and establish.

"But he challenged their attention to considerations more momentous than any which regarded merely their personal honour and character—the preservation of law, of liberty, and the Constitution. This house, said he, is a sanctuary; a citadel of law, of order, and of liberty; and it is here—it is here, in this exalted refuge—here, if anywhere, will resistance be made to the storms of political phrensy and the silent arts of corruption; and if the Constitution be destined ever to perish by the sacrilegious hands of the demagogue or the usurper, which God avert, its expiring agonies will be witnessed on this floor.*

"He then adverted to those affecting sentiments which attended a final separation—a dissolution, perhaps for ever, of those associations which he hoped had been mutually satisfactory. He consoled himself, however, and them, with the reflections that, though they separated, they would be engaged in the common cause of disseminating principles of freedom and social order. He should always regard the proceedings of that body with interest and with solicitude. He should feel for their honour and the national honour so intimately connected with it, and took his leave with expres-

* There was something prophetic in this prediction; for a few hours afterward, in the House of Representatives, Messrs. Nicholson and Randolph were betrayed into a violence of conduct which was noticed in our last.

Editor of the Washington Federalist.

sions of personal respect, and with prayers, and wishes," &c.

In this cold relation a distant reader, especially one to whom Colonel Burr is not personally known, will be at a loss to discover the cause of those extraordinary emotions which were excited. The whole Senate were in tears, and so unmanned that it was half an hour before they could recover themselves sufficiently to come to order, and choose a vice-president pro tem.

At the president's, on Monday, two of the senators were relating these circumstances to a circle which had collected round them. One said that he wished that the tradition might be preserved as one of the most extraordinary events he had ever witnessed. Another senator being asked, on the day following that on which Mr. Burr took his leave, how long he was speaking, after a moment's pause, said he could form no idea; it might have been an hour, and it might have been but a moment; when he came to his senses, he seemed to have awakened as from a kind of trance.

The characteristics of the vice-president's manner seemed to have been elevation and dignity—a consciousness of superiority, &c. Nothing of that whining adulation; those canting, hypocritical complaints of want of talents; assurance of his endeavours to please them; hopes of their favour, &c. On the contrary, he told them explicitly that he had determined to pursue a conduct which his judgment should approve, and which should secure the suffrage of his own conscience, and that he had never considered who else might be pleased or displeased; although it was but justice on this occasion to thank them for their deference and respect to his official conduct—the constant and uniform support he had received from every member—for their prompt acquiescence in his decisions; and to remark, to their honour, that they had never descended to a single motion of passion or embarrassment; and so far was he from apologizing for his defects, that he told them that, on reviewing the decisions he had had occasion to make, there was no one which, on reflection, he was disposed to vary or retract.

As soon as the Senate could compose themselves sufficiently to choose a president pro tem., they came to the following resolution :—

"Resolved, unanimously, That the thanks of the Senate be presented to *Aaron Burr*, in testimony of the impartiality, dignity, and ability with which he has presided over their deliberations, and of their entire approbation of his conduct in the discharge of the arduous and important duties assigned him as president of the Senate; and that Mr. Smith, of Maryland, and Mr. White be a committee to wait on him with this resolution.

Attest. SAM. A. OTIS, Secretary.

To which resolution Colonel Burr returned the following answer to the Senate :—

"Next to the satisfaction arising from a consciousness of having discharged my duty, is that which is derived from the approbation of those who have been the constant witnesses of my conduct, and the value of this testimony of their esteem is greatly enhanced by the promptitude and unanimity with which it is offered.

"I pray you to accept my respectful acknowledgments, and the assurance of my inviolable attachment to the inter ests and dignity of the Senate.

A. BURR.

TO JOSEPH ALSTON.

Philadelphia, March 22, 1805.

The enclosed paper will show you what is doing here. The subject of convention is about to divide this state into new and inveterate parties. The old names and the old animosities of federal and republican will be lost, but the passions will have full scope in the new.

I am not wholly free from apprehension that you take no

interest in any thing but a rice-field. Fame says that you are about to degenerate into a mere planter. If so, it is to be lamented that you have any thing above common sense, and that you have learned any thing more than to read and write, for all above common sense and school education spoils the planter.

Though in my former letters I did not, in express terms, inform you that I was under ostracism, yet it must have been inferred. Such is the fact. In New-York I am to be disfranchised, and in New-Jersey hanged. Having substantial objections to both, I shall not, for the present, hazard either, but shall seek another country. You will not, from this, conclude that I have become passive, or disposed to submit tamely to the machinations of a banditti. If you should you would greatly err. —— and his clan affect to deplore, but secretly rejoice at and stimulate the villanies of all sorts which are practised against me. Their alarm and anxiety, however, are palpable to a degree perfectly ridiculous. Their awkward attempts to propitiate reminds one of the Indian worship of the evil spirit. God bless you ever.

A. Burr.

TO THEODOSIA.

Philadelphia, March 29, 1805.

I arrived here on the 21st instant, and shall remain here yet ten days. John W. Smith is now here. He married Miss Duer a few weeks ago, and will take her, with Frances, &c., to Orleans next month. Ann does not go; but one younger than Susan, whose name I forget. Miss Dallas is to be married in a few days to a handsome young man, just admitted to the bar: no fortune, but said to possess talents. Poor La R. quite pale and emaciated; the fruit of dissipation. Celeste as heretofore, abating the influence of time, which is a little too visible; courteous even to flattery. La Planche a recluse. Miss Binney is to be married next week to Mr. Wallace, a young lawyer of this city of good character and prospects.

People who are occupied are never dull, never melancholy. I learn, then, from your letter of the 10th, that you have been a little lazy. To be sure, if that letter was written for publication, it would do credit to the author; but to me, *en particulier*, other reflections might have occurred. The story, however, is prettily told, and I kiss your hand for some other pretty things. But let me see more of the effects of those precepts and that example.

I am apprehensive that your milk diet will not carry you through the summer. You will want stimulus of some kind. For this purpose something is used in all warm countries. In the West Indies they drink rum and they die. In the East Indies and China, ginseng is the panacea. Try ginseng. Some decoction or (bitter) infusion. When my stomach is out of order or wants tone, nothing serves so effectually as a cup of chamomile tea, without sugar or milk. I think this would give you an appetite. Make the experiment. Bathing in seawater is a grand preservative. If your bath be in the house, the best time is an hour or two before dinner. Tepid bath; none of your cold baths for such a machine as yours. If you have no convenience for a warm bath in the house, set a mason to work to-morrow and make one in each of your country houses. It is a high evidence of the barbarism of our Southern states that, in an extent of three hundred miles, filled with wealthy people, and in a hot climate, there should not be, in any one private family, a convenient bathing-room. Perhaps, indeed, some ruined French refugee may have expended fifty dollars to furnish himself and family this luxury, as essential to comfort and cleanliness as to health.

In ten or twelve days I shall be on my way westward. My address, till further orders, is at Cincinnati, Ohio, to the care of the Hon. John Smith. As the objects of this journey, not mere curiosity, or *pour passer le tems*, may lead me to Orleans, and perhaps farther. I contemplate the tour with gayety and cheerfulness. The most weighty solicitude on my mind is your health and that of your boy. My letters have given you some advice as to yourself. You will have a letter from Pittsburg, and from other points as opportunities may offer, though I shall seldom be far from the route of some mail. God bless you

A. Burr.

TO THEODOSIA.

Philadelphia, April 10, 1805.

I rejoice that your nerves are in better tone, for truly, in some of your letters, I could scarcely recognise my daughter. As to the boy, I beseech you not to undertake to teach him the various sounds of the letters abstractedly from the words in which those sounds are found. This must be learned arbitrarily. Go on with his a, b, &c.; and when he shall have learned the language, and not till then, can you teach him (or ought it to be attempted) the principles of the construction of that language.

My ostracism is enlivened by a constant succession of visiters from New-York and New-Jersey. Swartwout and Bunner have just now come in, and I have not been a day without some *one*, *two*, or more. They stay generally two or three days with me, and I am privileged to take them with me wherever I dine. Major Powell, the friend of Miss Keene, and the lover of her mother, returned lately from Europe and died here last week. He has left an estate of ten or twelve thousand guineas per annum.

I met Miss Sumter (overtook meaning) at Wilmington last winter, and thence to Baltimore we rode together in the stage. She is a frank, sensible, amiable girl. May make a very interesting companion. I was so much pleased with her, that I went several times to see her (two miles), though I visited no lady. I took her to General Van Ness's, where I made her at home. She plays on the piano in a style which may be called superior, and has a most uncommon fine voice, which has been neglected.

A. Burr.

TO THEODOSIA.

Pittsburg, April 30, 1805.

Arrived in good order yesterday. Find my boat and hands ready. The water high and weather fine. Shall set off in two hours. Have therefore no time to give any account of my journey hither. My boat is, properly speaking, a floating house, sixty feet by fourteen, containing dining-room, kitchen with fireplace, and two bedrooms; roofed from stem to stern; steps to go up, and a walk on the top the whole length; glass windows, &c. This edifice costs one hundred and thirty-three dollars, and how it can be made for that sum passes my comprehension.

I find that Frankfort will be better than Cincinnati; so address to me, Frankfort, Kentucky, to the care of the Honourable John Brown.

A. Burr.

On the 30th of April, 1805, Colonel Burr and Gabriel Shaw, who had accompanied him from Philadelphia, left Pittsburg in their boat. At this period Colonel Burr commences, for the amusement of his daughter, a journal of his adventures, which contains some interesting details explanatory of the then situation of the western country. Extracts from this journal will be made. On the 2d of May they stopped at a little village on the north bank called M'Intosh. The next day "went on shore in the skiff (letting the ark float on) to see the town of *Wieling*, sometimes erroneously spelled *Wheeling*; a pretty, neat village, well situated on the south bank, containing sixty or eighty houses, some of brick, and some of a fine free stone found in the vicinity. Saw several well-dressed women, who had the air of fashion and movements of *vous autres* on the coast."

On the morning of the 5th reached Marietta, on the north side, "containing about eighty houses; some that would be called handsome in any village on the continent. After breakfast" (says Colonel Burr) "came in several gentlemen of the town to offer me civilities and hospitalities. We have been walking several miles to see the mounds, parapets, squares, and other remains of unknown antiquity which are found in this neighbourhood. I am astonished and confounded; totally unsatisfied with the conjectures of others, and unable to repose on any plausible one of my own. I shall continue to write to you journal-wise, but, having no copy, you must preserve the sheets, as I may wish to refer to them for facts and dates."

Arrived at Cincinnati on the 11th May, by the course of the river estimated to be 310 miles from Marietta. "Meeting here with General Dayton and several old army acquaintance, remained the whole day." In the evening started "for Louisville, which is at the rapids or falls of the Ohio. There it is proposed to take land, to ride through part of Kentucky, visit Lexington and Frankfort, and meet the ark again at the mouth of the Cumberland, which empties into the Ohio about fifty miles before its junction with the Mississippi."

TO THEODOSIA.

Lexington (Kentucky), May 23, 1805.

My journal has grown too big to be sent by mail. I have, therefore, only to assure you of my health and safety, without entering into any of those details which you will see anon. Shaw is with me. To-morrow we pursue our journey by land to Nashville in Tennessee, and thence down the Cumberland to Eddyville, where we expect to find our boat, and intend to go from that place to Orleans in ten days.

Arrived at Nashville on the 29th of May. "One is astonished at the number of sensible, well-informed, and well behaved people which is found here. I have been received with much hospitality and kindness, and could stay a month with pleasure; but General Andrew Jackson having provided us a boat, we shall set off on Sunday, the 2d of June, to navigate down the Cumberland, either to Smithland at its mouth, or to Eddyville, sixty or eighty miles above, at one of which places we expect to find our boat, with which we intend to make a rapid voyage down the Mississippi to Natchez and Orleans.

Left Nashville on the 3d of June in an open boat. Came down the Cumberland to its mouth, about 220 miles, in an open boat, where our ark was in waiting. Reached Massac, on the Ohio, sixteen miles below, on the 6th. Here found General Wilkinson on his way to St. Louis. The general and his officers fitted me out with an elegant barge, sails, colours, and ten oars, with a sergeant, and ten able, faithful hands. Thus equipped, I left Massac on the 10th of June, Shaw in company.

"On the 17th arrived at Natchez, being by water, as estimated, nearly eight hundred miles from Massac. Natchez is a town of three or four hundred houses; the inhabitants traders and mechanics, but surrounded by wealthy planters, among whom I have been entertained with great hospitality and taste. These planters are, many of them, men of education and refinement; live as well as yours, and have generally better houses. We are now going through a settled country, and, during the residue of my voyage to Orleans, about three hundred miles, I shall take breakfast and dinner each day at the house of some gentleman on shore. I take no letters of introduction; but, whenever I hear of any gentleman whose acquaintance or hospitalities I should desire, I send word that I am coming to see him, and have always met a most cordial reception.

"Edward Livingston was married about a fortnight ago to Madame Moreau, *veuve*, lately from St. Domingo, rich in beauty and accomplishments. I hear so many pleasant things of Orleans, that I should certainly (if one half of them are verified on inspection) settle down there were it not for Theodosia and her boy; but these will control my fate.

"On the 25th of June reached New-Orleans. The lady of your laughing friend is a charming woman. She was a widow from St. Domingo; *sans argent et sans enfants*. Without a single good feature, she is very agreeable. She is nearly the size and figure of Lady Nesbet. Fair, pale, with jet black hair and eyes—little, sparkling black eyes, which seem to be made for far other purposes than those of mere vision. Ph. Jones is to be married in a few days to a pretty little American, Miss Brown. The inhabitants of the United States are here called Americans. I have been received with distinction.

"The mark of attention with which I have been most flattered is a letter from the holy sisters, the Ursuline nuns, congratulating me on my arrival. Having returned a polite answer to this letter, it was intimated to me that the saints had a desire to see me. The bishop conducted me to the cloister. We conversed at first through the grates; but presently I was admitted within, and I passed an hour with them greatly to my satisfaction. None of that calm monotony which I expected. All was gayety, *wit*, and sprightliness. Saint A. is a very accomplished lady. In manners and appearance a good deal like Mrs. Merry. All, except two, appear to be past thirty. They were dressed with perfect neatness; their veils thrown back. We had a repast of wine, fruit, and cakes. I was conducted to every part of the building. All is neatness, simplicity, and order. At parting, I asked them to remember me in their prayers, which they all promised with great promptness and courtesy —Saint A. with earnestness.

"This city is larger than I expected, and there are found many more than would be supposed living in handsome style. They are cheerful, gay, and easy. I have promised to return here next fall. I go on the 10th instant (July) by land to Kentucky, and thence, probably, to St. Louis. *A la santé Madame* Alston, is generally the first toast at every table I have been. Then we say some evil things of Mr. Alston. *Encore*, adieu. I will ask Saint A. to pray for thee too. I believe much in the efficacy of her prayers. *Le pauvre* A. B. A., I can find nothing here to send him.

"Arrived at Nashville on the 6th August. You now see me safe through the wilderness, though I doubt (hussey) whether you knew that I had a wilderness to pass in order to get here. Yes, about four hundred and fifty miles of wilderness. The hospitality of these people will keep me here till the 12th instant, when I shall partake of a public dinner, given not to the vice-president, but to A. B. I shall be at Lexington on the 19th. I have directed Bradley's new map of the United States to be sent to you; this will enable you to trace my route, and I pray you to study the map attentively.

"I am still at Nashville (August 13th). For a week I have been lounging at the house of General Jackson, once a lawyer, after a judge, now a planter; a man of intelligence, and one of those prompt, frank, ardent souls whom I love to meet. The general has no children, but two lovely nieces made a visit of some days, contributed greatly to my amusement, and have cured me of all the evils of my wilderness jaunt. If I had time I would describe to you these two girls, for they deserve it. To-morrow I move on towards Lexington.

"I ought to tell you how I came hither. It was thus: I embarked in a little schooner at the mouth of the Bayou St. Jean on Lake Ponchartrain, and landed on the opposite side of the lake about ten miles below the mouth of the Chefonti, a traverse of about twenty-five miles, which I made in six hours. Took a guide, and went on next morning in a footpath; crossed the Chefonti about four miles above its mouth, and then turned northerly; crossed the 31st degree of latitude at forty-two miles from the Mississippi. Note;

this line has been actually run, and marked with great accuracy by commissioners on the part of the United States and of Spain, as the north bound of the Floridas and the south bound of the United States, till it strikes the St. Mary's. You will see on the map. Continued on to Natchez. From the mouth of the Chefonti to Natchez by this route is about one hundred and forty miles. I was four days from New-Orleans to Natchez. Passed near a week in the vicinity of Natchez, and saw some tears of regret when I left it; but I am *now* to give you the route; my journal will give you the incidents.

"The path from Natchez, going northward, keeps east of the Yazoo, and, I think, nearly on the dividing ridge between the waters of the Yazoo and those of the Tombigbee or Tambeckbee; a vile country, destitute of springs and of running water—think of drinking the nasty puddle-water, covered with green scum, and full of animalculæ—bah! I crossed the Tennessee; how glad I was to get on the waters of the Tennessee; all fine, transparent, lively streams, and itself a clear, beautiful, magnificent river. I crossed it, I say, forty miles below the muscle shoals, and three hundred and sixty above its mouth, reckoning by the meanders of the river. Thence to Nashville through the town of Franklin. On the map you will see laid down a road from Nashville to Natchez as having been cut by the order of the minister of war. This is imaginary; there is no such road.

"Arrived at Lexington on the 20th August, 1805. Left it for Frankfort, distant twenty-two miles, on the 31st. I am magnificently lodged at the house of John Brown, who married your old friend and neighbour Miss Mason, who is, you know, the sister of *my friend*, the priest (John Mason). She has two fine boys; the youngest, now four, I find something like A. B. A., and, of course, amuse myself with him a great deal. Mrs. Brown is still handsome, and speaks of you with attachment and respect.

"My plans for the two next months are now made up, or

rather imposed on me by letters received since I last wrote you, and by my previous engagements. On the 1st of September I leave this for St. Louis. My route is to Louisville, 55 miles; Vincennes, on the Wabash, 150 miles; Kaskaskias, on the Mississippi, 150 miles; St. Louis, 75 miles. These distances are probably inaccurate, but St. Louis is called 450 miles from this. I propose to be at Cincinnati on the 1st of October; at Chilicothe and Marietta from the 7th to the 15th; at Pittsburg about the 20th, and at Bedford till the 1st of November. If by that time I should hear nothing from you, shall take measures for going by land or water to Theoville, so that you see it must be late in November before I can see you.

"Arrived at Louisville (Falls of the Ohio) on the 2d of September, being sixty miles on my way to the Missouri. I have now again one hundred and fifty miles of wilderness to encounter. I will be at Berkeley Springs by the 20th of October, where I hope to meet you and Mari. Address to me at the city of Washington."

TO JOSEPH ALSTON.

Washington, November 29, 1804.

I came to Berkeley as was proposed. You were not there; no letter from you. I sent a messenger to Washinton city for intelligence, and waited his return in unpleasant suspense. At the termination of six days my messenger returned with letters advising that you would be at Hillsborough, whither I resolved immediately to go, but thought it best to take Washington in my way, in the hope of other letters. You were all at the Oaks, and no movement spoken of. You were to go alone to the legislature. Wife and child to be left at the Oaks.

Though oppressed with important engagements, I would nevertheless set off with the stage of this day for Georgetown and the Oaks if I could have been assured of finding preparations ready made for the contemplated journey of

Theodosia and the boy; but as you may have left home without attending to this point, it seemed probable that I might make a fruitless journey of nine hundred miles; fruitless, except the pleasure of passing one day at the Oaks, and even this with the alloy of your absence. My course will, therefore, be now to Philadelphia, where I have made appointments, and either at that place or this shall wait your reply, and we must endeavour to arrange our plans with precision. Address me at this place.

My solicitude about the health of Theodosia is no way relieved by the sort of recovery of which she advises me. The boy, too, has a relapse of the ague, a disease of all others the most fatal to the infant constitution. Great God! what sacrifices do you make, and to what end? These solicitudes poison all my enjoyments, and often unfit me for business. Being apprized from recollection of our personal communications last autumn, and of our correspondence last winter, of the engagements and ties which will prevent you, at least for some months, from leaving South Carolina, I determine, at any sacrifice, to rescue Theodosia and son.

There will be no war with Spain unless we shall declare it, which is not expected. England continues a course of malevolence, which will still continue and be borne. France, more courteous in words, under the pressure of her own affairs. Affectionately,

A. BURR.

The letters and extracts from the journal of Colonel Burr, which have been given in the preceding part of this chapter, sufficiently indicate that he was actively employed in travelling during the year 1805. From January, 1806, until August following, his time was principally spent in the cities of Washington and Philadelphia. During this period his correspondence* is voluminous, but in no manner develops

* Portions of the letters to and from Colonel Burr are interesting; many high-

any other views than such as relate to land speculations. Commodore Truxton, on the trial at Richmond, swore that Colonel Burr, in the latter end of July, 1806, informed him that he was about concluding a bargain for the Washita lands. In August Mr. Burr commenced his western tour. In the summer and autumn, and during that tour, he was brought before two different grand juries in Kentucky and discharged. So far as any testimony was produced, it went to prove an intention of settling the Washita lands. On the 3d of March, 1807, he was arrested, by order of the government, on a charge of treason, in the Tombigbee country, and transported to Richmond, Virginia, for trial.

CHAPTER XX.

A SEPARATION of the South American provinces from the government of Spain had long been anticipated. As early as the year 1796, while John Jay was governor, Colonel Burr had various conversations with him on the subject of these provinces. In these conversations Colonel Burr expressed his views in reference to South America, which, he said, he could revolutionize and take possession of. Governor Jay replied that the boldness of the project would contribute to its success; expressing his opinion that it was not impracticable. From this period until 1805, Mr. Burr's mind seemed to have been constantly engaged in reflecting on the feasibility of the measure, and the proper period for carrying it into operation.

As matter of history connected with this subject, but not generally known, it may not be improper to refer to an oc-

ly amusing; but the space yet remaining in which these memoirs are to be closed renders it absolutely necessary to exclude them from the work.

currence as early as the year 1797, 98. About this period General Miranda was in the United States. He formed an acquaintance with Generals Hamilton, Knox, and other distinguished Americans. To these gentlemen he communicated his project of revolutionizing South America. From the United States he proceeded to England, and presented himself to the British ministry. They entered into his views. The proposition was, that the United States should furnish ten thousand troops, and, in that event, the British government agreed to supply the necessary funds and ships to carry on an expedition. As soon as Miranda had completed his arrangements with the British minister, he addressed a letter to General Alexander Hamilton, dated April 6th, 1798, in which he says :—

"This, my dear and respectable friend, will be handed to you by my countryman Don ——, who is charged with despatches of the highest importance for the President of the United States. He will tell you, *confidentially*, all that you wish to know on this subject. It appears that the moment of our emancipation approaches, and the establishment of liberty on all the continent of the New World is confided by Providence to us. The only danger which I foresee is the introduction of French principles, which would poison our liberty in its cradle, and would finish by destroying yours."

So far did these arrangements advance, that Miranda again wrote General Hamilton, under date of the 19th of October, 1798 :—

"Your wishes are, in some sort, already accomplished, seeing that it has been agreed here on one side not to employ in the operations on land English troops; seeing that the auxiliary land forces are to be exclusively American, while the naval force shall be purely English. Every thing is smooth, and we wait only for the fiat of your illustrious president to depart like lightning."

48

On the same day (October 19th) General Miranda wrote General Knox as follows:—

"I cannot express to you, my dear general, with what pleasure I heard of your nomination* in the continental army of the United States of America. It would appear that your *wishes* are at length *accomplished*, and that every possible circumstance is united, at this moment, in our favour. Would to God that Providence would endow us with sufficient wisdom to make the most advantageous use of these circumstances."

At this time Mr. Adams, senior, was president of the United States, and declined entering into the arrangement. It is believed that no reply was made to the letter addressed to the president. Two questions here present themselves to the inquiring mind.

Was there any connexion between this plan of Miranda for the invasion of Mexico, and the raising of an army in the year 1798, under the pretext of resisting an attack upon this country by France?

Was the policy adopted by President Adams on that occasion any way connected with the imbittered warfare which subsequently ensued between Mr. Adams and Mr. Hamilton? These are questions for the consideration of speculative politicians, but not for discussion in this place.

It has been seen that Mr. Burr was actively engaged during the years 1805 and 1806 in traversing the western country. In his latter days Colonel Burr had no longer any motive for concealment; nor did he evince the least desire to suppress the facts in relation to any of his acts, even where the promulgation of those facts was calculated to affect his moral character. According to his representations, repeated at a time and under circumstances the most solemn† and

* In July, 1798, Generals Hamilton, Pinckney, and Knox were appointed major generals in the standing army raised that summer, *nominally*, for the purpose of repelling a French invasion, at a moment when France had not a ship of war on the ocean, and while British squadrons were hovering on her whole coast.

† On the 10th of June, 1835, Dr. Hosack, the friend and physician of Colonel

impressive, his views were twofold: viz., *First.* The revolutionizing of Mexico; and, *Second,* A settlement on what was known as the Bastrop lands. Burr, from early manhood, had a turn for speculation, and frequently entered into large contracts for the purchase and sale of lands.

At this period (1806) the difficulties with Spain in relation to the Mississippi and the right of deposite at New-Orleans created an opinion that a Spanish war was inevitable. Such a war would have been popular with the western people. Of these opinions and these feelings Burr took advantage, and undoubtedly, by innuendoes or otherwise, induced some to believe that his arrangements for the invasion of Mexico were with the knowledge, if not the approbation of the government.

Previous to the cession of Louisiana to the United States, Baron P. N. Tut Bastrop contracted with the Spanish government for a tract of land exceeding thirty miles square near Nachitoches. By the terms of the contract he was, within a given period of time, to settle upon these lands two hundred families. Subsequently Colonel Charles Lynch made an arrangement with Bastrop for an interest in this contract. Burr purchased from Lynch nearly four hundred thousand acres, lying between the Sabine and Nachitoches. On the trial at Richmond this purchase was established, and the actual payment to Lynch by Burr of five thousand dollars was also proved.

General Adair possessed the confidence of Colonel Burr in relation to his western movements in a greater degree than any other individual. Burr was introduced to Adair by General Wilkinson. In a letter dated March, 1807, General Adair says, and there is no doubt truly says—" So far

Burr, supposed that he could not continue but a few days, perhaps a few hours. Mr. Burr was so informed, and was then asked by M. L. Davis whether at any time he had contemplated a separation of the Union. His reply was—" No; I would as soon have thought of taking possession of the moon, and informing my friends that I intended to divide it among them." While making the reply his indignation seemed to be aroused.

as I know or believe of the intentions of Colonel Burr (and my enemies will agree I am not ignorant on this subject), they were to prepare and lead an expedition into Mexico, predicated on a war between the two governments; without a war he knew he could do nothing. On this war taking place he calculated with certainty, as well from the policy of the measure at this time as from the positive assurances of Wilkinson, who seemed to have the power to force it in his own hands. This continued to be the object of Colonel Burr until he heard of the venal and shameful bargain made by Wilkinson at the Sabine river; this information he received soon after the attempt to arrest him in Frankfort. He then turned his attention altogether towards strengthening himself on the Washita, and waiting a more favourable crisis. I thought the first of these objects honourable and worthy the attention of any man; but I was not engaged in it, my political as well as private pursuits forbidding me from taking a part until it was over; nor did I ever believe, notwithstanding Wilkinson's swaggering letters to me on that subject, which may be seen, that a war would take place."

The grant of the Spanish government to Bastrop amounted to 1,200,000 acres. Six tenths of this grant was conveyed to Colonel Lynch, and cost him about one hundred thousand dollars. As the time within which two hundred families were to be settled on the land was rapidly drawing to a close, Lynch conveyed one half his right to Burr for fifty thousand dollars. In this purchase many private citizens of worth and respectability were interested. The two projects, however, became in some degree blended. The great object of Burr was the conquest of Mexico. With this view he conferred with General Wilkinson, who was ardent in the cause. Wilkinson's regular force, about six hundred men, was intended as a nucleus, around which the followers of Burr were to form. They were the only disciplined corps that could be expected. As Wilkinson was the American commander-in-chief, and stationed upon the borders of Mexico, he possessed the power, and was pledged to strike the blow whenever it should be deemed expedient. This commencement of the war would thus have been apparently under the sanction and authority of the American government, and would have drawn to the standard of Burr numerous volunteers from the western states. Such, undoubtedly, was the plan; and Burr entertained no suspicion of Wilkinson's treachery towards him until his interview with Swartwout. As soon as he made that discovery, in the language of General Adair, "he turned his attention towards strengthening himself on the Washita, and waiting a more favourable crisis."

Daniel Clarke, of New-Orleans, entered into the Mexican project. He engaged to advance fifty thousand dollars; but subsequently, from disappointments, he was unable to fulfil his contract. General Wilkinson detailed to Colonel Burr all the information he possessed respecting that country, and pointed out the facilities which would probably be afforded by the inhabitants in effecting a revolution. Without Wilkinson's troops, Burr declared most solemnly, a short time before his death, that he would not have made the attempt on Mexico; that he was perfectly aware the men he would collect, so far as it respected military operations, would be at first little better than a mob.

Colonel Burr had repeated conferences on the subject with Mr. Merry, the British plenipotentiary resident in the United States. Mr. Merry communicated to his government the project of Mr. Burr. Colonel Charles Williamson, the brother of Lord Balgray, went to England on the business, and, from the encouragement which he received, it was hoped and believed that a British naval squadron would have been furnished in aid of the expedition. At this juncture Mr. Pitt died. Wilkinson must have heard of the death of the premier late in the spring or early in the summer of 1806. From this moment, in Mr. Burr's opinion, Wilkinson became alarmed, and resolved on an abandonment of the enterprise at the sacrifice of his associates.

On the suggestion of Wilkinson, Mexico was twice visited by Daniel Clark. He held conferences and effected arrangements with many of the principal militia officers, who engaged to favour the revolution. The Catholic bishop, resident at New-Orleans, was also consulted, and prepared to promote the enterprise. He designated three priests, of the order of Jesuits, as suitable agents, and they were accordingly employed. The bishop was an intelligent and social man. He had been in Mexico, and spoke with great freedom of the dissatisfaction of the clergy in South America. The religious establishments of the country were not to be molested. Madame Xavier Tarjcon, superior of the convent of Ursuline nuns at New-Orleans, was in the secret. Some of the sisterhood were also employed in Mexico. So far as any decision had been formed, the landing was to have been effected at Tampico.

During the year 1806 Colonel Burr was at the house of General Andrew Jackson for some days. Repeated and detailed conversations were held between them in relation to the expedition. Subsequently, General Jackson addressed a letter to Colonel Burr, in which he alluded to rumours that were afloat of his having hostile designs against the United States; adding that, if this were true, he would hold no communication on the subject; but, if untrue, and his intentions were to proceed to Mexico, he (Jackson) would join and accompany him with his whole division. To this the proper answer was given.

About the same time Colonel Burr wrote Senator John Smith, of Ohio, on the subject of these rumours, in which letter he says—"If Bonaparte, with all his army, was in the western country for the purpose of accomplishing that object, they would never again see salt water." It may be proper to state here that Colonel Burr's whole force at no time exceeded *one hundred and thirty men.*

This is a brief, but it is believed to be a true and faithful account of Colonel Burr's views and projects during the years 1805 and 1806. In the progress of these transactions many individuals were implicated. While the promulgation of their names might tend to gratify an idle curiosity, it could be productive of no possible good. The charge of treason, now that the storm has blown over, is so perfectly ridiculous, that one who investigates the subject will be astounded that it ever gained credence. It originated with the most corrupt and unprincipled, and was countenanced, propagated, and sustained by the most malignant. When the charge of treason was first spread abroad, Colonel Burr appeared to be deserted and abandoned by his confidential and devoted friends. Even his son-in-law, Governor Alston, seemed to shrink from the consequences of an intercourse with him. All those who were in any manner connected with the contemplated expedition disclaimed the idea of treasonable designs, averring that, if such were the views of Colonel Burr, they had been deceived. And what does all this prove? Does it not demonstrate that if his object was a separation of the Union, that object was to be accomplished without the knowledge or aid of his friends and associates? Can any thing place the charge in a more ridiculous point of view?

Colonel Burr was arrested as a traitor on the Tombigbee river, Mississippi territory, and transported to Richmond, where he arrived on the 26th of March, 1807. He was bailed until the 22d of May, when the court was to convene. A description of the outrages and cruelty which he endured would fill volumes. A calm and dispassionate detail of the means which were adopted by Mr. Jefferson to obtain an opportunity of shedding his blood, under colour of law, would be revolting to the philanthropist and the patriot, while it would not change public opinion of this philosopher.

In October, 1806, Mr. Swartwout delivered to General

Wilkinson a letter from Burr, written in cipher. That letter Wilkinson *altered*, and then deciphered it. The forgery was detected before the grand jury, and he compelled to acknowledge the fact, although he had sworn to the translation as being correct in all its parts. Notwithstanding Mr. Jefferson's knowledge that Wilkinson was a Spanish pensioner, which fact Mr. Derbigny had stated to Secretary Gallatin in a letter, and subsequently swore to its truth; and notwithstanding his perjury before the grand jury, yet did the president sustain and countenance the general as a fit instrument for his purposes.

Other arrests were made during this military reign of terror, *viz.*, Generals Adair and Dayton, Blennerhassett, Swartwout, Alexander, Smith, Bollman, Ogden, &c. Burr and Blennerhasset alone were brought to trial. On the 22d of May, 1807, came on the cause of Aaron Burr before the Circuit Court of the United States, Judge Marshall presiding. No indictment was found by the grand jury until the 25th of June, when two bills were presented against Burr; one for treason, and the other for a misdemeanour. On the 30th of June he was committed to the penitentiary for safe keeping until the third day of August. From the 5th until the 17th of August the court was engaged in obtaining a jury and discussing points of law. On that day the treason case was opened, and an examination of witnesses on the part of the government commenced. Colonel Burr had more than thirty witnesses in attendance, but deemed it unnecessary to call any of them.

On the 1st day of September, 1807, the jury retired, and in a short time returned with the following verdict, which was read by Colonel Carrington, their foreman.

"We of the jury say that Aaron Burr is not proved to be guilty under this indictment by any evidence submitted to us. We therefore find him not guilty."

This verdict was objected to by Colonel Burr as informal. He observed that, whenever a verdict is informal, the court will either send back the jury to alter it, or correct it itself; that they had no right to depart from the usual form, &c.

Mr. Hay thought the verdict ought to be recorded as found by the jury, which was substantially a verdict of acquittal; and that no principle of humanity, policy, or law forbade its being received in the very terms used by the jury.

Mr. Martin said that it was like the *whole play*, "Much ado about Nothing;" that this was a verdict of acquittal; that there was nothing to do but to answer the question of guilty or not guilty; that it was the case with every jury in every instance; they had or had not evidence before them.

Colonel Carrington, one of the jury, observed, that it was said among themselves that, if the verdict was informal, they would alter it; that it was, in fact, a verdict of acquittal.

The court then directed that the verdict should remain as found by the jury; and that an entry should be made on the record of "*Not Guilty.*"

On the 9th of September a jury was empannelled to try Colonel Burr on the indictment for misdemeanour, which consisted of seven counts; the substance of which were, that Aaron Burr did set on foot a military enterprise, to be carried on against the territory of a foreign prince; *viz.*, the province of Mexico, which was within the territory of the King of Spain, with whom the United States were at peace.

After the prosecution had examined some of their witnesses, and the court had decided that the testimony of others was not relevant, the district attorney, Mr. Hay, made a motion that the jury be discharged. To this motion Colonel Burr objected, insisting upon a verdict. This was on the 15th of September. The court being of opinion that the jury could not in this stage of the case be discharged without the consent of the accused, and that they must give a verdict, they accordingly retired, and very soon returned with a verdict of "*Not Guilty.*"

Previous to the trial for treason it was industriously circulated that Commodore Truxton had most honourably repelled Colonel Burr's advances, and pointed out the infamy which awaited him. He was subpœnaed on the part of the United States, and on his examination said—"That Colonel Burr told him (some time in July, 1806) that he contemplated an expedition to Mexico in the event of a war with Spain, which he thought inevitable. He asked me if the Havannah could be easily taken in the event of a war. I told him that it would require the co-operation of a naval force. Mr. Burr observed to me that *that* might be obtained. He asked me if I had any personal knowledge of Carthagena and La Vera Cruz, and what would be the best mode of attacking them by sea and land. I gave him my opinion very freely. Mr. Burr then asked me if I would take the command of a naval expedition. I asked him if the executive of the United States were privy to or concerned in the project. He answered *emphatically* that he was not: I asked that question because the executive had been charged with a knowledge of Miranda's expedition. I told Mr. Burr that I would have nothing to do with it; that Miranda's project had been intimated to me, but I declined to have any thing to do with such affairs. He observed to me that, in the event of a war, he intended to establish an independent government in Mexico; that Wilkinson, the army, and many officers of the navy would join. I told Mr. Burr that I could not see how any officer of the United States could join. He said that General Wilkinson had projected the expedition, and he had matured it; that many greater men than Wilkinson would join, and that thousands to the westward would join. I told Colonel Burr that there would be no war. He was sanguine there would be war. He said, however, that if he was disappointed as to the event of a war, he was about to complete a contract for a large quantity of land on the Washita; that he intended to invite his friends to settle it; that in one year he would have a thousand families of respectable and fashionable people, and some of them of considerable property; that it was a fine country, and that they would have a charming society, and in two years he would have double the number of settlers; and, being on the frontier, he would be ready to move whenever a war took place."

On his cross examination Commodore Truxton added "that he was very intimate with Colonel Burr; that in their conversations there appeared to be no reserve; that he never heard Colonel Burr speak of a division of the Union; that Burr said his Mexican expedition would be beneficial to the United States; that, so far from doubting Burr's intention to settle the Washita lands, he was astonished at hearing he had different views, which accounts were contained in newspapers received from the western country."

From among numerous instances of Mr. Jefferson's idea of *honour* and *morality*, as practised by him and by his order pending that trial, only one will be selected as a *sample*. Dr. Erick Bollman, the friend of Lafayette, was arrested by the order of Wilkinson as a co-conspirator with Burr. He was called as a witness on the part of the United States; and in open court, the district attorney, Mr. Hay, by order of Mr. Jefferson, tendered him a pardon, which he indignantly refused, asserting his innocence of any act requiring a pardon. Immediately after the trial, he published, under his own signature, an account of what occurred between himself and the president. From that publication, which was never controverted, sufficient will be extracted to show Mr. Jefferson's *feelings* and *principles*.

Bollman says, "In the month of December, 1806, I was seized and arrested at New-Orleans by order of General Wilkinson, but in the name of the United States. When I arrived at Charleston, Annapolis, and Washington, the newspapers represented Colonel Burr as being at the head of two thousand men, and they were ringing at the same time with reports of his *pretended treason*.

"These circumstances occasioned in my mind great indignation with regard to the reports just mentioned, and great solicitude lest General Wilkinson's conduct and Burr's situation might lead to occurrences which Colonel Burr would deprecate, and which involuntarily would put him in the wrong.

"I therefore requested an interview with the president of the United States for two decided objects. 1st, To remove from his mind the false impressions he had received with regard to treason. 2d, To endeavour to convince him that the interests of the United States would be best consulted by going to war with Spain, and giving countenance to the expedition which Colonel Burr had planned.

"It appeared to me that this step might do some good, could do no harm, and, in my situation, ought to be attempted. I saw the president, together with Mr. Madison; and having first, when questioned on that point, declared to the former that I had no *personal motives* for this interview, spoke to them to the effect just mentioned. The day after the interview I received the following note from the president, the original of which, in *his own handwriting*, now remains in my possession:—

"'The communications which Doctor Bollman made yesterday to Thomas Jefferson were certainly interesting; but they were too much for his memory. From *their complexion and tendency*, he presumes that Doctor Bollman would have no objection to commit them to writing, in all the details into which he went yesterday, and such others as he may have then omitted, Thomas Jefferson giving him *his word of honour* that they shall never be used against himself, and *that the paper shall never go out of his hand.*'

January 25, 1807.

"I immediately complied with the president's request; and considering the communication, in conformity with the tenour of his note, as *strictly confidential*, I had no motive to be unusually guarded, or to weigh every expression with more than ordinary care. The paper, containing nearly twenty pages, was hardly finished, when I immediately sent it to the president. I borrowed it from him some time afterward when in prison, in order to take a copy, and then returned it.

"The whole of it goes to the two points above mentioned, *viz.*, to disprove treason, and to show the expediency of war. It can give no other ideas to an unbiased reader, unless one or two expressions, improperly used, and for which the allowance ought to be made, that the English is not my native tongue, are singled out, are considered disconnectedly with what precedes and follows, and construed in a hostile manner.

"The president had given '*his word of honour*' that this paper should not be used against myself; and yet *on it* was predicated the pretended necessity of a *pardon* for my personal safety. The attorney for the district (Mr. Hay), in open court, when offering me the patent pardon, referred to it. Nay, when I indignantly refused that pardon, he reminded me of the *horrors of an ignominious fate*, in order, if possible, to change my determination. Is a paper not used against me when, on account of its contents being misunderstood, I am thus assailed with the *tender of a badge of infamy?* Is *life*, in Mr. Jefferson's opinion, *all;* and *character* and *reputation*, which alone can render it desirable, *nothing?* The great inquest of the nation, after hearing a great variety of testimony, and particularly that of General Wilkinson, *by an opinion nearly unanimous on my subject, have absolved me from guilt!* No indictment has been preferred against me, though they have indicted various gentlemen in different parts of the United States. Was it, then, becoming the first magistrate of the Union, whom I had approached with some degree of confidence, and with regard to whom neither my conduct nor my language have ever been unfriendly—was it becoming in *him*, in a measure, to forestall the opinion of the grand jury, and to stigmatize me as a pardoned criminal ?

"The paper was never to get out of the president's hands, but it is *now* in the hands of the attorney for the Virginia district. On the 23d of June, an occurrence of which the prints have taken no notice, the grand jury came into court. Their foreman stated that one of the witnesses had mentioned to him an important paper, written by another witness, which was in the possession of Mr. Hay, and of which they wished the delivery. Mr. Hay replied, that this referred to my letter to the president, which was in his possession, but that he did not consider himself warranted to give it to the grand jury. He also declared it to be his firm persuasion that the paper was written in my own handwriting; it has further appeared that he had occasioned General Wilkinson to read it. Through him he had brought what is falsely stated to be its contents insidiously before the grand jury. General Wilkinson, when before that body, and, of course, on his oath, did assert that he knew the paper in Mr. Hay's hands; that it was my handwriting and my signature.

"The history of the proposed pardon will have flown over Europe, and the impression of treachery to a friend—this more detestable, more odious crime than any infraction of the laws of the country, because essentially fraught with turpitude, will be blended with my name in the minds of men who may never see *this* letter. And if all this injury could be inflicted by Mr. Jefferson without *ill will*, merely from want of consideration, under the disturbing influence of *passion and resentment against Colonel Burr*, notwithstanding his mature age and the dignity of his station, it will amount to strong proof, at least, that I, in my humble sphere and with a more youthful imagination, may have become warmed with the beautiful prospect of the emancipation of an enslaved kingdom; a project which Mr. Jefferson himself approved of and connived at when planned, not by Colonel Burr, but by Miranda; and that I may have engaged in it without meaning any harm to the United States or their president.

"But since the measure of the pardon has proved abortive and ridiculous, and since the fact of his breach of the '*word of honour*' can no longer be denied, their tone is changed. As usual, I am abused, not for the wrong I did, but for the wrong which has been committed upon me. They insinuate, among other things, that at Washington I had *obtained promises* from Mr. Jefferson, and had *agreed* with him for a pardon; that I refused it at Richmond, in order to have a pretext for withholding testimony, on the ground that it would criminate myself, though it is well known that such promise, such agreement never took place; and that before the grand jury, during an examination of upward of two hours, I answered, *without a single exception, every question that was asked me.*

"When party spirit and passion go so far, it would be improper to remain silent; and should what I have said in my defence operate to the prejudice of Mr. Jefferson or wound his feelings, it is not my fault.

"Erick Bollman."

CHAPTER XXI.

The excitement produced by Mr. Jefferson, Mr. Eaton, and Mr. Wilkinson in relation to Burr's movements, exceeded any thing that can be well imagined. That grave and dignified body, the Senate of the United States, were *terrified*, or they were *used* for the purpose of *terrifying* the good people of the country. On the 22d of January, 1807, Mr. Jefferson sent a message to Congress developing the treasonable designs of Burr and his associates. On the 26th, with the aid of General Wilkinson, a second message was transmitted on the same subject; and, by *accident*, about the same time that this message of the president was received by the House of Representatives, that honourable body received a message from the Senate also, announcing that they had passed a "*bill for suspending the writ of habeas corpus*," and asking the concurrence of the house. This was carrying the *farce* too far, and a motion was therefore made and adopted to reject the bill on its *first reading*. Ayes 113; nays 19. Thus the bill was rejected.

During the years 1806 and 1807 Herman Blennerhassett kept a private journal, in which are recorded the principal incidents arising out of his connexion with Colonel Burr. Portions of it are interesting and amusing. The entries confirm in every particular the statements of Truxton, Bollman, and others, and repudiate the idea of treasonable designs. That journal, having been transmitted from England, is before me. From it a few brief extracts will be made. It appears that in December, 1805, Blennerhassett addressed a letter to Colonel Burr, expressing a wish to participate in any speculation in the western country that might present itself to Burr. A Spanish war was hourly anticipated, and Blennerhassett proposed to join Burr in any expedition that might be undertaken against the Spainish dominions.

In August, 1806, in consequence of this overture, Burr visited Blennerhassett at his house on the Ohio, and the next day rode with him to Marietta, and there they separated, Burr being on his way to Chilicothe. From Marietta to Blennerhassett's was about fifteen miles. Some time after Burr returned to Blennerhassett's. Burr said that an expulsion of the Spaniards from the American territory or an invasion of Mexico would be pleasing to the administration, if it could be accomplished without an open formal war, which would be avoided as long as possible, from parsimony on the one hand and the dread of France on the other.

Blennerhassett tendered his services to Burr generally. Blennerhassett states that General Jackson and others were to join, and that the general was in readiness to march whenever he should think himself authorized by the position of the government.

Extracts.

"The vivacity of Burr's wit, and the exercise of his proper talents, now (at Richmond) constantly solicited here, in private and public exhibition, while they display his powers and address at the levee and the bar, must engross more of his time than he can spare from the demands of other gratifications; while they display him to the eager eyes of the multitude, like a favourite gladiator, measuring over the arena of his fame with firm step and manly grace, the pledges of easy victory."

"August 17, 1807. This led me to praise a pamphlet, *Agrestis*, which Alston yesterday brought me, being two letters on Wilkinson's proceedings at New-Orleans, which, for its arrangement and strength, as well as for the imagery of the language, I observed would not be unworthy of a Curran; at the same time inquiring who was the author. Alston said that was not known. I then repeated the question to Colonel M'Kee, who said it was a friend of ours; at least, Mr. Alston was suspected. I mention this trifling occurrence for the sake of observing that Alston was now silent, thereby appropriating to himself the merit of the book, which his *wife*, I have no doubt, might produce. To suppose Alston* the author would be preposterous."

"August 23, 1807. My revery was soon broken in upon by the appearance of Mr. Douglas with a stranger. I should rather have said by two apparitions; for it was now near nightfall, and Douglas no sooner appeared than he turned on his heel, saying, 'Colonel Duane, sir,' and ran down

* At this period Blennerhassett was at war with both Colonel Burr and Alston, on the subject of their pecuniary transactions.

stairs. The surprise of this interruption the stranger, whom I had never before seen, did not suffer to endure long enough to allow me to invoke the angels and ministers of grace for my protection. I was already within the grasp of this Gabriel of the government. He seized my hand, and bade me dismiss my surprise, however natural it might be, on his appearance before me. I handed him a chair, and said 'I had lived long enough in this country to be surprised at nothing it could produce or exhibit, but yet desired to learn from what cause I had the favour of this visit.' 'Having heard Mr. Douglas observe,' said he, 'that you would be pleased to see me—' 'Sir, Mr. Douglas has made a mistake; he must have meant somebody else.' 'No matter,' continued he; 'having known and seen your present situation, I could not as a man, as an Irishman' (here he digressed to show me how he both was and was not an Irishman), 'I would not leave this town (Richmond) without warning you of the sacrifice now preparing to appease the government by your friends, of which you are destined to be the victim. You cannot desire any other key to my meaning than the course the defence has this week taken. But if you think the government will not cease to pursue that justice they possess the means of ensuring, and suspect, as you ought, the designs of those you have too long thought your friends, it might yet appear no better on my part than a nominal service to give you these cautions: I have therefore sought you, not to tender you words, but deeds. The only return on your part will be that care of yourself which will find a shield in *my honour*' (here he very awkwardly struck his breast, and grinned a ghastly smile), 'and that confidence I can *command* in the government whose good faith is not misplaced in the zeal I have testified to serve it.' To this harangue he added violent protestations of his wishes to serve me, saying, that for that purpose he would put off his journey back to Philadelphia, which otherwise was irrevocably fixed for Wednesday, and would now, or at any time hereafter, go to Washington for me, where *nothing he should ask would be refused him.* In thanking him for the frankness and zeal with which he cautioned me against my friends and a negligence of my safety, I assured him I was not afraid to meet the prosecution, as I expected I should before my arrival here, without counsel or friends ; but, from present appearances, I was more curious than interested to learn what were those means the said government possessed of ensuring justice. Finding by his answer that he was now disposed to allure me into a confession of having written certain papers in the hands of the prosecutors, I told him, the warmth of his offers to serve me could not make me forget either his situation or my own with relation to the government; that I cared not what writings should be charged upon me ; that I should admit none till fairly proved, which, if any such should ever appear, I would justify, if necessary, on the scaffold. He now summed up the objects of his mission, whatever produced it, with abuse of Burr, Tyler, and Smith, *acknowledging that he had been served gratis by Burr in the most handsome manner ;* that the others were more concerned against the government than I was; but swearing that he believed, if I did not follow his advice, they would make a scapegoat sacrifice of me for their deliverance."

"August 25, 1807. I asked Alston, 'Would you wish to see my notes of what passed between Duane and me?' 'Yes,' said he, 'very much.' I then read to him the minutes I had taken on Sunday evening, with which he seemed highly pleased, and said they ought to be published. To this I told him I could not accede. * * * * * * I informed him that Duane had intimated that government had got possession of one of his letters to me. 'One of my letters,' cried he ; 'I never wrote to you but two upon business of a private nature ; and, by G—d, any other letter they can have of mine must be a forgery.' 'To be sure,' said I ; 'or, at all events, from the favourable course things are now likely to take, such a letter could do no harm.' 'But what did the rascal,' continued he, 'state to be the purport of the letter?' 'Nothing more,' said I, 'than that you and myself were equally involved in all Colonel Burr's projects.' He then abused Duane, and repeated his wish that my notes were published."

"September 13, 1807. I visited Burr this morning. He is as gay as usual, and as busy in speculations on reorganizing his projects for action as if he had never suffered the least interruption. He observed to Major Smith and me, that in six months our schemes could be all remounted; that we could now new model them in a better mould than formerly, having a better view of the ground and a more perfect knowledge of our men. We were silent. It should yet be granted, that if Burr possessed sensibility of the right sort, with one hundredth part of the energies for which, with many, he has obtained such ill-grounded credit, his first and last determination, with the morning and the night, should be the destruction of those enemies who have so long and so cruelly wreaked their malicious vengeance upon him."

"September 16, 1807. I was glad to find Burr had at last thought of asking us to dine with him, as I was rather curious again to see him shine in a *partie quarrie*, consisting of new characters. We therefore walked with him from court; Luther Martin, who lives with him, accompanying us. * * * * * The dinner was neat, and followed by three or four sorts of wine. Splendid poverty! During the chit-chat, after the cloth was removed, a letter was handed to Burr, next to whom I sat. I immediately smelt musk. Burr broke the seal, put the cover to his nose, and then handed it to me, saying—'This amounts to a disclosure.' I smelt the paper, and said, 'I think so.' The whole physiognomy of the man now assumed an alteration and vivacity that, to a stranger who had never seen him before, would have sunk full fifteen years of his age. 'This,' said he, 'reminds me of a detection once very neatly practised upon me at New-York. One day a lady stepped into my library while I was reading, came softly behind my chair, and giving me a slap on the cheek, said, "Come, tell me directly, what little French girl, pray, have you had here?" The abruptness of the question and surprise left me little room to doubt the discovery had been completely made. So I thought it best to confess the whole fact; upon which the inquisitress burst out into a loud laugh on the success of her artifice, which she was led to play off upon me from the mere circumstance of having smelt musk in the room.' I have given this anecdote a place here only to convey an idea of that temperament and address which enables this character to uphold his ascendency over the sex. After some time Martin and Prevost withdrew, and we passed to the topics of our late adventures on the Mississippi, in which Burr said little, but declared he did not know of any reason to blame General Jackson, of Tennessee, for any thing he had done or omitted. But he declares he will not lose a day after the favourable issue at the Capitol (his acquittal), of which he has no doubt, to direct his entire attention to setting up his projects (which have only been suspended) on a better model, 'in which work,' he says, 'he has even here made some progress.'"

"September 20, 1807. I found Burr, just after a consultation with his counsel, secretly writhing under much irritation at the conduct of Judge Marshall, but affecting an air of contempt for his alleged inconsistencies, as Burr asserted he (the judge) did not, for the last two days, understand either the questions or himself; that he had wavered in his opinions before yesterday's adjournment, and should, in future, be put right by *strong language.* I am afraid to say *abuse,* though I think I could swear he used that word. I learned from Major Smith to-day a confirmation of what Colonel de Pestre had also mentioned to me, that Burr sets off immediately for England after his liberation to collect money for reorganizing his projects."

"September 22, 1807. I have seen a complete file of all the depositions made before the grand jury in Burr's possession. It must be confessed that few other men in his circumstances could have procured these documents out of the custody of offices filled by his inveterate enemies. Burr asserted to-day, in court, that he expected documents that would disqualify Eaton as a witness."

"September 26, 1807. Wilkinson, in his examination, confessed that he had altered the cipher letter, and sworn that there were no alterations."

"Of Dudley Woodbridge,* it must not be concealed from those who may have access to these *notes* that, although he is reputed to have given a fair, candid, and to us an advantageous testimony, *he has not yet told the whole truth, having suppressed my communication to him of our designs being unequivocally against Mexico*, which I suppose he kept back because he embraced and embarked in the plan on the first mention of it to him, though he afterward receded from it upon his own reflections or counsel of others. Such is the address with which ingratitude and dishonesty are made to pass in the garb of integrity, like towcloth under fine muslin."

"October 8, 1807. I called on Burr this morning, when he at last mentioned to me, during a short tête-à-tête, that he was preparing to go to England; that the time was now auspicious for him, and he wished to know whether I could give him letters. I answered that I supposed, when he mentioned England, he meant London, as his business would probably be with people in office; that I knew none of the present ministry, nor did I believe I had a single acquaintance in London. He replied, that he meant to visit every part of the country, and would be glad to get letters

* Former mercantile partner of Blennerhassett, and contractor for building Burr's boats on the Muskingum.

to any one. I said I would think of it, that I might discover whether I had any friends there whom it would be an object worth his attention to know, and took leave. We can only conjecture his designs. For my part, I am disposed to suspect he has no serious intent of reviving any of his speculations in America, or even of returning from Europe if he can get there."

After Colonel Burr's return to the United States from Europe, he received several letters from Blennerhassett; in two of them he refers to a suit which he commenced against General Andrew Jackson, in Adams county, Mississippi territory, for a balance due Burr. In reply to an inquiry made on the subject under date of the 4th of October, 1812, he says, "I allude to an account between yourself and Andrew Jackson, in his own handwriting, on which appears a balance in your favour of $1726 62," &c. He then speaks of other papers, and adds, "As to the manner in which I obtained the papers, it happened to be discovered that the portmanteau you left with me, to be transmitted to Mr. Alston, which lay at my disposal in the house of Mr. Harding, near Natchez, was broken open by his servants. On this discovery I called for the portmanteau, found the lock torn off, and some papers tumbled and abused, which had seemingly been all opened. I observed and took out the above document. The rest, with a silk tent, await the disposition of your orders."

In another letter, in a paroxysm of passion, he threatens the publication of a book, which he says is to be entitled,

"A review of the projects and intrigues of Aaron Burr during the years 1805, 1806, and 1807, involving therein, as parties or privies, Thomas Jefferson, A. Gallatin, Dr. Eustis, Governor Alston, Daniel Clark, Generals Wilkinson, Dearborn, Harrison, Jackson, and Smith, and the late Spanish ambassador Yrujo, exhibiting original documents and correspondence hitherto unpublished. Compiled from the notes and private journal kept during the above period by Herman Blennerhassett, LL.D."

It has been seen that General Wilkinson *altered* the letter written in cipher by Colonel Burr, and then swore that the translation was a true copy of the original. This alteration was for the purpose of establishing *treasonable* designs in Burr and his associates, to which fact the general had also sworn. But while he was thus urging the charge of *treason* at home, he had to give his Spanish employers a different account of the movements and object of Burr. Accordingly, after the trial at Richmond, General Wilkinson despatched Captain Walter Burling, his aid, to demand of the vice-king of Mexico the repayment of his expenditures and compensation for his services to Spain in defeating Burr's expedition against Mexico. The modesty of this demand, being only about *two hundred thousand dollars*, is worthy of notice. The development of this fact places in a new point of view Mr. Jefferson's confidential friend (General Wilkinson)—that friend whom he recommended to Congress on the 22d of January, 1807, as having acted "with the *honour of a soldier and the fidelity of a good citizen.*" The documents are presented without comment.

State of Louisiana, City of New-Orleans.

Before me, William Young Lewis, notary public in and for the city of New-Orleans, duly commissioned and sworn, this day personally appeared Richard Raynal Keene, Esq., attorney and counsellor at law of this city, who delivered to me, the said notary, and requested the same to be annexed to the current records of my office, the following documents, *to wit* :—

First. A certificate of the vice-queen of Mexico, dated at Madrid on the twenty-fourth day of January, eighteen hundred and sixteen.

Second. A letter from the said Richard R. Keene to the

Reverend Dr. Mangan, dated at Madrid on the twenty-first day of July, eighteen hundred and twenty-one.

Third. The reply of the Reverend Dr. Mangan to the aforesaid letter, dated at Madrid on the twenty-third day of July, eighteen hundred and twenty-one.

All of which said documents I have accordingly annexed to my current register, there to remain and serve as the case may be, after having marked the same *ne varietur*, to identify them with this act.

Done and passed at New-Orleans, this twenty-fourth day of December, eighteen hundred and thirty-six, in presence of William T. Lewis and Gustavus Harper, both of this city, witnesses, who have hereunto signed their names with said, and me the said notary. Signed, Richard R. Keene, William T. Lewis, Gustavus Harper.

W. Y. Lewis, Not. Pub.

Certificate of the Vice-queen.

"Whereas his excellency, the Marquis of Campo-Sagrado, minister of war, has been pleased to accede to the request of Richard Raynal Keene, colonel of the royal armies, addressed to him under date of the 12th instant, with the view of obtaining my declaration respecting the mission sent by the Anglo-American brigadier, James Wilkinson, to my late husband, Don Jose Yturrigaray, lieutenant-general of the royal armies in Mexico, during the period of his command as viceroy in that country; now, for the purpose required, I do declare and certify, that, having accompanied my said husband to Mexico, and stayed there with him during the time of his command as viceroy in that country, to wit, from the year 1802 to the year 1808, I recollect perfectly well the aforesaid mission, which was carried into effect by a person of the name of Burling; and although I cannot now undertake to relate all the details of that mission, nevertheless my memory enables me to state that, in substance, the exposition made by Keene to the minister of war, of the artifices and stratagems resorted to by Wlikinson on that occasion, through his confidential agent, is just and true.

The interested views manifested by Wilkinson *in his reclamation of large sums of money for his alleged disbursements* in counteracting the hostile plans of the American vice-president, Burr, against Mexico, appeared to the viceroy to be no less incompatible with the rights of his majesty than they were *irreconcilable to the honour of an officer and patriot* of a foreign state. The viceroy, therefore, did not give a single ducat to Burling, but took immediate steps for having him removed from the country.

This is what I declare, in compliance with the requisition of his excellency the minister of war. Madrid, January 24, 1816.

MARIA INES JAUREGUI DE YTURRIGARAY.

Madrid, July 21, 1821.

REV. SIR,

I send you an exposition of the vice-queen Donna Maria Ines Jauregui de Yturrigaray, of the 24th January, 1816, relative to the intrigue which the brigadier Wilkinson attempted to carry into effect in 1806 or 1807, through the agency of Mr. Burling, for the purpose of getting money from the vice-king of Mexico. The vice-queen told me, in the different conversations I had with her on this subject, that you enjoyed the full and entire confidence of her husband, and that he, besides speaking with you unreservedly about this affair, commissioned you to interpret the letter which Wilkinson sent him through Mr. Burling, the said letter having been written in English. The vice-king, had he not died suddenly, would have given me the same exposition which his widow gave me. It being then, in some sort, a matter of justice that you should give your declaration relative to the aforesaid exposition of the vice-queen, I therefore pray you to do so.

I will merely add that, in one of my conversations with

the vice-king, he told me that, in the aforesaid letter, Wilkinson, in speaking of his service rendered in frustrating what he called the invasion of Mexico by the ex-vice-president, Mr. Burr, likened himself to *Leonidas in the pass of Thermopylæ.* Be assured, reverend sir, of my profound respect.

RICHARD RAYNAL KEENE,
Colonel in the service of H. C. M.

Rev. Dr. MANGAN, *Rector of the Irish College in Salamanca.*

Madrid, July 23, 1821

MY DEAR SIR,

I have carefully read the exposition you enclosed me in your esteemed favour of the 21st instant, of the former vice-queen of Mexico, La Senora Donna Maria Ines Jauregui de Yturrigaray, relative to the famous *embassy* of General Wilkinson to her husband Don Joseph de Yturrigaray, viceroy of Mexico.

As his excellency was pleased to make use of me as interpreter in the interview he granted Mr. Walter Burling, the bearer of a letter from the aforesaid General Wilkinson, and commissioned by him to manifest to the viceroy the importance of his embassy, I candidly confess that, to the best of my recollection, the exposition of the vice-queen is perfectly correct, for the object of the famous embassy of Mr. Burling was to display to the viceroy *the great pecuniary sacrifices* made by General Wilkinson to frustrate the plan of invasion meditated by the ex-vice-president, Mr. Burr, against the kingdom of Mexico, and to solicit, in consideration of such important services, a pretty round sum of *at least two hundred thousand dollars.*

I cannot help observing that the viceroy, Don Joseph de Yturrigaray, received this communication with due contempt and indignation, bidding me to tell Mr. Burling that General Wilkinson, in counteracting any treasonable plan of Mr. Burr, did no more than comply with his duty; that he (the viceroy) would take good care to defend the kingdom of Mexico against any attack or invasion, and that he did not think himself authorized to give one farthing to General Wilkinson in compensation for his pretended services. He concluded by ordering Mr. Burling to leave the city of Mexico, and had him safely escorted to the port of Vera Cruz, where he immediately embarked for the United States.

This is, believe me, the substance (as far as I can recollect) of the famous embassy of General Wilkinson to the viceroy of Mexico, Don Joseph de Yturrigaray, who certainly was not mistaken in the passage he mentioned to you of Leonidas, as I recollect well that General Wilkinson, after displaying in a pompous style the great difficulties he had to encounter to render Mr. Burr's plan fruitless, concluded by affirming—"*I, like Leonidas, boldly threw myself in the pass*," &c.

I return you the original exposition of the vice-queen, Donna Maria Ines Jauregui de Yturrigaray, and remain yours, PATRICK MANGAN,

Rector of the Irish College of Salamanca.

RICHARD R. KEENE, *Colonel in the service H. C. M.*

I hereby certify that the foregoing is a true copy of the originals annexed to my current register. In witness whereof I grant these presents, under my hand and seal, at New-Orleans, this 26th day of December, 1836.

WILLIAM Y. LEWIS, Not. Pub.

The following short extracts from the letters of Colonel Burr to his daughter, while he was imprisoned in Richmond, will serve to show the state of his mind under circumstances thus oppressive and mortifying.

TO THEODOSIA.

"Richmond, March 27, 1807.

"My military escort having arrived at Fredericksburgh on our way to Washington, there met a special messenger, with orders to convey me to this place. Hither we came forthwith, and arrived last evening. It seems that here the business is to be tried and concluded. I am to be surrendered to the civil authority to-morrow, when the question of bail will be determined. In the mean time I remain at the Eagle tavern."

"April 26, 1807.

"Your letters of the 10th and those preceding seemed to indicate a sort of stupor; but now you rise into phrensy. Another ten days will, it is hoped, have brought you back to reason. It ought not, however, to be forgotten that the letter of the 15th was written under a paroxysm of the toothache.

"You have read to very little purpose if you have not remarked that such things happen in all democratic governments. Was there in Greece or Rome a man of virtue and independence, and supposed to possess great talents, who was not the object of vindictive and unrelenting persecution? Now, madame, I pray you to amuse yourself by collecting and collating all the instances to be found in ancient history, which you may connect together, if you please, in an essay, with reflections, comments, and applications. This I may hope to receive about the 22d of May. I promise myself great pleasure in the perusal, and I promise you great satisfaction and consolation in the composition."

"May 15, 1807.

"Respecting the approaching investigation, I can communicate nothing new. The grand jury is composed of twenty democrats and four federalists. Among the former is W. C. Nicholas, my vindictive and avowed personal enemy—the most so that could be found in this state (Virginia).

The most indefatigable industry is used by the agents of government, and they have money at command without stint. If I were possessed of the same means, I could not only foil the prosecutors, but render them ridiculous and infamous. The democratic papers teem with abuse against me and my counsel, and even against the chief justice. Nothing is left undone or unsaid which can tend to prejudice the public mind, and produce a conviction without evidence. The machinations of this description which were used against Moreau in France were treated in this country with indignation. They are practised against me in a still more impudent degree, not only with impunity, but with applause; and the authors and abettors suppose, with reason, that they are acquiring favour with the administration."

"June 3, 1807.

"Still waiting for Wilkinson, and no certain accounts of his approach. The grand jury, the witnesses, and the country grow impatient. It is an ungracious thing, and so deemed, after having for six months been branded as a traitor; after directing that Burr and his followers should be attacked, put to death, and their property seized; after all the violations of law and constitution which have been practised, that government should now say it has not proof!

"Busy, busy, busy from morning till night—from night till morning, yet there are daily amusing incidents; things at which you will laugh, also things at which you will pout and scold."

"June 18, 1807.

"On Saturday morning General Wilkinson, with ten or eleven witnesses from New Orleans, arrived in Richmond. Four bills were immediately delivered to the grand jury against Blennerhassett and Burr; one for treason and one for misdemeanour against each. The examination of the witnesses was immediately commenced. They had gone through thirty-two last evening. There are about forty-six. General Eaton has been already examined. He came out of the jury-room in such rage and agitation that he shed tears, and complained bitterly that he had been questioned as if he were a villain. How else could he have been questioned with any propriety?

"Poor Bollman is placed in a most awkward predicament. Some days ago Mr. Hay, the district attorney, in open court tendered him a pardon under the great seal and with the sign manual of *Thomas Jefferson*. Bollman refused to receive it. Hay urged it upon him. Bollman said that no man could force on him such a badge of infamy. Hay insisted that he was a pardoned man, whether he would or not; and this question will, probably, also come before the court in argument to-day or to-morrow."

"June 22, 1807.

On Friday Mr. Hay complained that Burr had so constantly occupied the court for the four weeks past with his extraordinary motions, that he (Mr. Hay) could not get an opportunity of making *one* on his part; he therefore gave notice that he should, at the first interval, move for leave to send to the grand jury interrogatories for their instruction, to be put to the witnesses, in order that the *whole truth* might come out.

"Burr said it was a thing without example, and which the court could not permit without his assent; but he thought there was reason in the proposal of Mr. Hay, and that he should cheerfully assent, with the condition only that he (Burr) should also send interrogatories, to be put to the same witnesses, the better to extract the '*whole truth*.'

"The court said that it certainly could not be permitted to Mr. Hay to send interrogatories, being against usage and reason; but as Mr. Burr had assented, there seemed to be no objection that both parties should send in interrogatories; and such permission was granted, whereupon Mr. Hay withdrew his motion."

"June 24, 1807.

"While we were engaged to-day in the argument of the question for an attachment against Wilkinson, the grand jury came into court with bills against Blennerhassett and myself for treason and misdemeanour. Two bills against each of us. These indictments for treason are founded on the following allegations: that Colonel Tyler, with twenty or thirty men, stopped at Blennerhassett's Island on their way down the Ohio; that though these men were not armed, and had no military array or organization, and though they did neither use force nor threaten it, yet, having set out with a view of taking temporary possession of New-Orleans on their way to Mexico, that such intent was treasonable, and therefore a war was levied on Blennerhassett's Island by *construction ;* and that, though Colonel Burr was then at Frankfort on his way to Tennessee, yet, having advised the measure, he was, *by construction of law*, present at the island, and levied war there. In fact, the indictment charges that Aaron Burr was on that day present at the island, though not a man of the jury supposed this to be true.

"This idea of *constructive war* is, by this jury, carried far beyond the dictum advanced by Judge Chace in the case of Fries; for Chace laid down that the actual exertion of force, in a hostile or traitorous manner, was indispensable to establish treason. Yet the opinions of Chace in this case were complained of by the whole republican party, and condemned by all the lawyers of all parties in Philadelphia, as tending to introduce the odious and unconstitutional doctrine of *constructive treason.*

"Out of fifty witnesses who have been examined before the grand jury, it may be safely alleged that thirty at least have been perjured.

"I beg and expect it of you that you will conduct yourself as becomes my daughter, and that you manifest no signs of weakness or alarm."

"June 30, 1807.

"Of myself you could expect to hear nothing new; yet something new and unexpected was moved yesterday. The counsel for the prosecution proposed to the court that Aaron Burr should be sent to the penitentiary for safe keeping, and stated that the governor and council had offered to provide me with an apartment in the third story of that building. This is extremely kind and obliging in the governor and his council. The distance, however, would render it so inconvenient to my counsel to visit me, that I should prefer to remain where I am; yet the rooms proposed are said to be airy and healthy."

"July 3, 1807.

"I have three rooms in the third story of the penitentiary, making an extent of one hundred feet. My jailer is quite a polite and civil man—altogether unlike the idea one would form of a jailer. You would have laughed to have heard our compliments the first evening.

"*Jailer.* I hope, sir, it would not be disagreeable to you if I should lock this door after dark.

"*Burr.* By no means, sir; I should prefer it, to keep out intruders.

"*Jailer.* It is our custom, sir, to extinguish all lights at nine o'clock; I hope, sir, you will have no objection to conform to that.

"*Burr.* That, sir, I am sorry to say, is impossible; for I never go to bed till twelve, and always burn two candles.

"*Jailer.* Very well, sir, just as you please. I should have been glad if it had been otherwise; but, as you please, sir.

"While I have been writing different servants have arrived with messages, notes, and inquiries, bringing oranges, lemons, pineapples, raspberries, apricots, cream, butter, ice, and some ordinary articles."

"July 6, 1807.

"My friends and acquaintance of both sexes are permitted to visit me without interruption, without inquiring their business, and without the *presence of a spy*. It is well that I have an antechamber, or I should often be gênê with visiters.

"If you come I can give you a bedroom and parlour on this floor. The bedroom has three large closets, and it is a much more commodious one than you ever had in your life. Remember, no agitations, no complaints, no fears or anxieties on the road, or I renounce thee."

"July 24, 1807.

"I want an independent and discerning witness to my conduct and to that of the government. The scenes which have passed and those about to be transacted will exceed all reasonable credibility, and will hereafter be deemed fables, unless attested by very high authority.

"I repeat what has heretofore been written, that I should never invite any one, much less those so dear to me, to witness my disgrace. I may be immured in dungeons, chained, murdered in legal form, but I cannot be humiliated or disgraced. If absent, you will suffer great solicitude. In my presence you will feel none, whatever may be the *malice* or the *power* of my enemies, and in both they abound."

"July 30, 1807.

"I am informed that some good-natured people here have provided you a house, and furnished it, a few steps from my *townhouse*. I had also made a temporary provision for you in my townhouse, whither I shall remove on Sunday; but I will not, if I can possibly avoid it, move before your arrival, having a great desire to *receive you all in this mansion*. Pray, therefore, drive directly out here. You may get admission at any time from four in the morning till ten at night. Write me by the mail from Petersburgh, that I may know of your approach."

[On this letter is endorsed, in Theodosia's handwriting,

"*Received on our approach to Richmond. How happy it made me!*"]

The following was written after Theodosia had left Richmond and returned to South Carolina.

"Richmond, September 28, 1807.

"It is impossible to predict when this business may terminate, as the chief justice has gradually relaxed from former rules of evidence, and will now hear any thing, without regard to distance of time or place. Wilkinson has been examined, and had partly gone through the cross-examination when we closed on Saturday. *He acknowledged, very modestly, that he had made certain alterations in the letter received from me, by erasures*, &c., *and then swore it to be a true copy.* He has not yet acknowledged the substitution of names."

"October 9, 1807.

"Major Bruff, who was produced as a witness on my behalf, deposed that, in a conversation with Dearborn and Rodney, the attorney-general, in March last, he accused Wilkinson of several crimes, and gave the names of witnesses who would establish the charges. Those gentlemen replied that General Wilkinson *had* stood very low in the estimation of the president, but that his energetic conduct at New-Orleans had raised him in estimation; that he now stood very high, and that the president would support him; that if the government should now prosecute Wilkinson, or do any thing to impair his credit, Burr would escape, and that was just what the federalists and the enemies to the administration wished."

"October 23, 1807.

"After all, this is a sort of drawn battle. The chief justice gave his opinion on Tuesday. After declaring that there were no grounds of suspicion as to the treason, he directed that Burr and Blennerhassett should give bail in three thousand dollars for further trial in Ohio. This opinion was matter of regret and surprise to the friends of the chief justice, and of ridicule to his enemies—all believing that it was a sacrifice of principle to conciliate *Jack Cade.* Mr. Hay immediately said that he should advise the government to *desist from further prosecution.* That he has actually so advised there is no doubt.

"A. Burr."

CHAPTER XXII.

On the 7th of June, 1808, Colonel Burr sailed from New-York on board the British packet for England, via Halifax. The personal and political prejudices which the influence of power and the death of Hamilton had excited against him, rendered, as he conceived, a temporary absence from this country desirable; and, at the same time, believing that the political situation of Europe offered opportunities for accomplishing the object he had long contemplated, of emancipating the Spanish American colonies from the degrading tyranny of Spain, it was his design to solicit the aid of some European government in such an undertaking. With these views he embarked for England.

During his residence in Europe he regularly corresponded with his daughter, Mrs. Alston, and also kept a private diary; but probably from the apprehension that his papers were at all times subject to the supervision of the government police, his memoranda are in a great measure restricted to occurrences private and personal. An amusing volume* *might* be made of these daily records of his privations and personal adventures during his protracted and forced residence in

* It is highly probable that portions of Colonel Burr's journal, with his correspondence while in Europe, may hereafter be published in a single volume, as a separate and distinct work.

Europe, but the limits of the present work compel us to pass hastily over this period of his life.

He arrived in Falmouth on the 15th, and in London on the 16th July; and on the same day, with characteristic promptitude, he presented his letters of introduction, and, among others, to John Reeves, Esq., then in the department of the secretary of state, through whom he seems to have hoped to gain access to the ministry.

During the next three months he made, through Mr. Reeves and others, various unsuccessful efforts to approach the government; but there were two obstacles in his way, both of which were insuperable. The Spaniards were then in the commencement of their noble resistance to the invasion of Napoleon, and the enthusiasm of the British nation in favour of the Spanish patriots, as well as the policy of the British government, were absolutely opposed to any scheme for separating the colonies from Spain. But, in addition to this obstacle, Colonel Burr, from the moment of his landing in England, was an object of suspicion and distrust to the government. The alien-bill was then in stern operation, and apprehensions were entertained of the emissaries of France; and it is not to be doubted that the same hostility which, as we shall see, openly displayed itself in the conduct of the United States' agents towards Colonel Burr in France, had been excited to misrepresent and anticipate him in his negotiations with the British government. After various interviews, that led to nothing, with Mr. Canning, Lord Mulgrave, and Lord Melville, on the 6th November, 1808, the following communication from A. Merry put an end to all hopes of assistance in his plans from the English ministry :—

Sunday morning, November 6.

DEAR SIR,

Although I could not see Mr. Canning yesterday, from his being gone into the country, to stay till Tuesday morning, for the recovery of his health, I conversed with another person of nearly equal authority, who told me he was sure that what you proposed to me yesterday could never be consented to, pointing it out in every way to be impracticable. I beg you to excuse the haste in which I write, and believe me to be, dear sir,

Your most faithful humble servant,

A. MERRY.

In private life in England Colonel Burr received much attention, and from no one more than *Jeremy Bentham*, with whom he formed a warm and intimate friendship. In a letter to his daughter of the 8th September, 1808, he speaks of Mr. Bentham :—"I hasten to make you acquainted with Jeremy Bentham, author of a work entitled 'Principles of Morals and Legislation' (edited in French by Dumont), and of many other works of less labour and research. You will well recollect to have heard me place this man second to no one, ancient or modern, in profound thinking, in logical and analytic reasoning. On the 8th of August I received a letter from him, containing a most friendly invitation to come and pass some days with him at a farm (where he passes the summer) called Barrowgreen, near Gadstone, and twenty miles from London. I was not tardy in profiting of this invitation. He met me at the gate with the frankness and affection of an old friend. Mr. Bentham's countenance has all that character of intense thought which you would expect to find; but it is impossible to conceive a physiognomy more strongly marked with ingenuousness and philanthropy. I have passed twelve days there, and shall return to-morrow, to stay most probably till he returns to town. His house in the city, which I now occupy solely and exclusively—[N. B. Three servants in the house at my command] —is most beautifully situated on St. James's Park, with extensive gardens, and built and fitted up more to my taste than any one I ever saw. In his library I am now writing."

The friendship of Mr. Bentham was uniform and constant; and if it did not preserve his friend from severe pecuniary privations and distress in Colonel Burr's second residence in England, it was because the extent of these privations was industriously and ingeniously concealed from him. "The benevolent heart of J. B." (Burr remarks in his diary, when apprehending an arrest for debt) "shall never be pained by the exhibition of my distress." Bentham, long after Burr's return to the United States, continued to correspond with him.

With William Godwin Mr. Burr also formed an intimate and friendly acquaintance. In a visit to Edinburgh in the winter of 1809, he seems to have been treated with great distinction; and his diary is sprinkled with the names of visiters the most distinguished in rank, fashion, and letters of the Scottish metropolis. He writes to his daughter 12th February, 1809: "Among the literary men of Edinburgh I have met M'Kenzie, author of the Man of Feeling, and Scott, author of the Minstrel. I met both frequently, and from both received civilities and hospitality. M'Kenzie has twelve children—six daughters, all very interesting and handsome. He is remarkably sprightly in company, amiable, witty—might pass for forty-two, though certainly much older. Scott, with less softness than M'Kenzie, has still more animation; talks much, and very agreeably."

While in Edinburgh Colonel Burr was informed by Lord Justice Clarke that Lord Melville had mentioned in a letter that it would be necessary for Mr. Burr to return to London. The government began now to evince great distrust of him. He seems at one time, and before he had abandoned all hope of receiving assistance in his political schemes, to have resolved to resist the operation of the alien bill, by claiming the rights of a British subject. He probably suggested this singular claim at the instance of his friend Reeves. The ground he took was that, having been born a British subject, he had a right to reassume his allegiance at pleasure; or rather that it was indefeasible, and never could be parted with. The claim appears to have caused some sensation among the crown lawyers. It was certainly unfounded and injudiciously asserted. Lord Liverpool pronounced it monstrous ; and it probably increased the suspicion and distrust already existing.

On the 4th April, 1809, the government took active measures against him. He writes in his journal of that day—"Having a confused presentiment that something was wrong, I packed up my papers and clothes with intent to go out and seek other lodgings. At one o'clock came in without knocking four coarse-looking men, who said they had a state warrant for seizing me and my papers, but refused to show the warrant. I was peremptory, and the warrant was produced, signed 'Liverpool,' but I was not permitted to read the whole. They took possession of my trunks, searched every part of the rooms for papers, threw all the loose articles into a sack, called a coach, and away we went to the alien office. Before going I wrote a note to Reeves, and on our arrival sent it in—waited one hour in the coach—very cold, but I refused to go in. Wrote in pencil to Reeves another note. He came out. We had a little conversation. He could not then explain, but said I must have patience. After half an hour more orders were that I must go with one of the messengers to his house. On this order I first went into the office to see Brooks, the under secretary, whom I knew [you may recollect the transaction in July, which must have fixed me in his memory]. He did not know me—none of them knew me—though every devil of them knew me as well as I know you. Seeing the measure was resolved on, and having inquired of the sort of restraint to which I was doomed, I wrote a note to Koe, which Brooks took to show to Lord Liverpool for his approbation to forward it—arrived at my prison, 31 Stafford Place, at four." In two days, however, he was released, and his papers returned unopened; but he was informed he must leave the kingdom. Some days afterward, as he still lingered, a message was conveyed to him:—"Lord Liverpool expects you to leave London to-morrow, and the kingdom in forty-eight hours." And on the 24th April, 1809, he sailed from Harwich in his B. M. packet Diana for Gottenburgh.

On leaving England Mr. Burr seems to have been undetermined as to his future movements. He was unwilling to renounce the projects which had carried him to Europe; and all hope of assistance from England being ended, he looked next for aid to Napoleon, whose policy, from the resistance of Spain and the preponderancy of the British navy, was now in favour of the independence of the Spanish American colonies. He finally resolved to wait in Sweden till he received advices from America, and then proceed to Paris to communicate with the emperor.

We must pass over his residence in Sweden, and his subsequent tour through Germany to Paris, during the whole of which period he kept a journal. He visited Hamburgh, Hanover, Saxe-Gotha, Weimar, and Frankfort; and, though travelling without letters or introduction, it appears from his itinerary that he was everywhere treated with distinction and attention. At Hamburg, where he arrived the 20th November, 1809, De Bourrienne, since known as the author of the Memoirs of Bonaparte, was the French minister. It will be amusing, perhaps, to compare the following extracts from De Bourrienne's work with a brief memorandum from Colonel Burr's diary, showing in what light they reciprocally regarded each other.

" At the height of his glory and power, Bonaparte was so suspicious that the veriest trifle sufficed to alarm him. I recollect that about the time the complaints were made respecting the *Minerva* (newspaper), Colonel Burr, formerly vice-president of the United States, who had recently arrived at Altona, was pointed out to me as a dangerous man, and I received orders to watch him very closely, and to arrest him on the slightest ground of suspicion if he should come to Hamburgh. Colonel Burr was one of those in favour of whom I ventured to disobey the orders I received from the restless police of Paris. As soon as the minister of the police heard of his arrival at Altona, he directed me to adopt towards him those violent measures which are equivalent to persecution. In answer to these instructions, I stated that Colonel Burr conducted himself at Altona with much prudence and propriety; that he kept but little company, and that he was scarcely spoken of. Far from regarding him as a man who required watching, having learned that he wished to go to Paris, I caused a passport to be procured for him, which he was to receive at Frankfort; and I never heard that this dangerous citizen had compromised the safety of the state in any way."—*Bourrienne's Memoirs of Napoleon*, vol. iv., p. 108.

In his journal of November 24, Burr writes:—

"I learn that A. B. is announced in the Paris papers in a manner no way auspicious. Resolved to go direct to the French minister, to see if he had any orders to give or refuse me passports. Sent in my name, but did not get out of my carriage; after some minutes the servant returned, saying his excellency was then much engaged, but would be glad to see me at three. At three, to minister's; begged to call to-morrow at twelve. November 25. At twelve, the minister's; was at once received; he is the transcript of our *Mari*,* only fifteen years older, but marked with the same characters. His reception was courteous, but with a mixture of surprise and curiosity. At once offered me passports to any frontier town, but has no authority to do more. Passports to go to Paris must come from Paris, and to that end I must write. Advises that I direct reply to be transmitted to Mayence. Asked me to dine at his country-house to-morrow."

At Mayence, however, he found no passport; and he was

* Joseph Alston, son-in-law of Colonel Burr.

detained in suspense there and at Frankfort for a month, before permission could be obtained to go to Paris.

On the 16th February, 1810, he arrived in Paris.

He commenced here a long and most vexatious and wearisome course of attendance on the minister of foreign relations and other high officers of state, endeavouring in vain, by personal solicitations and memorials, to obtain an audience of the emperor and an answer to his propositions. He attended the levees of the Duc de Cadore, the Duc de Rovigo, Jerome Bonaparte, King of Westphalia; but uniformly failed in his efforts, and was turned off with unmeaning professions. He records in his diary, with gratitude, the friendly attentions of Volney, Denon, and the Duc de Bassano; but, with these exceptions, he seems to have been treated with great coolness, even by those to whom his hospitality had been freely tendered in America. He always suspected that the alienation and immutable discountenance of the emperor were to be ascribed to the representations of *Talleyrand* and the representatives of the United States in France.

Several months neglect and inattention at length discouraged him, and he resolved to return home; but, on applying for a passport to the United States, he was informed by the police that he could not have a passport to go out of the empire. "Me voila [he writes in his journal], prisonier d'Etat! et presque sans sous." This event changed the course of his solicitations; and for the next year we find him, having abandoned all projects of ambition, limiting himself to solicitation for permission to go home, and without success. A memorial which he addressed to Napoleon sets forth in these manly terms the harshness and injustice of his treatment.

"While in Germany last winter I saw in the *Moniteur* an expression of your majesty's assent to the independence of the Spanish American colonies. Believing that I could be useful in the execution of that object, I hastened to

Frankfort, and there addressed myself to your majesty's minister, Monsieur Hedouville, who, at my request, wrote to the minister of exterior relations, stating my views, and asking a passport if those views should be deemed worthy of your majesty's attention. A passport was transmitted to me. On the day of my arrival in Paris I announced myself to the Duc de Cadore, and on the day following had an audience, in which I explained, as fully as the time would admit, the nature of my projects and the means of execution. Further details were added in subsequent conversations had with one of the chiefs of that department. Afterward, at the request of the Duc de Cadore, they were reduced to writing, of which memoir one copy was delivered to the Duc de Cadore and another to the Duc de Rovigo, to be submitted to your majesty's perusal. After the lapse of some weeks, having received no reply, nor any intimation that my views accorded with those of your majesty, being here without occupation and without the means of support, I asked a passport to return to the United States, where not only the state of the country, but my personal concerns, demand my presence. This passport has been refused; for nearly four months I have in vain solicited. The only answer I receive is—'His majesty has not signified his assent.'

"After conduct so frank and loyal on my part, it is with reason that I am hurt and surprised at this refusal. Not only did the motives of my visit and my conduct since my residence in France deserve a different return; at all times I have deserved well of your majesty and of the French nation. My home in the United States has been always open to French citizens, and few of any note who have visited the United States have not experienced my hospitalities. At a period when the administration of the government of the United States was hostile to France and Frenchmen, they received from me efficient protection. These, sire, are my crimes against France!

"Presuming that a proceeding so distressing and unmerited—so contrary to the laws of hospitality, to the fame of your majesty's magnanimity and justice, and to that of the courtesy of the French nation, must be without your majesty's knowledge, and that, amid the mighty concerns which weigh on your majesty's mind, those of an individual so humble as myself may have escaped your notice, I venture to intrude into your presence, and to ask either a passport to return to the United States, or, if in fact your majesty, with the expectation of rendering me useful to you, should wish a further delay, that I may be informed of the period of that delay, that I may take measures accordingly for my subsistence."

This memorial passed without notice.

The following correspondence between Colonel Burr and Mr. Jonathan Russell, then Chargé d'Affaires at Paris, and Mr. M'Rae, American Consul at Paris, will show the conduct of representatives of the United States to an American citizen in want and in a foreign land.

TO MR. RUSSELL.

Paris, October 25, 1810.

Mr. Burr presents respectful compliments. As a citizen of the United States, he requests of Mr. Russell an official certificate to that effect, and will have the honour of calling for the purpose at any hour which he may be pleased to name. The fact of Mr. Burr's citizenship being sufficiently known to Mr. Russell, it is presumed that other proof will be deemed unnecessary.

FROM MR. RUSSELL.

Paris, October 25, 1810.

In reply to Mr. Burr's note of this morning, Mr. Russell begs leave to inform him that the province of granting passports to citizens of the United States belongs to the consul, to whom all wishing for that protection must apply.

TO MR. M'RAE.

Paris, October 29, 1810.

Mr. Burr presents compliments. Having addressed himself to Mr. Russell for a certificate of citizenship, has been informed by him that the business of granting certificates was transferred to the consul. He therefore repeats the request to Mr. M'Rae. If a personal attendance be deemed necessary, Mr. Burr will wait on Mr. M'Rae for the purpose at any hour he may be pleased to appoint.

FROM MR. M'RAE.

Paris, October 29, 1810.

Mr. M'Rae answers to Mr. Burr's note of this morning, that his knowledge of the circumstances under which Mr. Burr left the United States renders it his duty to decline giving Mr. Burr either a passport or a permis de séjour. If, however, the opinion Mr. M'Rae has formed and the determination he has adopted on this subject be erroneous, there is a remedy at hand.

Although the business of granting passports and permis de séjour generally is confided to the consul, the chargé des affaires unquestionably possesses full authority to grant protection in either of those forms to any person to whom it may be improperly denied by the consul.

TO MR. RUSSELL.

Paris, November 1, 1810.

On receipt of Mr. Russell's note, Mr. Burr applied to the consul; a copy of his reply is herewith enclosed. It cannot be material to inquire what are the "*circumstances*" referred to by the consul, nor whether true or false. Mr. Burr is ignorant of any statute or instruction which authorizes a foreign minister or agent to inquire into any circumstances other than those which tend to establish the fact of citizen or not. If, however, Mr. Russell should be of a different opinion, Mr. Burr is ready to satisfy him that no circumstances exist which can, by any construction, in the slightest degree impair his rights as a citizen, and that the conclusions of the consul are founded in error, either in point of fact or of inference. Yet, conceiving that every citizen has a right to demand a certificate or passport, Mr. Burr is constrained to renew his application to Mr. Russell, to whom the consul has been pleased to refer the decision.

FROM MR. RUSSELL.

Paris, November 4, 1810.

Without subscribing to the opinion of Mr. M'Rae with regard to the appeal that lays from the erroneous decisions of the consul to the chargé d'affaires, Mr. Russell has no objection to judging the case which Mr. Burr has presented to him.

The man who evades the offended laws of his country, abandons, for the time, the right to their protection. This fugitive from justice, during his voluntary exile, has a claim to no other passport than one which shall enable him to surrender himself for trial for the offences with which he stands charged. Such a passport Mr. Russell will furnish to Mr. Burr, but no other.

In the winter of 1810 and 1811, being cut off from remittances from America, it appears from his journal that he suffered sad privations from the want of money.

In his diary of November 23, he writes—"Nothing from America, and really I shall starve. Borrowed three francs to-day. Four or five little debts keep me in constant alarm; all together, about two Louis."

December 1, 1810. "—— came in upon me this morning, just as I was out of bed, for twenty-seven livres. Paid him, which took literally my last sous. When at Denon's, thought I might as well go to St. Pelasgic; set off, but recollected I owed the woman who sits in the passage two sous for a segar, so turned about to pursue my way by Pont des Arts, which was within fifty paces; remembered I had not wherewith to pay the toll, being one sous; had to go all the way round by the Pont Royal, more than half a mile."

His journal for a year is filled with similar details, and would be a melancholy narration were it not that it exhibits him under every vicissitude, suspected and watched by the French government, misrepresented by the representatives of his own country, treated with almost universal coldness and neglect, cut off from all communication with America, without money, without occupation, and without any reasonable hope of a termination of his troubles, uniformly composed, firm, and cheerful. Not a discontented or fretful expression is to be found in his voluminous memoranda.

At length, in July, 1811, a ship being about sailing in ballast for America, with Napoleon's permission, Colonel Burr, through the influence of the Duc de Bassano, received permission to leave Paris. He arrived at Amsterdam on the 3d of August; and after a month's delay, apparently from the capricious tyranny of the French authorities, he sailed for America in the ship Vigilant on the 20th of September; and, escaping from the toils of one of the great belligerants, he fell into the power of the other, and was on the next day captured by an English frigate and carried into Yarmouth.

The Vigilant and the effects of her passengers were taken possession of by the government for trial in the admiralty; and as Burr had paid for passage to America, and was reduced very low in funds, he was obliged to remain in England. He continued in England from the 9th of October, 1811, till the 6th of March, 1812, when he sailed for America in the ship Aurora, and arrived in New-York, via Boston, on the 8th of June, 1812, just four years after his departure from America. During his second sojourn in England he enjoyed the society and friendship of Bentham and Godwin; but the latter could not alleviate his pecuniary distress, and the former was probably never fully aware of it. The diary contains a protracted record of privations, sometimes threatening absolute and hopeless want, but endured throughout with undisturbed and characteristic fortitude and gayety. He seems to have missed the attentions and society which he found on his first visit to London, and the following extract from his journal of 26th March, 1812, shows that he left England without feeling affection or regret.

"I shake the dust off my feet. Adieu, John Bull! Insula inhospitabilis, as you were truly called 1800 years ago."

CHAPTER XXIII.

IMMEDIATELY after Colonel Burr's arrival in the city of New-York, he opened an office and commenced the practice of law. The high and distinguished reputation with which he had retired from the bar in 1801 secured to him, on his return, an extensive and profitable business. A few individuals of the profession, under the influence of former prejudices, some of them hereditary, and as ancient as the 4th of July, 1776, endeavoured to throw impediments in his way; but these efforts were of short duration, and productive of but little effect. In general, he was courteously, if not kindly received, by gentlemen of the profession. In reference to this subject it was his request, that while no individual should be censured, the name of his friend, Colonel Robert Troup, should be recorded as meriting and receiving his most grateful acknowledgments. It has been seen that their intimacy was formed while they were yet but boys, at a period and under circumstances "that tried men's souls." On Burr's opening his office, Colonel Troup, having abandoned the practice of law, generously tendered him the use of his library until it should be required for his

(Troup's) own son; which, to Burr, was a most acceptable kindness, as he was destitute of the means of supplying even his most pressing wants. His prospects, for the moment, were cheering and auspicious. But they were soon "o'er-clouded with wo."

In his daughter (Mrs. Alston) and her son were centred all his hopes, all his affections, all the ties that bound him to this life. The following appears to have been the first letter, after his arrival in the United States, that Burr received from his son-in-law Alston.

FROM JOSEPH ALSTON.

July 26, 1812.

A few miserable weeks since, my dear sir, and in spite of all the embarrassments, the troubles, and disappointments which have fallen to our lot since we parted, I would have congratulated you on your return in the language of happiness. With my wife on one side and my boy on the other, I felt myself superior to depression. The present was enjoyed, the future was anticipated with enthusiasm. One dreadful blow has destroyed us; reduced us to the veriest, the most sublimated wretchedness. That boy, on whom all rested; our companion, our friend—he who was to have transmitted down the mingled blood of Theodosia and myself—he who was to have redeemed all your glory, and shed new lustre upon our families—that boy, at once our happiness and our pride, is taken from us—*is dead.* We saw him dead. My own hand surrendered him to the grave; yet we are alive. But it is past. I will not conceal from you that life is a burden, which, heavy as it is, we shall both support, if not with dignity, at least with decency and firmness. Theodosia has endured all that a human being could endure; but her admirable mind will triumph. She supports herself in a manner worthy of your daughter.

We have not yet been able to form any definite plan of life. My present wish is that Theodosia should join you, with or without me, as soon as possible. My command here, as brigadier-general, embarrasses me a good deal in the disposal of *myself*. I would part with Theodosia reluctantly; but if I find myself detained here, I shall certainly do so. I not only recognise your claim to her after such a separation, but change of scene and your society will aid her, I am conscious, in recovering at least that tone of mind which we are destined to carry through life with us.

I have great anxiety to be employed against Quebec, should an army be ordered thither, and have letters prepared asking of the president a brigade in that army. From the support which that request will have, if not obtained now, I doubt not it will be at the first increase of the military force, which, if the war be seriously carried on, must be as soon as Congress meet. Then, be the event what it may, I shall at least gain something. Adieu.

Yours, with respect and regard,

JOSEPH ALSTON.

The effect upon Burr of this blow may be imagined by those who have noticed his constant and unceasing anxiety for his grandson, Aaron Burr Alston. In his intercourse, however, with the world, and in his business pursuits, there was a promptitude and an apparent cheerfulness which seemed to indicate a tranquillity of mind. But not so in his lone and solitary hours. When in the society of a single friend, if an accidental reference was made to the event, the manly tear would be seen slowly stealing down his furrowed cheek, until, as if awakening from a slumber, he would suddenly check those emotions of the heart, and all would again become subdued, calm, dignified.

During this autumn (1812) Theodosia's health continued to be precarious. Deep-settled grief, in addition to her protracted disease, was rapidly wasting her away. She continued to correspond with her father; but at length, in November, it was determined that she should join him in New-

York. A few short extracts of letters will unfold and close this melancholy tale.

FROM TIMOTHY GREEN.

Charleston, S. C., December 7, 1812.

I arrived here from New-York on the 28th ult., and on the 29th started for Columbia. Mr. Alston seemed rather hurt that you should conceive it necessary to send a person here, as he or one of his brothers would attend Mrs. Alston to New-York. I told him you had some opinion of my medical talents; that you had learned your daughter was in a low state of health, and required unusual attention, and medical attention on her voyage; that I had torn myself from my family to perform this service for my friend. He said that he was inclined to charter a vessel to take her on. I informed him that I should return to Charleston, where I should remain a day or two, and then proceed to Georgetown (S. C.) and wait his arrival.

Georgetown, S. C., December 22, 1812.

I have engaged a passage to New-York for your daughter in a pilot-boat that has been out privateering, but has come in here, and is refitting merely to get to New-York. My only fears are that Governor Alston may think the mode of conveyance too undignified, and object to it; but Mrs. Alston is fully bent on going. You must not be surprised to see her very low, feeble, and emaciated. Her complaint is an almost incessant nervous fever. We shall sail in about eight days.

TIMOTHY GREEN.

FROM JOSEPH ALSTON TO THEODOSIA.

Columbia, S. C., January 15, 1813.

Another mail, and still no letter! I hear, too, rumours of a gale off Cape Hatteras the beginning of the month! The state of my mind is dreadful. Let no man, wretched as he may be, presume to think himself beyond the reach of another blow. I shall count the hours till noon to-morrow. If I do not hear then, there will be no hope till Tuesday. To feelings like mine, what an interval! May God grant me one word from you to-morrow. Adieu. All that I have left of heart is yours. All my prayers are for your safety and well-being.

January 19, 1813.

Forebodings! wretched, heart-rending forebodings distract my mind. I may no longer have a wife; and yet my impatient restlessness addresses her a letter. To-morrow will be three weeks since our separation, and not yet one line. Gracious God! for what am I reserved?

JOSEPH ALSTON.

FROM JOSEPH ALSTON TO COL. BURR.

Columbia, January 19, 1813.

To-morrow will be three weeks since, in obedience to your wishes, Theodosia left me. It is three weeks, and not yet one line from her. My mind is tortured. I wrote you on the 29th ult., the day before Theo. sailed, that on the next day she would embark in the privateer *Patriot*, a pilot-boat-built schooner, commanded by Captain Overstocks, with an old New-York pilot as sailing-master. The vessel had dismissed her crew, and was returning home with her guns under deck. Her reputed swiftness in sailing inspired such confidence of a voyage of not more than five or six days, that the three weeks without a letter fill me with an unhappiness—a wretchedness I can neither describe nor conquer. Gracious God! Is my wife, too, taken from me? I do not know why I write, but I feel that I am miserable.

Charleston, January 31, 1813.

A call of business to this place for a few days occasioned your letter of the 20th not to be received till this morning. Not a moment is lost in replying to it. Yet wherefore? You ask of me to relieve your suspense. Alas! it was to you I looked for similar relief. I have written you twice since my letter of December 29. I can add nothing to the information then given. I parted with our Theo. near the bar about noon on Thursday, the last of December. The wind was moderate and fair. She was in the pilot-boat-built schooner Patriot, Captain Overstocks, with an experienced New-York pilot, Coon, as sailing-master. This vessel, the same which had been sent by government last summer in pursuit of Commodore Rodgers's squadron, had been selected as one which, from her reputed excellence and swiftness in sailing, would ensure a passage of not more than five or six days. From that moment I have heard nothing of the schooner nor my wife. I have been the prey of feelings which you only can imagine. When I turned from the grave of my boy I deemed myself no longer vulnerable. Misfortune had no more a blow for me. I was wrong. It is true, I no longer feel, I never shall feel as I was wont; but I have been taught that there was still one being in whom I was inexpressibly interested. I have in vain endeavoured to build upon the hope of long passage. Thirty days are decisive. My wife is *either captured or lost*. What a destiny is mine! and I live under it, engage in business, appear to the world as though all was tranquil, easy. 'Tis so, but it cannot endure. A short time since, and the idea of capture would have been the source of painful, terrible apprehension; it now furnishes me the only ray of comfort, or rather of hope, that I have. Each mail is anticipated with impatient, yet fearful and appalling anxiety. Should you hear aught relative to the object of this our common solicitude, do not, I pray, forget me.

JOSEPH ALSTON.

FROM JOSEPH ALSTON.

February 25, 1813.

Your letter of the 10th, my friend, is received. This assurance of my fate was not wanting. Authentic accounts from Bermuda and Nassau, as late as January 30, connected with your letter from New-York of the 28th, had already forced upon me the dreadful conviction that we had no more to hope. Without this victim, too, the desolation would not have been complete. My boy—my wife—gone, both! This, then, is the end of all the hopes we had formed. You may well observe that you feel severed from the human race. She was the last tie that bound us to the species. What have we left? In surviving the 30th of June* I thought I could meet all other afflictions with ease, yet I have staggered under this in a manner that I am glad had not a witness. Your letter of January 28 was not received till February 9. The Oaks, for some months visited only at intervals, when the feelings the world thought gone by were not to be controlled, was the asylum I sought. It was there, in the chamber of my wife, where every thing was disposed as usual; with the clothes, the books, the playthings of my boy around me, that I sustained this second shock, doubled in a manner that I could not account for. My son seemed to have been reanimated, to have been restored to me, and to have just perished again with his mother. It was the loss of both pressing upon me at the same moment.

Should it be my misfortune to live a century, the 30th of June and the 10th of February are so impressed upon my mind that they will always seem to have just passed. I visited the grave of my boy. The little plans we had all three formed rushed upon my memory. Where now was the boy? The mother I cherished with so much pride? I felt like the very spirit of desolation. If it had not been for a kind of stupefaction and confusion of mind which followed, God knows how I should have borne it. Oh, my friend, if there be such a thing as the sublime of misery, it is for us that it has been reserved.

You are the only person in the world with whom I can commune on this subject; for you are the only person whose

* The day on which his son died.

feelings can have any community with mine. You knew those we loved. With you, therefore, it will be no weakness to feel their loss. Here, none knew them; none valued them as they deserved.` The talents of my boy, his rare elevation of character, his already extensive reputation for so early an age, made his death regretted by the pride of my family; but, though certain of the loss of my not less admirable wife, they seem to consider it like the loss of an ordinary woman. Alas! they know nothing of my heart. They never have known any thing of it. Yet, after all, he is a poor actor who cannot sustain his little hour upon the stage, be his part what it may. But the man who has been deemed worthy of the heart of *Theodosia Burr*, and who has felt what it was to be blessed with such a woman's, will never forget his elevation.

JOSEPH ALSTON.

This distressing correspondence between Colonel Burr and Governor Alston was continued during the year 1813; but the unfortunate Theodosia was never again heard of, except in idle rumours and exaggerated tales of her capture and murder by pirates. These reports, it is believed, were without foundation. The schooner on board which she had taken passage probably foundered, and every soul perished in a heavy gale which was experienced along our whole coast a few days after her departure from Georgetown.

Colonel Burr, on his return to the United States, mingled but little in society. He only knew those who first recognised him. In the ordinary conflicts of the political parties of the day he seemed to feel but little interest, and rarely interfered. From them he sought neither honour nor emolument. He pursued his profession, however, with great ardour and some success; but was continually embarrassed, and sometimes experienced great difficulty from the pressure of his old debts. The following extract will afford some general idea of his situation.

TO JOSEPH ALSTON.

New-York, October 16, 1815.

I have found it so difficult to answer that part of your letter which regards myself and my concerns, that it has been deferred, though often in my mind. At some other time I may give you, in detail, a sketch of the sad period which has elapsed since my return. For the present, it will suffice to say that my business affords me a decent support. If I had not been interrupted in the career which I began, I should, before this, have paid all my debts and been at ease.

My old creditors (principally the holders of the Mexican debts) came upon me last winter with vindictive fury. I was held to bail in large sums, and saw no probability of keeping out of prison for six months. This danger is still menacing, but not quite so imminent. I shall neither borrow nor receive from any one, not even from you. I have determined not to begin to pay unless I see a prospect of paying all.

A. Burr.

When any great political question agitated the country, such as a presidential election, Mr. Burr seemed to feel it his duty to express his opinion to those whom he supposed confided in his discernment or his patriotism. On these occasions he spake with great freedom and boldness. Many of his letters exhibit all that sagacity and talent for which he was so pre-eminently distinguished. It has been seen by the extract from Blennerhassett's private journal, that he did not complain in 1807 of any act done by General Andrew Jackson. The following will show that he remained under the influence of similar feelings in 1815.

TO GOVERNOR JOSEPH ALSTON.

New-York, November 20, 1815.

A congressional caucus will, in the course of the ensuing month, nominate James Monroe for President of the United

States, and will call on all good republicans to support the nomination.

Whether we consider the measure itself, the character and talents of the man, or the state whence he comes, this nomination is equally exceptionable and odious.

I have often heard your opinion of these congressional nominations. They are hostile to all freedom and independence of suffrage. A certain junto of actual and factitious Virginians, having had possession of the government for twenty-four years, consider the United States as their property, and, by bawling "Support the Administration," have so long succeeded in duping the republican public. One of their principal arts, and which has been systematically taught by Jefferson, is that of promoting state dissensions, not between republican and federal—that would do them no good—but schisms in the republican party. By looking round you will see how the attention of leading men in the different states has thus been turned from general and *state* politics. Let not this disgraceful domination continue.

Independently of the manner of the nomination and the location of the candidate, the man himself is one of the most improper and incompetent that could be selected. Naturally dull and stupid; extremely illiterate; indecisive to a degree that would be incredible to one who did not know him; pusillanimous, and, of course, hypocritical; has no opinion on any subject, and will be always under the government of the worst men; pretends, as I am told, to some knowledge of military matters, but never commanded a platoon, nor was ever fit to command one. "*He served in the Revolutionary War!*"—that is, he acted a short time as aid-de-camp to Lord Stirling, who was regularly * * * * * * * *. Monroe's whole duty was to fill his lordship's tankard, and hear, with indications of admiration, his lordship's long stories about himself. Such is Monroe's military experience. I was with my regiment in the same division at the time. As a lawyer, Monroe was far below mediocrity.

He never rose to the honour of trying a cause of the value of a hundred pounds. This is a character exactly suited to the views of the Virginia junto.

To this junto you have twice sacrificed yourself, and what have you got by it? Their hatred and abhorrence. Did you ever know them to countenance a man of talents and independence? Never—nor ever will.

It is time that you manifested that you had some individual character; some opinion of your own; some influence to support that opinion. Make them fear you, and they will be at your feet. Thus far they have reason to believe that you fear them.

The moment is extremely auspicious for breaking down this degrading system. The best citizens of our country acknowledge the feebleness of our administration. They acknowledge that offices are bestowed merely to preserve power, and without the smallest regard to fitness. If, then, there be a man in the United States of firmness and decision, and having standing enough to afford even a hope of success, it is your duty to hold him up to public view. that man is *Andrew Jackson*. Nothing is wanting but a respectable nomination, made before the proclamation of the Virginia caucus, and *Jackson's* success is inevitable.

If this project should accord with your views, I could wish to see *you* prominent in the execution of it. It must be known to be *your* work. Whether a formal and open nomination should now be made, or whether you should, for the present, content yourself with barely denouncing, by a joint resolution of both houses of your legislature, congressional caucuses and nominations, you only can judge. One consideration inclines me to hesitate about the policy of a present nomination. It is this—that Jackson ought first to be admonished to be passive: for, the moment he shall be announced as a candidate, he will be assailed by the Virginia junto with menaces, and with insidious promises of boons and favours. *There is danger that Jackson might be wrought upon by such practices.* If an open nomination be made, an express should be instantly sent to him.

This suggestion has not arisen from any exclusive attachment to Jackson. The object is to break down this vile combination which rules and degrades the United States. If you should think that any other man could be held up with better prospect of success, name that man. I know of no such. But the business must be accomplished, and on this occasion, and by you. So long as the present system prevails, you will be struggling against wind and tide to preserve a precarious influence. You will never be forgiven for the crime of having talents and independence.

Exhibit yourself, then, and emerge from this state of nullity. You owe it to yourself, you owe it to me, you owe it to your country, you owe it to the memory of the dead.

I have talked of this matter to your late secretary, but he has not seen this letter.

A. Burr.

Your secretary was to have delivered this personally, but has changed his course on hearing that Jackson is on his way to Washington. If you should have any confidential friend among the members of Congress from your state, charge him to caution Jackson against the perfidious caresses with which he will be overwhelmed at Washington.

A. B.

New-York, December 11, 1815.

A copy of the preceding went under cover to Dr. Wragg. Since that date things are wonderfully advanced, as your secretary will write or tell you. These will require a written message (letter) from yourself and others (or yourself alone, but three names would look more formal), advising Jackson what is doing; that communications have been had with the Northern states, requiring him only to be passive, and asking from him a list of persons in the Western states to whom you may address your letters.

A. Burr.

FROM JOSEPH ALSTON.

Charleston, February 16, 1816.

Your letter of the 20th of November, intrusted to Mr. Phillips, was received through the postoffice about the middle of last month. It was, of course, too late, had circumstances been ever so favourable, to be acted upon in the manner proposed. Had it even been received, however, in due season, it would have found me utterly incapable of exertion. On my way to Columbia, in November, I had another severe attack of illness, which rendered absolutely impracticable either the immediate prosecution of my journey or my attendance during the session of the legislature. As soon as I was able to bear the motion of a carriage, I was brought by short stages to this place, where I have been confined ever since. Yesterday was the first time for two months that I have been out of the house. So much for the miserable remnant of myself.

With regard to the subject of your letter of the 20th of November, I fully coincide with you in sentiment; but the spirit, the energy, the health necessary to give practical effect to sentiment, are all gone. I feel too much alone, too entirely unconnected with the world, to take much interest in any thing. Yet, without the smallest solicitude about the result, I shall certainly not fail to discharge my public duty, whenever the opportunity occurs, by giving a very strong and frank expression of my opinion on the subject suggested.

Vanderlyn, I perceive from the papers, has returned to New-York. Nothing, I trust, has prevented his bringing back the portrait* you left with him. Let me again entreat you to use your influence with him in procuring me a good copy. I received some days since, through the kindness of Mr. John B. Prevost, a miniature, which appears to have been taken from Vanderlyn's portrait. The execution is

* The portrait of Theodosia.

good, but in expression it is by no means equal to the portrait. There was a small portrait of Natalie which you took with you, of which, if Vanderlyn embraces that kind of painting in his present plan, I should be glad also to obtain of him a copy. The original picture, I think, was the best portrait I ever saw.

Yours affectionately,

JOSEPH ALSTON.

In this depressed state of mind and debilitated state of body Governor Alston remained until summer, when he died. Whatever may have been appearances to the contrary, it is highly probable that, after the death of his son and wife, he never enjoyed happiness. Their loss continually preyed upon him. To Colonel Burr, and, it would seem, to him alone, he unbosomed himself. All his letters breathe a deep and settled gloom, bordering on despondency—a gloom which time could not subdue or change.

FROM WILLIAM A. ALSTON.

Rosehill, near Georgetown, October 4, 1816.

SIR,

It was enjoined on me, and my brother John A. Alston, verbally, by our late brother Joseph Alston, to send a certain trunk to you, which he never had the courage to open, containing, as he said, some things that belonged to your daughter Theodosia; and to send a certain collection of other articles (of dress, I believe), that had also been hers, to the eldest daughter of Mr. J. B. Prevost. Pray point you out the way, sir, in which our trust is to be executed.

In his will, of which a copy shall be sent you if desired, my brother has given all demands up to you that he had against you. Very respectfully,

WILLIAM A. ALSTON.

P. S. These are alone the words relating to you in the will: "To my father-in-law, Aaron Burr, I give, devise, and bequeath all demands I may have against him, whether by judgment or otherwise."

The trunk and other articles above referred to were subsequently transmitted to Colonel Burr. Among the private papers of Theodosia there are some fragments and scraps of much interest. In the summer of 1805 she was dangerously ill, and she appears, from the following letter, to have been greatly depressed in mind.

FROM THEODOSIA TO JOSEPH ALSTON.

August 6, 1805.

Whether it is the effect of extreme debility and disordered nerves, or whether it is really presentiment, the existence of which I have been often told of, and always doubted, I cannot tell; but something whispers me that my end approaches. In vain I reason with myself; in vain I occupy my mind, and seek to fix my attention on other subjects; there is about me that dreadful heaviness and sinking of the heart, that awful foreboding, of which it is impossible to divest myself. Perhaps I am now standing on the brink of eternity; and, ere I plunge in the fearful abyss, I have some few requests to make.

I wish your sisters (one of them, it is immaterial which) would select from my clothes certain things which they will easily perceive belonged to my mother. These, with whatever lace they find in a large trunk in a garret-room of the Oaks house, added to a little satinwood box (the largest, and having a lock and key), and a black satin embroidered box, with a pincushion; all these things I wish they would put together in one trunk, and send them to Frederic, with the enclosed letter. I prefer him, because Bartow's wife would have little respect for what, however trifling it may appear, I nevertheless deem sacred.

I beg Sister Maria will accept of my watch-ring. She will find a locket which she gave me, containing the hair of her mother; she had better take it. If the lace in my wardrobe at the Oaks will be of any use to Charlotte, I beg she will take it, or any thing else she wishes. My heart is with those dear amiable sisters, to give them something worth preserving in recollection of me; but they know that a warm friendship is all I have to give.

Return to mamma the eagle she gave me. Should an opportunity to Catharine Brown ever occur, send her a pearl necklace, a small diamond ring, a little pair of coral tablets, which are among my trinkets at the Oaks. I pray you, my dear husband, send Bartow's daughter some present for me, and to himself and Frederic a lock of my hair. Return Natalie the little desk she gave me, accompanied by assurances of my affectionate recollection, and a ring of my hair. Remember me to Sally, who is truly amiable, and whom I sincerely esteem.

I beg, also, you will write immediately to New-York, forwarding some money for the comfortable support of *Peggy* until my father can provide for her. Do not permit grief at the loss of me to render you forgetful of this, for the poor creature may expire of want in the mean time. I beg this may be attended to without delay.

To you, my beloved, I leave our child; the child of my bosom, who was once a part of myself, and from whom I shall shortly be separated by the cold grave. You love him now; henceforth love him for me also. And oh, my husband, attend to this last prayer of a doting mother. Never, never listen to what any other person tells you of him. Be yourself his judge on all occasions. He has faults; see them, and correct them yourself. Desist not an instant from your endeavours to secure his confidence. It is a work which requires as much uniformity of conduct as warmth of affection towards him. I know, my beloved, that you can perceive what is right on this subject as on every other. But recollect, these are the last words I can ever utter. It will tranquillize my last moments to have disburdened myself of them.

I fear you will scarcely be able to read this scrawl, but I feel hurried and agitated. Death is not welcome to me. I confess it is ever dreaded. You have made me too fond of life. Adieu, then, thou kind, thou tender husband. Adieu, friend of my heart. May Heaven prosper you, and may we meet hereafter. Adieu; perhaps we may never see each other again in this world. You are away, I wished to hold you fast, and prevented you from going this morning. But He who is wisdom itself ordains events; we must submit to them. Least of all should I murmur. I, on whom so many blessings have been showered—whose days have been numbered by bounties—who have had such a husband, such a child, and such a father. Oh pardon me, my God, if I regret leaving these. I resign myself. Adieu, once more, and for the last time, my beloved. Speak of me often to our son. Let him love the memory of his mother, and let him know how he was loved by her. Your wife, your fond wife,

THEO.

Let my father see my son sometimes. Do not be unkind towards him whom I have loved so much, I beseech you. Burn all my papers except my father's letters, which I beg you to return him. Adieu, my sweet boy. Love your father; be grateful and affectionate to him while he lives; be the pride of his meridian, the support of his departing days. Be all that he wishes; for he made your mother happy. Oh! my heavenly Father, bless them both. If it is permitted, I will hover round you, and guard you, and intercede for you. I hope for happiness in the next world, for I have not been bad in this.

I had nearly forgotten to say that I charge you not to allow me to be stripped and washed, as is usual. I am pure enough thus to return to dust. Why, then, expose my person? Pray see to this. If it does not appear contradictory or silly, I beg to be kept as long as possible before I am consigned to the earth.

[Directed—"*My husband.* To be delivered after my death. I wish this to be read *immediately,* and before my burial."]

Although Colonel Burr seldom interfered in the politics of his own country, yet he continued to feel a deep and abiding interest in the emancipation of South America. He was constantly projecting some measure which in his opinion was calculated to promote this object. He encouraged the friends of freedom in that benighted land. He corresponded with those who were connected with any enterprise favouring the revolution, and consulted and advised with all who visited the United States, and sought his advice on the subject. The following letter will show the wishes of distinguished Mexicans in the year 1816.

FROM GENERAL TOLEDO.

TRANSLATION.

New-York, September 20, 1816.

SIR,

Although I have not the honour of knowing you personally, the reputation of your talents and good wishes for the cause of America have made your name familiar among us; and since this will dispense the accustomed forms of introduction, I dare present to your consideration the actual state of our revolution, our evils, and the remedies which we believe may be applied to them.

It is six years since that, almost simultaneously, the standard of liberty was raised by different provinces of Spanish America, and the cry of independence was heard from the territory of Mexico to the extremities of Chili. The inhabitants, determined to resist their European oppressors, formed themselves in groups under the name of armies, and placed at the head of them persons of the first reputation. Hundreds of battles have been fought, decided solely by dint of valour, without the assistance of military art or skill; the youth and most illustrious families have been sacrificed, and even entire populations have disappeared in a struggle so just, but unfortunately conducted with inaptitude or marked with cruelty.

I, among others, have been honoured with the confidence of the command of the Mexican troops; and at the close of so many sacrifices we have only come to a knowledge of the character of the people and of ourselves. Both are well disposed, and there is only wanting, to complete our wishes, that these dispositions be directed with calculation and wisdom for the public good.

My voyage to this country has for its object not only to obtain the means for continuing the war, but to seek the person best capable of employing them. This is the desire of that people; and I can assure you that their wish and mine would be satisfied at the same time, if we should have the fortune of your assuming the management of our political and military affairs in the dangerous crisis in which we find ourselves.

I hope that, in behalf of the cause of America and of humanity, you will accept this offer, which I have the honour to make you in the name of that people, and

I am, sir,
With the greatest respect and consideration,
Yours,
JOSE ALVAREZ DE TOLEDO.

The invitation of General Toledo was not accepted. Colonel Burr, however, continued to act with his accustomed zeal in behalf of the South American patriots; and in 1819 the Republic of Venezuela granted him the following commission:—

TRANSLATION.

Republic of Venezuela,
Palace of the Governor, Angostura, October 9, 1819.

John Baptiste Arismendi, of the Order of Liberators,

Captain-general of the Armies, and Vice-president of the State, &c., &c., &c.

Whereas Aaron Burr, citizen of the United States of North America, has proved, to the satisfaction of this government, his ardent love for the cause of liberty and independence, and his desire to be actively employed in its service, as one most worthy of a freeman and a philanthropist, and most glorious for an American who has fought for the rights of his native land:

Therefore, in compliance with his (noble) praiseworthy wishes, and in fulfilment of a duty imposed upon me by the absence of the president of the republic in the territory of New Grenada, and impressed with the necessity of rendering assistance to all other countries of South America and Mexico now contending against the civil and religious tyranny of the Spanish government,

I hereby authorize the above-named Aaron Burr (without violation of established laws and customs) to raise troops for sea and land service, to aid this government or any other now struggling in the same cause against the despotism of Spain; provided that, in thus contending against the common enemy, he conform to established ordinances, the laws of nations, and the acknowledged usages among countries that aspire to emancipation and liberty.

And I declare that, it not being possible to organize *gratuitously* naval or land expeditions in all parts of the country, the property taken from the enemy being insufficient to defray the expenses, this republic and any other that may be benefited or assisted by the said Aaron Burr shall hold their funds responsible for any debts contracted by him in the premises.

Therefore, that he may proceed with that order which the exigence of the case requires, the "*commissioned*" (A. B.) shall render an account, and advise of all contracts entered into by him in the fulfilment of his commission, in order that they may be examined and approved in anticipation (of payment).

But it will be understood that the government is unable at this time to pay its troops regularly; and the latter will not be justified in relying on any thing more than a bare subsistence or an occasional provision, more or less, according to circumstances. This notice to be given to *all* enlisting under his banners. This measure is rendered necessary, lest the good faith of the government should be compromised An account of all military stipends will be kept by the government, that they may be liquidated in proportion to the increase of its resources. The republic exacts this service only during the continuance of the war. At its termination each soldier shall receive as a bounty a landed estate of the value of five hundred dollars; and all officers shall be paid in proportion, in conformity with the provisions of the law, or the decree for the division of national property, in addition to the personal rights with which the gratitude of Venezuela constitutionally recognises the services performed in its cause.

And that the above-named Aaron Burr may legally exert himself in favour of the emancipation and liberty of Venezuela and New Grenada, and all other countries of South America and Mexico now contending against the arbitrary and oppressive power of Spain, without in any manner giving offence to friendly or neutral powers, so long as they shall preserve their amity and neutrality, I grant to him this commission, signed with my hand, sealed with the provisional seal of the republic, and countersigned by the secretary of state and foreign affairs, in the place, day, month, and year above named.

J. Baptiste Arismendi.

(Seal)

Juan G. Roscw, Secretary of State and F. A.

It was thus that Colonel Burr was employed after his return from Europe until near the close of his life. During his leisure hours, if any such he had, his mind was occupied for several years in directing the education of two young ladies (Misses Eden) who were his wards, and for whom, in a protracted lawsuit, he had recovered a valuable estate. His regular and constant correspondence with these ladies, pointing out their errors, their improvements, and the studies which they were to pursue from day to day, was to them invaluable, and well calculated to "teach the young idea how to shoot." Copies of these letters are preserved, and it was originally intended to have published portions of them in this work, but no space remains. They would form a pleasing and interesting treatise on female education.

Although Colonel Burr's pecuniary means were limited, yet he was not destitute. He had an annual income of a few hundred dollars, in addition to his half-pay as a colonel in the revolutionary army. For two or three years before his death he suffered under the effects of a paralysis. Much of the time he was in a measure helpless, so far as locomotion was concerned. His general health, however, was tolerably good, by using great precaution in his diet. He had long abstained from the use of either tea or coffee as affecting his nervous system. His mind retained much of its vigour, and his memory, as to events of long standing, seemed to be unimpaired. Few octogenarians had as little of what is termed the garrulity of age as Colonel Burr. He never was a great talker, and in the decline of life retained much of that dignified sedateness which had characterized his meridian. When visited by strangers he received them with courtesy, unless his pride became awakened by a suspicion that the visit was one of idle or impertinent curiosity. On such occasions his manner was formal, cold, repulsive. Under sufferings of body or mind he seldom complained; but, during the last year of his life, he became more restive and impatient. The friends of his youth had gone before him. All the ties of consanguinity which could operate in uniting him to the world were severed asunder. To him there remained no brother, no sister, no child, no lineal descendant. He had numbered fourscore years, and was incapable, from disease, of moving abroad, or even dressing himself. He therefore became restless, and seemed anxious for the arrival of the hour when his eyes should be closed in everlasting sleep. At length that hour came, and his mortal career terminated without a struggle on Wednesday, the 14th of September, 1836, in the eighty-first year of his age, on Staten Island, Richmond county, state of New-York, whither he had been removed for the benefit of pure air during the warm season. In conformity with his wish, his body was removed to Princeton, New-Jersey. The New-York Courier and Enquirer of the 19th of September gives the following account of his funeral.

From the Courier and Enquirer.

"On Friday morning, the 16th of September, the body of the late Colonel Aaron Burr was put on board a steamboat at Staten Island, and conveyed, with a number of his friends and relatives, from New-York to Amboy. Here it, with the followers, was received by the railroad cars and taken to Hightstown, nine miles from Princeton. A hearse and carriage having been previously prepared, the remains, with the friends of the departed, proceeded immediately to Princeton College, where the body was deposited until the hour of interment should arrive—half past three o'clock.

"At the appointed hour, the professors, collegians, and citizens having assembled, the ceremony commenced by a prayer to the Throne of Grace. It was succeeded by a most eloquent, appropriate, and judicious sermon, delivered by the president of the college; after which the procession was formed on the college green, and proceeded to the burying-ground under an escort of the military, accompanied by martial music. He was interred with the honours of war. The firing over the grave was performed by a well-disciplined infantry corps, designated as the Mercer Guards. The professors and students of the college, and some of the clergy and citizens, united with the relatives and friends of the deceased in the procession.

"The interment was in the college burying-place, near the tombs of his ancestors, in his native state, under the superintendence of the fathers of that seat of learning where the budding of his mighty mind first displayed itself, where it was cultivated and matured, and where the foundation was laid for those intellectual endowments which he afterward exhibited on the great theatre of life. He has shed a halo of literary glory around Nassau Hall. Through a long pilgrimage he loved her as the disciplinarian of his youthful mind. He vaunted that he was one of her earliest and most attached sons. He joyed in her success and sorrowed in her misfortunes. In this her last act of respect to his memory, she has repaid those kind feelings in which he indulged during a long life; and heartless must be the friend of the deceased who remembers not with gratitude this testimony of regard for the giant mind of him who must fill a large space in the history of his country. Peace be to his manes."

Extract from the Minutes of the Cliosophic Society.

"The Cliosophic Society having this morning received the mournful intelligence of the decease of Colonel Aaron Burr, formerly Vice-president of the United States, an eminent member, and one of the founders of our institution, would, in consideration of his eminence and talents, as well as the zeal with which he has promoted the interests of our association, pay to his memory a tribute of respect expressive of our admiration of his greatness and regret at his demise. Be it therefore

"*Resolved*, That the efforts of this individual in behalf of our society during her infant struggle, and the affectionate interest which he has at all times manifested for her success, claim from us an expression of condolence for his loss and gratitude for his services.

"2d. That the whole society follow his remains to the grave as mourners.

"3d. That, as a feeble testimony of our respect, the members wear crape on the left arm for the space of thirty days.

4th. "That these resolutions be published in the Princeton Whig, New-York Courier and Enquirer, New-York Gazette, Commercial Advertiser, United States Gazette, and United States Telegraph."

THE END.

LaVergne, TN USA
03 March 2010
174807LV00005B/49/P

9 781117 236568